D1611969

Words That Matter

Words
That
Matter

Linguistic Perception in
Renaissance English

Judith H. Anderson

Stanford University Press
Stanford, California

Stanford University Press
Stanford, California

© 1996 by the Board of Trustees of the
Leland Stanford Junior University

Printed in the United States of America

CIP data are at the end of the book

Stanford University Press publications are distributed
exclusively by Stanford University Press within the United
States, Canada, Mexico, and Central America; they are
distributed exclusively by Cambridge University Press
throughout the rest of the world.

Original printing 1996
Last figure below indicates year of this printing:
05 04 03 02 01 00 99 98 97 96

Acknowledgments

This book has many debts, some longstanding. It could not have been written without the generous support of two great research libraries during the past ten years: The Huntington Library supported my research with a Huntington-NEH Fellowship and a Mayers Foundation Fellowship; the Folger Shakespeare Library awarded me a Dulin Fellowship and invited me to teach a seminar for the Folger Institute that further enabled my reflection on this project. Indiana University provided supplementary support on these occasions. I cannot overstate my gratitude to these institutions.

I am also grateful to Rick Smith and Jennifer Vaught for their assistance in preparing the manuscript of this book for publication. I have benefited as well from the advice, suggestions, and counsel of numerous other scholars and friends, several of whom will be mildly surprised by the company they keep in what follows. In various ways, often through a casual observation or question, Anne Prescott, Jim Riddell, Susanne Wofford, Ken Gross, Mary Carruthers, Mary Thomas Crane, Ed Weismiller, Sandra Fischer, David Evett, Tom Greene, John Hollander, Bill Oram, Don Wayne, Don Cheney, Tim Heninger, Debora Shuger, Peter Lindenbaum, Peter Blayney, Tamara Goeglein, and Brian Strier have all stimulated my thinking about the substantiality of language. Talbot Donaldson, my late husband, selflessly encouraged this project in ways that were crucial. Many others — they will recognize the reference — have provided the support of friendship in the last decade. But I would single out Nancy Cridland and Harry Berger for particular thanks. Nancy has patiently and wittily read and listened to my rambling and has often contributed her unsurpassed expertise as a librarian to my researches. Harry's interest in the manuscript of this book rescued it from my lingering discontent, and his provocative suggestions and queries have helped me to extend or to clarify my arguments. I can thank him for the fact that this project is finished and that it has a definite form. I do so most warmly.

Portions of two of the following chapters have appeared earlier in slightly or considerably altered form. Part of the discussion of Spenser's language in Chapter 4 has been taken from " 'Myn auctour': Spenser's Enabling Fiction and Eumnestes' 'immortall scrine,' " in *Unfolded Tales: Essays on Renaissance Romance*, ed. George M. Logan and Gordon Teskey (Ithaca, N. Y.: Cornell University Press, 1989), pp. 16–31. Portions of my treatment of Donne's sermons in Chapter 5 appeared originally as "Patterns Proposed Beforehand: Donne's Second Prebend Sermon," *Prose Studies* 2 (1988): 37–48; and "Life Lived and Life Written: Donne's Final Word or Last Character," *The Huntington Library*

Quarterly 51 (1988): 247–59. I am grateful to Cornell University Press, Frank Cass & Co. Ltd., and the Henry E. Huntington Library and Art Gallery, respectively the holders of copyright, for permission to reprint these materials.

J. H. A.

Contents

A Note on Editions
and Citations

When possible, I have cited references to facsimile or other modern editions of Renaissance texts, since they are more readily accessible than the various editions in the specialized research libraries in which most of this book was written. In several instances, I have cited more than one edition of a text, usually because of relevant variants or, in the case of illustrations, because of the legibility (or illegibility) of the page involved.

I have also expanded abbreviations, including ampersands, that occur in my quotations from Renaissance or medieval texts. If a translation is not otherwise attributed in the Notes or in the Works Cited, it is my own.

Words That Matter

Prologue

I magine a scholarly world without the *OED*, bereft of the definitions, the detailed etymologies, and the explanations of origin it offers. Worse yet, imagine one without the ubiquitous desk dictionary. How would we determine meaning? Is it even conceivable that our theories of signification and practices of analysis would remain the same? When I began this project, its impetus lay in these questions, in part induced by annoyance at the excesses of verbal ingenuity that characterized the early heyday of deconstruction, a theory and practice that otherwise has my respect. My fantasy was to deprive readers of the technological support the modern lexicon offers and then to see what we could do on our own.

Constructively, what this led to was an interest in the status and influence of dictionaries in the early modern period and more specifically in the Renaissance, when dictionaries really began to come into their own, with editions and reprintings often running into the double digits. Dictionaries led in turn to correlative interests in printing, education, and language and then to an interest in words as such, whether verbal units such as proverbs, inscriptions, and biblical quotations — frozen syntagms in structuralist terms — or individuated words themselves, lexical entries, Latin tags, verbal icons, and other foci of the equivocal "thingness" of language. To my mind, what has proved especially fascinating in the period is the interplay of language with the growing cultural emphasis on externalized expression and on the material world, coupled with the considerable evidence that this interplay is an historicized perception rather than simply a modern one.

The very emphasis in the period on words and wordlike units may profitably be seen as an extension of Ian Hacking's thesis that "ideas then, and sentences now, serve as the interface between the knowing subject and what is known." Hacking argues that words function as signs of ideas in the later seventeenth century and implies the origin of this view in the essences and first principles of the Greeks and Scholastics, which, of course, also provide the fundaments of Renaissance thought.[1] He goes on to distinguish the autonomy of modern sentential discourse, which actually lacks a knowing subject, from the referentiality of the early modern period; I would add "whether ideationally or objectively referential" to this description. But here Hacking's argument, adapted and extended to the Renaissance, fails to acknowledge or account for the linguistic fiction in Renaissance wordplay: the sense, both anxious and liberating, that words themselves could be or become autonomous. This sense will figure conspicuously in the chapters that follow, which, like linguistic perception in the Renaissance, will focus on words and similar sub-sentential units.

The fact that modern linguists and stylisticians regard the sentence as the fundamental unit in English expression even when they analyze early modern texts could actually be used to support Hacking's distinction between modern discourse, which the analysts practice, and perception in the early modern period.[2] Renaissance grammar is word-based as well as centered in Latin, and

Renaissance rhetorics, which do treat English systematically, deal with tropes and schemes, or figures of thought and speech; therefore they prioritize word and figure rather than sentence. This prioritizing, moreover, has significant consequences for representation. While an analysis of Renaissance style founded on modern linguistic assumptions can be illuminating, it does not substitute for a more historical one. The most basic structures of meaning understood by one age are not translated into those understood by another without the elision of substantial differences.

The first of the chapters to follow offers an overview of linguistic speculation in the Renaissance through an examination of Rabelais's fable of the frozen words and its radiating implications, which specifically include the impact of printing and the prevalence of sententious or "meaning-full" expressions. If the word *sentential* is understood, with Hacking, to imply a grammatical "séntence" and the word *sententious* is understood to imply a semantic "senténce," as in Middle English, then sentent ious expressions, even when grammatically isolable or complete, can function as sub-sentential units like the other rhetorical figures of thought and speech with which they were classed during the Renaissance.[3] Turning to early modern printed books that focus on words and wordlike units, the second chapter considers the relation of Latin to English in the period as a prelude to the discussion of dictionaries, since comprehensive monolingual English dictionaries did not as yet exist and Latin was generally the language on which dictionaries that included English were based. This chapter explores the implications of alphabetical organization, a nonphonetic and nonreferential ordering of language increasingly normative in dictionaries, and it especially highlights the fictional awareness of words that does not merely co-exist with but is also enhanced by the lexical fixing of language. Chapter 3, continuing the discussion of dictionaries as characteristic Renaissance publications, focuses on etymology and definition, referentiality and abstraction, tracking signs in the period of the momentous shift from essence to word and logic to lexicon. The fourth chapter pursues the definitive word and its etymological basis into Ben Jonson's *Forrest* and Edmund Spenser's land of Faerie, and the fifth takes up the materiality of magical language, its bearing on the iconicity of the sermons of Lancelot Andrewes, and the reflection of that iconicity in various writings of Spenser and Shakespeare. The sixth and last chapter aligns disparate but defining Renaissance texts that centrally and conspicuously engage the substantiality of language and render insistent the questions of how, and how much, words weigh. The texts chosen are the fifth book of Spenser's *Faerie Queene* and Donne's sermons, specifically the second Prebend sermon and "Deaths Duell": Spenser's text is a skeptical, if not disillusioned, poem by the Elizabethan artist par excellence, and Donne's is an affirmation, in prose and a more popular genre, by a writer characteristic of the Stuart period. This final chapter circles around once more to Rabelais, and its ultimate point is that all these writers — the poet of Faerie, the cynical and the idealistic Donnes, and the irreverent monk Rabelais — share a single linguistic universe. It is a universe shaped only in part but in *significant* part by print and lexicography.

This summary tour of the chapters should suggest the extent to which my concerns are historical. They focus on verbal practices in the Renaissance, whether issuing in treatises, grammars, poems, rhetorics, anthologies, logics, dictionaries, or sermons. In relation to them, I should broach two further subjects: one, the old New Criticism, and the other, the term *Renaissance*. At times the arguments that I make will be reminiscent of such a central New Critical statement as this one by W. K. Wimsatt, Jr.:

> Poetic symbols — largely through their iconicity at various levels — call attention to themselves as symbols and in themselves invite evaluation. What may seem stranger is that the verbal symbol in calling attention to itself must also call attention to the difference between itself and the reality which it resembles and symbolizes. . . . Iconicity enforces disparity.[4]

If poetic symbols are considered verbal symbols more generally and "evaluation" is not understood as a moral imperative, my only quarrel with Wimsatt's perceptive statement is that it belongs to a general theory of style or of meaning, and pays no attention to the epistemological and technological changes that at any given point in history might validate it. The fact that it particularly, perhaps peculiarly, fits the Renaissance and even more that cynosure of New Criticism, John Donne, in itself argues the unrecognized and unacknowledged historicity of New Critical concepts. In a sense my own argument locates the historical origin of New Critical insight in the early modern period, while it also suggests the still perceptible relevance of that insight to half-buried roots in our own culture. We of the twentieth century's *fin de siècle* should have no difficulty understanding what Renaissance theorists of language — among whom I number its creatively critical artists — wanted language to do or why they thought that it mattered so much.

The term *Renaissance* also relates to the historicity of my project. I have read and largely assented to Leah Marcus's balanced and thoughtful discussion of this term in *Redrawing the Boundaries*, and I feel free to use *Renaissance*, where clear, interchangeably with *early modern*.[5] Subsequently, however, I will most likely use *early modern* either to imply cultural extension or else to indicate a specific connection with language, since I have known the term in this latter context since the early seventies, when plans for the early modern English dictionary, a proposed successor to the *MED*, were being discussed, and, if memory serves me, were to have included a broader chronological range than the word *Renaissance* suggests, extending through the seventeenth century and well into the eighteenth. In abstracts for papers at recent conferences, I have seen *early modern* extended forward to the end of the eighteenth century and backward to the eighth![6] A broader range of reference is the considerable advantage that the term *early modern* offers, but if a more specific and more historicized chronology is intended, in my case the reigns of the Tudor and Stuart monarchs prior to the Commonwealth, *Renaissance* is simply more accurate.

A problem, duly noted or endnoted where pertinent, that I have had with several otherwise distinguished treatments of Renaissance culture has involved their diachronic insensitivity, particularly to the medieval period. Much of my own scholarly career has engaged the continuities and distinctions between these two periods, and the following pages have been written with frequent glances over my shoulder at what has preceded the parameters of time I have set for my project. My use of the word *Renaissance*, which, in the interest of clarity, has been capitalized to indicate a chronological rather than an evaluative designation, is meant to require at least the awareness of defining relationships between this period and the many medieval centuries that preceded it. Distinctions between these two periods are — indeed, have to be — heuristic. There is no such "thing" as a "period." Such reifications are fictive. This assertion granted, distinctions between the medieval period and the Renaissance can nonetheless be made, often subtly; they are almost always both gradual and irregular, but they are also cumulative, demonstrable, meaningful, material, and technologically graphic. The Renaissance, in other words, is both traditional and fundamentally in transition, and this most interesting and definitive historical phenomenon on the threshold of modernity needs clearer delineation rather than dismissal in the name of the big historical blur.

Chapter 1

Frozen
Words

I n the *Moralia*, Plutarch recounts a humorous story about frozen words that came to be applied to Plato's writings: "In a certain city words congealed with the cold the moment they were spoken, and later, as they thawed out, people heard in the summer what they had said to one another in the winter; it was the same way with what was said by Plato to men still in their youth; not until long afterwards, if ever, did most of them come to perceive the meaning, when they had become old men."[1] Plutarch's version of this story concludes his description of the "ostentatious and artificial" kinds of discourse that first attract but then mislead students of philosophy, which he conceives as the knowledge of virtue. Such discourse includes "disputations, knotty problems, and quibbles," the concerns of the natural sciences, and the sophistries of formal logic; most emphatically, however, it consists of collections of apophthegms and anecdotes. Like Greeks who "never . . . put their money to any use save to count it," collectors of such *sententiae* are, according to

Plutarch, "for ever foolishly taking . . . inventory of their literary stock" and never laying up anything "else which would be to their own profit."[2] It is at this point that Plutarch, scornful of knowledge that is in some way objectified, formal, and unessential rather than centered in "character and feeling," tells the story of the frozen words that do not thaw until their relevance has passed.

In the sixteenth century both Calcagnini and Rabelais repeat versions of Plutarch's story, and Castiglione provides an analogous tale about the words of Russian fur traders that freeze in the air until they are warmed by fire.[3] Like Plutarch's, Calcagnini's version concerns the acquisition of knowledge, but in a reversal of Plutarch's point, it favors "hard knowledge"—frozen words that do not evaporate on first hearing, even though they are not readily accessible to understanding.[4] Rabelais's version, which might have been known to John Donne, is of still greater interest, because it occurs in an episode of the *Quart Livre* that explores signification and the meaning of language.[5] Based in large part on Plutarch's story, Rabelais's fable of the frozen words interweaves ideas about language that are variously Platonic and Aristotelian, nominal and realistic, ideal and material, conceptual and referential. It serves to introduce the complexity of linguistic views active in Renaissance thought and to expose the underlying concern of the present study—namely, the extent to which Renaissance writers conceived of a substantiality in language and the terms, including frozen speech, in which they did so.

Rabelais's fable serves also to illustrate the ambivalence in linguistic contexts of the word *substantiality* itself, which embraces meanings ranging from the metaphysical to the conceptual and the purely material and often lacking neat boundaries. For example, in a rhetorical treatise roughly contemporary with Rabelais's work and subsequently influential in England, Julius Caesar Scaliger attributes to poetry, and to all formal speech ("oratio"), "two *substantial* parts, matter and form (duabus . . . partibus substantialibus, materia et forma)," which he identifies as the spoken or written words on the one hand and the idea (or Idea) and arguments on the other.[6] Like Rabelais's fable, his treatise draws on an uneasy mix of Platonic and Aristotelian positions, along with their medieval and Renaissance mutations. In such a swirl of conceptual possibilities, two other terms common in Renaissance discussions of language, *thing* (Latin *res*) and *matter* (including subject matter, or *res*), share a similar breadth and instability of meaning, as Rabelais's fable will make dramatically clear.

In Rabelais's fourth book, when Pantagruel and his companions, most notably Panurge, are traveling by sea to the oracle of the Holy Bottle, suddenly they hear the sound of voices in the air. While Panurge reacts with fear, the more philosophically minded Pantagruel speculates about the origin of the voices. He first remembers having read ("leu"), not simply heard, that

> a Philosopher named Petron believed there were several worlds touching one another in the form of an equilateral triangle, at whose base and center [*en la pate et centre*][7] was said to be the manor of Truth [*manoir de Verité*] and there to dwell the Words, Ideas, Patterns, and Images [*les Parolles, les Idées, les Exemplaires et portraictz*] of all things past and future: around them is the Age [*Siecle*].[8] And in certain years, at long intervals, part of these drops down upon humanity like catarrhs [*comme catarrhes*] or like the dew that fell upon Gideon's fleece; part remains there, reserved for the future, until the consummation of the Age.[9]

In Pantagruel's myth words participate in truth, much as Plato's Socrates first hopes they might in the *Cratylus*. But Pantagruel's comparisons also allude to the less optimistic end of the *Cratylus*, where the world of Heraclitan flux is compared to a leaky pot and to "a man who has a running at the nose," that is, to one who suffers from catarrh, Greek *katarrhoos*.[10] Simultaneously they suggest that the dregs ("catarrhs") of truth reach earth and yet that what does descend is a divine gift, a sign of favor like the dew on Gideon's fleece. The attitude toward language expressed in the myth as a whole is mixed, even if weighted strongly toward linguistic idealism.

Among Pantagruel's memories that are subsequently evoked by the voices are Aristotle's praise of Homer's winged words; the song of Orpheus that survived his death, issuing from his severed head and lyre as they floated down the river Hebrus to the sea; and Plutarch's comparison of Plato's teaching to frozen words, which motivates the entire episode in Rabelais. Each of these memories involves inspiration and art, and each indicates that words live or endure and again suggests that in some special way they communicate with truth. By including Plutarch's comparison in a chapter dominated by the myth of truth's celestial dwelling and descent to earth, Rabelais, like Calcagnini, gives Plutarch's comparison a positive thrust: Rabelais's frozen words melt only with time and are understood only with the wisdom of age ("*à peine* estre d'iceulx entendu lors que estoient vieulx devenuz"; my emphasis). Yet a trace of Plutarch's scorn also lingers in the likely futility of such knowledge for the aged.

M. A. Screech has argued persuasively that Rabelais's view of the origin of linguistic meaning is partly Aristotelian and partly Platonic, partly conventional and partly idealistic or iconic.[11] Like most of his contemporaries, Rabelais read Aristotle and Plato through the filter of the established commentaries on their works; Rabelais was especially influenced by Hermaeus Ammonius, whose fifth-century commentary on Aristotle's *De interpretatione* was standard from the time of its translation into Latin in the thirteenth century through at least the sixteenth century. Ammonius endeavored to reconcile the linguistic idealism commonly attributed to Plato (usually by reducing his linguistic view to that of his character Cratylus) with the linguistic conventionalism of Aristotle (another simplification, since Aristotle's theory of signification relies on universals—*universalia in rebus*). With Cratylus, Ammonius maintained that names have a real, natural connection with the thing named; with Aristotle, he also maintained that the meaning of words is the result of human convention. His mixed views additionally resemble those of Augustine and of Isidore of Seville, whose works were also well known in the Renaissance.[12] As Ammonius's views were irreverently explained by Agostino Niso in the early sixteenth century, a word such as "'*lapis*, (a stone)'" is inherently appropriate to the object named because it means "'*laedens pedem*, (hurting the foot)'"; at the same time, however, Ammonius could hold that words result from "'human decision (*institutum*).'" While variations are rung on such views in the Renaissance, a great many are similarly mixed, expressing neither Cratylism nor Aristotelianism exclusively.[13]

But Rabelais's fable of the frozen words suggests that his linguistic views were still more eclectic. They might also be described as partly skeptical and partly idealistic, partly nominal and partly real. Both Plato's character Cratylus and Aristotle were basically linguistic realists, the latter believing that our abstract conceptions of nature correspond to things that really exist and therefore that the words in which we express these conceptions refer to what is actually there. Nominalism rejects this view, since it regards such conceptions as being without basis in objective reality. Although Aristotelianism and nominalism both consider words conventional in origin, nominalism maintains that the universals, which are for Aristotle the ground of real knowledge, exist *only* as names, empty nominations, and that conceptual language thus lacks a true correlation with a reality consisting of individual things.

In Rabelais's fable, words are variously but decidedly real, initially in the idealized forms that dwell in the Manor of Truth and then in more earthly terms, since their expression occurs in the less disembodied forms of Homeric epic, Orphic song, and Platonic philosophy. When their reality is further pressed and pursued into increasingly material dimensions, however, it simply melts away. In the end, its evanescence thus enacts the distance between words and materially objective realities.

Materialism grounds the mnemonic flight of Pantagruel's linguistic idealism when the pilot of his ship informs him that the sounds they hear are only the frozen noises of a battle fought at sea during the previous winter — verbal ice cubes, so to speak — which are just now thawing out. Palpable, visible sound: this simpler idea excites Panurge's more materially oriented imagination, and he suddenly recalls Exodus 20.18: "the people saw the voices *sensiblement*" — that is, "sensibly."[14] In comic response, as if to dramatize the literalism of this recollection, Pantagruel promptly throws handsful of frozen words onto the deck, and these are said to resemble "crystallized sweetmeats of diverse colors."[15] The narrator describes them in greater detail, his attention at once on utterance, heraldic colors, and his stomach: "We saw there some words gules — 'gullet words' — some vert, some azure, some sable, some or.[16] When we warmed them a little between our hands, they melted like snow, and we really heard them." Then Panurge asks Pantagruel to give him some more words, and Pantagruel quips that the giving of words is the act of lovers. "Sell me some then," says Panurge, and Pantagruel retorts, "That's what a lawyer does."

Relenting, Pantagruel tosses more words on deck, among them "some very sharp" — "bloody words that sometimes return to the place from which they have been uttered, but with a cut throat; some hair-raising words, and others unpleasant enough to look at." Clearly these are words with material consequences. Play with the melting words continues, next including onomatopoeic sounds and unintelligible battle cries in barbarous tongues, and the narrator proposes to preserve some choice "*motz* [modern *mots*]" in oil and straw. The irrepressible Panurge then provokes the vociferous ire of his fellow pilgrim Frère Jean by unexpectedly "taking him at his word" — catching him off his verbal guard in a perversely literal sense and thereby perpetrating word-theft or entrapment. The episode ends in a sexual slur and an inarticulate gesture of derision, thus completing the catarrh-like descent from the words that dwell with celestial truth to the lower signification of matter.

Screech explains the bearing of all these palpable, visible, literal (literally, letter-all) words in the fable on a number of contemporary legal questions, such as whether a deaf-mute's testimony can be allowed and in what legal sense a word can be seen, rather than heard: for example, "I see what you mean" (pp. 433–34). What seems even more obvious, however, is the extent to which Rabelais's frozen words — visible, gustatory, multicolored, audible, shaped, consequential, and affective — explore the relation of words to things and, broadly conceived, the materiality of language.

In another national context, the definition in English of a noun in "Lily's Latin *Grammar*," the most authoritative text for English schools during the Renaissance, offers a surprisingly telling illustration of the problems that beset the relation of word to thing:

A noune is the name of a thinge, that may be seene, felte, hearde, or vnderstande [i.e., understood]: As the name of my hande in Latine is MANUS: the name of an house is DOMUS: the name of goodnes is BONITAS.[17]

In its English section, Lily's *Grammar* thus characterizes a noun as the mere label for a thing and thereby encourages the identification of word with thing, whether physical or moral thing, that obscures the nature of language as a system of signification.[18] This is the usual reading, which rightly finds in Lily an early symptom of the problem of referentiality that becomes more acute in the following century, with its desire for so many words, and only so many, as things.

The uncertainty inherent in the syntax of Lily's English definition of a noun—an uncertainty that the superfluous comma between "that" and its antecedent merely accentuates—invites a closer look, however.[19] The possibility that the relative pronoun "that" modifies "name," hence "noune," rather than "thinge," is distractingly present. Momentarily, it suggests that the noun itself might be what can be seen, felt, heard, or understood, or, in Rabelaisian terms, frozen, savored, sold, exchanged, believed, preserved, or seized upon.[20] The immediately succeeding examples ("As the name of my hande . . . is MANUS") graphically enforce this possibility. What it involves is reification of the word itself, the word as entity or "thing"; it is a displacement of the referent, a grab for power, as it were, by language. Such reification exaggerates the substantiality of words, whereas the substitution of word for thing stresses the function of words as (ideally transparent) referential markers and ultimately would endeavor to deny it. The latter view inclines to identify the thing as the word's real substance, and the former, its inverse, to identify the word itself as a kind of substance or thing: in the latter case, the word might be said to disappear into the referent; in the former, reality itself to be constituted or reconstituted in language. Have we only melting words or also the recovery of muted voices in Rabelais's fable? Are the frozen words analogous only to the dissolution of Herbert's "Church-monuments" or also to the construction of an antique image in Spenser's *Faerie Queene*?[21]

The Latin section of Lily's *Grammar* offers an alternative definition of the noun, which differs notably from the English one: "Nomen, est pars orationis, quae rem significat, sine vlla temporis aut personae differentia."[22] The difference between a noun that in some sense takes the place of a thing and a noun defined as a part of speech that is not a verb and that *signifies* a thing is important.[23] With G. A. Padley, I would give Lily's Latin definition of a noun the benefit of the doubt and read in the verb *significat* some sense of "a linguistic sign divisible into signifying and signified facets" instead of simply "an item of nomencla-

ture."[24] Lily's "pars orationis," or "part of speech," also implies the
relationship of the noun to a larger structure of meaning ("orationis"), and the Latin definition of the noun as being "without
any difference of time or person" ("sine vlla temporis aut personae differentia"), hence different from the verb, suggests some
awareness of formal grammatical criteria.[25] Like Lily's English
definition, this one draws, via Renaissance sources, on classical
and medieval definitions.[26] But it also represents the persistence
in Renaissance conceptions of language of some balancing sense
of language as a system, rather than as merely an assemblage of
names and nouns—although this sense has been greatly weakened.[27] Without such a sense, a functioning language would be
difficult to conceive at all.

Aside from the possibility that contemporary readers of Lily
were insensitive to the discrepancy between the noun's "thingness" in the English definition and its greater structural integra-
tion in the Latin one, a partial explanation of this discrepancy is
that a committee rather than a single individual compiled the
Grammar and drew on numerous sources, which included but
were by no means limited to the work of William Lily.[28] Often in
the Renaissance, outside strictly logical contexts, seemingly dis-
crepant alternatives are both retained, perhaps because both are
items of potential worth in a store of knowledge still conceived as
being essentially cumulative. Moreover, even within logical linguistic contexts, such as Ammonius's commentary on Aristotle,
an amalgam of opposing views that disorients a modern reader
could be maintained without acknowledgment of any tension.
Part of a work could also be considered valid apart from its modifying conclusion, as, for example, Socrates' initial agreement with
Cratylus apart from his later rejection of Cratylism.

Lily's English definition of a noun signifies more than the
mentalité of inveterate collecting, however. It represents the dominant conception of grammar in England throughout the Renaissance period. This definition, read as encouraging the identifica-

tion of word with extralinguistic thing, transparent label with referent, reflects the tendency "to confound the real world," increasingly conceived in material terms, with "the linguistic symbolization of it." Additionally, it foreshadows more extreme attempts to establish a radically "isomorphic relationship between language and nature" later in the seventeenth century — a relationship whose logic implied that things themselves should effectually be words and thereby obviate the need for language.[29] But read, even playfully, as encouraging the notion that the word per se has a substantial existence, that a noun or name is a thing to be seen or understood to an extent in itself, the English definition further suggests the projection of the semiautonomous "word-world" that Leo Spitzer long since attributed to the Renaissance period and specifically to the work of Rabelais:

> The appearance of this intermediate [word-world in the Renaissance] . . . is conditioned by a belief in the reality of words, a belief which would have been condemned by the "realists" of the Middle Ages. The belief in such vicarious realities as words is possible only in an epoch whose belief in the *universalia realia* has been shaken. It is [in] this phantasmagoric climate . . . [that] Rabelais will move easily and naturally, with a kind of comic independence.[30]

Perhaps it is really (or only) the noun that can be seen, felt, heard, or understood or that can be frozen, savored, sold, exchanged, believed, preserved, or seized upon. After all, had not St. Augustine himself said that words are things (*res*)?[31]

Poised between linguistic realism and nominalistic skepticism, between the idea that words really refer to something out there and the idea that they don't, the imagined world of words Spitzer describes is a fabric of possibilities with an uncertain relation to truth. Conceptually it bears comparison with Sidney's golden world or with "that happy land of Faery" that Spenser "so much do[es] vaunt, yet no where show[s]."[32] Bacon surely had such a fictive world specifically in mind when he likened the cultivation of "eloquence and copie [i.e., *copia*] of speech" to Pygmalion's frenzy, "for words are but the images of matter; and . . . to fall in love with them is all one as to fall in love with a picture."[33] For Bacon at least, words without material warrant have simply become unreal.

Characterizing Erasmus's conception of the relation of language to thought, particularly in *De copia rerum*, Terence Cave describes a coalescence of *verba* and *res* (words and subject matter) that results in "word-things." Through this coalescence, language and thought become two aspects of "a single domain" — language — rather than remaining distinct. Language thus attains a new status but loses its secure basis in things. Cave's hybrid word-things bear a suggestive resemblance to Spitzer's world of words, to Rabelais's fable, and to the equivocations of Lily's humble noun.[34]

The "isomorphic relation" between words and things that I earlier associated with increasingly material conceptions of language in the seventeenth century might also result in a poem that looks like — hence visually is — an exaggeration of the substantiality of language, the reification of the word as reality that Spitzer describes. Yet it is conceptually the other kind of reification, the identification of word with thing that would eliminate the tendency of language to self-referential autonomy; this may be why Herbert's "Easter Wings" does not look like *The Faerie Queene*.[35] "Easter Wings" is a literalizing of the reference of word to thing. It is the depiction of a relationship whereby language is literally *shaped* by matter. "Easter Wings" is not primarily an abstract or mystical thing; like program music, it is representational, and if a hieroglyph, it is also a striking materialization of conventional English. Although "Easter Wings" may strive for a symbolic rendering, the visible thing finally dominates the word. Its domination is even more evident when the lines of the poem are printed vertically, as they were in all the early editions. In Rabelais's terms, this is frozen language.

"Easter Wings" is also a lyrical oddity, something of a *tour de force* whose extreme artifice is infrequently matched and often questioned in Herbert's poetry, as it poignantly is in the ironic self-reflection of "Church-monuments." As stanzaic, syntactical, and even verbal form disintegrates in "Church-monuments," the monumental impulse of Renaissance art—so celebrated in the gestures toward immortality of Shakespeare's sonnets—bows to matter.[36] "Church-monuments" reinstates what is missing—namely, the body and its mortality—from the illustrations of severed hands holding pens that Jonathan Goldberg has found in Renaissance manuals on handwriting, itself the mainstay of monumental fiction.

While Herbert thus tends to privilege the thing and Spenser the word, the line between them is thin, and what they share is finally more important in defining the linguistic character of the age. The concerns their textual practices engage are basically similar, their linguistic universe the same, the continuum between them essentially unbroken.[37] Their poems, if aligned, might be said to debate the relation of words to things and, in particular, the substantiality of language apparent in even the authorized grammar of the time. In both cases their practice heightens the reality of language and thereby reifies it, though inversely: the one by identifying word with *res*, the referential "thing," the other by circumventing or subsuming this identification. The mockery (and self-mockery) of Rabelais's seemingly inexhaustible play with the frozen words suggests how interrogatory and self-reflexive such practices can be and, in the fictive writing of this period, are likely to be.

As we have seen, when Rabelais writes of the words that dwell with truth, the living ("animées") words of Homer, the immortal words of Orpheus, and the enduring words of Plato, his fable suggests that language can transcend impermanence and that metaphysically it has substance. His carefully introducing, within the context of Truth's dwelling, Plutarch's comparison of Plato's wisdom to frozen words further emphasizes the accessibility of truth to human language. As an immediate sequel to this context, Panurge's invocation of Exodus — "le peuple voyoit les voix sensiblement" — could even glance, though I should suppose ironically, at the Kabbalistic belief that the mystical secrets depicted in the very letters and accents (the letteralism) of Hebrew Scripture were revealed to Moses on Mount Sinai.[38] And when, instead of being conceived as intimations of celestial truth, words tumble, frozen, by the handful onto the deck, Rabelais also explores the fact that human language has not simply intelligible substance but also material dimensions, whether as *vox*, voice or sound; as a spatial object, the frozen speech of printed or written record; as the virtual stand-in for its referent, the thing itself; or as a medium of exchange, a tender between lovers, and, in the instance of lawyers, a venal commodity. But as noted before, the substance of language in the fable, when regarded materially, melts paradoxically away, like so many thawing cubes of ice. Rabelais's fable thus plays variously on the distinction (or lack of distinction) between matter and substance, which includes substances born of mind or spirit. This is a distinction that materialist philosophies, ancient or modern, reject, but it is also one that bedevils modern attempts to deal with Renaissance notions about language, since, as Rabelais's fable suggests, it is operative in them.

In an obvious sense, the fable also concentrates attention on the freezing and fixing of language, formulaic varieties of which are everywhere prominent in the Renaissance. Indeed, the reified verbal forms of the fable provide the very occasion and ground for interrogating the nature of language. Within it, the *mots* preserved in oil and straw surely glance at the volumes of *sententiae* published during the period — apophthegms, adages, proverbs, maxims, and other wise sayings preserved for posterity. Citation of the verse from Exodus, which is similarly a recognizable unit of meaning, makes light not only of literalism but also of the assumption that such a unit is a portable object, a sound bite that will play uniformly despite its environment. Much the same is true of set expressions like "Give me your word" or "I take you at your word" when they are found amid a sea of frozen but melting linguistic forms, where their literal meanings become suddenly and absurdly volatile.

An immediate context that extends the application of Rabelais's frozen words still further occurs in Juan Luis Vives' *In Pseudodialecticos*, an attack on the contemporary teaching of logic and dialectic.[39] Vives' play in this work on the words *rigore* — rigidity, hardness, inflexibility — and *frigore* — coldness, frigidity, iciness — suggests another form of freezing, to which writers such as Rabelais and Erasmus were equally sensitive. Vives' treatise vehemently attacks the "senseless inanities" of the logicians of the Sorbonne and pleads for a more useful knowledge and a more natural way of expressing it. Sounding much like Erasmus, he decries the formulas, the straitjackets of thought and expression, that dominate the schools.[40] He takes particular aim at the logicians' distinction between a statement's being false according to common sense and its being true *ad rigorem*. Making this distinction, the logicians "are lacking in common sense, and they speak only *in rigore*, a rigor more frigid [*frigidiore*] than ice" (pp. 54–55). "Let them speak *in frigore* if they so desire, and in ice itself," he exclaims on another occasion (pp. 60–61). Vives' criticism, like that in Plutarch's story, is directed primarily at the substitution of "ostentatious and artificial" kinds of discourse for a more humane engagement with "character and feeling."[41] But the numerous examples of formulaic inanity he cites (e.g., "Varro, though a man, is likewise not a man because Varro is not Cicero"; "Socrates and this ass are brothers"; "Nothing and No-man bite each other in a sack"), along with his awareness that both logic and dialectic have "to do precisely with words" and his repeated comparison of the Sorbonnistes' formulations to ice, indicate his specific concern with the freezing of language as well as of thought. As Vives emphasizes, language is not to be "twisted to

suit the rules [Latin *formulae*], but rather the rules follow . . .
language" (pp. 36–37). What is particularly interesting in his
discussion is not merely the fact of the freezing of language but
once again a contemporary *perception* of it as having frozen forms.
To a greater or lesser extent, the freezing and reifying of language conspicuous in Renaissance works characterize many cultures and, at some level, culture itself. Working in the field of
linguistics, for example, William E. Cooper and John Robert
Ross have analyzed the fixed order — what they term "freezes" —
of phonological and semantic elements in brief conjuncts of current speech, such as "bigger and better" and "fore and aft," and
also in more complex constructions such as proverbs.[42] Nigel
Barley, similarly concerned with proverbs and maxims, both current and Anglo-Saxon ones, describes such formulaic expressions
as "templates" and "portable paradigms," which incorporate new
situations into existing categories.[43] In a popular mode, these
expressions serve a function analogous to that of Sorbonniste
logic in Renaissance schools. Indeed, Roland Barthes has loosely
characterized any "utterances of the cultural code," a description that extends to logical formulas in the Renaissance, as "implicit proverbs." Following Saussure, he has also suggested that
stereotyped modes of writing like proverbs constitute "a real *linguistics of the syntagm*"; that is, they are fixed syntagms, frozen
chains of utterance "out of reach of the combinative freedom of
speech [*parole*]," and they therefore belong to language as system (*langue*).[44]

Writing in the middle of the twentieth century, William Empson broached an idea broadly similar to that of a cultural code: "A
word [or phrase] may become a sort of solid entity, able to direct
opinion, thought of as like a person; . . . also it is often said
(whether this is the same idea or not) that a word can become a
'compacted doctrine,' or even that all words are compacted doctrines inherently."[45] What is popularly known as a buzzword affords an extreme example of the kind of complex word Empson

describes, which comes to be thought of as "a sort of solid entity." A proverb is an example of a phrase to which comparable solidity might attach; to cite a case both ironically and literally in point, *Verbum sat sapienti*, "A word [is] enough for a wise man."

Received codes themselves, as the implicit metaphor in the term suggests, are instances of freezing, and there is an obvious sense in which any semiotic system involves an element of freezing as well. George Lakoff and Mark Johnson describe the "metaphors we live by" — for instance, the notion, ancient and modern, that linguistic expressions are containers or arguments are buildings — as cultural encoding.[46] Such a code is a form of psychological and epistemological programming, a mind-set or fixing of perception that is inscribed in language. The programming appears to be culturally specific, although particular metaphoric codes may occur within broad temporal or geographic boundaries and the *grounding* of the most basic codes in direct physical experience, including spatial orientation, is very likely universal.[47] Not surprisingly, Lakoff and Johnson consider the human process of conceptualization itself to be fundamentally metaphorical, and they invoke Aristotle as a precursor, since he understood that "the greatest thing by far is to be a master of metaphor."[48]

Conceptual thought likewise requires some degree of reification, a fact evident in its penchant for conspicuous nominalization — "-ists," "-isms," "-ations," and "-ologies."[49] Among those conceptually inclined, a seemingly natural tendency to hypostatize language in this way appears meant to give us the impression that the concept really exists, or, in metaphorical terms, that it has "weight" and "substance." Consider the seeming solidity, the visual and audible claim, of words like "distanciation," "decontextualization," "euphemization," "discoursivization," and, my current favorite for sheer orthographical enactment, "reterritorialization." Such terms, not unlike Donne's more modest efforts in "A Valediction: forbidding Mourning" ("profanation," "trepidation," or even "inter-assured") testify to our own sense of the substantiality of language.

Nominal, or "nounlike," sentences bear on a frozen form of expression especially typical of Renaissance culture. Nominal sentences are distinguished by their general, sententious, and proverbial quality. Benveniste describes them as non-verbal assertions complete in themselves, "beyond all temporal or modal localization and beyond the subjectivity of the speaker." Absolute and inflexible, a nominal sentence like *verbum sat sapienti* or *omnis homo mortalis*, "every man [is] mortal," implies a nonvariable relationship "between the linguistic utterance and the nature of things."[50] It is an objectified saying, an entity, frozen, inscribed in stone: the sort of sentence commonly found on monuments. There is a striking coincidence of expression and perception, medium and message, in the fact that the lapidary epigraph becomes a favored artistic form in Renaissance sculpture, architecture, and painting, achieving, in John Sparrow's words, virtually an "independent existence" in the sixteenth century and in the seventeenth century developing into a kind of book related to the epigram.[51] Inscriptions are inherently monumental; they seem to guarantee the solidity and weight, the stability and objectivity of language.[52]

One of the most familiar expressions in this period of the tendency to fix and reify language involves a reconception of graphic space and an increasing emphasis on its visual character, developments Walter Ong has ably examined, notably followed by Murray Cohen, Elizabeth Eisenstein, Glyn Norton, and, more recently but variously, Martin Elsky and Jonathan Goldberg.[53] Although grids, diagrams, sectioning, and various techniques of visually emphasizing parts of a text (including underlining, the use of different scripts and colored inks, illustrations, and marginal notation) were frequently employed in the manuscript culture of the Middle Ages, such visual features so multiply and intensify in the production of printed texts as to validate the view that a significant shift in the perception and communication of data is occurring.[54] This shift is more than the result of the sheer quantity and quality of visual devices and the general cultural dissemination of them that the new technology of print made practical, although these developments too are important. Gradually and increasingly, it also reflects a different way of conceiving the character and purpose of representation on the page.

Visual devices become oriented increasingly to the presence of the page in its own right, to such immediate needs as legibility, reference, and comprehension — in short, to its there-ness, its character as an objective site, a locus of definitive meaning. Such a meaningful place is potentially more than a record of something outside itself or a symbolic witness to a transcendent truth, as was typically the case in the Middle Ages.[55] Although the roots of socially complex changes in attitude toward the page can be traced back to the Middle Ages, particularly to its later phases, in obvious ways the technology of print facilitated and accelerated these. In terms of manipulability, time, and cost, a quill pen bears on the choice of a style of writing and the very shapes of the letters themselves: a lucid medieval bookhand, for example, might be fine for an unpressured monk, but harried administrators would turn to the quicker, less distinct cursive. Standardized printing types have clear advantages of uniformity, legibility, and reliability over letters subject to the skill and circumstances of the individual scribe. Printing offers the possibility of investing more autonomous authority in the page per se, rather than only in certain pages and for special reasons.

Even the gradual movement away from abbreviated orthographical forms to fully visible words during the Renaissance is significant. There is evidence, according to M. T. Clanchy, that the system of abbreviating words in medieval manuscripts was mainly intended to cue someone reading aloud.[56] This evidence further suggests that writing primarily served a mnemonic function; indeed, it provided a "script" in the performative sense and not just in the literal one. The gradual displacement of medieval abbreviations thus suggests more than a lessened need to skimp on space and time, though these are relevant considerations. More important, it indicates a lessening sense of the function of letters as cues to predictable constructions and a growing sense of them as the locus of meaning, invention, and authority.[57] In a very small way, they are part of a greater emphasis on externalization and the material world, the same movement that informed a number of the most heated religious controversies of the period: those concerning the translation of the biblical *Logos* as either the ineffable *verbum* of Augustine or the articulated *sermo* of Erasmus; the primacy of Scripture, or the written page; the greatly elevated role of preaching, or sound; and the reality of bread (rather than its mere appearance) in the Sacrament.[58]

Controversies such as these register the difference between the Middle Ages and the Renaissance with particular sensitivity. Recently, for example, much has been made of the enhanced status of *vox*, understood as the sounded vernacular word, in Renaissance language theory, but little of the fact that conceptually it implied not only a socialization but also a materialization of language.[59] For the Scholastic critics of Erasmus's translation of *Logos*, materialization was the basic scandal from which the diachronic evolution and social mutability of language merely followed. Exceptions to any broad generalization about artificially demarcated historical periods necessarily exist and become more numerous near their putative borders. Yet, on the whole, theory in the Middle Ages gives radical precedence to the mind; it is not that the Renaissance does not often do, or try to do, the same or that medieval thinkers had no sense of matter, but that conceptually the reality of matter becomes more conspicuous, important, and indeed essential as time goes on.

Along with the significantly increased use of columns, maps, grids, and diagrams that printed books made possible during the

Renaissance, marginal identifications proliferate, seeming in the novel presence of tabular indices to function more as emphatic devices or advertisements than as mnemonic aids. By the turn of the sixteenth century, there had appeared a sufficient number of *sententiae* with forefingers pointing to them to elicit an exasperated complaint from the stylistically sensitive John Hoskyns. While Hoskyns is aware that such pointers might serve as mnemonic aids (their presumed function in an earlier period), and while he does not object to them for this purpose, he perceives them essentially as visual obstacles to understanding and as reinforcements of a corrupt, euphuistic style. His *primary* concern is with appearance and legibility as fundamental conditions for rhetorically effective writing. His attention is focused on the page itself, and that is the point.[60]

Earlier in the century and toward a different end, Nicholas Udall's translation of Erasmus's *Apophthegmes* had outdone even the pointings Hoskyns had in mind. Udall inserts trefoils (1542) or outstretched index fingers (1542, 1564) in the very midst of the Erasmian text to indicate the addition of his own explanatory glosses of proper names and historical, mythological, and proverbial allusions; he adds other reference marks such as asterisks, Maltese crosses, and double daggers within the text to signal further explanations in the margins; and he marks "the moralizacion[s] of Erasmus" with the typographical sign of a leaf (Fig. 1). In addition, Udall is at pains to explain that the text will present the apophthegm, or "saiyng self," in "a greate texte letter" (large type) and Erasmus's commentary in "a middle letter," his own contributions appearing in small type. Lest anything "should lacke" that might assist "the vnlearned reader," he also provides for the volume an extensive alphabetical index of names and subjects.[61]

Udall's employment of the page resembles medieval practices and doubtless derives from them, but in his hands the page itself has become a road map keyed less to cognitive debate and mne-

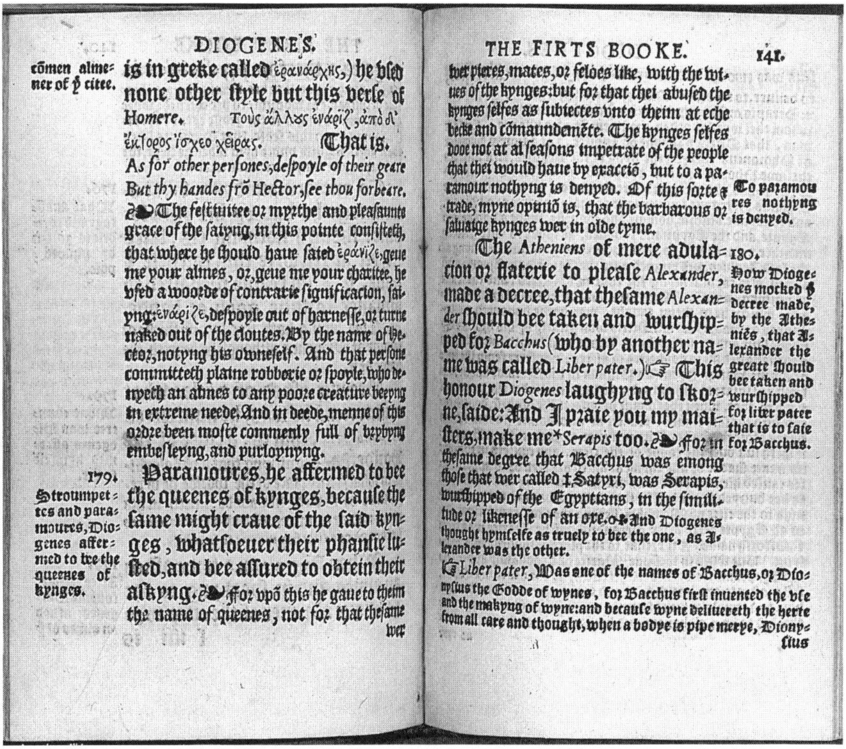

DIOGENES.

cōmen almes ner of þ citee.

is in greke called ἐρανάρχης,) he vsed none other style but this verse of Homere. Τοὺς ἄλλους ἐνάριζ', ἀπὸ δ' Ἕκτορος ἴσχεο χεῖρας. That is.

As for other persones, despoyle of their geare
But thy handes frō Hector, see thou forbeare.

☞ The festiuitee or myrthe and pleasaunte grace of the saiyng, in this pointe consisteth, that where he should haue saied ἐράνιζε, geue me your almes, or, geue me your charitee, he vsed a woorde of contrarie signification, saiyng: ἐνάριζε, despoyle out of harnesse, or turne naked out of the cloutes. By the name of Hector, notyng his owneself. And that persone committeth plaine robberie or spoyle, who denyeth an almes to any poore creature beeyng in extreme neede. And in deede, menne of this ordre been moste commenly full of brybyng embeslyng, and purloynyng.

179. Stroumpettes and paramoures, Diogenes affermed to bee the queenes of kynges.

Paramoures, he affermed to bee the queenes of kynges, because the same might craue of the said kynges, whatsoeuer their phansie lusted, and bee assured to obtein their askyng. ☞ For vpō this he gaue to theim the name of queenes, not for that the same wer

THE FIRTS BOOKE. 141.

wer pieres, mates, or felóes like, with the wiues of the kynges: but for that thei abused the kynges selfes as subiectes vnto theim at eche becke and cōmaundemēte. The kynges selfes doe not at al seasons impetrate of the people that thei would haue by exacciō, but to a paramour nothyng is denyed. Of this sorte & trade, myne opiniō is, that the barbarous or saluaige kynges wer in olde tyme.

To paramoures nothyng is denyed.

180. How Diogenes mocked þ decree made, by the Atheniēs, that Alexander the greate should bee taken and wurshipped for liber pater that is to saie for Bacchus.

The *Atheniens* of mere adulacion or flaterie to please *Alexander*, made a decree, that the same *Alexander* should bee taken and wurshipped for *Bacchus* (who by another name was called *Liber pater*.) ☞ This honour *Diogenes* laughyng to skorne, saide: And I praie you my maisters, make me **Serapis* too. ☞ For in the same degree that Bacchus was emong those that wer called †Satyri, was Serapis, wurshipped of the Egyptians, in the similitude or likenesse of an oxe. ☞ And Diogenes thought hymselfe as truely to bee the one, as Alexander was the other.

☞ *Liber pater*, Was one of the names of Bacchus, or Dionysius the Godde of wynes, for Bacchus first inuented the vse and the makyng of wyne: and because wyne delivereth the herte from all care and thought, when a bodye is pipe merye, Dionysius

Fig. 1. Desiderius Erasmus of Rotterdam, *Apophthegmes*, trans. Nicholas Udall, 1542: 140^{v}–141^{r}. By permission of the Folger Shakespeare Library.

monics than to textual properties.[62] In the Middle Ages, the layout of the standardized glosses typically found on the biblical page, for example, required no explanation, since anyone supposed to be reading them had been trained in their use. In contrast, Udall's concern for a more popular and secular audience, for a visually explanatory layout, and for the spatial, hence territorial, identification of authorial ownership is symptomatic of change.[63]

Additional examples suggest similar conclusions. More ubiquitous than marginal pointers in Renaissance texts is the employment of different typefaces, frequently to signal the appearance of another voice—for example, that of a different speaker or of a sententious quotation, biblical or otherwise.[64] Styles of lettering in other media, like styles of print, also contribute to an emphasis on visibility. The roman style that replaces the gothic one in Renaissance inscriptions and increasingly in typography achieves visual emphasis through clarity of form and increased legibility; the swirling flourishes of signatures in italic script, the privileged "Humanist hand," add graphic emphasis and distinction—a more authoritative presence—to the handwritten word, and italic refinements increase the sense, for writer and viewer alike, of what Jonathan Goldberg has described as "the materiality of letters themselves."[65] Even the periodic sentence, in its extension on the page, might be perceived to further the same effect.

My point, however, is not that the Renaissance page is simply more spatial or the Humanist hand more material than their counterparts in the Middle Ages. The *Glossa ordinaria* was bulky enough, and a medieval scriptorium real enough. As for the material conditions of writing, a quill pen certainly required as disciplined a hand on parchment as on paper, and, in addition to the instruments for writing in the Renaissance, the medieval scribe had also an awl for pricking holes, a knife or razor for preparing parchment, and a boar or goat's tooth for polishing the page; no milktoast he. Often medieval gothic inscriptions were more extensive than the later roman-style ones; that is, they literally took up more space and more material. The same is true of a paratactic style like Malory's, whose sentences are loosely but amply additive.

Aside from the sheer quantity of print that the press made available, Renaissance forms of written expression were in general more spatial or material than medieval ones only in the metaphoric sense in which "spatial" means something like "easily or dramatically visible"—that is, "legible" or "emphatic" to modern eyes—and "material" means "determinative" or "culturally focal."[66] I therefore refer to these qualities as impressions, as perceptions, or, *in extremis*, as illusions. The force of Goldberg's description of Renaissance writing as "material" may appear somewhat different, since he grounds the materiality of the letter in the hand that writes it, albeit with a simultaneous pun on the "hand," or script, that inscribes the body (*Writing Matter*, pp. 228–29). But unless this grounding is understood to mean a greater conceptual and societal emphasis on the hand per se, the medieval period, whose graphic production was scribal, would appear to be more material. The greater materiality of Renaissance writing (not writings) is based on quality rather than quantity, on style rather than physical extension and mass, on perception and utilization rather than purely material fact.[67] One John Done, presumably not the poet, puts the literalist's case more simply, writing in his miscellany: "Observe regularly the speech of man, and there is nothing almost spoken but by figure; as one sayes, this is my hand, for his handwriting: this is my deed, when it is but his consent thereto."[68] It is, of course, entirely in keeping with these views that Renaissance forms of writing, whether typographic, chirographic, or inscriptive, should also seem to be more spatial, material, and conceptually "weighty." In Lakoff and Johnson's phrasing, space, matter, and weight provide basic "metaphors we [have come to] live by," to see and understand by, and, as such, they concern us vitally. What "seems," for the practical consciousness, is often actual.

In conjunction with other related developments, the conspicuous concentration of visual techniques of organization and emphasis on the Renaissance page lent itself readily to the impression of objectivity and fixity. The quantity and replaceability of exact printed copies further heightened this impression by vastly increasing the likelihood that writings would endure once "set" in print. In this light the paucity of extant Renaissance manuscripts actually used for typesetting makes a certain lamentable sense, suggesting that the printing houses discarded them after they had been printed. Having first been marked for casting off, then corrected, smudged, and, in the words of Aldus Manutius, "delivered over to the printers to be ripped apart, and to die like vipers in the act of birth," the manuscripts themselves were deemed redundant.[69] Other contemporary cultural phenomena similarly suggest the perceived objectivity, perdurability, and fixity of the printed page, as, for example, the reformers' reliance on the principle *sola scriptura* or the obsessive emphasis in the period on the eternizing conceit: "so long as . . . *eyes can see* / So long lives this, and this gives life to thee." These lines by Shakespeare find a literalizing analogue in William Bullokar's *Booke at Large, 1580,* a treatise on spelling reform: "Letters," Bullokar writes in his metronomic verse, "for picture true, of speech, were first deuizd," and "man changing this mortall life, by picture leaues in minde, / the speciall gifts of God most high, to them that bide behinde."[70] Shakespeare's lines conclude a sonnet that uses metaphor to circumvent physical description of the beloved, and they roughly mean, "an impression of you lives in this poem so long as eyes can see it." Bullokar's more literally means, "speech lasts in the very letters that express it." In Bullokar's view letters accurately depict sound; they make it visible and, in effect, they freeze it. They *realize* speech, without the complicating duplicity evident in Shakespeare's couplet: the intervention of interpreting eyes (or subjective "I's") and the equivocation of the word "this" in the final line, which can be interpreted either as poetic response to the beloved or as the graphic form that perpetuates that response — in either case, an "impression." While the power of verse to confer immortality is an ancient motif, the consciousness of this potential in the perdurance of visible words and letters, whether in Shakespeare's subtleties or Bullokar's literalism, is peculiarly pronounced in the Renaissance.[71] Older habits of mind undoubtedly assert a strong influence throughout the period, and newer ones have roots in the past, but the cultural center of gravity is nonetheless shifting perceptibly.

Whereas to a great extent the medieval page remained the servant of memory and the inner word, the Renaissance page had—or at least seems to have—more autonomy, and the Renaissance word more literal weight. In the Middle Ages, as Mary Carruthers has observed, books were likely to be considered "memorial cues and aids" subservient to memory, and memory itself was thought to be "most like a book," with actual books its limited extramental reflection (p. 16). By the seventeenth century, however, virtually the reverse is entirely conceivable. In the following quotations from Donne's sermons, the written form has conceptual priority: "Our whole life is but a *parenthesis*, our *receiving* of our soule, and delivering it back againe, makes up the perfect sentence"; indeed, the person of Job is the "booke" in which to study "all the *letters* in this *Alphabet* of our life." Even the death of Christ "is delivered to us" not "as a *writing*" only but also as a "writing in the nature of a Copy to learne by; It is not only given us to reade, but to write over" again.[72]

The closest medieval parallel to Donne's sermon that I have encountered comes in a sermon from the twelfth century. Its nearness to and distance from Donne are alike illuminating and perhaps can afford an optimum summary of the relation of the Renaissance view of writing to that of the Middle Ages. The medieval sermon asks its hearers to "become scribes of the Lord," for

> the parchment on which we write for him is a pure conscience, whereon all our good works are noted by the pen of memory. . . . The knife wherewith it is scraped is the fear of God. . . . The pumice wherewith it is made smooth is the discipline of heavenly desires. . . . The chalk with whose fine particles it is whitened indicates the unbroken meditation of holy thoughts. . . . The ruler [*regula*] by which the line is drawn that we may write straight, is the will of God. . . . The tool [*instrumentum*] that is drawn along the ruler to make the line, is our devotion to our holy task. . . . The pen [*penna*], divided in two that it may be fit for writing, is the love of God and our neighbour. . . . The ink with which we write is humility itself. . . . The diverse colours wherewith the book is illuminated, not unworthily represent the multiple grace of

heavenly Wisdom. . . . The desk [*scriptorium*] whereon we write is tranquillity of heart. . . . The copy [*exemplar*] by which we write is the life of our Redeemer. . . . The place where we write is contempt of worldly things.[73]

Startlingly similar to Donne's, the claims of the medieval sermon differ significantly from them. The extended comparison in the medieval sermon is conventionally allegorical; it is openly contrived and motivated by a trope of resemblance.[74] Donne's metaphors have the same underlying structure, but they deny it. In the medieval sermon, writing is merely the illustration of a devout mnemonic process, whereas in Donne's it partakes of life's essence. There is an identity between life, death, and the perfectly written sentence for Donne. His metaphors make a claim that is literal and real; after all, are they not written? The life of Christ, too, is a writing, and, in every sense, as the saying goes, the word is the thing.

Even if it were true that "writing something down cannot change in any significant way our mental representation of it, [since] . . . the mental representation . . . gives birth to the written form, not vice versa," written or printed representations we encounter can so influence our perceptions as in time to alter them radically. At the very least, the cultural interaction of conception, representation, and production is more nearly and complexly reciprocal and dynamic than static and one-directional. They enable and shape one another incrementally.[75]

Hall's chronicle records a familiar story for the year 1529 concerning Cuthbert Tunstall (1474–1559), bishop of London, and William Tyndale, translator of the English Bible, that serves to illustrate both the *mentalité* of transition from a culture of manuscripts to one of print and the material reality of the new technology — the "letters and stampes" of the print shop itself. Tunstall, intent on destroying all copies of Tyndale's allegedly heretical translation, unwittingly employed one Packington, who sympathized with Tyndale, to buy up the remaining copies of the translation in order that the bishop might burn them. Tyndale, though aware of the bishop's intention, supplied Packington with "a hepe of newe Testamentes" and then used the bishop's money to pay off his debts and to bring out a corrected edition. Informed that the Bibles "came thicke and threfold into England" even after his bonfire, Tunstall sent for Packington and demanded an explanation. Packington explained that all available copies had been purchased, as agreed, but that Tyndale had simply printed some more. The wily Packington now advised the bishop to buy "the stampes" of the translation in order to stop the flood of books. At this point, however, the bishop, beginning to learn his lesson in technology, "smiled at him and said, well Packyngton, well," and so broke off the interview.[76]

The new technology clearly had a material persistence that had caught the bishop by surprise. This is a matter to which Spenser's first canto of *The Faerie Queene* also refers, when the monster Error disgorges a flood of books and papers in close proximity to a passage implicating the illimitable fertility of the material world.[77] Apprehension about an inability to control the output of the new technology, a sense of being overwhelmed by it, bears at once on dogmatic intransigence and on a desire to fix and freeze language. Apprehension, of course, was hardly the only Renaissance response to print or the only Spenserian one, but in celebrating technology it is the one we are likely to forget.

The commonplace book or collection of *sententiae* — variously proverbs, adages, aphorisms, maxims, apophthegms, and sayings, indeed, *mots* — figures among the most frequent of Renaissance publications, and it, too, reflects not only a desire to amass cultural treasure but also a pleasure in crystallized language. The taste in this period for what Plutarch nominated as his prime example of frozen words, sententious sayings, whether collected or selected, secular or sacred, classical or vernacular, appears insatiable. Erasmus's *Adagia*, a collection of proverbs with commentaries, saw ten editions and many enlargements between 1508 and his death in 1536, and by 1700 it had gone through 52 complete editions and 96 editions in epitomized or selected form. It was translated into numerous vernacular languages and proved the most popular book of the century. Its popularity was almost equaled by Erasmus's other sententious collections, the early *Adagiorum Collectanea*, the *Apophthegmata*, and the *Parabolae*, a collection of aphorisms based on similitudes, which was published in 38 editions during Erasmus's lifetime and in 22 others before 1600. As Margaret Mann Phillips has memorably written, this was a time when "Marguerite de Navarre embroidered *Ubi spiritus ibi libertas* on her hangings, and Montaigne had only to raise his eyes to the rafters of his study to find his own choice of proverbs."[78] Sir Thomas Elyot had sayings engraved on his plate and vessels; Sir Nicholas Bacon, the father of Francis, embellished the long gallery at Gorhambury with *sententiae*; Lancelot Andrewes was a student of proverbs, and George Herbert made a collection of them; William Cecil, Lord Burghley, sounding much like Shakespeare's Polonius, wrote sententious commonplaces to his son; and even John Hoskyns set Latin, Greek, and Hebrew inscriptions (presumably without pointers) in the buildings on his estate.[79]

This vogue has attracted various explanations. Since "sayings," albeit written, collected, and inscribed, suggest speech, it has been seen as evidence of the ingrained orality of Renaissance culture. More often, it has been interpreted as a vital engagement with traditional wisdom and particularly with what Hoskyns describes as "morall philosophie."[80] In terms of my earlier discussion, it also expresses the appeal for this period of culturally encoded templates such as proverbs, which Henry Peacham describes as "The

Summaries of maners" and "Images of humane life."[81] Developing
the social utility of *sententiae*, Frank Whigham and Mary Thomas
Crane have explained the period's fixation on commonplaces as
the conscious and deliberate "cultural capital" of humanism.[82]

Like the Renaissance inscriptions that frequently drew on collections of *sententiae*, the sententious vogue exhibits abundant
examples of nominal assertion—to take one from the collection
at Gorhambury, LONGUM ITER PER PRAECEPTA: BREVE
ET EFFICAX PER EXEMPLA, "Long the way by rules, short
and effectual by examples."[83] In words that again suggest the
monumentality of such inscribed authority Barbara Kirshenblatt-
Gimblett refers to "the *weight* of impersonal community con-
sensus" that the proverbial saying invokes, and Morris Palmer
Tilley observes in a curiously mixed metaphor how some proverbs "sound like *petrifications* of alliterative poetry." George Puttenham's explanation of a gnomic saying, "by the Latin . . . called
sententia," similarly suggests its substantiality: "In waightie causes
and for great purposes, wise persuaders use grave and weighty
speaches."[84]

In short, the sententious vogue tends to fix and reify language,
particularly in visual, syntactical, and rhythmic terms and particularly when examples of it are in some way isolated, as in inscriptions; unsituated historically or contextually, as in compilations;
or repeated ritually or programmatically, as in sermons.[85] Once
again, this is a vogue with similarities to and deep roots in medieval culture, but it is at the same time a development of them that
employs and adapts to a new technology and participates in a
larger process of cultural change.[86] Slowly and fundamentally,
this process involves interrelated perceptions of language and, in
both broad and narrow senses, of the material world.

There are signs in the period itself—even outside creative writing, where we might expect them—of an awareness of the way
sententiae operate as templates of meaning, freeze language, and
appear to solidify it. The notion of a template is implicitly present

even in Roger Ascham's confidence that "good precepts of learning, be the eyes of the minde, to looke wiselie *before* a man, which waie to go right, and which not"; precepts are, as it were, the spectacles through which new experiences are seen and hence understood.[87] The essential significance of an experience appears to be settled beforehand. Ascham's observation belongs to a context in which, while granting that experience is profitable, he insists it is so only "to him . . . that is diligentlie before instructed with preceptes of well doinge." Experience merely provides an occasion on which to fit the precept — *praeceptum*, "already possessed."

Ascham "proves" his point, moreover, with a flurry of sayings, among them several conspicuous for the solidity of their matter: "An vnhappie Master he is, that is made cunning by manie shippewrakes: A miserable merchant, that is neither riche or wise, but after som bankroutes. It is a costlie wisdom, that is bought by experience." In Ascham's employment of these sayings metaphorical and literal meanings, subject matter and the material world, the impression of moral solidity and its material basis become virtually indistinguishable. Such solid-seeming substance rests on an appeal not only to economic sense but also to linguistic and rhetorical senses: acoustic, syntactic, and figurative. To read Ascham's sayings is to experience, in Nigel Barley's phrase, a "prefabricated unit" for the construction of meaning (p. 741). Such a unit has become at once a piece of evidence and a kind of thing.

A more explicit and negative sense of the prefabricated fixity of the sententious commonplace appears in Gabriel Harvey's *Ciceronianus*, when he speaks scornfully of "such *domiciles* of argument [*argumentorum domicilia*]" and again of the "architects of the aforesaid domiciles." Harvey's choice of words implies the affected artifice of these constructions. In a way that recalls Rabelais and Vives, his making the rhetorical "places" actual houses, and pretentious ones at that, reifies and mocks reliance on them, to which he opposes the true "sources of reason."[88] Harvey's awareness is fitful, however, and it shows how readily one kind of Renaissance awareness of words shades into another, suggesting the significant extent to which such awareness is in flux and rendering an isolated quotation misleading. Often within the *Ciceronianus* Harvey's sense of the materiality of language is unreflective: for example, he speaks of "the architecture of clauses, the shaping of sentences," "the sinews in tropes," and "the muscles and tendons in figures" (pp. 53, 77). His extravagant deployment of these *commonplace* comparisons, moreover, is outdone by William Lewin's laudatory preface to the *Ciceronianus*, which was apparently written by one of like mind: "the body of a speech ought . . . to be like the human body, with some members longer and others shorter; for if anyone have feet the length of the lower legs or fingers the length of the forearms, people would call the fellow's appearance not merely misshapen but monstrous."[89] The corporeality of Lewin's extended comparison is so pronounced and literal that it is difficult not to visualize the actual metamorphosing of a multimembered sentence into a squirming monster. Spenser's monstrous Error come again — a clear case, it would seem, of words that have themselves become things.

But Harvey next sounds very much like Francis Bacon, when he speaks in the *Ciceronianus* of a need to keep Homer's winged words from flying away and endeavors to maintain their "equilibrium by the weightiness of the subject matter."[90] Here A. C. Howell's classic essay on the slippage of the word *res*, "things," toward an exclusively material meaning in Renaissance language theory affords a gloss on Harvey's phrasing: "the term *res*, meaning *subject matter*, seems to [have] become confused with *res* meaning *things*, and the tendency to assume that *things* should be expressible in *words*, or conversely, [that] *words* should represent *things*, not metaphysical and abstract concepts," is clearly discernible.[91] Howell describes the tendency to identify words with *material* things, whether this identity is conceived to be nominal or real, conventional or isomorphic.[92] This slippage is apparent in the particular use Harvey makes of the metaphor of weightiness in the quotation with which this paragraph begins: he attributes a surprisingly literal force to the word "matter" in the phrase "subject matter," the stuff required to ground those winged words of Homer. Harvey now seems to find things in language that are really out there in the world.

Vives, in *De tradendis disciplinis* (1531), intimates the materiality of sententious language in another, subtler way. He characterizes proverbs, *sententiae*, and "all those other precepts collected from the recorded [*annotata*: literally, 'noted down'] observation[s] of wise men which have remained among the people as public wealth in a common exchequer [*publicae opes in aerario communi*]."[93] Although Vives clearly assumes the traditional designation of memory as the treasury of knowledge (*thesaurus*, *scrinium*, *arca*, etc.), his attention focuses specifically on the riches of wisdom preserved in language and particularly in *written* language. He gives such treasure an externalized and impersonal emphasis — "public wealth," indeed, "material riches [*opes*]" and "common exchequer," the last a treasury in the specific sense of "a place for keeping public funds," a meaning associated with that of cognates like *aerarius*, "of, or connected with coinage, money."[94]

Vives' treasure, at once societal and material, is well on its way to Ascham's solid precepts; to Bacon's comparison of letters, words, and other semiotic signs to "currency" (moneys); and, indeed, eventually to Tilley's description of modern proverbial knowledge as "the small change of conversation," cultural capital devalued in a less traditional economy.[95] Fleetingly, Vives' image also touches Rabelais's jest about words as salable goods in the hands of lawyers, which alludes to a much older tradition of legal venality but subsumes it in a fable whose focal concern is language.[96] Vives' public treasury aligns itself as well with such quintessentially Renaissance *thesauri*, "treasuries," as Thomas Cooper's *Thesaurus linguae Romanae et Britannicae* and Robert Estienne's *Thesaurus linguae Latinae*, both popular printed dictionaries that graphically amass and circulate the necessarily rare or mnemonic achievements, the unique or interior treasures, of the classical and medieval past.[97]

There is further evidence in Renaissance treatments of language of an awareness of proverbial sayings as linguistically distinctive units, things that resist any simple equation with content and reference. Peacham, for example, defines *paroemia*, the proverb, unexceptionally as "a sentence [i.e., *sententia*] or forme of speech" that is "witty, and well proportioned, whereby it may be discerned by some speciall marke and note from common speech" (p. 29). The "well proportioned" form — the proverb — apparently possesses rhetorical or grammatical features that distinguish it from its linguistic surroundings. In 1565, Henri Estienne similarly characterizes the "propriety [*la propriété*]" of the words in proverbs that constitute their charm and force and render them essentially untranslatable: "Aussi en ha chascune langue quelsques-vns ['proverbes'], lesquels ne se peuuent pas mesmes traduire en sorte aucune, à cause de la propriété des mots esquels consiste la grace du prouerbe, ou l'energie." Inherently equivocal, the word *propriety* (Latin *proprietas*) basically means "property" and therefore both "appropriateness" and "possession." It implies entities, in this case verbal, that have identities and rights, again a kind of thingness. More than once Estienne urges the necessity "for great discretion" in translating proverbs, for a literal translation ("word for word from one language to another") either ruins their meaning or spoils their effect (their "grace"), even "as wine [is spoiled when] poured into an ill-smelling vessel."[98] Notably, Estienne does not report the same difficulty in translating individual words.

To take an additional example in English from the following century, in 1622 Joseph Webbe observes that "euery tongue hath proper and peculiar words, which are neither agreeable to other tongues, or lyable to translation; by which the eleganter sayings, the graver [i.e., 'weighter'] sentences [i.e., *sententiae*], and the more vsuall proverbs are especially composed." Elsewhere Webbe concentrates more on the syntax of sententious expressions than on their diction, but once again his point is that their constitution is both distinctive and frozen: "in euery tongue there are many things, which if wee should utter *by any other order* . . . would not run well . . . as euery man may iudge by the clauses, sentences, and especially Prouerbes, of his owne language: which, *transposed* . . . would for the most part lose their pleasing grace, delightful sound, and (many times) their sense, and meaning."[99] Webbe's admiration for the proverb's form and wisdom coincides with his sense of its fixity — what Erasmus describes as its gemlike quality, the integrity of its thingness.[100]

As Webbe employs the word *transpose* (Latin *transponere*), it also indicates his awareness that linguistic formations like proverbs cannot literally be transferred ("carried across" or "translated," Latin *translatum*) from one language to another. His view of proverbs, like Estienne's, contrasts, if only on a limited basis, with what Glyn Norton has characterized as the "age-old illusion" that words are objectively referential and therefore have equivalent meanings in any language: witness the objectivity implied by the idiom of translation — *reddere, vertere, transferre, transponere*, and *translatio* (p. 57). Explicit Cratylism aside, both Aristotelian and Augustinian (i.e., reason-based and will-based) theories hold that a reality external to language validates the meaning of words. Their position implies that differences among languages are merely superficial and do not affect meaning in any real way.[101] Throughout the Renaissance, this is the view dominantly and somewhat surprisingly *stated*, despite the many controversies about meaning attendant on translation of the Bible into the vernacular and the growing recognition of vernacular languages as equivalent in status — theoretically or de facto — to Latin. Change usually precedes the popular acknowledgment of it.

As we have seen, however, the view that meaning is prior to

language is also challenged — directly to an extent, and more widely and implicitly through textual practices. Questions about the nature and origin of language remain substantially open. In *A View of the Present State of Ireland*, for example, Spenser aims to re-form the minds of the Celtic-speaking Anglo-Irish by requiring them to speak English: since "the wordes are the Image of the minde," he writes, "the minde must be nedes affected with the wordes[,] So that the speache beinge Irishe the harte must nedes be Irishe."[102] Clearly, for him words constitute meaning to a considerable extent. The same holds true for Bacon, who endeavors to disabuse men of their belief "that their reason governs words," because "words react on the understanding."[103] And it would appear to apply to John Donne, when he observes that "a perpetual perplexity in the words cannot choose but cast a perplexity upon the things."[104]

To exemplify the "age-old illusion" of objective reference, Norton cites the listing by Renaissance language manuals of words such as Latin *arbor* and French *arbre* in columns of equivalents, which imply "an identical conceptual unity" (pp. 128–29). While this may have been — and most often still is — the case, other more distinctive kinds of listings lend themselves to somewhat different stories. A common practice in English-Latin dictionaries, for instance, is simply to reverse the order of Latin headword and English translation that is found in a Latin-English dictionary. This practice often leaves intact the remainder of the English entry, including such information as grammatical data about the Latin word (now the definition, rather than the term to be defined) or a string of defining English synonyms as an extension of the English headword.[105] It exhibits the extent to which in a lexical context the translation equivalents and the headword, quite apart from their referents, could be considered fixed entities and *in themselves* reversible objects. It thus suggests one way in which the popularity of the printed dictionary both reflected and affected ideas about the substantiality of language. As subsequent chapters will indicate, this was not the only way. Within the pages of Renaissance dictionaries a complexity of attitudes about language rivaling those of Rabelais can be uncovered. Some consideration of the relation of Latin to English during the period will precede my pursuit of them, however; in the absence of a comprehensive Renaissance dictionary solely in English, lexical Latin was normally (and normatively) the language on which bilingual English dictionaries were either modeled or based directly.

Chapter 2

Latin and
Lexicons

The frequent use of Latin, normally in a distinctive style or typeface, in Renaissance *sententiae* and inscriptions and in biblical and classical quotations can itself contribute to an impression of their authority and monumentality, their status not only as things but also as fixed and frozen things. While Latin remained the language of learning throughout the Renaissance period, its status was slowly shifting, and the perception of it as in some sense a "dead" language was emerging. The significance of its use in sayings and in citations embedded in vernacular texts — sermons, tracts, or poems — was bound to reflect these developments. Consider the use of the word *locus* even today in such a phrase as "the *locus* of meaning": in an English environment, the Latin word, although familiar, has distinction and emphasis; its associations imply learning, tradition, even logic, and it conveys an authority that most English equivalents would lack. It has "weight" and "substance" in a culture that (still) valorizes Latin.[1]

Even while Humanist education sought to revitalize society through the study of language, most commonly a reformed Latin, it contributed to the perception that Latin and life are not the same thing. The syntax of medieval Latin is closer to that of the various European vernaculars, and its diction less copious, than that of Humanist Latin, which sought to emulate classical models. According to Vivian Salmon, students in medieval schools "could often hear a form of Latin as a[n actually, as distinct from an artificially,] spoken language around them in everyday life," whereas in the Renaissance "the introduction of Classical Latin as a medium of communication demanded far greater attention to grammatical correctness and elegance" (pp. 19–20). To judge from the everyday phrases in the Tudor *Vulgaria*, students in the schools of Renaissance England were not learning Latin by describing their daily routines in Ciceronian periods; yet beginning Latin differs from the ideal of expression ultimately sought by the Humanists, and there remains considerable truth in Salmon's assessment. Aside from the more specific issues (then and now) raised by the celebrated debate between Bruni and Poggio about whether the commoners of ancient Rome could have mastered literary Latin, its very occurrence in early Renaissance Italy acknowledges the difficulty of a refined Latin style and suggests an uneasy awareness that the artifice of this style might be, even by Renaissance tenets, unnatural.[2] Notable in connection with it is a diagram in John Brinsley's *Ludus Literarius* (1612), an English treatise on methods of grammar school teaching, which distinguishes between what Brinsley calls "naturall order," or "*Ordo Grammaticus*," and "*Ordo Ciceronianus*," a Ciceronian or "artificiall" ordering of syntax.[3] The status of Latin intersects with a persistent and often anxious concern in the period with the relation of art to nature.

In Brian Stock's words, "Latin was the unique language of both grammar and scripture" in the Middle Ages, when "to teach grammar was to teach the letter of the Word" (*Text*, pp. 3–4). During the fifteenth and sixteenth centuries in England, however, medieval grammars were gradually replaced by wholly or partly vernacular ones in which Latin was treated as a foreign tongue. Grammatical treatises on Latin written wholly in English are extant from the first half of the fifteenth century, thus anticipating the more familiar grammatical works by Stanbridge, Horman, and Whittinton during the early Tudor period.[4] Speculating as to when Latin became a written as opposed to a spoken language, Beatrice White notes the growing importance of the vernacular and the increasing availability of textbooks in the sixteenth century, and she concludes that when Stanbridge and likeminded schoolmasters began to teach Latin "by means of English, they dealt a blow to its supremacy as a spoken language." White's view accentuates the reflection in Tudor grammars of anxiety about learning an artificial tongue and the resistance to its difficulty, as well as, of course, the continuing attraction of the learned language that seemed to offer access to authority. Her remarks suggest how significant an effort to regulate change was implicit in the royal authorization of Lily's dominantly Latin grammar and what was at stake—the absolutist state, Richard Helgerson might argue—in later debates about whether Latin grammar should be taught partly in English or entirely in Latin and whether a thorough grounding in English was a necessary preparation for instruction in Latin.[5] To teach Latin in English was to break fundamentally with the central tradition of the Middle Ages and much that it implied about language, both intellectually and socially.

The increasing popularity of polyglot vocabularies and dictionaries throughout the sixteenth century testifies to the growing importance of the vernaculars, as does the astounding number of bilingual Latin-vernacular or vernacular-Latin dictionaries published. According to Gabriele Stein, the number of these vernacular dictionaries appearing in the final 30 years of the sixteenth century "amply document[s] the shifting linguistic preoccupations of the time, away from Latin towards the vernaculars."

Not surprisingly, the primitive monolingual vernacular dictionary soon follows in the wake of the bilingual ones, appearing in English just after the turn of the century.[6] With its appearance, Latin as the metalanguage of lexicography and the very ground of meaning is for the first time fully, if as yet only symbolically, displaced.

Considering Latin a case in point, S. J. Tambiah has noted as linguistic features of world-religions either a radical disjunction between religious and profane tongues or else the presence of archaic or stylized elements within the religious idiom of a single mother tongue that serves a similar disjunctive function.[7] Both forms of disjunction bear on the power and authority of religious language itself, without necessarily accounting fully for it, and their effects are evident in the English Renaissance. Although England in the sixteenth century had become a Protestant country with a vernacular Bible, regular use of the Latin Bible in sermons continued, even though it provoked the objections of reformers sensitive to issues of symbolism and authority. Less directly, the disjunction Tambiah describes also illuminates the status of Renaissance Latin in a secular context as it becomes slowly but increasingly a language of specialized and privileged uses. In English-speaking countries the nominal sentence in Latin can be instanced as an obvious museum piece, yet it is a telling example in which the evolving status of Latin in a secular context is implicated.

The status of Latin is a focus of gradually developing cultural attitudes that illuminates the freezing and reifying of language in this period. Vives' *De tradendis disciplinis* again affords a useful point of departure, since it reflects a medieval inheritance and looks forward to later developments. Vives conceives of Latin not simply as the language of international communication but as the repository and very medium of civilization: "Language is the sacristy [*sacrarium*] of erudition, a storeroom, as it were, for what is to be concealed and what is to be brought forth. Since it is the treasury [*aerarium*] of knowledge and the instrument of society, it would be to the benefit of the human race that there should be one language [Latin] which all nations might use in common."⁸ As earlier noted, Vives attributes the traditional role of memory as the treasury of knowledge specifically to language and even more specifically to Latin, which is no longer a vernacular. The emphasizing of Latin rather than memory is significant, since it suggests the extent to which he has books and other documents, written language, in mind. He stresses the appropriateness of such a language being "sacred [*sacram*]" and "different from the common language," a kind of disjunctive code for the learned (*"doctorum"*: Latin, p. 287; English, p. 93). Through nuances, an awareness specifically of the Latin language as something sacred, enclosing within itself the treasures of the past, Vives' statements convey a sense of its universality that is protected, shielded, set apart from the mutable present. His views recall various medieval ones — evoking Dante's description of Latin as "perpetual and incorruptible" because grammatical, as well as the claims of the Modistae, medieval philosophers of language who thought that not merely grammar but preeminently Latin grammar mirrors the structure of reality as perceived by the human mind.⁹ Yet it is also notable that Vives does not base his elevation of Latin on abstract truth and grammatical speculation but on cultural richness and usefulness, values inherently more practical and open to change.

Toward the end of the century the mutable, vernacular present found a strong voice in Richard Mulcaster's *Elementarie* (1582), which describes the "soulish substance in eurie spoken tung, which fedeth . . . change," for "as all things else, which belong to man be subiect to change, so the tung also is." In effect Mulcaster opposes the "quikning" — that is, en*live*ning — spirit of a living language to Latin: "For if anie tung be absolute, and fre from motion, it is shrined vp in books, and not ordinarie in vse, but made immortall by the register of memory." Mulcaster surely "honor[s] the Latin" language, as he protests, but his views further exhibit not only a sense of its sanctity, "shrined vp in books," but also of its separation from the "quikning" processes of time.[10] To be immortal is also in human terms to be dead. Although similar to Dante's, Mulcaster's idealization of Latin is more qualified, and his sense of its fixity stronger.[11]

Alexander Gil, Mulcaster's immediate successor as headmaster of St. Paul's, similarly honors Latin, in this case for its universality and its "consecration" to spreading the knowledge of Christ — again its sanctity, if somewhat differently conceived. Gil identifies Latin with "that inviolable spirit of Christ which governs the universal company of Christian teachers" and which has established God's word "through the one language Latin, a language common to no people and therefore not liable to changes."[12] The gifted translator John Florio puts Gil's basic point more neutrally when he distinguishes between Italian, a living language into which new words come daily, and "*Latin, a limited toong, that is at his full growth*" and, in short, set and settled.[13]

In addition to learning, universality, and stability, the values of authority and tradition number among the associations Gil and others in the period bring to the Latin language, and these doubtless contribute to the disapproval by more radical Protestants of an admixture of Latin in English sermons.[14] The readiness with which Latin could be fixed and reified, appropriated to impressions of substance and effects of a spatial, ritual, or monumental sort, symbolically suggests the presence of Rome. More broadly, therefore, it engages the matter of iconicity, and its contemporary antithesis iconoclasm, as these pertain to language. When a substantial or seemingly substantial Latinate medium between the faithful and the Spirit is characterized by the reformers as needless, showy, and distracting, as it is by William Perkins, submerged motivations involving traditional authority and forms of representation underlie the more obvious ones of morality and decorum.[15]

Striking in this connection is Philip Stubbes's literal interpretation of the opening words of St. John's Gospel in an attack on the mystery plays in *The Anatomie of Abuses* (1583): "In the first of Ihon we are taught, that the word is GOD, and God is the word. Wherfore, who so euer abuseth this word of our God on stages in playes and enterluds, abuseth the Majesty of GOD in the same, maketh a mocking stock of him, and purchaseth to himselfe, eternal damnation." The abuse Stubbes has in mind is dramatic adaptation and embellishment. Michael O'Connell rightly observes that Stubbes's opposition to such embellishment is so profound as actually to lead him in this passage to identify "the *Logos* with the word of scripture, rather than with the preexistent Christ."[16] As O'Connell recognizes, Stubbes's view further concentrates the power the reformers found in the words of Scripture. Underlying it is the sense of language as a label substituting for the thing. This is a transparently referential language rather than one in itself substantial, the latter a denser and richer medium that invites embellishment or requires that its meaning be unfolded. Yet Stubbes's virtual hypostatization of the word of the text, which the emphatic typography of the name "GOD" in black-letter capitals reinforces, again suggests how difficult the distinction between substance and transparency could (and can) be to maintain (Fig. 2).

Lancelot Andrewes's response to complaints about the use of Latin and Greek words in sermons is as suggestive with respect to the contemporary significance of their use as are Stubbes's fulminations. Andrewes reports impatiently, "They must hear no Latin, nor Greek; no, though it be interpreted," and scoffs, "A mere imagination." He then explains that St. Paul used "terms as strange" in writing to the Corinthians as Latin and Greek are to speakers of English in his own day and adds that Paul "might easily enough have expressed [such terms] in their vulgar, but

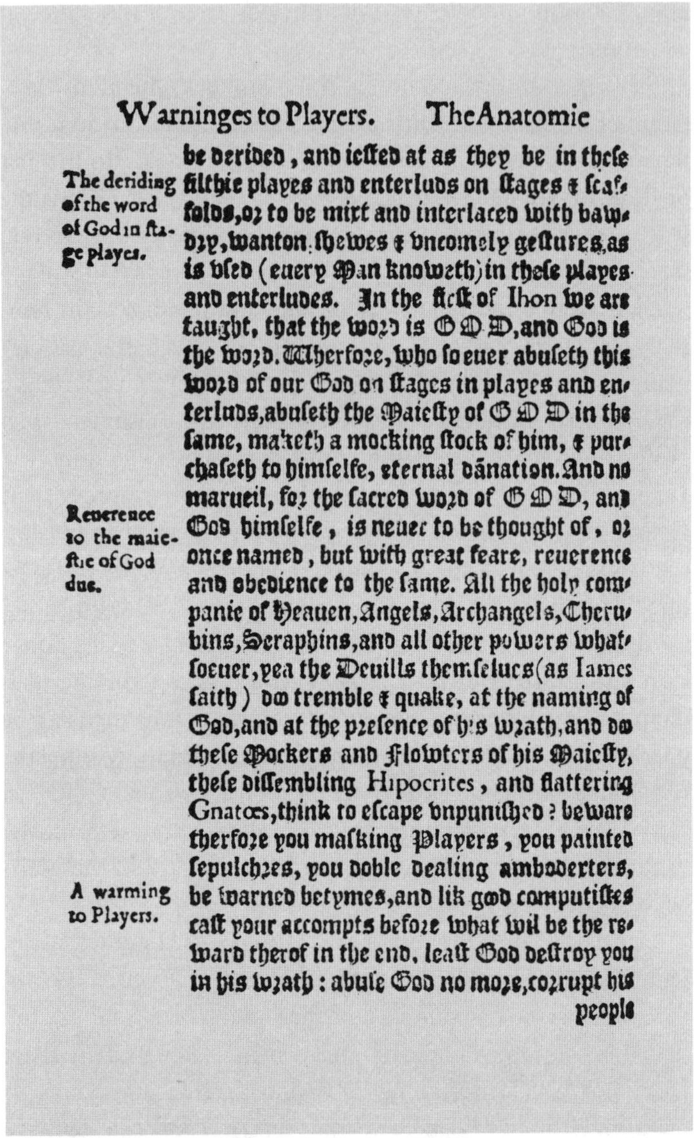

be deriued, and iested at as they be in these
The deriding filthie playes and enterluds on stages & scaf-
of the word folds, oz to be mixt and interlaced with baw-
of God in sta- dzy, wanton shewes & vncomely gestures, as
ge playes. is vsed (euery Man knoweth) in these playes
and enterludes. In the sirst of Ihon we are
taught, that the wozd is G O D, and God is
the wozd. Wherfoze, who so euer abuseth this
wozd of our God on stages in playes and enterluds, abuseth the Maiesty of G O D in the
same, maketh a mocking stock of him, & purchaseth to himselfe, eternal dānation. And no
marueil, foz the sacred wozd of G O D, and
Reuerence God himselfe, is neuer to be thought of, oz
to the maie- once named, but with great feare, reuerence
stie of God and obedience to the same. All the holy com-
due. panie of Heauen, Angels, Archangels, Cheru-
bins, Seraphins, and all other powers whatsoeuer, yea the Deuills themselues (as Iames
saith) doo tremble & quake, at the naming of
God, and at the pzesence of his wzath, and doo
these Mockers and Flowters of his Maiesty,
these dissembling Hipocrites, and flattering
Gnatoes, think to escape vnpunished? beware
therfoze you masking Players, you painted
sepulchzes, you doble dealing ambodexters,
A warming be warned betymes, and lik good computistes
to Players. cast your accompts befoze what wil be the re-
ward therof in the end, least God destroy you
in his wzath: abuse God no moze, cozrupt his
people

Fig. 2. Philip Stubbes, *The Anatomie of Abuses*, 1583: Lvᵛ. By permission
of the Folger Shakespeare Library.

that it liked him to retain his liberty in this point."[17] The learned
Bishop Andrewes describing Latin and Greek as "strange" — that
is, "alien," "foreign," "unfamiliar" — is itself first worth noting.
There is no reason in this case to assume that the "speakers" he
has in mind all belong to an uneducated class. Indeed, it is sober-
ing to align his description with the audience John Rider intends
for *Bibliotheca Scholastica* (1589), his mainly English-Latin dictionary, and specifically for the information about Latin grammar, such as the variable cases governed by certain verbs, that he
includes in the Latin index to the English entries concluding the
work. Rider's audience is to consist of "Courtiers, Lawiers, Ap-
prentices of London, Travailers, and al Discontinuers, who haue
lost the vse of their Grammar rules by discontinuance."[18] Like
Andrewes's acknowledgment that Latin and Greek are "strange"
to English ears, Rider's advertisement illuminates the increasing
potential of Latin for alienation and thus for iconic and monumental effects.

Andrewes proceeds right from asserting St. Paul's "libertie" to
classifying objections to citations and examples from the Apoc-
rypha, the Talmud, heathen authorities, and nature as vain "imag-
inations," like the objections to Latin and Greek. His procedure
suggests that he takes complaints about the use of classical languages similarly to be based on the supposition that they add in
an illicit way to the godly text, embellishing and in some way
blocking or changing its (allegedly transparent) meaning. Oddly,
what Andrewes does not say in defense of his own position on
classical citation is as interesting as what he does. He passes up
the opportunity to offer any number of reasons for the preacher's
employing it — those of Vives and Gil, for example, or one based
on the transmission of biblical texts, a subject with which, as a
major translator of the authorized version of the Bible, he was
well acquainted. Instead, he simply remarks Paul's preference for
"libertie" in the matter.

The word "libertie" in this context may indicate the hierarch's sense of privilege, but it simultaneously suggests a more open sense of the text than that of his critics and consequently a different understanding of what the preacher does with words to make the text yield its full meaning. Use of the word "liberty" in the anonymous "Translators to the Reader" of the authorized version of the Bible in 1611 supports this suggestion.[19] Noting the presence of variant readings in the margins, the translators explain that wise readers "had rather haue their iudgements at libertie in differences of readings, then to be captiuated to one, when it may be the other." They ask why they should be in bondage to one translational word when they might use "another no lesse fit, as commodiously?" In subsequent uses of the word "liberty" they explain that those who are not superstitious may translate a Hebrew or Greek word by various English equivalents, using "the same libertie in our English versions . . . for that copie or store that he [God] hath giuen vs" in the Bible. "Copy" or *copia* correlates with the sense that there are more words than things, in effect a sense that language has more to say than our objectivized philosophies can tell us.[20]

To judge from Andrewes's practice, his sense of the preacher's craft is essentially more provisional and creative than that of the radical Stubbes or the more reasonable Perkins. Although it might be silly to suggest that Andrewes's own faith in the *universalia realia* had been shaken, his position was not naive, uninformed, or unchallenged, and the faith of his audience was by no means reliably and uniformly certain.[21] Appropriately, perhaps, his attitude toward words is more complex, intuitive, and performative — in short, more tolerant of fiction — than it is literal and dogmatic, and, while authorized by Scripture, its expression is more congenial to the Renaissance word-world described by Spitzer in connection with Rabelais than is that of Stubbes and Perkins. The "intellectual and imaginative liberty" that Arthur Kinney attributes to Humanist fiction in the Tudor period lingers insistently in the copious Stuart sermons of preachers like Andrewes and Donne, where the warrant of truth, an ultimate referentiality, still persists as well.[22]

As we have seen to some extent already, the dictionary is a characteristic Renaissance publication that bears significantly on changing and developing attitudes toward the classical and vernacular languages. It bears as well on the fixing and reifying of words. Although specialized word lists, glossaries of manuscripts, topical vocabularies, and even comprehensive Latin and bilingual manuscript dictionaries existed in the Middle Ages, the dictionary as a normative publication and a fixture in schoolrooms and private libraries is essentially a Renaissance phenomenon.[23] The number of editions of the more popular dictionaries of the period repeatedly run well into the double digits. They afford one of the more radical examples of the extent to which the technology of print could influence the basic conditions and assumptions of meaning.

The impact of the Renaissance dictionary can be sampled in the highly systematic and systematically visual pages of Cooper's massive Latin-English *Thesaurus linguae Romanae et Britannicae*, which for 30 years after its initial publication (1565) was "the standard [Latin-English] reference dictionary."[24] The pages of Cooper's dictionary are clearly for reference rather than memorization.[25] They employ four different fonts to distinguish various kinds of lexical data: one font for the Latin headword itself, which is also indented; another font for such matters as stress and grammatical function, derivatives, sources of reference, and examples of use, these last further indented; a third font for the English equivalent of the Latin, and a fourth for cross-references. Cooper also separates different senses of a word from one another by colons or periods, marks proverbs with an asterisk, and employs a paragraph sign to indicate that "the signification, or use of the thing [word] differs somewhat" from that of the illustrative quotations preceding this sign.[26] The folio pages are divided into two columns. The main headwords are organized alphabetically, but cognate forms generally follow an "etymological principle" of organization.[27] To look at a word on Cooper's pages is to see it in a new environment, one that is essentially related to other words; the word is not merely part of a list but part of an elaborate verbal system. Thousands of words are conspicuously frozen — "fixed" for analysis — in long double columns of mechanically rendered print (Figs. 3, 4).

Cooper's *Thesaurus* features an unusual, not to say inordinate, number of illustrative examples of usage for the words defined. The word *locus*, for instance, is followed by well over 200 examples, each listed separately; *gravis* is followed by close to 100, *scribo* by about 50, and *nomen* by more than 220. This copiousness keeps the word in touch with its use but also conveys a sense of proliferation that is unreal because isolated from any actual context of use except the lexical one. Despite Cooper's elaborate typography, the main entry words or root forms can be difficult to locate without at least scanning through the many examples and experiencing some sense of drift in a Rabelesian sea of frozen word forms. The effect of Cooper's pages is finally double: they reify language and also display its seemingly self-generating variability. Looking at them, one can begin to conceive language itself as a subject with a substantial room of its own.

It would be idle to speculate as to whether Thomas Thomas, compiler of the immensely popular Latin-English dictionary that displaced Cooper's near the end of the sixteenth century and remained standard well into the seventeenth, actively set out to simplify the bifurcated effect of Cooper's *Thesaurus*, but in comparison to it Thomas's *Dictionarium linguae Latinae et Anglicanae* affords very few illustrative examples.[28] In it, words mainly stand apart from usage. Relatively streamlined, it *looks* very much like a standard modern dictionary (Fig. 5). Not surprisingly, its alpha-

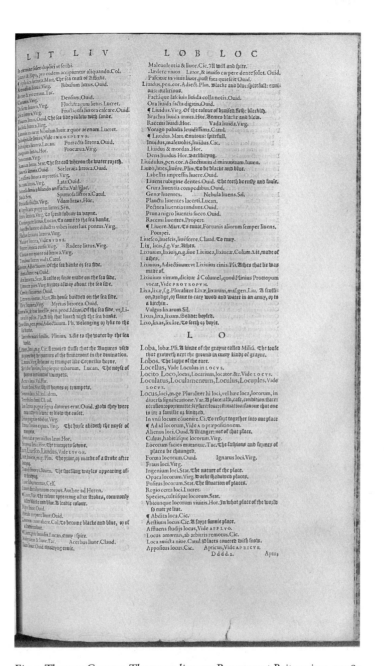

Fig. 3. Thomas Cooper, *Thesaurus linguae Romanae et Britannicae*, 1578: D.ddd.2ʳ. By permission of the Folger Shakespeare Library.

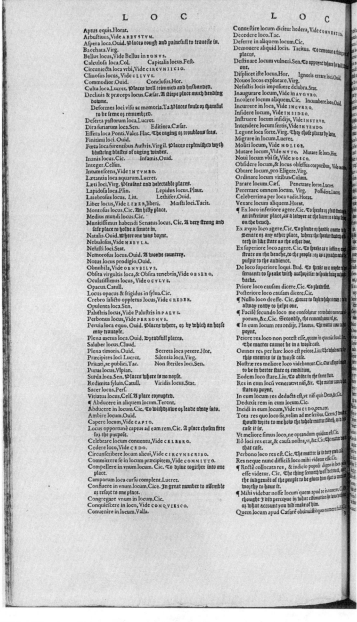

Fig. 4. Thomas Cooper, *Thesaurus linguae Romanae et Britannicae*, 1578: D.ddd.2ᵛ. By permission of the Folger Shakespeare Library.

56

ditate,aviditate,& similibus rapi.
To be carried or led away with, &c.
¶Aliquem in jus rapere,Plau,*To
arrest one, and bring him before a
Judge.* ¶Rapere se ad urbem, *To
goe hastily to.* ¶De luce rapi,Stat.
To be taken out of the world,to die.
Rápio,ŏnis,m.g. Pompon.vide
raptor.
Rápd,onis,m.g. Varro. ἁρπαξ.
A glutton.
Rapedus,a,um,particip.Virg.
*Taken,caried, or drawn with great
violence.*
Raptim,adverb. ἁρπάγδην,ἁρπα-
λίως,*Sodenly, hastily,swiftly,in hast.*
Raptio, onis, fœm. g. Terent.
ἁρπαγμός. *A violent taking of any
person: a snatching, a catching.*
Raptito,& rapto,as,frequent.
ᵱερσναρπάζω.*To snatch or pull oft,
to take or catch often by violence.*
Raptor,oris,m.g.Col. ἁρπακτής.
*A violent taker away, a robber,an
extortioner, a snatcher, catcher, or
spoiler : a ravisher.*
Raptum,ti, n.g. Liv. *A thing
snatcht or taken away violently.*
Raptúra,æ,f.g.Plin.Idem.
Raptus,a,um,part. *Taken away
suddenly,carried away perforce, pul-
led off or about: ravished.*
Raptus,us,m.g.verb. βία, *A ra-
vishing or deflouring of a vvoman
against her consent or will: a pulling
or stretching,a violent taking away.*
Raptus pronus, Aurel. ide quod
Emprosthotonus. ¶Raptus ner-
vorum, Aurel. i.q. Spasmus.
Rápulum,li,m.g.dimin. Horat.
ῥαφάνιον. *A little rape roote.*
Rápum,pi,n.g. Plin ᵱωγάλιαν.*A
rape roote or navew.*Porcinum vel
terræ rapum,Iun. Sovvbreade, or
Swinebread.
Rapum Genistæ,* *An excres-
cence comming from the roote of
broome,broome-rape, orobanche.*
Rápunctilus,li,m.g.Iun. *Wilde
rape roote.*
Rárè,rariùs,adver.Plin. ἀραιῶς,
ᵱερὶῶς.*Not oft,seldome: thinnely,not
thicke.*
Rárefácio, is, ēci, ctum,ēre, &

part. ens,Colum.ἁραιόω. *To make
thinne that which is too thicke, to
make scant or seld.*
Rárefáctus,a,um,part. Lucan.
Made thinne, made scant and selde.
Rárēfio,is, ctus sum,ēri, Lucr.
ἁραιοῦμαι.*To be made thin or scant.*
Rárentèr,adverb. Cato. vide
Rarò.
Rárefco,is,ēre,Colum.ἁραιόομαι.
*To waxe scarce or small in number,to
waxe thinne or not thicke growen,
to be or happen seldome, to decrease
by litle and litle, to waxe lesse and
lesse.*
Rárípülus,a,um,Colum.λεπτός.
Thinne haired.
Rárissimè,adverb.superl.Suet.
Rárítas, ātis, ἁραιότης,ἁραίωσις.
*Seldomenesse, thinnesse, fewenesse,
scantnesse, spongie hollownesse.*
Rárítúdo,inis,f.g.Col. idem.
Rárò,adverb. ἁραιῶς.*Se'dome,
rare, fewe times, long betweene, not
so often.*
Rárus,a,um,ior,issimus, ἁραιὸς,
ἁραιῶς.*Not thicke, thinne, not thicke
growen or set, seld, seldom seene, not
often: also excellent, pretious, rare.
Rarus in potu,Plin. Vseth not to
drinke much.* ¶Facie rarus,Ovid.
Of rare and excellent beautie.¶Ra-
rum cribrum,Ovid. *A coorse or
wide sieve.*¶Racemirari,Virg.*A
fewe clusters here and there one.*
Rásilis,le,Plin. ξυστὸς.*That may
be shaven, easie to be shaven, scraped, plained,made smooth, polished.*
Rasis,Colum. *A kinde of raw
pitch.*
Rásito,as, frequ. à rado, Gell.
ξυσσάω.*To shave or scrape often.*
Rásor,ōris,m.g.verb ξυστής. *A
scraper, a shaver,a barber, a fuller, a
clooshwor̄ker.*
Rásōnius,a,um.* κυφαλὶς.*Belonging to shaving or scraping.*
Rasta,* *A dutch mile.*
Rastellum, li, n.g. & in plural.
Rastelli, Varro. τὸ σμινυδιον & θρε-
λίσμον.*A litlerake or harrow, &c.*
Rastrum,stri, n. g. & in plural.
Rastri, vel rastra, orum, Terent.
ξύσρον,λίσρον. *A rake,a harrow,a drag*

alsò an instrument to weede corne,
and to treade away earth from vines.
Rásūra,æ,f.g.Colu. ξυσμὸς. *A
scraping,a shaving.*
Rásus,a,um, à rador, *Shaven,
scraped out,made smooth, swept and
made cleane.*
Ratiaria,vel ratiāria navicula,
Virg. *A boat called a lighter.*
Ratiárius,ii, m.g. à ratis, Paul.
ὁ τὴν σχεδίαν νεως ἀγων̄ισς. *A lighter
man,or he that occupieth a lighter or
barge, to transporte marchandise
from place to place.*
Ratihabitio,onis,f.œ.g. Digest.
*An approouing or confirming of a
thing.*
Rátio,onis, fœ. g. λόγος,λογισμός.
*Reason, purpose, counsell, care, re-
spect, consideration,advisement,re-
gard: the cause,the matter,the state:
the meanes,the way : the fashion, the
forme, the proportion: a rule : the
trade, the state: the maner and sort:
a minde: a counsell,advise,or fanta-
sie : an account or reckening:busines:
the quantitie,value: affaires.Habe-
re rationem cum terra , To have
to doe with: also to labour & occupy.
Pro ratione pecuniæ, According
to the value of.*
Rátiōcinátio,onis,f.g. verbal.
λογισμός. *Reasoning, debating of a
matter.*
Rátiōcinátivus,a,um, συλλογιστι-
κὸς. *Belonging to reasoning or debating of a matter in argument.*
Rátiōcinātor,oris, m.g. verb.
συλλογιστὴς.*A keeper of reckenings,
an auditour,a reasoner,a caster of an
account :a disputer, a caster and ex-
aminer by reason.*
Rátiōcinium,ii,n.gen Colum.
λογισμὸς. *A reasoning or disputing.*
Rátiōcinor,aris,d pon. συλλογί-
ζομαι. *To debate or reason togither
in argument, to dispute, to recken,
to account.*
Rátiōcinābilis,Quint.& Rationalis,le,ad Heren λογικὸς. *Reasonable , that hath the vse of reason,
done with reason. Rationales Cæ-
saris, Lamprid. The Emperours re-
ceivers.*

Fig. 5. Thomas Thomas, *Dictionarium linguae Latinae et Anglicanae,*
1596: Bbb1ʳ. By permission of the Henry E. Huntington Library.

betical ordering is much more conspicuous than that in Cooper's *Thesaurus*, where alphabetical order, although conceptually primary, can nonetheless be obscured by a flood of examples or interrupted by an etymological principle of order. Since Thomas's dictionary proved even more attractive to contemporary users than Cooper's, doubtless in part because of its more convenient size and lower cost, the implications of its emphatically alphabetical organization of language are worth pursuing.[29]

Although the vast majority of dictionaries in England in the Renaissance period were alphabetical, some ambivalence about this method of organization existed. John Baret expresses it, for example, in the 1574 edition of *An Alvearie*, and his concern engages several relevant issues, among them the way in which letters, hence words, represent language, whether materially and literally or symbolically and conventionally. Defining the letter *A*, Baret first identifies it as the initial character in the Greek, Latin, and English alphabets and then adds,

> But whether this common vsuall order in our Alphabet or crosrewe, was so placed and appointed by counsell and learning from the beginning, or was shuffled togither by ignorance: neither am I able, nor at this time haue I sufficient leysure to determine. But *howsoeuer the reast* of the letters were driuen to this order, it is of many supposed that nature hath taught A. to stande in the first place, as *(they say)* we may easily perceyue by the first voyce or confuse crying of yong infants, which soundeth in the eare most like to A.[,] beinge also the first letter in the name of our great graundfather *Adam*, as *Abba* signifying father, which woorde children gladly heare and learne. *Rom.8.Galat.4.* And the Prophet *Ieremy* being commaunded of God to preache to the people, and tell them boldly of their sinnes, aunswered againe *A, A, A, Domine Deus ecce infans sum, nescio loqui, Ierem.1.* So speaking like a childe. *S.Iohn* also seemeth to prooue the same by Gods owne witnesse: *Ego sum α et o[,] id est primus et nouissimus. Apoc.22.* Some therefore haue thought it good to dispose Dictionaries rather with the

woordes of the fiue vowels set first in order, and then such as beginne with Diphthonges to folow them: and last of all, such as begin with Consonants in their place. But concerning this matter all men are not of one opinion. Wherefore in the meane time vntill it be better agreed vpon among the learned, I thinke it best to vse *the accustomed and long receyued order.*[30]

Both Baret's relative detachment regarding efforts to connect letters to a natural origin ("they say" and "howsoeuer the reast") and his persistent desire for biblical authorization of lexical order are noteworthy, but finally more telling is his explicit, conclusive awareness that the customary way to order lexical material is alphabetical.[31] He is concerned enough about the implications of alphabetical order to question its rationale, but he is not worried enough or impractical enough to reject it.

Baret, a schoolmaster, was more strongly influenced than most other lexicographers by the views of the radical spelling reformers, Sir Thomas Smith and John Hart, who, like Bullokar, thought that letters are quite literally "the figures and colours wherewith the image of mans voice is painted" and thus, in effect, the visible and palpable sound of Rabelais's fable. These orthoepists believed that language was physically grounded in nature.[32] Much as Baret would have liked each letter of the alphabet to represent a single sound, his position as a lexicographer is typically more balanced, conservative, and representative than theirs. Dictionaries are preeminently meant for use and are aimed at a market of users. Their proliferation and striking popularity in the Renaissance make them valuable indices of attitudes toward language and the character of its substantiality.

Some degree of alphabetical order had been known in lexical works since at least the eighth century, but the alphabet only became the undeniably dominant principle of lexical organization during the Renaissance.[33] In its dominance it comes to suggest, as Roy Harris has observed, that "orthographic form is more basic than phonetic form"; it suggests as well that writing is linguistically more basic than speech.[34] Increasingly it also subordinates or entirely replaces other principles of lexical organization — for example, the "natural" one that Baret first mentions or the religious one that particularly attracts his attention.

In this period, however, the alphabetical organization of lexicons is a significant indication of the changes affecting thought about language rather than a decisive codification of its consequences. In a rhetorical treatise written close to the decade in which the alphabetically ordered dictionary of Thomas Thomas ran through five editions, for example, Peacham describes

> *Catacosmesis*, in Latin *ordo*, ["order," as] . . . a meete placing of words among themselues, wherof there be two kinds, the one when the worthiest word is set first, which order is *naturall*, as when we say: God and man, men and women, Sun and Moone, life and death. And also when that is first told that was first done, which is necessary and seemly. . . . The use of this first kind of order, doth most properly serue to the proprietie and elegancy of speech, and due observation of nature and dignitie: which forme is well represented in the ciuil and solemne customs of nations, where the worthiest persons are always first named and highest placed. (pp. 118–19; my emphasis on "naturall")

Here Peacham favors an order based on a putatively natural principle of hierarchy, for which a topical arrangement in lexicography would be fitting. But he also defines "the other kind of order [that] is *artificiall*, and in forme contrarie to this, as when the worthiest or weightiest word is set last" (p. 119; my emphasis). His description of artificial order, which refers to a traditional rhetorical scheme for amplifying, namely, *incrementum*, remains hierarchical, although in reverse. As the reverse it is not unnatural, which would be disorderly, but merely artificial. Order remains the underlying principle; nonetheless, its result no longer duly observes "nature and dignitie" and therefore no longer corresponds *properly* to the order of things. In the swerve of Peacham's thinking from "natural" to "artificial" a crack opens for a broader conception of artificial order that is less firmly rooted in the moral and social order or in what the period generally conceived of as "things."

This potential is enforced elsewhere in Peacham's treatise. When Peacham initially treats the origin and rationale of tropes, for example, he bases them on a lack—a want of "words to expresse the nature and propertie of diuerse things"—and the consequent borrowing of "the name of one thing, to signifie another" that resembles it in some way. He then observes that men, seeing matters well expressed by this means, began to refuse "such words as were proper" and to substitute their own inventions for the nature of things. But instead of proceeding next to reflect on human perversity, as we might expect, he explains that "proper" words either "had litle sweetnesse, or could not declare the nature of the thing so well." Lest any reader now doubt this assertion of the superiority of artfully "translated speech" he reinforces it, concluding that men borrowed words "from like things, both for the grace sake of the similitude, and also *for the cause of perspicuitie of the thing* [subject matter or existent thing] *expressed*" (pp. 1–2; my emphasis). Far from being merely a necessary evil, tropological art apparently outstrips the shortcomings of "natural" language.[35]

If tropology is artificial, alphabetical order is quintessentially so. It ignores similitude and bypasses not only the hierarchical or religious ordering of language but also its organization according to etymology or historical relationships and to topical, logical, or grammatical categories, such as nouns and verbs, the specialized lists of "Nominales" and "Verbales" familiar to the Middle Ages. In addition to this purely artificial order, earlier periods had applied all these other ordering principles to lexical materials, conceiving them to be rational rather than arbitrary and in some way to reflect objective reality.[36] Although these alternative principles certainly do not vanish during the Renaissance, from around the time that the comprehensive dictionary begins to flourish they become increasingly subject to alphabetical organization and their grounding in objective reality also becomes, if at times anxiously or extravagantly reasserted, less self-evident. Little wonder that some serious thinkers of the sixteenth and seventeeth centuries sought either to ground the alphabet itself more firmly in objective reality or else to replace it altogether with a new system of artificial notation that did correspond to nature, to the order of things. In their efforts the desire for a language clearly subordinated to objective reality reasserts itself, along with its corollary, words conceived as transparent labels for things.[37]

The reasons given for projecting or actually compiling dictionaries in the period reflect nearly as broad a range of linguistic views as that in Rabelais's fable of the frozen words. They include philosophical, rhetorical, orthoepic, and pedagogical concerns as well as those more broadly social and economic. The need of *copia*, copiousness, is often remarked and is coupled with an emphasis on synonymy and illustrative examples (as in Cooper); there is a great deal of emphasis on verbal propriety and decorum, on finding or knowing the right word for the occasion. Not coincidentally, there is frequent citation of predictable authorities, who, although their larger systems of thought might have conflicted, were thought to have maintained in some way that words have a connection with truth or knowledge: thus Plato, Aristotle, Galen, the Bible, Varro, Festus, Cicero, Quintilian, and Isidore are cited, as well as a number of latecomers such as Valla, Fungerus, and both Scaligers.[38]

Of particular interest here, however, is the lexicographer's connection of words with matter, or the material out of which discourse is, building-like, constructed. The preface to a 1578 edition of Robert Estienne's influential *Thesaurus linguae Latinae* affords a representative example:

It stands not otherwise with the man who purposes the construction and completion [*exaedificationem constructionemque*] of a speech, for it is necessary that he first have a formal plan and then a material one. . . . Truly, he will have planned everything in vain unless he finds fitting matter [*materiam*] out of which the speech might be constructed and in which its form might shine forth [*eluceat*]; for the material [*materia*] of discourse is partly in the words and partly in the things themselves.³⁹

Here the "words" cannot mean subject matter, since "the things themselves" do. In a literal sense, the force of "words" is considerably more material and materially more real. It embraces the dimension of sound but clearly includes that of space as well and suggests additional qualities, in the period variously conceived as mass, weight, scope, force, and magnitude. Apart from things, words themselves thus have a substantial status.⁴⁰ As the preface puts it, the primary concern of Estienne's dictionary is with words as such — "verborum simplicium," words pure and simple. Despite the presence of illustrative examples, these are separated from actual use as subject matter, a fact the preface acknowledges. They are, as words, reified.

The sense of discourse as something tangible, particularly as a construct or building, that is evident in this preface is a commonplace in the period and, as indeed Lakoff and Johnson have noted, in our own. The idea that words are material in more than an audible sense is much older than the Renaissance, yet during this time it is peculiarly emphasized, made focal apart from philosophic contexts, and also embodied literally for the first time in thousands of mechanically rendered lexical pages. It is crucial that the comprehensive dictionary seeks to present the essential word-stock of a language, not just a practical or specialized slice of it. As is evident in a number of early modern dictionaries, efforts are made before long to admit or to exclude words that do or do not "belong" in the language. In this way, too, the comprehensive dictionary encourages the idea that language is "a specific, identifiable system of words," and language comes eventually "to be seen as constituting, in principle, a finite system of elements at any given time."[41] Somewhat paradoxically, there are already ironic foreshadowings of this relatively modern structural principle in some of the universal language schemes of the mid-seventeenth century. The conspicuous artificial systematism of these schemes, notwithstanding the blatantly referential intentions of their inventors, foreshadows the realization that language, far from providing natural labels for things, is not autonomously or even primarily referential.[42]

In the Renaissance itself there is an awareness of the lexical standardization of English usage and correlatively, it appears, of the inevitable association of dictionaries with writing. In 1589, for example, George Puttenham, presumably referring to bilingual dictionaries, cautions the aspiring writer against verbal impurities and ostentation, noting that "herein we are already ruled by th'English Dictionaries and other bookes written by learned men."[43] Puttenham thinks of the dictionary as the arbiter of verbal correctness, quite apart from variations on the printed standard. This is an idea that might at first seem alien to the openness of wordplay characteristic of Elizabethan and Jacobean literature, but this very openness thrives on the deliberate violation of verbal propriety — the properties and "rights" of words — and is likely to be indebted to the newly heightened awareness of it.

Nearly two decades earlier than Puttenham's invocation of lexical standards, Peter Levins tries in his English-Latin dictionary to fix the meaning of English words by marking and regularizing their accents. In such a practice, which is modeled on Latin, the conception of accent may coincide with modern stress: "Wheras," Levins explains, "oftentimes one worde maye haue diuers significations, as, [English] *differ*, [i.e., 'defer'] *differre, id est, prolongare*: and [English] *differ, differre, id est, discrepare*, . . . we haue . . . *set* the accent . . . in that place . . . where the sillable must go vp and be long."[44] As if predicting the postmodern fascination with the coincidence of origin in the words *differ* and *defer*, Levins's example gives a historical edge to the fact that lexicalization would eventually contain the wholly free play of language — arguably, perhaps, "contain" it in both the word's senses.[45] Levins's accentual method of stabilizing English is a lexical innovation in 1570, although it is one contemporaneously endorsed by proponents of orthoepic reform and earlier used in classical lexicons. An additional connection with these lexicons is also noticeable in Levins's reliance on Latin equivalents — *prolongare* and *discrepare* — to discriminate between the meanings of the two English words. Although language in this period appears to be immensely more flexible and fluid than in modern times, the pressures and the means to stabilize it were building. Somewhat paradoxically, they were both reflecting and contributing to a sense of its always ambivalent substantiality, its elusive manageability, its equivocal "thingness."[46]

The words in which William Bullokar and Richard Mulcaster phrased their innovative calls for a dictionary focusing exclusively on English express a similar desire to stabilize language. Bullokar promises "a perfite Dictionarie in time to come, and alreadie purposed: To the perfite staie and easie use of Inglish speech, as long as letters endure." The word "staie" asserts a strong claim here: although it can mean "support," in the context of Bullokar's subsequent explanation it more precisely means "stability," implying order and permanence. Literally it means a standstill. Bullokar would "fix" English words with a vengeance.[47] If we were to assume that his reference to "letters" is a loose expression for language in general, the full title of his proposal — namely, *A short Introduction or guiding to print, write, and reade Inglish speech* — would swiftly correct our assumption and clarify the extent to which he has writing specifically and literally in mind. Indeed, the way Bullokar uses the word "speech" in these quotations indicates that it does not necessarily even mean spoken, as distinct from written, discourse.[48] His usage is similar in this respect to our own, since we regularly refer to a book's "saying" what we read in it.

Bullokar's meaning is further emphasized in another publication, the *Booke at Large* of 1580, in which he explains his plans for a dictionary in greater detail. If he were to be consulted about an English dictionary, he promises, "there should be means [in it] for [indicating] difference in equivoces [homonyms]." Writing or printing, that is, would resolve — indeed, "fix" — the equivocations of speech. Bullokar then adds that "perfect *writing and printing* keepeth euery language in *continuance* of perfect vse, and perfect sense and signification: And though the common sort doe neglect it, yet it may be the touchstone for the wise and learned, to be aided thereby in matters of great *waight*" (p. 22; my emphasis). Once again Bullokar's interest in spatial representation, in writing and printing, and simultaneously in stability, continuance, and "fixing," is pronounced. His association of these with weight, a metaphor tottering on the brink of literalism, seems only natural.

Within two years of Bullokar's proposal to set his reformed orthography in a dictionary, Richard Mulcaster, a conservative and sensible voice among orthoepists, also advocates a dictionary devoted to the vernacular. As Mulcaster envisions this project, "besides the right writing, which is incident to the Alphabete," the learned compiler "wold open vnto vs therein, both . . . [the] naturall force [of words], and their proper vse: that . . . we might be as able to iudge of our own tung, . . . as we ar of others" (p. 187). Mulcaster too thinks of a dictionary in connection with writing, although in comparison to the reformers of orthography he is more interested in etymology and propriety, "naturall force" and "proper vse," and, in short, right words for things. When faced with radical proposals for the reform of orthography, he explicitly defends linguistic custom and the prerogative of language to change, but he also adheres to the notion that the word in some way corresponds to "the propertie [of] the thing," and he wants to see such etymological correspondence, as well as "right writing," or the established spelling of words, stabilized in an English dictionary (pp. 187–88). Like Bullokar, most of whose other views Mulcaster opposes, he recognizes that a dictionary is essential to the rationalization—the stability and in some sense the "fixing"—of language. On the threshold of the decades in which the dictionary becomes a popular form with far-reaching potential for influencing attitudes to language, he appears also to have sensed that "orthographic developments rest . . . with the printer," or, more exactly, with the books that issue from his press, which will inevitably "set" current usage, variously reflecting and forming it.[49]

Whereas Bullokar wished radically to reform the orthography of English words and Mulcaster merely to tidy it up, the implications of Mulcaster's more conservative views are ultimately more profound. In proposing a dictionary that would accept traditional spellings that fail to correspond to pronunciation (phonetic value), or at least in recognizing the practical necessity of accepting them, Mulcaster implicitly sanctioned the existence of a written form of language relatively independent of the oral form—a kind of ideograph with a semiautonomous realm of its own.[50] Again one thinks by analogy of the semiautonomous word-world that Spitzer found in Rabelais.

In 1598, virtually at the turn of the century, John Florio published an impressively inclusive Italian-English dictionary called *A Worlde of Wordes*, subsequently revised in 1611 as *Queen Anna's New World of Words*. Florio, whose translations display a fine sensitivity to idiom, appears to have chosen his title with care, and he is at pains to emphasize its appropriateness. He attributes the choice to his "Mistresse Muse" herself and offers this explanation of it:

> Since as the Vniuers containes all things, digested in best equi-
> paged order, embellisht with innumerable ornaments by the vni-
> uersall creator. . . . And as *Tipocosmia* imaged by *Alessandro Cit-*
> *tolini*, and *Fabrica del mondo*, framed by *Francesco Alunno*, and
> *Piazza vniuersale* set out by *Thomaso Garzoni* tooke their names of
> the vniuersall worlde, in words to represent things of the world:
> as words are types of things, and euerie man by himself a little
> world in some resemblances; so thought she [the Muse], she did
> see as great capacitie, and as meete method in this, as in those
> latter, and (as much as there might be in Italian and English) a
> modell of the former, and therefore as good cause so to entitle it.[51]

Florio understands words as "types of things" here, not just as
labels or, in Padley's phrase, "items of nomenclature." Types are
figures, signs, or symbols, as the traditional comparison of the
human microcosm to the macrocosm suggests, rather than mere
names and literal substitutes for things. They imply the complexity of relationship rather than simple identity. The titles of the
books by Citolini, Alunno, and Garzoni—respectively, a "Type
or Figure," a "Fabric or Frame," and a "Piazza"—and the verbs
with which Florio refers to these—namely, "imaged," "framed,"
and "set out" (this last in reference to the piazza, an architectural
construct or conception)—also suggest an artificially oriented
understanding of signification rather than a merely substitutive
one. "Types of things" implies a degree of substance and even
iconicity that can readily become problematic.

As a gifted translator of Montaigne, Florio knows that *"every*
language hath it's [sic] *Genius and inseparable forme; without* Py-
thagoras *his* Metempsychosis *it can not rightly be translated. . . .*
The sense may keepe forme; the sentence is disfigured; the finenesse,
fitnesse, featenesse diminished: as much as artes nature is short of na-
tures arte, a picture of a body, a shadow of a substance."[52] Here the
picture, the inferior imitation, is the rendering in one language of
another language rather than a direct depiction of nature. Logically in Florio's statement, the original language is therefore

comparable to "natures arte," "a body," and "a substance." The language of translation then appears to be at two removes from nature and implicitly, at least, the original language at one. The original language is surely more natural and lifelike than its translation, but it is nonetheless an "arte" and, however natural, a human construct. Hardly transparent, moreover, it has body and substance. The supplemental relation of art to nature everywhere evident in Renaissance thinking is here doubly compounded by an explicit art of translation. This doubling, an implicit duplicity, appears both in the art by which Florio turns Italian to English and in that of the metaphor — the figure itself called *translatio* — that he invokes to describe what he fashions in translating: "a picture of a body, a shadow of a substance." Little wonder in this cultural milieu that the serpentine character of Spenser's Error should have taken both verbal and natural forms.

Florio's practice in his dictionary and in his translation of Montaigne's *Essais* recognizes that words are not literally translatable or portable, that they do not simply substitute for things but have their own integrity within a particular linguistic context: so "*the Tuscan altiloquence, the Venus of the French, the sharpe state of the Spanish, the strong significancy of the Dutch cannot . . . be drawne to life* [in English]." Each language has a different character, a different perspective, or in Florio's words, a different "forme" and "Genius." Perhaps not surprisingly, when Florio's explanation of the title *A Worlde of Wordes* continues, it suggests that words and the models made from them do not simply itemize reality but shape and to an extent create it. Having noted both that words are types of things and that his dictionary images the universe, Florio continues, "If looking into it [*A Worlde of Wordes*], it looke like the Sporades, or scattered Ilands, rather then one well-ioynted or close-ioyned bodie, or one coherent orbe: . . . an armie ranged in files is fitter for muster, then in a ring; and iewels are sooner found in severall boxes, then all in one bagge." Whether ranged in files or rings, an army "ranged" is artificially ordered, and jewels, as used here, are cut and polished artifacts, not raw lumps; they have been arranged, moreover, systematically in boxes.[53] The world of words that Florio as dictionary maker translates, and that he imagines, is not so very different from the world that, as the translator of Montaigne, he must try to re-create. Both have a kind of integrity or autonomy of their own; this approaches the notion that words themselves have substance and that a world of them is a created form or constructed entity. Florio's pages evidence again the sense that words occupy a room of their own rather than simply stand for things. This is the essentially artistic, the poetic, or (in both broad and narrow senses) the *fictional* awareness of words that we have also observed in Rabelais and in Andrewes. The space it inhabits is conceptual, but it is constructed from visible words, and it is perceived as being real in some sense. Moreover, it coexists with—here, in fact, emerges from—the lexical fixing of language.

Chapter 3

The
Definitive
Word

The large number of dictionaries issued and reissued in the Renaissance and the increasing use made of them correlate suggestively with a phenomenon familiar to readers of English Renaissance literature, namely, the conspicuous, thematic use of key words or phrases — for example, "nothing," "honest," or "honor" in Shakespeare; "care" or "errant" in Spenser; "dwell" in Jonson; "issues" in Donne; "service" in Herbert. While this phenomenon is hardly unique to the Renaissance period, the centrality and complexity of its occurrence are among the characteristic features of Renaissance writing. Many factors besides dictionaries foster or reflect a nearly obsessive attention to individual words in the period: the unsettled state of the vernacular language itself, the shifting cultural values it registers, and, in more traditional contexts, such procedures as the "word-by-word approach" to teaching grammar and lexical techniques of biblical exegesis.[1] Even a traditional technique can acquire an added edge in the context of new uncertainties and opportunities, of which the dictionary is symptomatic and to which it is in good part a response. Cultural practices such as the making and using of dictionaries *are* perceptions.

The word *trouth* in Wyatt's writing affords a familiar and revealing example of lexical instability in the period. This word is well on its way to becoming a diminished thing, shifting from the medieval meaning, which encompasses personal, epistemological, and spiritual realities, to a modern one, in which these separate into a personal *troth* and a largely objective *truth*, the latter conceived as a conformity to fact and actuality.[2] In Wyatt's lyrics *trouth* serves, via Thomas Greene's sensitive reading, as a "focus of their moral disorientation" and as a further distillation of Wyatt's refrain "What vaileth trouth?" In such a climate the increasingly popular dictionary was to become not only a standard pedagogical tool and a sign of spreading literacy, widening trade, and growing nationalism, but also a kind of cultural touchstone. There comes to be something reassuring, reliable, even "scriptural" about an authoritative book that contains the meaning of words.

As we have seen already, the dictionary heightens emphasis on individual words, and it thereby both registers and disseminates "the illusion," as Ricoeur calls it, that words have meaning apart from a statement, that is, apart from an actual context of syntactical and intentional use (p. 85). In most dictionaries examples of usage (not quite use) counteract these tendencies, but only to a limited extent. When a word is "listed" in a dictionary, it is at once abstracted from discourse and situated in a reifying format.[3] It appears discrete, autonomous, independent of the contexts of actual speech, and this appearance influences our perception of language. While the occasional isolation of individual words for analysis or discussion is ancient and widespread, the dictionary provides the space in which words truly come into their own.

An increasing interest in etymology evident in Renaissance dictionaries likewise highlights individual words, and the lexical presentation of etymological data in the list-like fashion of a work such as John Minsheu's *Ductor in Linguas* (1617), rather than in the discursive prose of a Varro or an Isidore, makes it appear still less a narrative about meaning and a process that develops over time than a fixed equation—something given.[4] This development accentuates the "proprieties," the rights and possessions, of individual words and presages a later interest in historical linguistics proper. Even the sections of Varro's and Isidore's works closest to Minsheu's listings (e.g., Varro, V.xx.101; Isidore, X) employ as a constant refrain such phrases as *fit dictum, dictus, dicitur,* and *dicimus,* which insistently intimate the fact that naming is a human process, at once inventive (*fit*) and cultural (*dicimus*). These sections, in addition to being embedded in larger discursive frameworks, typically have a more continuous, conversational quality than Minsheu's entries, which are more abbreviated and abstracted in form. Radically favoring analytical method over narrative, system over story, Minsheu's listings facilitate reference, but they are simply and significantly less readable.

Presumed to reflect a reality prior to language, etymology—derived ultimately from Greek *etumos,* "true"—can be correlated either with the desire for a natural language or with that for a mystical one, in either case, with "truth." In order to create a natural language Bishop John Wilkins (1614–72) sought the structural correspondence of language, thought, and things—that is, marks "so contrived, as to have such a *dependance* upon, and relation to, one another, as might be sutable to the nature of the things and notions which they represented." But Wilkins also entertained the wish for a more material reflection of things in words themselves, even though he recognized the improbability of its attainment: "It were exceeding desirable that the *Names* of things might consist of such *Sounds,* as should bear in them some Analogy to their *Natures*; and the Figure or Character of these Names should bear some proper resemblance to those *Sounds,* that men might easily guess at the sence or meaning of any name or word, upon the first *hearing* or *sight* of it. But how this can be done in all the particular species of things, I understand not; and therefore shall take it for granted, that this Character must be by *Institution*," that is, by the creation of an artificial character with a real relation to things. Thus Wilkins would strive so to order "the *Names* of things . . . as to contain such a kind of *affinity* or *opposition* in their letters and sounds, as might be some way answerable to the nature of the things which they signified; [and] This would yet be a farther advantage superadded . . . [that] we should, by learning the *Character* and the *Names* of things, be instructed likewise in their *Natures*."[5] Wilkins might aim for the simulation of an isomorphic relation of words to things rather than for the recovery of an original, etymological one, but these alternatives prove not so very far apart in practice. Renaissance etymology, for instance, often invokes as its basis analogy, "affinity," or occasionally even opposition between words and things, one that is graphic, onomatopoeic, or otherwise.[6] The goal of either Wilkins's or the etymologist's alternative is to ground the word in the thing, whether an ideal or material thing. Its effect is to make the word potentially a substitute for the thing and thus, as Socrates recognized centuries before in the *Cratylus*, to make the word the thing itself. Ironically, in such a literal instance of translation, the word achieves substantial status — absolutely the last "thing" Wilkins wanted.

Expressing an essentially representative Adamic view, Agrippa's *De occulta philosophia* (1531) will serve to clarify the relation between the natural philosopher's desire and that of the mystical one. The *De occulta philosophia*, familiar during the Renaissance and translated into English shortly before the publication of Wilkins's *Essay* (1668), more simply but comparably affirms that "*Adam* . . . gave the first names to things, knowing the influencies of the Heavens, and properties of all things" and therefore "gave them all *names according to their natures*, as it is written in *Genesis*" (my emphasis, excepting proper names). By and large, Agrippa has etymology in mind, the notion that true meaning is contained, perhaps even "hidden," in a word. More conspicuously conflating this view with a magical one, however, he also maintains "that proper names of things are certain rayes of things, every where present at all times, keeping the power of things, as the essence of the thing signified"; such names are "proper, and living Images" of things.[7] For Agrippa, names are not merely icons but efficacious ones — in short, verbal amulets. Here Agrippa parts company most dramatically with Wilkins, although his belief in the Adamic origin of contemporary verbal meaning also differs markedly from the bishop's.[8] Throughout the early modern period less radical versions of Agrippa's and Wilkins's views shade into a generally more pedestrian concern with etymology.[9] Yet the presence of ideas like theirs charges this concern with latent tensions and dimensions of meaning and further ensures a probing attention to individual words.

Robert Estienne's Latin *Thesaurus*, an influential work in Tudor England, affords a relatively early example of the etymological impulse in a Renaissance lexicon. Aside from the formal etymologies that Estienne includes after headwords (e.g., *ratio* from the supine *ratum*), many of his general definitions are more etymologically and causally motivated than those of a modern dictionary. Repeatedly he endeavors to explain long-established figurative meanings and thus to resolve dead metaphors into their origins. In the following example of his practice, I am going to offer a literal and sometimes awkward translation, since to a greater extent it will resemble some characteristics of entries in Latin-English dictionaries subsequently to be discussed, wherein the English translation equivalents of Latin words are at times either contextualized or ungrammatically literal.

Defining *gravis*, "heavy" or "weighty," Estienne starts with Valla's view that *gravis* in its own nature [*suapte natura*] . . . signifies heavy: as a heavy stone, a heavy bundle, weighty arms, a weighty shield, clearly because it burdens us [*grauat nos*] in bearing it and because it is carried with difficulty and vexation [*cum molestia*]. Thence we transfer it tropically [literally, through abuse, catachresis: *per abusionem transfferimus*] to age, illness, labor, grief: because these who feel the vexation of age, illness, and other things are oppressed, as it were, by an intolerable burden, which, even as a heavy weight, they ardently wish to put from them. And this transference [*translatio*] is applied not only to bodily vexations but also to those of the mind, as a severe reproach [*grauis contumelia*], a grave injury, a burdensome sorrow, a heavy loss, which oppress the spirit with a certain kind of weight. And thus one sense [of *gravis*] is to name the heavy things that are a vexation to the body or mind. And for the same reason *molestia*, "vexation," has been named from *moles*, that is, from a huge mass, heavy in weight. Another sense of the word is, for instance, because [*quod*] heavy rocks and huge tree trunks are not easily moved from a place but stand fixed in all changing times: similarly, constant persons endowed with wisdom are justly and figuratively called grave [*graues*], because neither by entreaties, nor bribes, nor vainglory, nor promises are they budged from fairness and justice — as are these whom we call light [*leues*], who in likeness of dust and straws are stirred by every breeze.[10]

Estienne's effort to identify not only a root meaning but also an objectified one is notable: a reproach is heavy because it is like a stone; judgments have weight because they are fixed and constant like rocks or tree trunks. He also looks to the sense of a word that "names," rather than merely "designates," things heavy and that thereby identifies something in their natures. He seeks a meaning that corresponds closely to things. In his definition passive constructions progressively displace active ones ("transfferimus"), and metonymy displaces radical metaphor or catachresis ("abusionem"): thus nature appears to displace art, and tradition to replace invention.

Estienne also tends to personalize and to contextualize lexical meaning: a bundle "burdens us"; "these," not those, who suffer illness or "these" who prove to be unwise and inconstant lightweights. A figurative meaning, moreover, "is because" or, perhaps, "is that" heavy rocks are hard to move, rather than "arises because" or "is based on the fact that." Literally translated to English, this last example seems to lack a conceptual step; in it, a distancing syntactical structure is weakened or gone. Translation suggests Estienne's tendency to efface the structure of the sign, paradoxically revealing both that figure, *figura*, in his Latin has become fact and that meaning itself is fundamentally tropic: after all, is it not like "dust and straws," that moral lightweights "are stirred by every breeze"? Conceptually, the compression of syntactical elements in Estienne's Latin construction is analogous to that in the nominal sentence and similarly reflects an effort to ground the linguistic utterance in the nature of things.[11] At the same time, however, like the rest of his definition or, indeed, like the gold threads in Busyrane's — *[A]busio*'s — tapestry in *The Faerie Queene*, it "vnwillingly" displays a commitment to interpretation, translation, and human making — to *fictio*, or fiction (*FQ* III.xi.28).

Of the six most popular comprehensive Latin and Latin/English dictionaries of the period in England — in order of original publication, Calepine, Estienne, Elyot, Cooper, Thomas, and Rider-Holyoke — Elyot and Cooper devote only slight attention to the etymologies of Latin words, Thomas and Rider-Holyoke somewhat more, and Calepine and Estienne a great deal (e.g., Estienne's *gravis*).[12] In England the supreme example of etymological concern, however, is Minsheu's massive *Ductor in Linguas (Guide into the Tongues)*. Minsheu's *Ductor* tackles the etymologies of some 12,550 primitive forms of English words, plus secondary derivatives. In addition to the etymology of the English headword, each entry in the *Ductor* offers parallels to the headword in up to eleven languages, often with additional etymologies, and it sometimes gives explanations of headwords or illustrative quotations. Grandly, Minsheu promises that by the "Etymologies vnder the *Name* [one might] *know the* Nature, Propertie, Condition, Effect, Matter, Forme, Fashion or End of things."[13] Like most etymologists of the period, however, he is also wary, or at least intends to be wary, of etymological excesses. His *Prima epistola lectori* denies that Valla intended to censure true etymologies when he rejected absurd ones, acknowledges that Varro's etymologies are often based on facetious puns and ridiculous illiteracies that result from too exclusive a reliance on Latin alone, and singles out Peter Lombard as an example of similar faults: *"vt Tellus a tollendo, Mons a mouendo,"* for instance.[14] Switching to English examples, Minsheu explains that it is equally laughable to suggest "Anglice *Fire* quasi *Flie higher*, *Cloake* quasi *cleaue oake*." From start to finish, he gives his project a scientific cast. Whereas Isidore had allowed that not all words had originally been imposed according to the nature of the things but also certain ones at whim ("Non autem omnia nomina a veteribus secundum naturam inposita sunt, sed quaedam et secundum placitum"),[15] Minsheu considerably refines this view, introducing a third category into it, as well as the more scientific notion of categories — indeed, *genera* — themselves. He explains that there are three kinds of etymons ("Etymorum genera [genuses of etyma]") — the true, the verisimilar, and that based on mere opinion ("Vera, verisimilia, et ad placitum") — and he expresses his confidence that the true and the verisimilar are susceptible of demonstration ("probari posse"). It is a sign of the times that Francis Bacon, John Donne, and Lancelot Andrewes, along with King James, are all known to have purchased the *Ductor in Linguas*.[16]

As earlier intimated, to read one of Minsheu's entries is to encounter an object (very much an object) of definition rather than a component of actual discourse (Fig. 6). The form these entries take is analytic and taxonomic.[17] Distinguished by three different typefaces (roman, italic, and black-letter), plus Greek,

:. H.P.Lodóſo. I. *Lotéſo*,
s. T. **Drꜩckicht**, **Rettig**.
Gr. ῥοπβοράφνς. Vi. Etym:

ndo, *quòl ſterecra in vnum lo- ıı coact lia concinnat & facit*, **per**, & **Plaiſterer**.
ı, obſcurus, denſam & ſpiſ-, *ὰ σκία*, ı. vmbra, & *ſκούς*,

ntenſ: part: & **dupſter**, *i.ob- - & **finſter**, *i. obſcurus*. G. *ab ob & fuſcus, i. genus co-*, & *uéλας,i* niger. *συνκοτά-* ıecheſchich.

'. **Uerfinſterung**. G. Of- P.Offuſcaƒio. L.Offuſcátio.

ön, à *κόνις,i.*puluis. ¶ Cruſ- ıol *autem per additionem arti-* ı. Vi. **Powder**.
Poudréux. I. *Poluerófo*. H. **taub**,*i.puluis*. B. **Stofach**- ς vel κονιόρτΘ·, i. puluis.
meel, *à* **ſtupf**, *i. puluis*, & ı *inſtar puluiſculi tenuiſſimi*, *à molendinis in quibus farina* ıica namque *farina eſt, molen-* ſole *dicitur*. I. *Farina che ſe ıuha*. L. **Póllen**, *à palande* ıtlabunda vagatur : vel quòd :,*farina tenuiſſima, à* πάλλω, *purgatiſſima. Hæc autem fa- ıe facie diſpellitur*.

ll *matters appertaining to the* ee *of the* Chancelour *of that* he Fourth *his daies, who ob-* Second, *and hauing the* Dut- *mother, he was ſeized thereof,* rties, Franchiſes, *and* Iuriſ- ıng, *by his grand* Seale, *and* ns *of* Euerwicke, *and of the* ıch *had deſcended to the* King Henry the Fourth *by authori-* e *poſſeſſions, liberties, &c. of* vne. *Yet* Henry the Seuenth ry the Fifths *daies*. ¶ Crom- *nzing to this* Court, *are the* rall, Clerke *of the* Court, *the* ıſtants *of this* Court, *as one* f *the* Dutchie *in the* Chaun- *ıâ of Counſell with the* King *in*

* **Pygmeus**. Pygmei *ſunt ſemicubitales, qui tertio anno perfectæ ætatis ſunt, ſeptimo ſeneſcunt, & dicuntur pugnare cum gruibus, & armati deſerti ab ipſis, à* πυγμ̀, *i.* pugnus, *nam tota cohors pede non eſt altior vno: the talleſt ſcarce à* foot high. Gr. Νᾶνὸς, *à* μὴ *particula priuatiua, &* ἄνω, *i.* ſurſum, *minimè enim augentur in altitudinem, ſed ſunt pumila plane ſta-* tura. Heb: גַּמָּדִים *gammadim, i. pigmæi, à* גֹּמֶד *gomedh, i. menſura cubiti, a..z ſecundum* ¶ Hieronym: *menſura palma manus. Hinc* Gammadim *dicti* Pygmæi, *quaſi* cubitales, *vel* palmares, *homunculi paruæ ſta- ture inſtar* brachiorum. Gr. *etiam dicuntur* απ Δαμάΐοι, à απ Δαμάὶ,*i.* ſpi- thama, *a* ſpan. ¶ Heſych: *vocat* Νόβας. Vndè Gal: Nabót, *i. Nanus*, ¶ Guich: *a dwarfe, dumplin, a* Nobedie.

b *a* ſhe **Dwarfe**. T. **Zwergin**. B. **Dwerghinne**. G. Naíne, Nain- treſſe. P. Nảna. H. Enana. I. L. Nana. Gr. Ναυῖς.

c **Dwarfeciſus**. Vi. **Sunflower**.

3586 to **Dwell**, *videtur corruptum à* Gr. αὐλὴ,*i.* aula, ſtabulum, ſtatio, ha- bitatio, εναυλίζομαι, habito, εναύλισμα, habitatio, domicilium, *vt ſit quaſi* εναυλίζω, *vel à* Goth: **Dualc**, *quod idem ſignificat*. G. Demeurér, habitér. I. *Dimoráre, Habitáre*. H. P. Morár, Habitár. L. Morari, à μόρθ, *i.* portio, *quòd ibi vbi* portionem *habeamus, morari ſolemus*, habi- tare, *ab* habendo, *quòd ibi ſedem fixam, & firmam habeamus,vbi* habita- mus, à Gr. μένω,οἰκέω,ab οἶκΘ,*i.*domus. B. **wonen**. T. **wohnen** à Gr. *valew*, ἐνναίνειν, ı. habitare, *niſi malis ab* Heb. בָּנָה banah, *i.* ædi- ficare. *Alludit & ad* מָעֹן maon, *habitaculum, manſio, & ab* Gr. μονὴ, idem à μένω, *i.* manere. & Heluig: *vel ab* Heb: נָוָה nauah, *habitauit*. ¶ Vander-myl: Heb: שָׁמַע gnamadh, *i. ſtetit, habuit ſtationem fixam & firmam*. נָוָה nauah. *Vnde* veteo, habito, ¶ Guich: יָשַׁב jaſchabh, *i.* ſedit, *habitauit*.

b *a* **Dweller**. T. **Einwohner**. B. **Inwooner**. G. Habitánt. I. *Habi- tatóre*. H. Habitadór, Moradór. P. *Moradór*. L. Habitator. Græ: οἰκητὴς.

c *to goe or* **Dwell** *in another place*. G. Tranſmigrér. H. P. *Tranſmudár*. I. L. Tranſmigráre, migráre : *quod vſitatius dicitur autem* tranſmigro, q. trans meum agrum eo, *vel ab* Heb: נֶגַל magar, *idem*. ¶ Aucn: T. **Au- ziehen**, *ab* aw, *i.* ex, & **ziehen**, *i.* proficiſci. B. **Uerhupſen**, *à* ver , *quòd transmutationem denotat*, & **hups**, *i.* domus. Gr. μετοικέω, à ἐΔ, trans, & οἰκέω, habito. Heb: גָּלָה ghalah.

d *a* **Dwelling**. T. **Wohnung**. B. **Wooninghe**. G. Demeuránce, De- méure. I. *Dimoránza,Dimóro,Dimóra*. H. P. Morada. L. Manſio,com- moratio. Gr. μονὴ. *Dicitur* & L. Habitaculum, Domicilium, *à* Domo, *quod tamen propriè ſignificat* locum habitandi, *ſeu* domum *in qua quis* ha- bitat.

e *a* **Dwelling-houſe**. Vi. **Houſe**, *or* **Manſion**.

3487 **Dy**. *Quæcunque vocabula reperiuntur ſcripta cum* **Dy**, *inuenies in* **Di**, *vt* **Dyall**,*Vi.***Diall**, **Dybble**.*Vi.* **Dibble**. **Dyc**.*Vi.* **Die**.**Dye**, *Vi.* **Dice**. & *ſic de cæteris quibuſcunque*.

3588 **Dyer**, *was à* learned Lawyer, *and* Lord chiefe Iuſtice (*del com- mon banke*) *of* the common plees, Hee *liued in the daies of* Queene Eliza- beth: Hee *writ a* booke *in great eſtimation and accompt amongſt vs, called his* Commentaryes *or* Reports *in* Law French.

E

E Quinta eſt litera Alphabéti, *vicem vocalis obtinet tam apud* Græcos, *quàm* Latinos, *aliaſque nationes, & vocatur* Aram: vu. Aſſyr: Ethi- mi, Sclau: ieſt. Vand: ed. Iacob: e. Armen: æ jee. Ægypt: eni: Hebræi *autem* E literam non habent, *ſed vocáles duas breuem vnam al-*

Fig. 6. John Minsheu, *Ductor in Linguas, The Guide Into Tongues*, 1617: p. 164 (quartern). By permission of the Folger Shakespeare Library.

Hebrew, and Saxon characters, they lie in very densely printed double-column folio pages, well over 500 of them. As a rule, they are syntactically fragmentary. Primitive entries are numbered, as well as alphabetically ordered, and their derivatives are also listed alphabetically; certain classes of terms (law, offices, titles) are indicated by pointing index fingers, and other indicators like asterisks and paragraph signs are similarly schematized.

Any decontextualization of words is simultaneously a recontextualization, and the radically methodical form of Minsheu's dictionary strives to decontextualize language in order to recontextualize it as linguistic science. To an extent, however, Minsheu's method backfires, proving variously incongruous with both the linguistic and more broadly causal or rational explanations of origin he offers, which are often borrowed from the more encyclopedic and philosophically oriented dictionaries originating considerably earlier in the Renaissance, such as that of Calepine. His enumerations of alternative etymologies when he is clearly unsure of the origin of a word (or more likely lacks a prior lexical source for it) suggest a faltering purpose and an arbitrariness at odds with the claims of his format. Similar enumerations do not have the same weakening effect in the more discursively narrative prose forms that characterize important etymological works in earlier periods, which, by a suggestive coincidence, are also topically or associatively and not alphabetically ordered.[18] Like the effect of Cooper's *Thesaurus*, that of the *Ductor* is finally and doubly two-sided, at once to freeze language and to display its irrational if productive mutability, and at once to substantiate its referentiality and its own thingness, its objectivity as a self-contained system or an entity in a world of things.

Minsheu most often goes badly wrong in dealing with words of nonclassical derivation, and these instances prove more revealing in some respects than those in which his etymologies are accurate. When wrong, he relies far more conspicuously on coincidences of meaning and form than on coincidences of sound or even such practices of derivation (addition or excision of letters or syllables) as passed for etymological principles in the Renaissance, although he does not hesitate to employ these as well. The word *heaven*, for example, he derives from "**heaue**, i[d est,] eu-ehere, eleuare, quia euehitur et eleuatur super omnia." Next he offers parallels in other languages: "*Sax*[on:] *Hefon*. *B*[elgick:] **Hemel**. *T*[eutonic:] **Himmel**. . . ."[19] Then the entry continues with alternative derivations, Greek, Hebrew, and Germanic, and further parallels. What is striking about it, however, is that *heaven* is actually derived from Old English *heofan* — Minsheu's Saxon *hefon* — a possibility (in 1617 largely speculative) to which his search for a *rational* cause of the word blinds him.[20]

Another non-Latinate headword, *dwell*, Minsheu suggests is a corrupt form of Greek "αὐλὴ, *i[d est,] aula, stabulum, statio, habitatio*," unless it comes from "*Goth*[ic] **Duale**," which, he assures us, "means the same thing" ("quod idem significat"). Throughout this entry, which has some interest in relation to Jonson's *Forrest*, Minsheu's guiding principle is meaning, namely, that *dwell* indicates the habitation, the possessing ("*habendo*"), of a "sedem fixam, et firmam," that is, "a firm and fixed seat" (see Fig. 6). This principle is the basis of his combined lengthening and shortening of the presumed Greek original, and with a fine linguistic irony, it gets him closer to the etymological origin of *dwell* — "to delay," from Old English *dwellan* — than apparently he ever realized or than the seeming absurdity of "aule, aula, stabulum" and the like would ever have seemed to make likely.

In Rabelais's comic epic, when Panurge first meets Pantagruel (II.ix) he expresses his bodily needs in a babble (or Babel) of fourteen different real and imagined tongues. Until he speaks French, however, Pantagruel and his companions are unable to understand him, despite their sharing with him a common ground or (subject) matter: his basic human need of food and drink. Here the joke is that a language requires a community of speakers who recognize its conventions if it is to be comprehensible. Minsheu's underlying assumption appears to be just the opposite; words in the twenty or more "languages," including several dialects, that his dictionary recognizes and variously employs are fundamentally related if their meanings are similar, or, as the *Guide* puts it in an etymologically accurate entry, "**TRANSLA-TION**, *or* **transportinge**. *G.Translation*. *H*.translacion. *P.translaçaō*. *I*.translatione. *L.translatio*, a Trans et Fero, fers, *tuli*, supinis *latum, latu. est* enim *Translatio ex* vna lingua in alium *vel* ex vno loco in alium." That is, the word *translation* derives from *trans*, "across," and *fero*, "carry," for it is the *transporting* of meaning from one language to another or from one place ("loco") to another: some referential thing need only be identified and lugged across. And there is always an etymological key, so long as an objective meaning can be located, and its location appears to reside in the individual, presyntactical, hence precontextual, word.

Perhaps the clearest and most important way in which the Renaissance dictionary puts emphasis on individual words is by connecting them, definitively and irrevocably, with the very nature of definition. Pertinently, Roy Harris asks, "What might we mean by 'definition' if we did not have the model of the dictionary constantly before us?" And in reply he cites W. V. O. Quine's splendidly terse reflection on the fate of the Greek doctrine of essence in the modern world: "Meaning is what essence becomes when it is divorced from the object of reference and wedded to the word."[21] Classical definition is a matter of logic, and it is concerned with the truth or falsity of propositions about the nature of things. It is essentially concerned with objects rather than words, and it is the basic form of conceptualization that the Renaissance inherits from the Middle Ages.[22]

In view of this fact, we might ask just when definition is divorced from the object of reference. Harris has in mind the monolingual dictionary in a modern vernacular language, whose roots and early manifestations are present in the Renaissance but whose full emergence belongs to a later period. As he evidently sees it, the vernacular monolingual dictionary takes a further step away from things and into a self-enclosed system of signs (à la Saussure) than does the bilingual or multilingual dictionary or even the monolingual Latin dictionary, because these are not "monuments to . . . nascent nationalism" (pp. 128–29). Valuable as Harris's work is on the whole, this historicized explanation seems puzzling at best and more likely simplistic: if ever there were a self-contained linguistic system, it is that of the monolingual dictionary of a nonvernacular or monumentalized language, in this case Renaissance Latin.[23] The Renaissance monolingual Latin dictionary is largely distinguished from a modern one not by nationalism or monolingualism but by its radical commitment to linguistic origins and to a fiction of objective meaning, as Estienne's definition of *gravis* has already suggested.

Lexical developments are more complicated and linguistically more nuanced in the Renaissance than Harris's assumptions suggest. Puttenham's observation, cited earlier, that "we are already ruled by th'English Dictionaries and other bookes written by learned men" indicates that the polyglot and bilingual dictionaries (as yet the only learned ones available) did indeed function as arbiters of the proprieties of English words — that is, as containing linguistic institutions. Conceptually, moreover, the bilingual dictionary in Latin and English (or the reverse) also anticipates and approaches the enclosure of the monolingual vernacular dictionary, although without full coincidence. In comparison to a more discursive and necessarily more interpretive translation of a text from one language to another (e.g., Montaigne's *Essais*), the bilingual dictionary must rely on more reductive equivalents such as *arbor* and *arbre* or *sheep* and *mouton*. It therefore relies to a relatively greater extent on the assumption that some thing (a tree, a sheep) is the identical referent for two words in different languages.[24] By definition, it is more objectively and deceptively referential than either a translated text or a monolingual dictionary.

This is not the whole story, however. The bilingual dictionary in fact equates words, not extralinguistic things, on its pages. Moreover, when the popular bilingual dictionaries of the English Renaissance offer a great many English words as apparently synonymous or proximate translations of a Latin word (or vice versa), these equivalents in themselves implicitly approach the cognitive perspective of the monolingual dictionary. Defining the noun *Integritas*, for example, Thomas's *Dictionarium* offers the following equivalents: "Integritie, innocencie, honestie: without corruption, entirenes, vprightnes in al points, purenes, perfectnes, soundnes, healthfulnes: good state, when no part is out of frame and order." In an adaptation of the procedure already employed in the period to turn Latin-English into English-Latin dictionaries, one of the English words, such as *integrity* or even *innocencie*, need only be moved to the position of headword, the other English words becoming its equivalents, in order to approximate a definition in a monolingual dictionary. An alphabetical listing of words and their defining equivalents virtually invites such transpositions, as more discursive and less fully reified forms of presentation would not. Notably, in transpositions such as these objective reference is minimally involved; words mainly interact with other words.

Although the bilingual dictionary may inevitably be based on a stronger assumption of objective reference than the monolingual dictionary, it nonetheless makes the definition of words themselves systematic and abstracts their meaning from specific reference or actual use in a particular argument, thereby decontextualizing them. In most cases by reference to the fixed or unchanging language of Latin, the bilingual dictionary also defines — literally sets boundaries to — the meanings of words in English or in some other vernacular language. The dictionary thus becomes a conspicuous model of definition whose essential allegiance is to the word. When Latin is the defining equivalent, the word is also peculiarly detached from its normal context, since Latin belongs only artificially to "vulgar," vernacular, every-day speech.

Various kinds of definition existed, of course, long before the early modern period, and from the beginning etymology pertains to them. Whereas in the *Topics* (I.5, 102a) Aristotle regards "A definition . . . [as] a phrase signifying a thing's essence," in the *Rhetoric* he describes definition less strictly as the commonplace "defining your terms" (II.23, 1398a). In the *Posterior Analytics*, he distinguishes between "an account of what the name . . . signifies" and an account that demonstrates syllogistically "what a thing is" (II.10, esp. 93b29–31, 94a11–13; cf. 7, 92b26–27). Cicero in his *Topica* is close to Aristotelian logic and dialectic when he describes a definition as "a statement which explains what the thing defined is" and then extends his description in terms of enumeration and analysis and genus and species. But the procedure he recommends remains loosely methodical rather than strictly logical, and definition blends with hardly a break in his discussion into argumentation based on etymology.[25] Quintilian, invoking Cicero, makes the rhetorician's concern with an etymological basis for definitive argumentation explicit: "We find room for etymology," he explains, "when we are concerned with definitions."[26] Centuries later, Erasmus too understands the relation of etymology to definition this way in his immensely influential *De duplici copia verborum ac rerum*, where he declares that "etymology . . . is a kind or species of definition."[27] From the beginning, etymology is involved in defining reality, explaining *things*.

Over time, a concern with etymology bears on the shift Quine and Harris describe in the dominant model of definition from logic to lexicon, essence to meaning, objective reality to words. In 1551, Thomas Wilson's *Rule of Reason* suggests how this might have developed. In accordance with Aristotle's *Posterior Analytics*, Wilson distinguishes carefully between the definition of a word and the real definition of a thing and simultaneously recognizes that there are two legitimate forms of definition, one substantial and logical and one verbal and etymological:

> A definicion is twoo waies considered, for either it is a definicion of a woord, or of a substaunce. A definicion of a woorde, is any maner of declaracion of a woorde, as, a realme is so called, because it is by a king ruled. . . . A woman hath her name so geuen her, because she bringeth woe vnto manne.
>
> A difinicion of the substaunce, is a speache, whiche sheweth the very nature of the thing, and euery perfeicte difinicion, is made perfeicte by the generall woorde, and his difference ioigned together.[28]

Whereas a substantial definition is a true proposition indicating the genus and species of a thing, a verbal definition is concerned with terminology and ideally with the essential definition of a word. The one is necessarily a speech, a complete statement; the other, a declaration or clarification, may be more fragmentary.

Wilson's examples of verbal definition (a realm, a woman) indicate his desire to define words etymologically. His conception of verbal meaning is basically essentialist insofar as he endeavors, through etymology, to maintain a firm connection between the word and its object of reference. At the same time, however, he might be said to transfer essential meaning in such a definition to the word. Wilson's verbal definition affords a glimpse into the conceptual process by which the model of definition might have evolved. The Renaissance dictionary expresses a quantum leap in this process by systematizing and spatializing the meaning of words and thus making words seem in themselves more autonomously real.

Like Peacham's two kinds of order, Wilson's two kinds of definition, one logical and the other lexical, illustrate how the Renaissance can be both thoroughly traditional and fundamentally in transition. On the one hand, Wilson merely endorses Aristotle's position; on the other, his relative emphasis on the word and his etymological examples impute to the word a rational connection with its referent; he thereby empowers the word in a way that lends itself to the incipient shift from logic to lexicon. The conception — indeed even the traditional definition — of definition is thus drawn into flux, and as the period unfolds it is increasingly at issue. A later and more radical instance of the way it is shifting occurs in Bacon's explanation of the "Idols of the Market-place," false images resulting from the linguistic conventions that shape human consciousness: "The remedy for this evil (namely, definitions) is in most cases unable to cure it; for definitions themselves consist of words, and words beget words."[29] Conceivably in this proto-Derridean sentence Bacon could be speaking merely of definitions of words rather than of real definitions of substances, but elsewhere he clearly extends the same criticism to logical definitions, for "syllogisms consist of propositions, and propositions of words; and words are but the current tokens or marks of popular [i.e., inaccurate] notions of things."[30] In Bacon's skepticism, both of Wilson's two kinds of definition have become *essentially* verbal and by this token unreal.

But Bacon hopes for a third kind of definition based more securely in matter, the object itself, than is the case with the inherited tradition of logical propositions. His hope is for a science free of the tyranny of words and, like Wilkins after him, for a transparent language accurately moored in some way, if only nominally and conventionally, to things. What is curious is the extent to which his memorable but derogative description of current language as "an Idol" — that is, an image — acting on the mind reflects as powerful a conception of its seeming substance as that of any Renaisance rhetorician or lexicographer. Although Bacon is best known as a herald of the age to come, his own language and hence his thinking often recall his birth as an Elizabethan and a contemporary of Spenser, Shakespeare, Jonson, and Donne. The very strength of his perception of the substantiality of language and consequently of its idolatrous intervention accounts for the intensity of his linguistic iconoclasm, which is rooted deeply in Calvinist thinking: for "man's nature," as Calvin explains, "is a perpetual factory of idols."[31]

Wilson belongs to a considerably earlier state of linguistic transition than Bacon, but his ordering of words in *The Rule of Reason* is similarly revealing and in this case suggests the extent to which a logical purpose still dominates his conception of language. Anne Ferry has remarked how Wilson "seems indifferent" to grammatical distinctions between parts of speech and has pointed to his definitive lists "blurring the grammatical division between noun and verb" as evidence of the oddity of linguistic awareness in the English Renaissance (pp. 64–65). Since the contexts of Wilson's lists are relevant to our perception of them, I shall quote one of them involving the logical definition of an accident at some length:

> Accident (that is to saie, a thing cleauyng, or chauncying, or comyng to a substaunce) is that whiche dooeth not stande by him selfe, nether is the parte of a substaunce, but rather is after soche sort in the substaunce, that it maie bothe be awaie and be there, sometimes more, and sometimes lesse, without destruction or losse of the subiecte, or substaunce, *as mirthe, sorowe, to ronne, to sitte, to be well colored,* all these maie be awaie, and yet the man maie be on liue, in whom thei were before. (p. 18; my emphasis)

Within an Aristotelian logic like Wilson's, a verb in and by itself may be termed a noun or a name and regarded as substantival; it is, strictly speaking, only a verb when used in a proposition.[32] An infinitive, lacking person, number, tense, and functioning substantivally (e.g., "To run is natural"), further straddles the grammatical line between noun and verb. Rather than indicating Wilson's indifference to grammatical categories, his illustrative combination of nouns and infinite verbs in the preceding passage indicates his proper inclusion of grammatical categories that are indifferently subsumed under the logical category of accidents. The point is not that he is insensitive to grammatical categories (a possibility his training in Latin should have precluded in any case) but that in the context of Aristotelian logic grammatical categories are not the point.[33]

At midcentury in Tudor England, the instance of Wilson still suggests the conceptual priority of logic over language; nearer the turn of the century, certain features of definition in the standard dictionary of Thomas Thomas, like those in Estienne's *Thesaurus*, also indicate that even within a linguistic context lexical abstraction (decontextualization) is far from complete. In the Thomas dictionary, for example, some definitions, particularly those pertaining to Roman society, employ verbs in the past tense. As in a number of earlier lexicons, other definitions make use of personalized references — for example, of first-person pronouns, of an observer's point of view, of the author's opinion, or of an implied moral engagement. Gabriele Stein notes the following instances: *Atnepos*, defined, "The sonne of my nephewes nephew"; *Citerior*, defined, "Nigher, or nearer to vs, or to our time"; *Delinquo*, in part defined, "To omit that we shoulde doe"; *Glaucus*, in part defined, "commonlie taken for blew and graie . . . but I thinke it is rather red with brightness" (pp. 323–24).

Elsewhere Thomas, like his predecessors, occasionally defines a word in a way that does not correspond grammatically to the headword — for example, the noun *Homonymia*, defined, "When diuerse thinges are signified by one word."[34] Since Thomas's careful indication of grammatical categories after headwords (e.g., gender, declension, or part of speech) demonstrates his obvious regard for them, we might explain these differences from modern standards of detemporalized, impersonal lexical definition simply as reflections of everyday usage, for the most part still current today. In the specific context of a dictionary, however, they are further significant as nearly submerged indications of a transitional state of lexical abstraction and of a residual linguistic awareness resistant to it.

In a study of cognitive growth Jerome Bruner has described linguistic representation in a way that illuminates Thomas's practices. Discussing a gradual process of linguistic acculturation, Bruner cites the example of a child's definition — "A hole is to dig" — that is ungrammatical in a way broadly analogous to some of Thomas's definitions or to Estienne's definition of *gravis* ("a sense of the word is because") examined earlier. He characterizes it as a definition in words of "the process of hole making" and as a practical representation of action in linguistic symbols. It "account[s] for the early process by which the child brings overt behavior under the control of language."[35] Obviously there are later stages in this process, of which another example might be found in the word *Drama*, defined as follows in Thomas's dictionary: "When in a Comedie or tragedy diuers persons are brought in, some tarying, and some departing." Other examples can be found in some of Thomas's personalized definitions already cited — "nearer to vs, or to our time," defining *Citerior*, for instance. The point here is not that Thomas or Estienne is a child (or a "primitive") but that lexical abstraction and the cultural amplifiers that elicit and encourage it are still visibly developing. In Thomas's case, which is fairly representative of lexicographers of the period, I would add that the process of decontextualization (or recontextualization) is far advanced, and the majority of his definitions do not show these traces of alternatives to lexical abstraction.

In fact there are further signs in his definitions and in those of his competitors of the shift from a logical focus to a lexical one and from Wilson's proposition to the definitive word. If Thomas's inclusion of explanatory definitions rather than just translation equivalents accounts in part for the lasting popularity of his dictionary, as Stein has suggested, it obviously also indicates the importance for his readers of defining the meaning of *words* and, in short, of defining meaning lexically (p. 320). Under

Magistratus, for example, where Thomas's entry might simply have translated "A magistrate" it instead continues, "a great or head officer, one in authoritie or gouernance of the people," and only then adds definitively, "*also* the authoritie, office, power, dignitie of a ruler." Under *Melancholia* the entry reads, "Melancholia, blacke choler, a kind of madness rising of melancholie," and next specifies *Melancholia hypochondrica, sive flatulenta, aut flatuosa* as "Melancholie or black choler vnder or about the short ribs, or windie melancholie, which is bred of ach and sorenes about the saide partes, from whence a black fome arising doth hurte and trouble the minde." Both the definition of *magistratus* and that of *melancholia* are similar to definitions of *magistrate* and *melancholia* or *melancholy* to be found today in a dictionary of English words. Both intimate reassuringly that language has things under control.

Another reason for Thomas's popularity is very likely his inclusion of numerous synonymous or related terms in translation equivalents, thus turning them into indications of a word's range of meaning quite apart from specific contexts of usage. Under the participial adjective *Distinctus*, for example, the entry reads, "Deuided, distinguished, separated, pointed, noted, marked, distinct, discerned by or differing in, beset with, orderlie"; and under the verb *Recreo*, "To recreate, to renew, to make againe: to refresh, to make lustie, to recover his old strength and nature, to gather his spirits: to comfort and delight." (The partial contextualization of the latter definition — "his old strength" and "his spirits" — is incidentally notable as well.) Unlike the definitions of *magistratus* and *melancholia*, however, those of *distinctus* and *recreo* differ significantly from those of *distinct* and *recreate* in two standard modern desk dictionaries I checked, *Webster's New World Dictionary* (1974) and the *American Heritage Dictionary* (1985). The modern definitions are more analytical and summary, hence more abstract. Thomas offers a range of translation equivalents meant to cover possible nuances of meaning whose definitive effect is more tentative and secondary. At moments, his copious equivalents suggest a world of words, rather than either an actual or a fully lexical one.

In comparison to standard modern definitions, those in the dictionaries of Thomas and his competitors are generally less thorough. Yet this is a statement no sooner made than necessarily qualified. If we take Thomas's dictionary together with other Renaissance dictionaries of comparable coverage, their definitions add up to something approximating the modern form. This is all the truer if their examples of usage, extensive in the instances of Calepine and Cooper, are considered the precursors and roughly the equivalents of the more decontextualized specifications and extentions of meaning in the standard modern version.[36] In other words, the tradition of lexical definition that would combine these features in a more summary and analytic form was still in a relatively early stage of codification, with less than a hundred years to its credit. Relevant cultural amplifiers were very much in an evolving process of change — a heightened, generative, and unsettling state.

The relative focus, inclusiveness, and abstraction of definitions in Renaissance dictionaries compared to modern ones can be further clarified by turning again to specific examples, here the words *homo / human being*, *substantia / substance*, and *ratio / reason*. Since these words are familiar in logical contexts, they cast additional light on the relation of verbal to logical definition and thence on the increasingly focal role of the definitive word. Defining *homo / human being*, Cooper and Thomas are essentially representative of Calepine, Estienne, Elyot, and Rider-Holyoke. Cooper offers the more logical definition: "A lyuinge creature subiecte to death and indued with reason, man, woman or childe: or man kinde comprehending, man, woman and childe"; he follows this definitive statement with numerous examples of usage carrying a variety of applications: for example, "Iniquitas hominum," "Sator hominum atque deorum," "Maritimi homines,"

"Nobilissimus omnium homo," "Nauus et industrius homo." Calepine and Estienne, the two relevant continental lexicographers who precede Cooper, similarly cite examples of usage but also include in their most general and summary definitions quotations from authors such as Vergil, Cicero, and Ovid characterizing the human condition. Calepine cites this Ovidian passage: "And, though all other animals are prone, and fix their gaze upon the earth, he gave to man an uplifted face and bade him stand erect and turn his eyes to heaven."[37] In dramatic contrast to such expansive definitions, Thomas's definition is simple and terse — "A man or woman: *also* humanitie or sense of mans nature" — and it includes no examples of usage.

For the purpose of lexical comparison, the most useful modern equivalent of *homo* is to be found in arguably outdated meanings of *man*, defined, for example, as follows:

> **1.** a human being; person; specif., *a*) a primate (*Homo sapiens*) having an erect stance, an opposable thumb, the ability to make and use specialized tools, articulate speech, and a highly developed brain with the faculty of abstract thought: the only living species of a worldwide family (Hominidae) *b*) any member of several extinct species of this family, as Neanderthal man **2.** the human race; mankind: used without *the* or *a* **3.***a*) an adult male human being *b*) sometimes, a boy **4.***a*) an adult male servant, follower, attendant, or subordinate *b*) a male employee; workman *c*) [*usually pl.*] a soldier, sailor, etc.; esp., one of the rank and file *d*) [Archaic] a vassal **5.***a*) a husband *b*) a lover **6.***a*) a person with qualities conventionally regarded as manly, such as strength, courage, etc. *b*) manly qualities.[38]

Here, in the modern monolingual dictionary, the definitive word is fully emergent. The apparatus of definition is also conspicuous: **1**, **2**, and **3** typographically emphatic, for example, and *a* and *b* also distinctive typographically.

Additional specialized meanings of *man* follow those just cited. There are no examples of usage apart from common idiomatic phrases. Although meanings appropriate to *homo / human being* merge with those appropriate to *vir / man* in this example, it nonetheless suggests the difference in abstraction and analysis that exists between dictionaries in Renaissance and modern times. Yet many elements in the modern example are represented in Cooper's rationally abstractive definition and extensive examples of usage, and if we discount scientific data unknown to the Renaissance, they are at least implicit in Thomas's translation equivalents. Visible in them are the ghostly lineaments of the definitive word.

The definition of *substantia / substance*, although as familiar in philosophical and logical contexts as *homo*, does not elicit a similarly abstractive definition from Cooper and therefore suggests some inconsistency in his methods. Cooper's simple equivalents — "Substance: mattier. . . . Goods: riches" — which are based, he notes, on Quintilian, fairly represent those in Elyot, Thomas, and Rider-Holyoke's Latin-English section. In this section, however, Holyoke, perhaps to cover his plagiaristic tracks, reorders and shortens the Cooper-Thomas version to "goods, riches, matter" and thereby obscures its rational progression from the more to the less abstract meaning. In Rider-Holyoke's English-Latin section, moreover, Holyoke retains Rider's translation equivalent for *substance* — "*Substantia.hypostasis.* . . . The substaunce, or beeing of a thing. *Ousia*" — and thereby includes Rider's philosophical nuancing.[39]

This time Minsheu, whose primarily etymological purpose commits him to a search for the rational causes of words, offers the most logical explanation of *substance*, which largely repeats those in Calepine and Estienne: "It is what subsists by itself and provides a foundation for accidents, which cannot subsist for that purpose."[40] The definitions of both Minsheu and Estienne also refer specifically to *substance* meaning "matter, and as it were the essence and solidity and sinews of whatever thing" and, along with Calepine, they relate this sense to rhetorical substance:

in the clause Minsheu borrows from Calepine and cites for this purpose, "Also when *substance* is posited of the matter and argument [*materia et argumento*] around which the hinge of the whole thing [*totius rei*] is swung."[41] The implication of language ("materia et argumento") in essential being ("substance") and necessarily in changing conceptions of it is so obvious in the Calepine-Minsheu definition as to qualify as a lexical fact. If only incidentally, the substance of Rabelais's frozen words can be seen congealing around the edges of their definition.

A modern dictionary defines *substance* quite similarly and in doing so establishes the ambivalence of the concept:

> 1. the real or essential part or element of anything; essence, reality, or basic matter 2. *a*) the physical matter of which a thing consists; material *b*) matter of a particular kind or chemical composition 3. *a*) solid quality; substantial character *b*) consistency; body 4. the real content, meaning, or gist of something said or written 5. material possessions; property; resources; wealth 6. *Philos.* something that has independent existence and is acted upon by causes or events — **in substance** 1. with regard to essential elements 2. actually; really.

The modern definition includes a specialized philosophical sense but subsumes it under a more general one and even presents what is properly an example of common usage, "in substance," in abstracted form. Again the range of definitive meaning the modern summary offers is fuller and more analytically detailed than those in the Renaissance lexicons, but the difference between the two is otherwise slight.

Even so, it is notable that the connection in the modern version between the first, most inclusive sense (essence, reality) and the fourth, rhetorical sense (real content, meaning, gist) is not as explicit as in the Calepine-Minsheu version. As a result, the implication of verbal argument in essential being is less emphatic. Paradoxically, while modern words may more clearly constitute meaning, they may also be less clearly substantial than Renaissance ones. The slippage in the meaning of the word *substantial* between the two periods, although less dramatic than that of the word *truth*, may suggest a similar story. In both, a breadth of meaning is fragmented and restricted.

The definition of *ratio / reason* affords a final example, which, with the preceding ones, suggests movement within the Renaissance itself from definitions belonging to an external context — logic, nature, or the like — to those within the definitive purview of language. It will be useful to start with the modern definition of *reason* as a point of reference:

> **1.** an explanation or justification of an act, idea, etc. **2.** a cause or motive **3.** the ability to think, form judgments, draw conclusions, etc. **4.** sound thought or judgment; good sense **5.** normal mental powers; a sound mind; sanity **6.** *Logic* any of the premises of an argument, esp. the minor.

From a Renaissance point of view, the order of definition in the modern entry would be backwards. The definitions of Calepine and Estienne differ in significant respects from the modern one. For Calepine, *ratio* is "the most noble faculty of the soul, by which alone man is distinguished from the animals and from which he is called rational." Similarly for Estienne, it "is that power of the intellect, by which man is separated from the other animals, surpasses them in power, and rules over them."[42] Both definitions are discursive in style and logical and philosophical in origin, and they reflect a worldview somewhat different from our own. Both tell more of a story about reason than does the modern version. These characteristics are further emphasized in successive quotations from Cicero, Augustine, and the like, describing, defining, or reflecting on reason. Since both entries cite the same passage from Cicero's *De officiis*, it affords an appropriate example: "Now we find that the essential activity of the spirit is twofold: one force is appetite . . . which impels a man this way and that; the other is reason, which teaches and explains what should be done and what should be left undone. The result is that reason commands, appetite obeys."[43] Properly speaking, the general definitions in both dictionaries are encyclopedic and reminiscent of the *summae* and great encyclopedias of the Middle Ages. Significant here, however, is also the fact that both are found in a *dictionarium*, the word-book, rather than in a *summa*, the perfecting epitome of knowledge, or in an *encyclopaedia*, the course in general education. It represents another small step in the increasing institutionalization of the transfer of meaning from essence and object to meaning and word.

In both Calepine's and Estienne's dictionaries, such overarching definitions are followed by a number of specific designations of usage, as well as by extensive examples of it. These designations of the various senses of a word operate as headings for the examples grouped with them: "Sometimes it means 'cause' [*ponitur pro causa*, literally, 'is set down, put for']," or "Sometimes it means 'consideration' and 'proposition,' " or, in another, simpler designatory style, "Reason, mode, way, and form." By modern standards, such specifications are proto-analytic, but they subordinately follow generic definitions more suited to a textbook or an anthology of sayings than to a (modern) lexicon. Primarily they belong to a context of things external to the lexicon rather than to one essentially of words.

For both Calepine and Estienne, *ratio* has a direct and very real referent, not just a conceptualized meaning, in a world they conceive in logical, philosophical, and religious terms. What is supposed to be a true statement about the nature of things dominates and contextualizes lexical concerns. The word answers first to something outside language as such.[44] Nonetheless, the fact that their definitions are organized beneath a word rather than beneath a topic, a symbol, or an object, and in abstractive form rather than in a series of propositions, a narrative, or some other discursive framework, is a notable shift from the dominant emphasis of the preceding period. Again paradoxically, even as words seem to become more directly referential as a result of dictionaries such as Calepine's and Estienne's, they become part of a system of words that is emphatically self-contained. As we have often observed in this study, the situation of words produces a fertile ambivalence in the Renaissance: on the one hand frozen reifications and on the other variable, mutable, arbitrary openness.

In comparison to Calepine and Estienne, Elyot, Cooper, Thomas, and Rider-Holyoke define *ratio* lexically. Elyot and Cooper are the parents of this definition, which Cooper's *Thesaurus* illustrates and refines in several folio columns of examples; Thomas is the greatly expansive son. Rider-Holyoke subsequently reduces Thomas's version by half, making it nearly identical to Elyot and Cooper, although, like Thomas, Rider-Holyoke omits examples. I cite Thomas's entry under *ratio* as the fullest:

> Reason, counsell, purpose, care, respect, consideration, advisement, regard: the cause, the matter, the state, the meanes, the way, the fashion, the forme, the proportion, a rule, the trade, the feate, the manner, and sorte: a minde, counsell, advise, or phantasie: an account or reckoning, busines: the quantitie, value: affayres. *Habere rationem.* To have to do with: *also* to labour and occupie.[45]

Thomas's list seems again to aspire to absorption in a world of words, and again it is not hard to imagine a Baconian despair of linguistic precision in reading his extensions and synonymies of meaning. Amid these, the notion that every word should have a single meaning, and every meaning its own word, seems far distant.

Yet Thomas is well on his way to abstraction and analysis and, in short, to rationalization. He separates different levels of meaning with a colon, and he represents usage abstractively, even citing "*Habere rationem*," as it might be cited in a modern desk dictionary.[46] In citing this idiom, which is hardly a predictable translation equivalent of *ratio*, Thomas exposes his reliance on examples of usage in other lexicons and his penchant for decontextualizing them. Half knowingly, perhaps, he signals his interest in defining the meaning of *ratio* and not merely in translating it. What is most significant about his definition, however, is its purely linguistic character. Although his dictionary, like Calepine's and Estienne's, presumably attempts only to define the possible nuances of a Latin word, it does so exclusively through other words, without significant reliance on contexts.

Thomas's lexical practice, consistent where Cooper's is varied, is notably innovative. In the definition of meaning it suggests movement from a logically and philosophically contextualized allegiance to a primarily linguistic one. Yet it is also transitional both in itself and in relation to other dictionaries of the period. Although the dictionaries of Estienne and Calepine were originally composed at much earlier dates than that of Thomas, they continued to be highly popular long after the latter's was published. It is therefore difficult to conclude, although tempting to do so, that their inclination toward logically and philosophically embedded definitions represents at this stage an outdated lexical conception and concomitantly an earlier kind of linguistic awareness, rather than simply an alternative one. As the modern definitions I have cited also indicate, logical and philosophical meanings of words continue today to be of interest to lexicographers. But as such meanings are represented in modern dictionaries, they are precisely that — meanings or senses of words, not definitions of reality. If implicitly we think of them as the latter (and we commonly do), then meaning is indeed what essence has become once "divorced from the object of reference and wedded to the word."

Predictably, Minsheu's etymological interests, merging easily in their search for rational causes with logical and philosophical ones, intersect conspicuously with the etymologically rich dictionaries of Calepine and Estienne, from whom he borrows time and again. Minsheu is not just a belated etymologist, however.

His influence is considerable in the remainder of the seventeenth century and after, and it is also paralleled to an extent in Thomas's chief competitor, Rider-Holyoke, whose etymologies are more numerous and consistently provided than are Thomas's own.[47] Etymology, of course, also continues to be a feature of the modern dictionary, but once again with a difference. A modern dictionary defines *etymology* as "The origin and historical development of a linguistic form as shown by determining its basic elements, earliest known use, and changes in form and meaning, tracing its transmission from one language to another, and identifying its cognates in other languages." For a modern linguist, etymology is thus (to illustrate Quine's contention that the modern dictionary defines reality) the historical study — or perhaps simply the story — of the development of words, whereas for Minsheu it is an ahistorical and associative dissection of them. In his *Ductor in Linguas* it is an attempt to find the reality — the thing itself — at their core. Minsheu nevertheless made an effort to catalogue the content of words in a systematic, comprehensive, and analytical way and thereby to make of their study a science. The format of his dictionary, like that of others in the period, tends to isolate and to reify the individual word; as my own metaphors ("dissected," "content") have implied, its focus on the word itself is radically, but also ambivalently, substantial.

Stones
Well
Squared

Definition in 'The Forrest'
and 'The Faerie Queene'

The Renaissance dictionary sheds light on the ways that the practices of such different poets of the period as Spenser and Jonson are fundamentally lexical — that is, specifically concerned with the meanings of individual words. Characteristically, if variously, both poets give a distinctive weight to the word, even though both also typically compose a poetry that represents a distinctive content — *res*, or subject matter — Spenser favoring Neoplatonized ideals, and Jonson favoring the Baconian "nature of things," a rationally perceived reality. Unlikely as it may seem, Jonson, the poet of the plain style and contemporary experience, rather than Spenser, the etymologizing archpoet of Fairyland, is more concerned with words as such. Words themselves, strikingly, can be the nodal points of meaning or the objectives of a process of definition in Jonson's poems, as they are recurrently in his poetic miscellany, *The Forrest*. Despite the seemingly inexhaustible verbal density of the Spenserian text, typically its words do not operate this way. There is not in Spenser's writing the same insistence of and on the word on the page itself that there is in Jonson's.

Yet in *Timber, or Discoveries; Made upon Men and Matter*, Jonson specifically endorses Bacon's strictures in *The Advancement of Learning* and *Novum Organum* on "the study of words" — mere words: unless words serve matter, they are merely the heady froth of an intellectual imbalance and "the first distemper of Learning" (VIII, 592, 627). Elsewhere in *Timber*, however, Jonson's own statements reflect a number of the same tendencies to substantiate words that we have earlier encountered, and they indicate an inconsistency or ambivalence in his regard for them. Recurrently and extensively, for instance, he compares a verbal construct to a dwelling: "For as a house, consisting of diverse materialls, becomes one structure, and one dwelling; so an Action, compos'd of diverse parts, may become one *Fable Epicke*, or *Dramaticke*" (VIII, 648). He also invokes the relation of mind or soul to body in order to clarify that of matter (or "sense") to words and describes the stature, figure and feature, skin and coat, and flesh, blood, and bones of various styles of writing — the fleshly style, with blood and juice, though in danger of fat, or the bony and sinewy style, "not lesse blood, but lesse flesh, and corpulence" (VIII, 592–93, 621, 625–27). Although such comparisons are basically conventional, he develops them with a gusto that recalls the linguistic materialism of Gabriel Harvey and John Hart.

Like Erasmus, Philip Sidney, and most other writers of the early modern period, Jonson seems at times to belittle language by externalizing it in the imagery of clothing; yet in an age when clothing was considered so intrinsic to status and identity as to require legislative control, his comparisons of language to it effectively blur the boundary between what is inside and what outside a person, what essential and what merely apparent: "*Language* most shewes a man: speake that I may see thee. It springs out of the most retired, and inmost parts of us, and is the Image of the

Parent of it, the mind" (VIII, 625–26).[1] The nature of the relation of body to mind and image to source involves basic issues of
representation and belief and is hardly simple, clear, and stable in
this period — or, for that matter, in Jonson's own life. Correspondingly, there is an appreciable difference between Jonson's
writing that "his mind [cannot] be thought to be in tune, whose
words doe jarre" and the assertion that this discord results merely
from the speaker's failure to fit his words to his preexistent thinking (VIII, 628). Although carefully hedged with the verb "be
thought," rather than the more absolute claim "is," Jonson's assertion accommodates a constitutive function for language. As Bacon put it, "men [may] believe that their reason governs words;
but . . . words react on the understanding."[2]

Elsewhere in *Timber*, where Jonson seems clearly to deny to
language a power so substantial, his own words undercut him:
the Jonsonian writer "must first thinke, and excogitate his matter; then choose his words, and examine the weight of either.
Then take care in placing, and ranking both matter, and words"
(VIII, 615). If the writer is somehow to cogitate — indeed, to
ex-cogitate — without language, his thoughts lack structure until
they are verbal, and once they are, the words expressing them
carry their own "weight." Jonson's statement recalls both J. C.
Scaliger's view that poetry has two *substantial* parts, ideas and
words, and the advice in Estienne's *Thesaurus linguae Latinae* to
the man purposing "the construction [*exaedificationem constructionemque*] of a speech," who is to be mindful that "the material
[*materia*] of discourse is partly in the words and partly in the
things themselves." Without such rationalizing parallels, Jonson's
statement would merely suggest a basic instability in his conception of the relation of mind to matter.

Jonson indicates a sense of words as separate entities — things
in themselves — even more sharply in another of his architectural
images for composition. He refers in this case to a paratactic

style: "The congruent, and harmonious fitting of parts in a sentence, hath almost the fastning, and force of knitting, and connexion: As in stones well squar'd, which will rise strong a great way without mortar" (VIII, 623). Here the axis of comparison is fitting and fastening, and the parts of a sentence could include not only words but also complex units such as phrases and clauses. But the image of the "stones well squar'd" remains the most memorable part of the sentence, and stones are not usually thought of as complex units; the image primarily and powerfully suggests individual words — words, moreover, "well squar'd" or carefully shaped by a skillful craftsman in accordance with his conception of the whole building.[3] Although a prose style as unlike Jonson's model as Malory's is also paratactic, as I termed it earlier, Jonson's squaring, shaping, and design pay infinitely more attention than Malory's to definitive words. Jonson, annotating his *English Grammar*, embraces the traditional view that "Dictionis natura prior est, posterior orationis" ("Words are prior, speech posterior"), an opinion that incidentally casts light on his endorsement of Bacon's view that words unsquared are "the *first* distemper of Learning."[4]

A final passage from *Timber* with particular relevance to Jonson's *Forrest* adds to the evidence of tropic supplementation in his pronouncements on language. Jonson observes of decorum that the "Elegance, and Propriety" of words are seen "when wee use them fitly, and draw them forth to their just strength and nature, by way of Translation, or *Metaphore*" (VIII, 621). Continuing, he explains that such translation must serve necessity (the absolute lack of a word) or "commodity, which is a kind of necessity" (the lack of a fit word). Not only can a commodious metaphor "avoid loss," but it can also effect a "gaine in the grace and property, which helpes significance." By the time Jonson has finished, the ground of his argument has shifted somewhat, and he sounds a little like Peacham: metaphor has progressed from an extension of verbal propriety (i.e., property) to something required by it, namely, a "gaine in property" itself and therefore a gain in the very basis of significance. If we assume that Jonson, who told Drummond that "he wrott all his [verses] first jn prose," has preconceived the conclusive word "dwells" in "To Penshurst," his notion of drawing words forth through metaphoric translation, in this case transference to an entire estate and entire poem, affords a convenient way into *The Forrest*.[5]

Hardly an interpreter of *The Forrest* fails to comment on the import of its title, which, in its refusal of literal meaning and its nominal relation to *Timber* and *The Under-wood*, conspicuously invites glossing. In fact, Jonson himself became its primary glossator in the familiar headnote to *The Under-wood*, explaining it by reference to a genre consisting of miscellaneous pieces:

> *With the same leave, the Ancients call'd that kind of body* Sylva, *or* Ὕλη, *in which there were workes of divers nature, and matter congested; as the multitude call Timber-trees, promiscuously growing, a* Wood, *or* Forrest: *so am I bold to entitle these lesser Poems, of later growth, by this of* Vnder-wood, *out of the Analogie they hold to the* Forrest, *in my former booke.*[6]

In part this headnote translates that to *Timber*, as printed in the 1640 Folio; that headnote is drawn from commentary based on Aulus Gellius, Cicero, and Quintilian in a 1616 edition of Statius, according to Herford and Simpson, Jonson's modern editors (XI, 213; VIII, 557–58).

Among other pertinent glosses of Jonson's title, none of which excludes the alternatives to it, Richard Peterson has invoked a passage in Bacon's *Advancement of Learning* where young minds are described as yet "emptie and unfraught with matter, . . . that which *Cicero* calleth *Sylva* [*De Oratore*, III.26.103] and *Supellex* [*Orator*, 24.80], stuffe and varietie."[7] In a fuller exploration of Jonson's title, Alastair Fowler has noted the resemblance to *The Forrest* of J. C. Scaliger's characterization of *silva* as a poetic form, and he has also seen in *silva* an allusion to "the *selva oscura*, the entangling forest of error" or even to "formless chaos, hyle waiting to be formed."[8] Nearly all these glosses associate *silva* with matter, understood either as subject matter or as the material world or as both.

To them I would add the specific association of *silva* and *hyle* with language. Most relevantly, Scaliger, whose work Jonson knew well, entitles the second book of the *Poetice* "Hyle" ("Poetic Matter") and explains this to be "litera, syllaba et dictio" or more simply "dictio" — words.[9] In Jonson's own translation of the *Ars Poetica*, Horace's *silva* is associated both with uncultivated wilderness — raw material — and with Orpheus, the poet as civilizer; still more tellingly, it is associated specifically with words:

> As woods [*silvae*] whose change appeares
> Still in their leaves, throughout the sliding yeares,
> The first-borne dying; so the aged state
> Of words decay, and phrases borne but late
> Like tender buds shoot up, and freshly grow.
> Our selves, and all that's ours, to death we owe.[10]

This passage belongs to a discussion of the effects of time and change on human works and specifically on language. Although it is translated rather than original with Jonson, its paralleling of the "state of words" with that of human culture as a whole is a constant theme in Jonson's writing.

As thoroughly and perceptively as the language of *The Forrest* has been studied, the extent to which this collection is directly concerned with words — is even in a sense about them — bears further emphasis and development.[11] Since my purpose is to discuss verbal configuring in *The Forrest* rather than the "stuffe and varietie" of the collection as a whole, I shall start with Jonson on Penshurst, an actual building that is potentially also an image of writing, and, more exactly, with the end of "To Penshurst": "dwells." This ending, in which the idea of abiding inheres, is itself a nice touch; that its strength should reside in the simplicity and utter integrity of one word is another. The entire course of the poem comes to this focal point, a single word that is the final, encapsulating achievement of a process of definition:

> Now, **Penshvrst**, they that will proportion thee
> With other edifices, when they see
> Those proud, ambitious heaps, and nothing else,
> May say, their lords haue built, but thy lord dwells.

The difference between building and dwelling that the poem has constructed is hardly the same as that the two verbs would have if the final line or even the final sentence were to stand alone. The content (*res*) of the hundred or so lines that compose the characterization of Sir Robert Sidney's residence is transferred — translated, in effect — to the last word of the poem, thus imparting to it substance or "weight."[12] This transfer is basically a metaphorical one. It represents things as the cause of words, but words as the final, defining form of things. It might be said in this way to ensure the poet's place.

Both the outset and end of "To Penshurst" define this place — historical, rhetorical, and poetic — conspicuously through difference: "not . . . to enuious show," "nor . . . a row / Of polish'd pillars," "no lantherne," and, climactically, not "built" but "dwells."[13] Such a definition by difference registers the constructive function of language more assertively than would a nondifferential one, which would more easily give the impression that it is looking through the word to the referent. In a differential definition, the referent isn't there at all or exists as a relation with something other than itself, to which it is therefore connected. A major way "dwells" is defined is by not being "built."[14] The fact that the opening definition of Penshurst is also patterned or schematized renders more substantial the difference it expresses.

The depiction of nature at Penshurst is more indirectly and complexly differential: for example,

Each banke doth yeeld thee coneyes; and the topps
Fertile of wood, **Ashore**, and **Sydney's** copp's,
To crowne thy open table, doth prouide
The purpled pheasant, with the speckled side:
The painted partrich lyes in euery field,
And, for thy messe, is willing to be kill'd.
And if the high-swolne *Medway* faile thy dish,
Thou has thy ponds, that pay thee tribute fish,
Fat, aged carps, that runne into thy net.
And pikes, now weary their owne kinde to eat,
As loth, the second draught, or cast to stay,
Officiously, at first, themselues betray.
Bright eeles, that emulate them, and leape on land,
Before the fisher, or into his hand.   (25–38)

Some years ago, Raymond Williams asked of these lines, "What kind of wit is it exactly—for it must be wit; the most ardent traditionalists will hardly claim it for observation—which has birds and other creatures offering themselves to be eaten?" (p. 29). While fat carp and cannibalistic pike hardly occasion much sentiment, Williams is surely right in finding something unsettling about these lines, although I am not persuaded that eating (even broadened metaphorically to economic consumption) is what triggers our discomfort with them. For me the trouble lies in a violation of codes, a deliberately heightened sense of dislocation, an uncertainty as to what this place is and where it is that the wit of the passage sharpens rather than resolves.[15]

Although the lines in question describe the bounties of nature at Penshurst, nature is not-nature in them because it is idyllic pastoral, and yet it is not-pastoral because it is all too real: even amid ardently suicidal fish the word "betray" carries a jolt. The language of the passage is so heavily laced with that of conquest and politics that at moments it sounds as if the land of milk and honey had been invaded by Roman legions ("yeeld," "crowne," "kill'd," "tribute") and subsequently colonized by the court of

Shakespeare's Claudius and Polonius — "weary their owne kinde to eat . . . Officiously . . . themselues betray." Potentially, *yield* and *crown* have innocent meanings, but in this verbal context they cannot be exclusively innocent. The word *officiously*, meaning "obligingly" but also "obtrusively" in this period, radically personifies the fish, attributing a witty perversion of the pathetic fallacy to them. Without its impersonating effect on the fish, the word *betray* would be less forceful, since it would not be the final, finishing stroke in a developing impression of specifically human corruption. Throughout this description of nature a human hand is heavily felt, and at the end of it, while Penshurst emerges as a microcosm of the best that can naturally be, again it is so in relation to what qualifies or negates it.

The generous yet self-betraying fish give way to a description of the peasantry that reflects and continues both piscine generosity and denial. As if to neutralize the exclusionary nature of the walls surrounding Penshurst Place, "The blushing apricot, and woolly peach / Hang on . . . [its] walls, that euery child may reach." In a further exclusion so conspicuous as to advertise the pressure of displacement, the walls themselves, "though . . . [they] be of the countrey stone,"

> They're rear'd with *no mans* ruine, *no mans* grone,
> There's *none*, that dwell about them, wish them downe;
>   But all come in, the farmer, and the clowne:
> And *no one* empty-handed, to salute
>   Thy lord, and lady, though they haue *no sute*.
>   (43–50; my emphasis)

Seldom has differential definition had an equal. In a suggestive reading of these lines, Don Wayne has found them disguising the "exploitation [that] has gone into the rearing of . . . [the] walls" and thereby suppressing "the force and function of labor." In his view, all the "giving" in them merely idealizes the "real relations of exchange at Penshurst" (pp. 65, 75). While this reading is invited by the affective phrase "no mans grone," it might better be argued in relation to the obvious Jonsonian pun on "suit" — petition or garment — than to the rest of the passage, albeit with the inconvenience for an ideological critique of the poet's awareness of his own meaning: thus the peasants' self-abnegating lack of self-interest ("no sute") would be defined differentially against the suits (petitions/possessions) of courtiers and property owners like Penshurst's lord.[16]

Wayne's reading fails to account for the concession of *though* in the line "And though thy walls be of the countrey stone" or for the phrase "no mans ruine" in the line that follows. Why should the wall's being of "countrey stone," rather than of some other material, be important enough to emphasize? And if "grone" suggests labor, it equally suggests devastating grief, which "ruine" — an unlikely word to characterize the labor of constructing an English boundary wall (after all, not the Great Wall of China) — enforces. These lines strongly suggest that the parts of them in question refer to the common practice of despoiling existing structures, architectural and social — "ancient piles," whether ancient monasteries and manors or tenant walls and cottages — to build the "envious show[s]" of the privileged and *nouveaux riches*.[17] In contrast to such despoliation, the walls of Penshurst, specifically the orchard wall erected in 1612, were built of stone newly taken from local quarries.[18] Jonson relies not only on the antiquity of Penshurst Place but also on its unpretentious resource-fullness to warrant its validity. Perhaps for this reason, the word *dwell*, which anticipates the poem's conclusion, occurs first in connection with the peasants, the suitless backbone, as it were, of what keeps Penshurst going.[19]

Like definition through difference, the conclusive word of "Penshurst," *dwell*, in itself affords Jonson an unusually clear opportunity to shape the language that translates and thereby defines reality. A fairly common if sonorous word, it is one whose use he appears to have weighed carefully, from whatever historically linguistic angle his choice is assessed. While no word is a clean slate, *dwell* comes close to being one. It carries little connotative baggage, and Jonson can control or "square" it to a remarkable extent. Within a seventeenth-century lexical context in England, *dwell* also has no easily legible etymological story and, in this significant sense, no history within it of which Jonson is likely to have been aware or, if aware, to have endorsed. The word "likely" is worth emphasizing, however. Although in speaking with Drummond, Jonson characterized Minsheu as a rogue, his acquaintance with Minsheu's work-in-progress or with other etymological sources is certainly possible and has suggestive relevance to his use of *dwell* in several poems of *The Forrest*, even though he makes no obvious or explicit display of etymology in them.[20]

As earlier noted, Minsheu identifies *dwell* as a corruption of Greek *aule*, since it refers to the inhabiting or possessing of "a firm and fixed seat." This explanation applies both to "Penshurst" and to the poem addressed "To Sir Robert Wroth" that follows it, in which dwelling takes a distinctly inward turn: "Thy peace is made; and, when man's state is well, / 'T is better, if he there can dwell" (93–94). But the word *dwell* is actually derived from Old English *dwellan*: "to lead astray, hinder, delay; to go astray, err; to be delayed, tarry, stay."[21] Whether Jonson would have had access to this information is difficult to assess, but it seems to me unlikely. Since the first printed dictionary of Old English words was not published until 1659, the major sources of Old English meanings in Jonson's lifetime were Latin glosses of individual words and Laurence Nowell's manuscript "Vocabularium Saxonicum" (ca. 1567), subsequently enlarged by William Lambarde, and the Joscelyn-Parker manuscript, contemporary with Nowell's and indebted to it.[22] For a time John Selden had possession of the Nowell-Lambarde manuscript, however, and his possession could have provided an opportunity for Jonson to inspect it.[23] Had he done so, it is at best questionable whether he, any more than Minsheu, would have recognized an etymological relation between early modern *dwell* and Old English "*dwelan*," in Nowell glossed, "To seduce, to bring into errour . . . to erre," or Old English "*dwolian*," glossed, "To erre, to be in a false opinion or heresie. To wander out of the waye."

But Jonson is more likely to have been exposed to medieval uses of *dwell* meaning "to delay, procrastinate, be tardy, tarry, linger," which reflect its Old English value, although he might have regarded them simply as instances of a former "custom" — usage — rather than as etymological indicators. These meanings occur regularly in medieval writers such as Lydgate, Wyclif, Malory, and Chaucer — for example, in *Troilus and Criseyde* and in the *Nun's Priest's Tale*: "But that tale is al too longe to telle, / And eke it is nigh day, I may nat dwell [delay]."[24] While the association of *dwell* with inertia and pride in the penultimate poem of *The Forrest* — "Ode. To Sir William Sydney, on his Birth-day" — could well be the fortuitous result of further definition through difference, here specifically a contrast in meaning, it almost uncannily reflects the historical implication of the word in errancy and belatedness.

In this ode, the poet warns young Sidney that there is little difference between one who backslides from his high birth and one "whose will / Doth vrge him to runne wrong [off course], or to stand still" (27–30). Here the phrases "runne wrong" and "stand still" realize the historically negative meaning of the Old and Middle English versions of the word, and predictably, perhaps, this meaning is confirmed in the following stanza. Now Jonson counsels Sidney,

> [not to] rest
> On what's deceast.
> For they, that swell
> With dust of ancestors, in graues but *dwell*.
> (37–40; my emphasis)

If Jonson did not already know the etymological story underlying *dwell*, in this stanza and the last one he has managed to invent it. Differential definition is peculiarly a condition of language, and *The Forrest* — *silva, hyle* — is a natural site for its defining, formative work.

Although in Jonson's lifetime the word *dwell* could simply mean "live" (i.e., "reside") without sounding as formal or poetic as it would now, it was nonetheless distinctively associated with biblical contexts. This association might be described as an available resonance rather than an intrusive or necessary one, and would readily lend itself to "squaring." It was one well suited to the godly family within the mansion of Penshurst, to the inner peace Wroth possesses in the third poem, and to the spiritual condition Jonson himself desires in the final one: all involve dwelling.

Thomas Wilson's *Christian Dictionary* affords a fair contemporary indication of the significance the word *dwell* could tap into. Wilson devotes an extensive series of definitions to this word that suggests how often and how memorably it occurs in the English Bible.[25] Wilson's main entry, after which he glosses various occurrences of cognate forms and specific biblical phrases, defines *dwelling* as

> A true, mighty, and fixed presence, eyther for good or euill, according to the nature of the thing that dwelleth, *Ioh.* I, 14. *The word was made flesh, and dwelt among vs.* Thus the Spirit and the word are said to dwell in vs. 2 *Cor.* 5, 16. *Colos.* 3, 16. *Eph.* 2. *Christ Dwelleth in our hearts,* that is; they be conuersant with vs, and do keepe mansion in our hearts, ruling and ouer-ruling vs, as a Maister ruleth and guideth his house. Also sinne dwelleth in the regenerate. *Rom.* 7, 17. *Not I, but sinne that dwelleth in me.* (pp. 141–42)

What Jonson and his contemporaries might have called the "weight" of the word *dwell* is striking in Wilson's definition. A dwelling is a constant, stable, enduring presence; as Wilson glosses this word in subsequent entries, it is "To remaine, abide, and continue," for "*Hee that eateth my flesh, dwelleth in me, and I in him.*" One biblical verse after another — 27 in all, in my count — is summoned to occasion or illustrate versions of this meaning.

More than once Wilson associates or actually equates *dwelling* with a mansion, a word derived from Latin *manere*, "to remain," "to abide," "to tarry," or, indeed, "to dwell," as in the extensive quotation above ("do keepe mansion") or when he characterizes the "*Dwelling of the Spirit in vs, or of Christ in his members*" as a continual presence, "not as of a guest, who lodgeth for a night in an Inne, and is gone next day; nor as a Soiourner that flitteth, but as an owner and possessor to abide for euer, as in *Iohn* 14" (pp. 142–43). For Wilson and his readers the social landscape is inseparable from religion. At one point, Wilson even identifies "dwelling, habitation, or mansion" synonymously as a "name given to the Tabernacle which *Moses* made and God dwelt in" and then as one given to Solomon's temple and heaven itself, each time citing relevant biblical passages (p. 143).

The progress of Wilson's glossing of the occurrence of *dwell* in biblical phrases bears suggestively on that of *The Forrest*, the mansion of Penshurst near its beginning, Wroth's dwelling in peace, and the indwelling of the spirit in the lyric "To Heaven" at its end: "Dwell, dwell here still: O, being euery-where, / How can I doubt to finde thee euer, here?" (15–16). There is no way that the word *dwell* could already have carried all Wilson's nuances at the end of "Penshurst," but Jonson there charges this word with emphasis and significance that give it a substance — a life, so to speak — of its own. While I do not suppose that the word *dwell* was the groundplot of *The Forrest*, I think that it became a generative, "weighted" focus for the matter — the *silva* — collected there.[26]

Two other, even commoner English words, *still* and *live*, the latter with its cognate forms, cooperate significantly with the word *dwell* in *The Forrest* to clarify what dwelling actually means.

Noticeably, given Jonson's classicism, both these words are also derived from Old English, and in the seventeenth century, therefore, they lack a readily discernible or persuasive etymology — a self-contained history that would give them shape.[27] Neither carries connotative weight specialized enough to gloss, but together, as they weave through the poems of *The Forrest* that succeed "Penshurst," they triangulate definitively with "dwelling" to form a kind of anaphoric field of meaning.[28]

It is not my intention to discuss every occurrence of *still* and *live*, and still less to claim that each is equally and automatically significant. Because Jonson's weighting of these common words in *The Forrest* is unobtrusive and cumulative, however, discussion of it will require a corresponding accumulation of the material evidence. This weighting emerges only gradually, starting with "To Sir Robert Wroth," the immediate sequel to "Penshurst." In this poem Wroth is told that he can "at home, in . . . [his] securer rest,"

> Liue, with vn-bought prouision blest;
> Free from proud porches, or their gilded roofes,
> 'Mongst loughing heards, and solide hoofes.
>
> (13–16)

Poised at the outset of a line and pointedly separated by two phrases from the verb *can* — "canst" in context — and by thirteen verses from the subject of "canst," the verb "Liue" is not only noticeable but also emphatic, appearing virtually an imperative.

Toward the middle of the poem, the infinitive *to live* similarly takes on an imperative coloring. Since Wroth can "make . . . [his] owne content" of his rural paradise — complete with "serpent riuer" — the poet urges him, "Striue, **Wroth**, to liue long innocent" (18, 65–66). The emphasis on the infinitive "to liue" results largely from its placing in the line, separated from its verbal sponsor by the naming of Wroth, for whom it provides the object and substance of striving. The end of the poem, "when thy latest sand

is spent, / Thou maist thinke life, a thing but lent," further enforces living as its subject matter.

The poem addressed to Wroth extends the notion of dwelling
found in "Penshurst." Wroth's *dwelling*, like Robert Sidney's, is
inseparable from his country estate, and yet an emphasis on re-
tirement and inwardness is more pronounced in it, as the lines
cited earlier suggest: "Thy peace is made; and, when man's state
[inward estate] is well, / 'Tis better, if he there can dwell." The
very fact that "Penshurst" is addressed to the place and "Wroth"
to the person is indicative of this difference.

"Wroth" is framed on its further side by a poem "To the
World," written for a woman who rejects the public world altogether and still more explicitly identifies a domestic space with
an inner one: the speaker's "strengths, such as they are" can be
found "Here in my bosom, and at home" (67–68).[29] This poem
includes two occurrences of *live/lives* that are not emphatic yet in
context are noteworthy: in one the ventriloquized woman determines to "liue exempt / From all the nets" the world can spread,
and in the other she dismisses "such as blow away their liues, . . .
Enamor'd of their golden gyues" (7–8, 22, 24). The dissipation
shunned by the speaker anticipates that of "Liuers, round about
the towne" in the poem "To Sicknesse" who "Liue . . . [such that]
Spittles, pest-house, hospitalls, / Scarce will take . . . [their]
present store" (9–11, 17). Again the concern is with living and,
more conspicuously than before, with not-living as well. Those
with windblown lives are still bound with gyves, and those who
disperse themselves "about the towne" are destined, like Vol-
pone, for enclosing paralysis: "Spittles, pest-house, hospitalls."
Dwelling is obviously more and other than mere stasis.[30]

The word *still* in "To the World," the poem identifying bosom
with home, operates as a focal pun: "Nor for my peace will I goe
farre, / As wandrers doe, that still doe rome" (65–66). Primarily,
still here means "always" or "ever," but it also suggests the para-

doxical meaning "at rest" or "motionlessly" — being, for example, physically still but emotionally wandering. "Still roaming" indicates an inner restlessness whose externalized reflection appears in the seventh poem: "Follow a shaddow, it still flies you; / Seeme to flye it, it will pursue" (1–2). This usage also finds a curious echo in "Epode," the eleventh poem, where by "subtle traines, / Doe seuerall passions still inuade the minde" and "He that for loue of goodnesse hateth ill, / Is more crowne-worthy still" (28–29, 87–88). To my ear, at this point in *The Forrest*, "passions still invad[ing] the mind" paradoxically suggest not only recurring waves of emotional turbulence but also the relentlessness, the ironic constancy of their recurrence — thus not only movement but its still-ness (persistence); and "crowne-worthy still" suggests stasis — stillness — as well as purity. The word *still* is itself taking on a potentially ironic value in *The Forrest* that is truer to a reality of differentiations than is any single occurrence of it. In itself, the word has acquired weight.[31] "Stones well squar'd . . . will rise strong a great way without mortar": Jonson's statement attributes a vestigial autonomy to words that may exceed his primary intention.

Paradox has never been identified as closely with Jonson as with Donne, but again and again his writing courts it. The epistle "To Elizabeth Countesse of Rutland," the twelfth poem in the sequence, challenges,

> let this drosse [gold] carry what price it will
> With noble ignorants, and let them still,
> Turne, vpon scorned verse, their quarter-face.
>
> (27–29)

If the comma after "still" in the authoritative edition of 1616, which Jonson saw through the press and which the most reliable modern editions honor, is to be justified as a metrical necessity, it nonetheless accentuates the words on either side of it, "still" and "turn." Jonson himself would have to have been deaf not to hear the echo of "still roam" from the fourth poem in *The Forrest*.[32] The idea of still turning seems, even at times in defiance of immediate context, to have fascinated him, as it does here.

In "Rutland," *live* and its cognates occur repeatedly in connection with the ability of Jonson's verse to extend immortality or, more exactly, monumentality to those worthy and thus to confer the final, defining form of things upon them. Although there were brave men enough before Homer brought some to Troy, he tells the countess, "none so liue: / Because they lack'd the sacred pen, could giue / Like life vnto 'hem" (53–57). He promises her that all who grace his muse shall have a "place" in his poems and then describes what hers will be:

> There like a rich, and golden *pyramede*,
>   Borne vp by statues, shall I reare your head,
> Aboue your vnder-carued ornaments,
>   And show, how, to the life, my soule presents
> Your forme imprest there: not with tickling rimes,
>   Or common places, filch'd, that take these times,
> But high, and noble matter.   (83–89)

Jonson's monument of and to the countess will not be constructed of clichés and trivial rhymes but of substantial matter (*silva, hyle*) — namely, her form in his soul and the words required to define it and thereby to ensure that its final form be lasting. Jonson's claims for his art are more masked in "Penshurst," which, after all, was not meant for a woman, but they are no less substantial or finally dependent on his ability to square words wisely and well.

The epistle addressed "To Katherine, Lady Aubigny" that follows "Rutland" occurs as the collection nears its end and proves of crucial interest. In it, words and life and the particular words *still* and *live* converge pointedly. Like so many of Jonson's poems of praise and patronage, this one imposes the claims of his art on those of its object: "My mirror is more subtile, cleere, refin'd, /

And takes, and giues the beauties of the mind" (43–44). "Takes and gives"—the paraphrases "registers and reflects" and even "receives and returns" stop short of the active reciprocity and formative claim of "giving."[33] Claims like these are enough to trigger a grammatical pun when Jonson approves Lady Aubigny's distance from "the turning world": "This makes, that wisely you decline your life, / Farre from the maze of custome, error, strife, / And keepe an euen, and vnalter'd gaite" (59–61, 64). Her declining—averting, withdrawing—her life from this maze is also the orderly, definite inflection of her life that Jonson's verse can take and give in "euen, and vnalter'd gaite."[34] Yet the word *decline* also means "depreciate," and this meaning, too, cannot be excluded: stillness, distance from the turning world, in some sense entails a withdrawal from "life" and, realistically, a loss.

The end of this poem praises the "name, and goodness . . . [of Lady Aubigny's] life"—or, in both typographical and moral senses, her character, which is that of the good wife (109). As Jonson defines this, Lady Aubigny is "still . . . depending" on her husband's "word, and will"—at once depending always and silently, "still" (113–14). He continues, "This makes, that your affections still be new" (118). Affections constant but ever new, and yet also in repose, stilled, and silent; the contrast with the "passions still invad[ing]" of false love depends on the senses of control, silence, and stilling (by her husband's willing) in the laudatory passage at hand.[35] Through the lady's enabling stillness, her soul "conspire[s]"—breathes together, cooperates—with her husband's as if they "now made one," and Jonson urges her emphatically,

> Liue that one, still; and as long yeeres doe passe,
> *Madame*, be bold to vse this truest glasse:
> Wherein, your forme, you still the same shall finde;
> Because nor it can change, nor such a minde.
> (119–24)

The words "Liue" and "still," now combined, suggest vitality and stasis, or as Richard Peterson has aptly glossed them, "movement amid fixity, . . . forward motion into the future (by the sense 'always') and the stillness of repose" (pp. 287–88). Quintessentially, stillness also suggests both the lasting life and monumentality through art that the poet promised the Countess of Rutland. In it, too, are endurance and silence: a life declined.

With the weighting of the words *live* and *still* to this point in mind, I would return to the final two poems of *The Forrest*, the birthday ode to William Sidney, Robert's eldest son, and the poet's seemingly personal lyric "To Heaven." For men, at least, the birthday ode offers a definition of living:

> he doth lacke
> Of going backe
> Little, whose will
> Doth vrge him to runne wrong, or to stand still.
>
> . . . .
>
> For they, that swell
> With dust of ancestors, in graues but dwell.
>
> . . . .
>
> And he that stayes
> To liue vntill to morrow' hath lost two dayes.
> So may you liue in honor, as in name,
> If with this truth you be inspir'd.
>
> (27–30, 39–40, 49–52)

As opposed to living, *standing* still — always, motionlessly, and silently (sound itself traditionally being motion) — is death, complete with "swelling" or putrefaction. Even deferral, "staying," is measurable loss. Living is active and moral, apparently the condition realized for Lady Aubigny through the addition of her spouse's concreative breath. The negation of dwelling is not building, as it was in "Penshurst," but now, more simply and essentially, lifelessness.[36]

In "To Heaven," dwelling is defined more explicitly in relation to stillness and living, although with some surprising turns. Here the qualification of silence (and the silence of its qualification) lingers significantly in stillness, and living becomes, if not differentiated from dwelling, then related to it in an equivocal way. "To Heaven" concerns the discontented speaker's relation to God, which is troubled by his sense of God's distance and possible indifference:

> Where haue I beene this while exil'd from thee?
> And whither rap't, now thou but stoup'st to mee?
> Dwell, dwell here still: O, being euery-where,
> How can I doubt to finde thee euer, here?   (13–16)

The speaker clearly has doubted the nearness of God and greets its qualified renewal with complaint and frustration as well as relief: "now [only now] thou but stoup'st [merely condescend'st] to me?"[37] His desire that God's indwelling presence be lasting is intense, and yet in the stillness — at once constancy, motionlessness, and silence — of that dwelling lies the ground not only of his comfort but also of his doubt.

Dwell implies a real and enduring presence, in Thomas Wilson's words, "A true, mighty, and fixed presence . . . [in which] the Spirit and the word . . . be conuersant with vs, and do keepe mansion in our hearts": presence, not distance; fixed, not fleeting; conversant, not indifferent — a lord who "keeps mansion," maintaining and abiding in the house that is his. In Jonson's "Heaven," however, immediately after the four lines I have cited, which are those in the poem addressed most directly and emotionally to God, the speaker turns from direct engagement to focus at length on his own wretchedness: "I know my state, both full of shame, and scorne, / Conceiu'd in sinne, and vnto labour borne" (17–18). His complaints occupy the rest of the poem and effectively deny the very possibility of God's still dwelling. He does not again gesture specifically toward God until the end of

the poem, whose last words, "not loue of thee," while technically
direct address, hardly seem so:

> Yet dare I not complaine, or wish for death
> With holy **Pavl**, lest it be thought the breath
> Of discontent; or that these prayers bee
> For wearinesse of life, not loue of thee.   (23–26)

The word *life* may occur at the end, but drained of the potent
affirmation "living" has expressed so often in this sequence, particularly in its verbal forms, which in this life at least imply movement—turning. As the word "weariness" witnesses, no vitality,
no movement, is here except the uneasy motion of discontent.
The poet seems to offer himself as a negative exemplum.

But in this final poem of *The Forrest*, even the title "To Heaven,"
rather than, say, "To God," seems a little odd, and the more so if
we try to substitute "Heaven" for "God" or "thee," the actual addresses in the poem. "Heaven," to be sure, can mean the power or
providence of God and, presumably by transference, God Himself.[38] The title "To Heaven" also associates divinity with place,
with many mansions, and affords an appropriate balance at the
end of *The Forrest* to the poems addressed "To Penshurst" and "To
Sir Robert Wroth" near its start, both of which celebrate real
places. I would repeat "real places." Even recalling Wilson's mansion in our hearts, for heaven to "Dwell, dwell here *still*"—always
and unchangingly—requires a place that squares oddly with the
serpent river in Wroth's rural paradise, the politicized fish in
"Penshurst," and poems like "To the World" or "To Sickness."
Again, "I know my state . . . Conceiu'd in sinne, and vnto labour
borne."

The speaker in "Heaven" seems to want an enduring intimacy
with God that literalizes the biblical metaphor of a mansion—a
place that remains (*mansio, manere*)—and, perhaps, also literalizes a figurative extension like Wilson's, which locates this mansion in the heart. Opposed to his desire, from one point of view,

is the speaker's weariness of life, but from another, this weariness is itself his recognition that what he wants is unlikely, indeed impossible here. His concern at the end is with not-living in a sense more literal than the dissipation in the poems "World" and "Sickness." Implicit in his desire for stillness is death: "Yet dare I not complaine, or wish for death / With holy **Pavl**," the speaker complains, alluding to Paul's impatient outcry, "Wretched man that I am! who shall deliver me from the body of this death?" (Rom. 7:24). At the end of *The Forrest* of this material world — of *silva* and *hyle* — death, the ultimate material fact of life, should be named and thereby included. Surprisingly and movingly, Jonson locates this reality, which has played here and there throughout the poems of the sequence, squarely in himself, thereby giving the whole matter of dwelling a differential turn — a swerve, an inflection, a final realistic declination. The lord of Penshurst may "dwell" in a mansion, and Wroth may live "long innocent," but the ultimate definition of dwelling — "dwelling still" — is not "here."

I remarked at the outset of this chapter that Spenser's writing does not typically display the same insistence of and on the word on the page that Jonson's does. At least briefly, I would pursue this observation and contrast some typically expansive wordplay in *The Faerie Queene* with the process of defining words in *The Forrest* — that is, with the squaring of them, the ascertaining of their limits. Differential definition is a condition of language, one honored in Jonson's own practice, and comparison is the appropriate way further to "square" this practice and thus to define the linguistic perception of his poems.

When, in a familiar instance of Spenserian wordplay, *care* and its cognate forms recur repeatedly in the second book of *The Faerie Queene*, the word itself wholly subserves the theme of temperance, the balance between caring too little (carelessness) or caring too much (selfish possession, hoarding).[39] What *care* means *qua* word and what it means to care refuse focal emphasis, although we incidentally learn something about both these matters. Definition, the exploration and setting of limits, is focused radically on the idea of temperance rather than on the key words that signify it. The distinction here concerns emphasis and is certainly not meant to imply that any idea exists outside language or that Spenser supposed that in this world it could. What it means in practical terms is that while Spenser was surely fascinated by words, he was probably not interested as long as Jonson in any one of them.

Spenser's deployment of words in the Mutability Cantos is especially relevant to Jonson's practice and again indicates a linguistic difference between them, albeit within a thematic likeness. A case in point is the word *permanent* in the phrase "records permanent," which refers to the Faerie records of Mutability's "antique race and linage ancient" that the poet consults in the opening stanzas (vi.2).[40] Through apparent contradiction, the word *permanent* is designed to attract attention: a permanent record of change is, after all, a curious notion and potentially, at least, an ironic one. *Permanent* is further notable because it is a rare word in Spenser's writing, never once occurring in *The Faerie Queene* until this point and then recurring twice, without variation in meaning, during the subsequent trial of Mutability's claims to sovereignty (vii.17, 56).[41] It therefore appears to be a deliberately chosen word, rather than an old standby or merely a cog in the rhyme scheme. In short, it asks for explanation; it even requires one that goes beyond the immediate context.

Like many other words in *The Faerie Queene*, *permanent* comes to Spenser with a relevant set of implications—a veritable thesaurus of memories and associations. Taken together, these compose a kind of story reaching deep into the past. The etymological citations of a modern dictionary offer a shortcut to this history and an introduction to the somewhat freer etymological associations available to the sixteenth century in classical sources. *Permanent*, deriving from Latin *per*, "through," and *manere*, "to remain," is cognate to the word *manor*, or "desmesne, domain, area of dominium," which comes from Latin *manere* by way of Old French *manoir*, "to stay" or "dwell." The Indo-European base of *manere*, namely, *men-*, is thought originally to have been identical with the Indo-European homonym *men-*, meaning "to think," which also underlies the word *mind*. The connection between *men-*, "to think," and *men-*, "to remain," is hypothesized to be the idea "stand in thought."[42]

While the finer points of Indo-European bases were hardly available to Spenser, classical studies of etymology were, and Varro's *De lingua Latina* bears suggestively on the striking occurrence of the word *permanent* in *The Faerie Queene*. Varro connects the ideas of remaining and thinking with one another and with the idea of remembering or memory (i.e., what remains), and Spenser follows suit in characterizing the secret, everlasting sources of his poem, the "records permanent" of Faerie Land. Varro uses the Latin word *mens*, or "mind," to bridge the ideas of remaining and remembering: thus, "*meminisse* 'to remember,' [derives] from *memoria* 'memory,' when there is again a motion toward that which *remansit* 'has remained' in the *mens* 'mind': and this may have been said from *manere* 'to remain.' "[43] Developing further the association of *manere*, "remain," with *memoria*, "memory," Varro explains the expression *Mamurius Veturius* as an appellative signifying "memoriam veterem," or what Spenser might have translated as an antique image, the plain truths and timeless admonitions that reside in memorial scrolls and permanent records. Such records, written in words and (re-*cor*-dari) in the heart, participate in Clio's "volume of Eternitie," the cultural, historical, and sacred volume that always surpasses yet ever illumines human memory (III.iii.4).

The rest of Varro's etymologies in this section of *De lingua Latina* read like a gloss on Mutability, on Spenser's explicit recognition in the final Cantos that mutability and mortality are part of the abiding records in Faerie Land and of the undying content of human memory. Varro's evolving derivations from *memoria*, "memory," also anticipate Spenser's recurrent interest in the idea that "moniments" (monuments) admonish, an idea relevant to Mutability and to the "records permanent" of her "antique race and linage ancient": from *memoria*, Varro explains, comes *"monere* 'to remind,' because he who *monet* 'reminds,' is just like a memory. So also the *monimenta* 'memorials' which are on tombs . . . *admonere* 'admonish' the passersby that they themselves were mortal and that the readers are too. From this, . . . other things that are written and done to preserve their *memoria* 'memory' are called *monimenta* 'monuments.'" Imprinted in the heart and embedded in the mind, enduring, memorial, admonitory, and written in the human past, "records permanent," and "mongst" them the memory of Mutability's origin, are thus the stuff that Spenser's Faerie romance is made on.

As so often in Spenser's writing, the expanses made to resound within the word and the stories that radiate out from it claim our attention as much as the word in its immediate context. Spenserian etymology, at its most characteristic, does not look simply through the word to the thing but via the word to another story: to take a briefer example, *carcass*, contextually a surprising word because it denigrates the godly character Contemplation's starved body, etymologically signifies "fallen flesh," in Spenser's culture a meaning that recalls and renews the fatal story in the Garden of Eden and the corruption of nature that it entails. Spenserian etymology often leads us between the lines, out to the margins, and virtually off the page in this way. There is a sense in which it might be said to look through the word. Or perhaps there are two senses, one conveying the sense "beyond," and the other "by means of." The expanding and (from another theoretical vantage point) receding horizons it discovers and invents (*invenio*) are far from the target of Jonathan Swift's parodic discourse in which men unpack a knapsack of objects and silently move them around on the ground like chess pieces whenever they want to have — no, cannot avoid — a conversation. Swift had Bacon's logophobic successors in mind, of course, men of simplicity like John Wilkins, who hoped somehow to replace language with things.

Rich, intricate, even sometimes unexpected as is Jonson's exploration of the limits of meanings, it is also more tightly controlled than Spenser's. In Spenser the word, whose meaning is neither random nor limitless, nonetheless opens out to a much wider context. Although Jonson also plays on etymological meanings in his writing, to do so at all, let alone expansively, is not his trademark. His dialogues with the classical past, as Thomas Greene has eloquently described them, adjust, attune, and greatly deepen his meaning, but this still remains essentially definitive, more concerned with boundaries and finely tuned differences than with open expanses.[44]

Typically, by contrast, the most striking words Spenser employs are richly allusive, seemingly selected less for definition or "squaring" than for the reminders — the associations or reminiscences — built into their history. Consider, for example, the arresting word *scrine*, from Latin *scrinium*, which first appears in the proem to Book I, where the poet asks his muse to "Lay forth out of" her "euerlasting scryne / The antique rolles" of Faerie Land. Thomas Cain has argued that *scrine* appropriates to Elizabeth I a customary reference to papal authority: *in scrinio pectoris omnia*.[45] While this meaning credibly adds another dimension to praise of the queen in the opening stanzas, broader applications of the word are primary both here and elsewhere in the poem, where *scrine* is tied intrinsically to the very idea of words, written records, and the mnemonic working of the human mind.

The word *scrine* comes to Spenser with a considerable history, or story, behind it. Cooper's *Thesaurus* of the Roman language defines *scrinium* as "A coffer or other lyke place wherin iewels or secreate thynges are kept." Estienne's *Thesaurus* derives *scrinium* from *secernendo*, "setting apart, secreting, secluding," and defines it as a place in which precious things and mysteries (*secreta*) are preserved and protected (*servantur*).[46] Not surprisingly in view of these definitions the word *scrine* also carries the more specific meaning "shrine" during the Middle Ages and the Renaissance.[47] Also in view of them, Spenser's description in Proem I of the rolls that lie in his muse's "euerlasting scryne" as "hidden still"—that is, hidden always, secretly, silently, motionlessly—makes sense, but it is primarily in relation to the sacred meaning "shrine" that the word *euerlasting* at this point does so. In the chamber of Eumnestes, or Good Memory, within the brain turret of the House of Alma, the word *still* recurs in the phrase "recorded still" describing Eumnestes' operation and carries with it something of its mysterious force in the first proem. In connection with Eumnestes' function, the word *scrine* likewise recurs, characterized in this second and final appearance not as "euerlasting" but, with added point, as "immortall" (II.ix.56).

Both Cooper and Estienne include among their illustrations of the meaning of *scrinium* Catullus's phrase "librariorum . . . scrinia"—the bookseller's containers of manuscripts or rolls.[48] Their illustration bears on the furnishing of Eumnestes' chamber, which is "all . . . hangd about with rolles, / And old records from auncient times deriu'd, / Some made in books, some in long parchment scrolles" (ix.57). The association of *scrinia*, or scrines, with books, records, and sacred relics goes deep into the past. Under the late Roman emperors, there were four types of public scrines for various kinds of historical records (*scrinia libellorum, memoriae, epistularum,* and *epistularum Graecarum*).[49] The scrines of monasteries or churches, whether chests, cupboards, niches, or rooms, were the places where the enabling instruments and authorizing documents that pertained to the rights of the institution were kept. In this context, the scrine is equivalent to the *secretum*, or "secret place," the treasury of the institution and, prior to the establishment of libraries, the depository for books.[50] Isidore of

Seville, whose *Etymology* was a notable source throughout the Renaissance, describes scrines as containers in which books or treasures are protected — "servantur libri vel thesauri" — and explains this to be the reason that those Romans who preserved the sacred books — "libros sacros" — were called *scriniarii*.[51]

From the ancient Roman past through the Middle Ages to the early modern period, the fortunes of the word *scrine* suggest, in addition to its association with books and archives, equally persistent associations with memory or with things worth remembering — things worth keeping *in mind* and things of value. Repeatedly and specifically *scrine* is associated with secrecy or seclusion (*secerno, secretum*), with a need to guard or preserve, and with the word and idea of a *thesaurus*, a treasure or treasury of writing and, more fundamentally, of words. One moves easily, induced by the context of Spenser's usage, from these associations to Sidney's commonplace observation that, "memory being the only treasure[r] of knowledge, those words . . . fittest for memory are likewise most convenient for knowledge"; and then back in time to Plato's more mystically oriented idea that all knowledge is memorial, a kind of remembering, an idea reflected variously in turn by Aristotle, by the Neoplatonists, and by Saint Augustine.[52]

The word *scrine*, in itself and as Spenser employs it, also conveys the idea of communal or racial content — of resources that span generations.[53] Such resources may be accessible to individuals in time but always exceed their direct and specific experience. Here, in connection with Spenser's two uses of *scrine*, one thinks of Bacon's traditional definition of history as both memory and experience and of Aristotle's and Aquinas's descriptions of experience itself as memory — as the fused product of many generations of memories of many things. When Aquinas considers the intellectual virtue of prudence, whose components the three sages of Alma's brain-turret represent, he follows Aristotle in explaining that *"intellectual virtue is engendered and fostered by experience and time*" and that "experience [itself] is the result of many memories." He concludes that "prudence requires the memory of many things," or, as he affirms elsewhere, "prudence requires experience which is made up of *many memories*." Similarly, for Bacon's wise and prudent historian, whose knowledge belongs to the faculty of memory, "history and experience" are "the same thing." Heirs of such definitions, the sages of Alma's brain-turret represent imagination, rational judgment, and memory — the last in the figure of Eumnestes; they look in turn to the future, the present, and the historical past, and together they constitute Spenser's allegory of prudence.[54]

The content of Eumnestes' "immortall scrine" appears to be considerably purer than the books and scrolls, "all worme-eaten, and full of canker holes," that hang about its walls. These physically decrepit records are explicitly contrasted with the disembodied purity and seeming transcendence of the content of memory, which derives from them. Well removed from physical worms, the content of Eumnestes' scrine belongs to a figure of "*infinite* remembrance," who

> things foregone through many ages held,
> Which he *recorded still*, as they did pas,
> Ne suffred them to perish through long eld,
> As all things else, the which this world doth weld,
> But laid them vp in his *immortall scrine*,
> Where they for euer *incorrupted* dweld.
> (II.ix.56; my emphases)

Like the content of any other shrine, including the body, the temple of the Holy Ghost, it is the content of Eumnestes' scrine — the "precious things and mysteries" — that is immortal, rather than the scrine itself, to which, in a way familiar to readers of *The Faerie Queene*, Spenser transfers the attribute of immortality. The immortal content of this scrine in which the past dwells uncorrupted is not far distant from the figurative use of *scrine* in Nich-

olas Udall's translation of Erasmus's *Apophthegmes*: "the mynde
or solle of manne is couered, and . . . housed or hidden within the
tabernacle or scryne of the body, and doeth in a mannes commu-
nicacion clerely appere, and euidentlie shewe it self" (106ʳ).[55]

Udall's translation would seem to apply to the House of Alma,
to the chamber of Eumnestes, and to Eumnestes' scrine itself,
with its transferred epithet "immortall": together, like so many
Chinese boxes, these recesses are always receding, always hidden,
but always there, always evident, always recorded — in memory,
in experience, and in words. As a gloss on Eumnestes' scrine,
Udall's translation also returns us to Estienne's derivation of
scrinium from *secernendo*, "setting apart, secreting, secluding,"
which, along with "the antique rolles, which there [in the muse's
scrine of Proem I] lye hidden still," suggests so hauntingly the
proem to Book VI:

> Such secret comfort, and such heauenly pleasures,
> Ye sacred imps, that on *Parnasso* dwell,
> And there *the keeping* haue of *learnings threasures*,
> Which doe all worldly riches farre excell,
> Into the mindes of mortall men doe well,
> And goodly fury into them infuse;
> Guyde ye my footing, and conduct me well
> In these strange waies, where neuer foote did vse,
> Ne none can find, but who was taught them by the Muse.
>
> Reuele to me the *sacred* noursery
> O vertue, which with you doth there *remaine*,
> Where it in siluer bowre does *hidden ly*.
> (2–3; except *Parnasso*, my emphases)

Secrecy, seclusion, the preservation of learning's treasures, the
welling or infusing of them into mortal minds, their sacred source
at once immanent and hidden still — all again are present. Though
all Spenser's muses are daughters of Dame Memory, his special
muse is Clio, History, which is memory itself, and the mnemonic

resources this muse preeminently figures are finally the reason that "vertues seat is deepe within the mynd" (VI.Pro.5). It is entirely appropriate that Spenser's mnemonic muse and Eumnestes should thus preside over the same scrine.[56]

It is notable, however, that by Spenser's sixth proem, just cited, the word *scrine* itself has disappeared, even while the ideas associated with it remain. The expansiveness of Spenser's poem is inseparable from the network of implications latent in words like *scrine*; many of his poem's richly linked ideas inhere in such words, yet for a reader of the poem's whole, they are occasioned by them, rather than lexically bounded or restrictively shaped by them. His poetry comes closer to reveling (revealing? reveiling?) in a world of words than to squaring and building one. Spenser "writ no language" was Jonson's judgment, but Harvey's more jocular dismissal hit nearer home in characterizing Spenser's work as "*Hobgoblin* runne away with the garland from *Apollo*."[57]

Discussing analogous phenomena in Scripture, Gerald L. Bruns describes two conceptions of a text, one ancient and one modern, which apply equally well to its verbal components: "On the one hand, the text is imagined to contain all that can be said, and a good deal more besides, since it recedes into the unspeakable source of all that can be put into words. . . . On the other hand, . . . the text is imagined to be univocal . . . [for it] withholds nothing of itself."[58] These two types of texts can roughly but suggestively be aligned with the characteristic deployment of words we have witnessed in Spenser and Jonson, despite the fact that the characterization "univocal" is too plain and much too simply nuanced to describe the subtlety of Jonson's language. Instead, his writing might be said to probe the limits, or rather the limitations, of univocity precisely by being attuned to it, and thus to aim for a Baconian standard while actually realizing its elusiveness. Witness *dwell*, *live*, and *still*: the more these words are emphasized and repeated in *The Forrest*, the more richly equivocal their interrelated meanings become.

The word *still*, which occurs 22 times in Spenser's Cantos of Mutability (as opposed to his earlier use of *scrine* twice), offers an irresistible final example of difference between the lexical practices of Spenser and Jonson. Frequently a pun in the Cantos, *still* is a primary intensifier of their central paradox of stability in flux, which anticipates Jonson's fascination with "still turning" and very possibly influenced it. In two consecutive stanzas of the Cantos, for example, there are no less than six occurrences of this word, two of which advertise their participation in paradox and pun:

> For, th'Ocean moueth still, from place to place;
> And euery Riuer still doth ebbe and flowe:
> Ne any Lake, that seems most still and slowe,
> Ne Poole so small, that can his smoothnesse holde. . . .
>
> (VII.vii.20)

The next stanza continues, "So likewise are all watry liuing wights / Still tost, and turned, with continuall change, / Neuer abyding in their stedfast plights." Like the last two verses in the preceding quotation, in this one the word "stedfast" underlines the pun. Retrospectively, in comparison to this remarkable display, which my quoting has actually curtailed, Jonson's punning seems to resist or to minimize — to contain — the equivocity of the word *still*, even while invoking it. Spenser's verses, by contrast, embrace and celebrate it.

In the Mutability Cantos, the crucial example of the paradox of stability in flux and flux in stability comes in the Spenserian narrator's description of "Great *Nature*, euer young yet full of eld, / Still mouing, yet vnmoued from her sted; / Vnseene of any, yet of all beheld" (vii.13). Throughout the Cantos, as in this instance, *still* participates in an irony that affirms the inescapability of change and denies its ultimate reality, and in this function resembles other puns that occur thematically, such as *universe*: *unus*, "one," univocal; and *versus*, "turned," changed, equivocal

(VII.vii.56). To judge from my own experience over a number of years, however, in reading the Cantos one can overlook all but a few instances of the recurrence of *still*, mainly those I have cited. In the Cantos, *still* does not have the progressively distinctive, discrete nodal function that it develops in Jonson's collection, and it is not appropriated to a process of definition in which the individual word, well squared, is crucial, as again is the case in *The Forrest*. The fact that Spenser's poem is a romance, a dramatized story in which the narrator shares center stage with other characters, also means that his own voice (insofar as it is his) and the words that give it substance and weight are less exclusively focal than are Jonson's in the lyric forms that constitute *The Forrest*.

As I have argued, the poems of *The Forrest* are fundamentally concerned with definition, mainly of a differential sort. Like Bacon's strictures regarding language, they have an iconoclastic relation to the etymologically charged medium of the Elizabethans, but a relation nonetheless. To an appreciable extent these poems engage the linguistic character of the early modern dictionary, endorsing its concerns and challenging its limitations. Particularly when measured by Spenser's expansive effort to look through the word (in both senses of *through*) to the secrets it contains, they can be read as participating in the early stages of a cultural shift of meaning from essence to word and logic to lexicon.

In Jonson's case as in Bacon's, this shift can also be aligned with other cultural pressures on language, including other iconoclasms whose extremes Jonson resisted. Discussing the "idols of the mind" castigated by iconoclastic religious reformers in England, Margaret Aston notes that even the use of mental imagery came to be considered impious and corrupting. Mental pictures were to be replaced by more abstract and therefore purer verbal forms, such as axioms and syllogisms, and verbal tags or brief précis were to be plotted on a page in the dichotomous schema characteristic of Ramist teaching. In this way, Aston concludes, "Words were structured to be their own reminders" (I, 457–58).

Her conclusion resonates suggestively in the context of Jonson's literally re-verberative writing. While Jonson ridiculed rather than embraced the views of religious radicals in his plays, he openly admired Bacon's secular efforts to reform the distempers of learning, among them the idols of the mind that conspicuously include an idolatrous attitude toward language. Jonson's own *English Grammar*, moreover, has been identified as an effort to apply Ramus's grammatical theories to English at a basic level.[59] The verbal principle Jonson employs focally in *The Forrest*, which is both anaphoric and reverberative, involves a restriction and tighter focusing of Spenserian *copia* — indeed, copiosity, if viewed from a Baconian perspective on writing. Aesthetically and culturally, it adds up to a plus and a minus, a modern differential distinction that Jonson himself would easily have understood.

Here a final recursion to Bacon's strictures on copiosity in *The Advancement of Learning* will highlight the underlying issue of materialism — or materialisms — in Jonson's and Spenser's uses of language. Criticizing the excessive pursuit of "eloquence and copie of speech" that has characterized recent Humanist learning, Bacon complains that "men began to hunt more after words than . . . after the weight of matter, worth of subject, [or] soundness of argument." His enumerating matter, subject, and argument in this order indicates that the phrase "weight of matter" carries a more simply and directly material meaning than "subject matter," the rhetorically oriented referent of the phrase that immediately follows. His conclusive summation of the vanities of Humanism, which echoes this earlier phrasing, conveys the same suggestion, for it was a time "bent . . . rather towards copie than weight" (VI, 119–20). In *copia* there is for Bacon the sense of words going beyond things, the fear of verbal constructs intervening (like statues) between perception and actuality, the danger of substantial words as an autonomous medium. Put another way, *copia* is implicated in fiction, in verbal constructs that do not simply mirror things, material *res*. From such a Baconian perspec-

tive, we should expect attitudes to fiction to correlate suggestively with those toward language in the period. When the next
chapter turns to the implication of linguistic substance (verbal
res) in magic, to the fictive language of Andrewes's sermons, and
eventually to the fictions of Spenser and Shakespeare, Bacon's
identification of the Humanists' desire for "efficacy of preaching"
as a major cause of their inordinate pursuit of "eloquence and
copie" will be worth remembering (VI, 119).

Chapter 5

Magic and Metaphor

Tree Rings in the
Renaissance Arboretum

Earlier, Agrippa's *De occulta philosophia* afforded a glimpse of the relative ease with which the Renaissance concern with etymology could pass from an Adamic view of the origin of language to a fully magical one. Magic has a broader bearing on the reification of language in the period than this instance suggests, however. At times the distinction is fine between a magical reification, which carries transitive power from agent or subject to object absolutely, and figures that are more simply, if also effectively, verbal or tropological. The latter might be rhetorically and psychologically powerful without being truly magical — as is the case with the "charmed speeches" of Spenser's Despair or with the "mighty magic" of Othello's courtship of Desdemona (*FQ* I.ix.30, *Oth.* I.iii.92).[1]

When Rabelais's fable of the frozen words describes a continuum between this lower world and Truth, it affords a synoptic point of reference for the relation of language to magic. The words, ideas, patterns, and images that drop down upon human-

ity from the manor of Truth loosely suggest a Neoplatonic ema-
nation, that is, the descent of celestial influence from a higher
level to successively lower ones, each of which is at once an adul-
teration and a materialization of the one above it.[2] As we have
seen, Rabelais's mutable world of Heraclitan flux, his world of
catarrhs, is also the world of Gideon's dewy fleece, a world endowed with divine favor. In it are the living ("animées") words
of Homer and Orpheus, which are receptacles and reifications of
truth, and also the frozen words of Plato's wisdom. Within it as
well is the quotation from Exodus that seems to glance (if ironically) at the kabbalistic belief in the presence of higher powers in
the very writing — the letters and accents — of Hebrew Scripture:
"le peuple voyoit les voix sensiblement" (p. 228; see Chap. 1, pp.
12, 19, above).

Rabelais's Neoplatonic precipitates, the living words of his
Orphic mage, and his allusion to kabbalistic power summon into
relevance the more pointedly magical views of Ficino and his
radical successor, Agrippa. But even aside from the pervasive,
elusive irony of Rabelais, there is a notable distinction between
his view of such higher powers in the fable and that of the magicians. In Rabelais, divine favor is a gift that drops down on humanity in certain years, at long intervals; from a human stand-
point, it simply happens. For Ficino, however, the human ability
actively to attract and to influence celestial powers is a deeply held
belief. In his eyes, appropriate words inscribed on talismans or
composed in songs serve to reify spirit, which is the basis and
medium of influence between celestial and human worlds.[3] Even
"the very matter of song," its existence as sound, is relatively pure
and heavenly, since it is "air, hot or warm, still breathing and
somehow living; like an animal, it is composed of certain parts
and limbs of its own and not only possesses motion and displays
passion but even carries meaning like a mind, so that it can be said
to be a kind of airy and rational animal."[4] Ficino has the words of
a song, perhaps even more than its melody, in mind, and when he

concludes that "Song . . . is full of spirit and meaning," he means "full" quite literally. Words themselves thus become animate objects and talismanic containers. They are infinitely more substantial than is mere matter, and they are so not in their own right but because they are pregnant with higher powers.

Agrippa, of course, goes further. As we saw earlier, he believes names to be not only "rayes of things" but also sources of essential knowledge, comparable to "proper, and living Images" of things (p. 153). Influenced by Kabbala, he takes the "two and twenty Letters" of the Hebrew alphabet to be "the foundation of the world," and its letters "the most efficacious of all, because they have the greatest similitude with Celestials, and the world" (pp. 162–63). They are "even as certain sacraments and vehicles of the things they unfold, carrying everywhere with them the essence and virtues of those things."[5] Therefore the manipulation of them has "intrinsic power."[6]

To a lesser extent, words in other languages such as Latin and Greek have power as well: "if this name *Abracadabra* be written, as is here expressed, *viz.* diminishing letter after letter backward, from the last to the first, it will cure the Hemitritean Feaver or any other, if the sheet of paper or parchment be hanged about the neck" (p. 374). Words, for Agrippa, are not only holy objects; they are also the repositories of a fully transitive power. They can "change not only the hearers, but also other bodies, and things that have no life" (p. 152). Affecting inhuman and inanimate objects, they empower changes that are more than emotional or psychic. A name accompanied by the pronunciation of "some occult thing," Agrippa reports, has been known to restore a young woman to life or to lead to the fall of a city, and "sacred words" can accomplish "many [other] wonderfull things, as we read of *Medea*" (pp. 153–54, 374).

It has often been noted that Agrippa's philosophy extends and exposes the magic more latent in Ficino's. In quoting Agrippa, I have cited some of the exotic conclusions to his statements that frequently disappear from arguments concerning the relevance of his views to mainstream thinking about language in early modern England. His views are certainly relevant, but they are so selectively and with qualifications. If they are read in their fuller context, it is easier to see why they might also have been greeted with caution, skepticism, or even disdain.[7]

This point granted, Agrippa's view on "the vertue of writting, and of making imprecations, and inscriptions" can profitably be both aligned with and distinguished from the relatively less exotic views advanced by the English advocates of basic spelling reform (p. 159). With the exception of Mulcaster's, the specific proposals of these spelling reformers were not, on the whole, influential, but their positions reflected, as well as exaggerated, some more commonly held. We have already noticed, for example, how Bullokar's adaptation of the eternizing conceit literalizes it, so that the very letters written are thought to make speech visibly present and enduringly real. In comparison, Agrippa maintains the following:

> The use of words, and speech, is to express the inwards of the mind, and from thence to draw forth the secrets of the thoughts, and to declare the will of the speaker. Now writing is the last expression of the mind, and is the number of speech and voice, as also the collection, state, end, continuing, and iteration, making a habit, which is not perfected with the act of ones voice [alone].[8] And whatsoever is in the mind, in voice, in word, in oration, and in speech, the whole, and all of this is in writing also. (p. 159)

Writing, in Agrippa's eyes, is the perdurance and perfection — indeed, the realization — of speech. It is both the ultimate reification of language and the furthest possession of the mind's secret powers. Given the considerable evidence that early printing invited associations with magic, Agrippa's references to writing plausibly embrace printing, much as references to speech (then and now) often comprehend writing. As Linda Woodbridge has suggested, "the press was a child of a magical age," and "print's exact repeatability . . . allied it to ritual."⁹ Similarly, for Agrippa the iterability of writing—its continuance—is its triumph over time, rather than the sign of its subjection to it.

If we set aside the mysticism of what Agrippa means by "the inwards of the mind" and "the secrets of the thoughts," his view of writing resembles Bullokar's and even more closely that of the more radical spelling reformer John Hart. Like Bullokar, Hart believes writing to be the painting of speech: *ut pictura, scriptio.* But in an amusing little "Allegorie," as Hart calls it, he carries the depiction of speech to a degree of literalism that makes Bullokar's look almost abstract (27ʳ).¹⁰ Hart compares "the liuely body of our pronunciation, which reason biddeth the writer to paint and counterfet with letters, vnto a man" who wants his figure painted. The man, dubbed Esop, asks the painter to portray his body and apparel "so liuely"—that is, "so lifelike"—as men might know him "as I now am." The obliging painter promises that he will depict Esop "as all the Painters of this countrie are accustomed to doe," and there follows Hart's parody of the arguments of his orthographical opponents, who sanction conventional spellings. The painter first explains that he will portray Esop without hose and shoes and thus alludes, unwittingly, to a spelling that employs too few letters properly to mirror pronunciation. His plans touch next on unnecessary letters that result from derivation, from distinctions among homonyms, or from etymology: your figure, he tells Esop,

> shall therefore haue painted other apparell, by a thirde more than you weare, and vpon euerie seuerall peece, I will marke and write, the countries name whence it came. And bicause your clothes, as well the cloth as the furre and silke, are of one colour, I will make them to be the better seene of diuers colors. I will also write in your forehead your fathers and mothers name that men may see of what stocke you are come of. (27ᵛ)

Hart's fiction now turns to the needless letters conventionally justified as indications of the length of vowels, to such "Vsurpation of power" as the *c* in *cat* sounding like a *k*, and to the misplacing of letters, such as the final *e* in *warre* or *g* in *apothegm*. His confident painter continues,

> Where as in some countries Painters doe use to make the nose, of like quantitie to that in the body, we set others at the endes of them. And for masking the littlenesse of the eyes, we make the compasse of the head greater, than the naturall, and double the eie browes. Then in the place of eares, we doe use to paint eyes. And last of all, I will chaunge the middell fingers and thombes in others places. (27^v-28^r)

At this point the painter asks expectantly, "How like you this, will it not doe well?" "Yes," replies the bemused but tactful Esop before requiring an explanation, which the painter has ready: "Bicause the Painters of this countrie, for time out of minde, haue vsed the like, . . . and bicause it is so commonly receyued as it is, no man needeth to correct it." "A good aunswere," adds Hart with an irony reminiscent of Thomas More's (28^r).

There is nothing specifically magical or talismanic about the reification of language that Hart so literally (and letterally) imagines. For a modern reader, his burlesque of his opponents' views may actually backfire, ironically suggesting the excess of his own fantasy about the palpability of words or even his lurking awareness that language does not really work this way. Wittingly, however, Hart is not joking about reification. It is the basis of his argument; the very terms in which he conceives the allegory of Esop are conspicuously material. To Hart's attack, a proponent of conventional spellings might simply reply that the exchange of thumbs for fingers has nothing whatever to do with language.

The reification of language Hart envisions is grotesquely physical: letters are not only like the human body; in his eyes they have become it.[11] His metaphors, like Ficino's and Agrippa's, cross into reality.[12] Hart is quintessentially a literalist, that is, a linguistic materialist. He even attempts to find a physical basis in the functioning of the mouth and throat for the sound of each vowel his orthography recognizes. When he compares the reformation of letters at considerable length to "thorder of Phisicke, which is, first to vnderstand the complexion, disposition and parts of the body," a reader might suddenly be reminded that Ficino too was a physician, whose interest in sympathetic magic was medical in origin (10^{r-v}).[13] Like Hart's spelling, Ficino's magic is a materializing of language, albeit in the interest of the mystical forces it is thought to contain. The material effect is the same, although its rationale and its meaning are significantly different.

Other related instances in the period belong to a curiously liminal space between what I have termed literalism, whether magical or more simply material, and the conventions of tropology. This liminal space is not unlike that in which Edgar Wind locates mottoes, and Roy Strong painted miniatures.[14] In it, reified words and literalized comparisons are neither quite magical nor in modern terms quite rational, that is, neither fully transitive in their (supposed) effects nor merely representational and expository in their functions.

A relatively conservative example of the many passages in Lancelot Andrewes's sermons that answer to this description occurs when Andrewes explicates the biblical clause "regeneravit nos in spem vivam," Christ "hath begotten us againe unto a lively hope." His explanation glosses *regeneravit* by explaining that this hope is a begotten or generated one:

> it is *spes generata*, which . . . is *per viam generationis*, and *generatio*, we know, *terminatur ad substantiam*, "brings forth a substance." So, this, a substantial hope, called therefore by Saint Paul, "the helmet" of hope, "the anchor" of hope, things of substance that will hold, that have metal in them.[15]

Exercising a certain liberty with biblical grammar, if not necessarily with a larger biblical sense, Andrewes first applies the force
of *(re)generavit*, "(re)generated," directly to *spem*, "hope," and, in
effect, makes *spem* the object of (re)generation. Now he argues
that the object or end of generation, begetting, is a substance and
therefore that hope is one. In this way, he can interpret hope as a
thing, a substantial thing, one with metal — indeed, with mettle,
or spirit — in it. The word "lively" with which he translates *vivam*
in the phrase *spem vivam* anticipates and clarifies the metal/mettle
pun: so lively a thing has substance in both the spiritual and
material senses, or as Andrewes puts it elsewhere, "Nay, *viva* is
more than *vivens*; 'lively,' than 'living.' Where *viva* is said of aught,
as of stone or water, the meaning is they spring, they grow, they
have life in themselves" (II, 373). As helmet and anchor a lively
hope is not simply materialized but more complexly substan-
tialized in metaphor and pun, or concept and language. Whereas
Ficino and Agrippa might etch an anchor of hope on a stone to
attract and concentrate spiritual power, Andrewes plumbs figurative and linguistic conceptions — the anchor of hope and *spes gen-
erata* in this instance — and in them he finds the emblematic substance of allegory.

By Renaissance standards, the grounds of Andrewes's embellishment of the biblical text are rational: namely, a belief in the
correspondence of grammar (verb to object) to reality and the
necessary pertinence of a final cause (an end or object) to an
action. Once Andrewes conceives hope as the effective object of
generation, the structure of his equation — verb is to object as
generation to substance — is homologous. Like many thinkers of
his time — philosophers, grammarians, orthographers, etymologists, magicians — Andrewes might be said to confound the real
world with the linguistic symbolization of it. Put more simply,
words are for him real, their relation to things isomorphic, although not in the sense of "things" or of "morph" (form) that a
materialist's might be.

But Andrewes's practice is distinctive insofar as it gives a curious priority to language; a reality of hope follows from figure, grammar, logic, and pun, rather than the reverse. Ultimately Scripture is his warrant, yet it is not so in an immediate and functional way. If we examine his practice without wearing the spectacles of faith, what we see is conspicuously language. Unlike the linguistic materialists of his time, he appears deliberately to exploit the perception that reality is verbal. Whereas they reduce words to matter, he locates meaning in the constructs — logical, etymological, and grammatical — of language.

Andrewes's position regarding the "real presence" in the Sacrament is similarly poised between metaphor and materialism, symbol and magic, and it is fundamentally verbal, as even the terms he uses to argue it indicate. Referring to Zwingli's sacramental memorialism, for example, he complains that "To avoid *Est* in the Church of Rome's sense, he fell to be all for *Significat*, and nothing for *Est* at all. And whatsoever went further than *significat* he took to savour of the *carnal presence*." Andrewes adds that if a Roman Catholic dislikes Zwingli for this reduction to a purely symbolic meaning, "so do we." He obviously wants to go further than *significat*, "it signifies," but he also rejects an unqualified Roman *Est*, "it is," or full identity.[16] His reifications of the Latin verbs *est* and *significat*, both of which function as compacted doctrines, are striking in themselves, but they are surpassed when he scornfully exhibits his Catholic opponent's French verb as a reified object, which is comically modified by an adjective and to which a subordinate construction remains incongruously attached: he dismisses "a wrong *Croyoit, comme contenant le vray et propre corps de Christ.*" Instead, Andrewes endorses Saint Augustine's spiritual understanding of the word *manducat*, "eats": in Augustine's words, which he cites approvingly, "*Etsi necesse est illud visibiliter celebrari, oportet tamen invisibiliter intelligi*" (Although it is necessary that the Sacrament [*illud*] be celebrated visibly, it nevertheless must be understood invisibly).[17] Both

Andrewes's reified verbs and his spiritual understanding are appreciably different from Ficino's talismans and his still more materialized sense of a world that lives and breathes, a world, according to D. P. Walker, whose vital spirit we can absorb if we "consume things which contain an abundance of pure cosmic spirit, such as wine, very white sugar, gold, the scent of cinnamon or roses."[18] Ficino's things contain spirit literally and physically; Andrewes's enable spiritual understanding.

Like the words *thing* and *substance*, the word *real* in a Renaissance context, particularly in relation to the word *presence*, is notoriously and significantly treacherous, and it remains so in a postmodern one. To assume that such verbal debates are immaterial or without reality would be a denial of history, which they materially affected. It would deny the cultural productivity of fiction and, more narrowly, of psychosomatic power. Indeed, such debates matter.

The relations between magic and reification and literalism and metaphor can be further clarified and extended by reference to intertextual examples from another of Andrewes's sermons, Spenser's *Shepheardes Calender*, and a Shakespearean sonnet and drama. Early in a sermon on the Passion, Andrewes specifically invokes the basic principle of figural interpretation: that Old Testament history contains "forerunning figures" of the life of Christ ("omnia in figura contingebant illis"), in preparation for his analysis of a text from Lamentations, and he thereby establishes the tradition of interpretation in which he works.[19] One phrase of the scriptural text that presently concerns us is *vindemiavit me*, which would normally be translated "he has gathered me as the grapes," or, "he has gathered me as the vintage," although it could more literally be rendered "he has removed me as the wine," or "he has removed me as the grapes." The latter meanings are closer to the Greek and Hebrew texts and to the less figurative Geneva and authorized rendering "hath afflicted me."

The association of Andrewes's text with affliction, along with the occasion of the sermon, Good Friday, probably explains why he does not pursue the Eucharistic, explicitly sacramental symbolism that reference to a vintage would invite. Instead he emphasizes the intensity of Christ's suffering, evoking his isolation to particular effect. Whether incidentally or by design, he thus manages to keep the fractious contention between *est* and *significat* at arm's length in this sermon. With respect to doctrine, his strategy defuses his treatment of the image implied by the phrase *vindemiavit me*.

Turning to the various versions of his text, he explains the Hebrew "importeth renting off, or bereaving"; the Latin "*Vindemiavit me*, as a vine whose fruit is all plucked off"; and the Greek "ἀπεφύλλισέ με, as a vine or tree whose leaves are all beaten off, and it left naked and bare."[20] Already in his translations of these words, his tendency to nominalize and to reify or personify is pronounced. If the English phrases are taken as translations of the Latin and Greek, for example, he does not gloss *vindemiavit me* as a verb and its object but as the noun "vine" plus a participle or verbal adjective; and already latent in his amplification of the Greek verb and object—a single tree left naked and bare—is an isolated or a naked person. Alternatively, if the English phrases are read as continuations, not translations, of the Latin and Greek (e.g., "me," who is "as a vine"), the same nominalizing tendency persists, since the English dilation of Latin *me* transfers figural emphasis from verb (*vindemiavit*) to pronoun (*me*) to noun, the denuded vine; and the English expansion of the Greek to emphasize the naked vine or tree only intensifies this transference. From the outset, Andrewes's attention is thus on *figura*—"the figure"—and not surprisingly so, since traditionally present in the figure of the tree is "the cross on which Christ was crucified."[21]

When Andrewes develops the meaning of the Greek and Latin words, he is again careful to signal that he is working with metaphor, or more exactly with allegory, in the simple rhetorical sense of an extended comparison. He introduces his embellishments by comparing Christ's isolation, his betrayal and abandonment even by his disciples, to a denuded tree: his state

> is *here in the* . . . *word* said to be like the tree, whose leaves and whose fruit are all beaten off quite, and itself left bare and naked both of the one and of the other. (145; my emphasis)

Andrewes really means "here in the word." The locus of meaning his statement intends is literally verbal, *vindemiavit*. The word is a metaphor and is recognized as such, but it is also understood as a verbal substantiation of the otherwise absent suffering of Christ. Additionally, of course, it is authorized by Scripture, its substance warranted, as it were, by the Holy Spirit, but this is a given, and here neither Andrewes's particular point nor my own.

While Andrewes locates meaning in the sacred word, he also limits its claims. The simple but important word "said," for example, here indicates a speech act with defining circumstances; its deletion would affect the meaning of the statement, making the biblical word in itself an absolute site. The word "like," a formal sign of comparison, similarly qualifies the implication of identity between Christ and the tree. The function of "like" is indirectly glossed in an earlier passage of the sermon when Andrewes considers the purpose of "a *sicut*," an expression meaning "just as," or "as." With respect to Christ's sorrow he reflects on the Latin phrase "*si fuerit sicut*; 'If ever the like were'" that he employs to gloss and to amplify the anglicized biblical text. He characterizes the components of the Latin phrase, which appears to be his own, as "words that have life in them, and are able to quicken our consideration, . . . for by them we are provoked, as it were, to 'consider' [*attendite*], and considering to see" (pp. 138–42).[22]

These words have life all right, but without being properly magical. Occasioned by reflection on the biblical text, they serve to enliven his audience's apprehension.

In Andrewes's subsequent amplifications of the biblical text, his explicit, rational glossing of the *figura* of the denuded tree he has glimpsed in the Greek and Latin words outweighs the incidence of untranslated metaphor to an extent difficult to demonstrate without quoting several paragraphs of the sermon. What follows is a partial but representative instance:

> But *Vindemiavit Me*, saith the Latin text; — even that [divine consolation] was, in this His sorrow, this day bereft Him too. And that was His most sorrowful complaint of all others; not that His friends upon earth, but that His Father from Heaven had forsaken Him; that neither Heaven nor earth yielded Him any regard, but that between the passioned powers of His soul, and whatsoever might any ways refresh Him, there was a traverse drawn, and He left in the state of a weather-beaten tree, all desolate and forlorn. (p. 146)

Such explication ensures that we do not take the figure of the tree for a fully transitive vehicle of grace or for a holy object with a magical identification with Christ, rather than for a conventionally, albeit strikingly, figurative one.

Yet Andrewes's naked tree is also progressively more than merely an illustration or a heuristic device. His text at once insists on a metaphorical structure and as a simulated process of perception, a performance, denies it. Thus the figural tree images truth and is supposed to convey it, if rightly understood. It is presented as a realization of suffering, and as such only so long as it is "realized" in both the subjective and objective senses. It is an objectified vehicle of insight and understanding. Insofar as the tree's effect might be termed transitive, it is affectively and psychologically so, or, if you will, it is so through faith. Faith aside, here it makes contact with the secular writing of the poets of the

English Renaissance: in Sidney's words, "so Poetry [fiction], being the most familiar to teach . . . and most princely to move . . . is the most excellent workman" (p. 94).

In the course of several paragraphs on either side of the passage from the sermon quoted just above, Andrewes's embellishments ask that we assent to a degree of substitution by the figurative word and to a degree of reification of it in the text exceeding that of a merely conventional metaphor — "what is left the meanest of the sons of men, was not left Him, not a leaf. Not a leaf!" The fickle crowds that followed Christ during his ministry are "but withered leaves," and of the twelve disciples, "the greenest leaves and likest to hang on, and to give Him some shade," there is "not a leaf left" (pp. 145–46). Reification and substitution so consistently sustained cross into allegory and potentially, at least, into mystification.

"But leaves are but leaves," Andrewes continues, then adding, "and so are all earthly stays." The word *stays* means "supports," but in conjunction with the word *leaves*, it gestures as well toward the meaning "waits" or "delays," thus broadening Andrewes's reflection to encompass our earthly existence more generally.[23] The pun on *stays* releases a still more contrived pun on *leaves* (foliage and departures) that dissolves and demystifies the increasing iconicity of the arboreal image.[24] The second pun serves as yet another reminder that this is human interpretation (human *cult*ivation) intervening between the seminal word and its realization. It has not been sufficiently recognized that Andrewes's more facetious puns often work to delimit his mysticism in this way. Whether expounding a text or a sacrament, Andrewes often seems to want it both ways — *via media*.

Only a moment after this punning the arboreal image is reasserted, figuring total desolation within and without. Now we learn that "the true fruit of the Vine," divine comfort, has also left him "in the state of a weather-beaten tree, all desolate and forlorn." The stripping of the fruit has entailed the utter abandonment that is internal isolation. His soul becomes the dry ground of deprivation and then the bare tree itself: this soul is "even as a scorched heath-ground, without so much as any drop of dew of divine comfort; as a naked tree — no fruit to refresh Him within, no leaf to give Him shadow without."[25] Parched within and exposed without, the naked tree that reemerges is emotionally and memorably silhouetted as a figure of suffering and as a highly charged sign. In the course of the entire arboreal passage, meaning quite literally exfoliates from the seminal words — Latin *vindemiavit me* and Greek ἀπεφύλλισέ με. The figurative word becomes the true ground of comprehension. Progressively, it is enabled to reveal itself as the focus of truth and understanding.

Yet it is still not the vehicle of sympathetic magic, even though the cultural memories of magic in Andrewes's methods and in the iconic figure he cultivates are strong. If, in comparison with Ficino's or Agrippa's use of images, Andrewes's use is less literal, less material, less objectively real, and, correlatively, less efficacious, it is more so than, say, Spenser's in the January Eclogue, where a stylized landscape is "made a myrrhour, to behold" the speaker's state of mind:

> You naked trees, whose shady leaues are lost,
> Wherein the byrds were wont to build their bowre:
> And now are clothd with mosse and hoary frost,
> Instede of bloosmes, wherwith your buds did flowre:
> I see your teares, that from your boughes doe raine,
> Whose drops in drery ysicles remaine.
>
> All so my lustfull leafe is dry and sere,
> My timely buds with wayling all are wasted:
> The blossome, which my braunch of youth did beare,
> With breathed sighes is blowne away, and blasted,
> And from mine eyes the drizling teares descend,
> As on your boughes the ysicles depend.   (31–42)

The "naked trees"—plural to begin with—that Colin, the pastoral speaker, sees in these lines are human enough: clothed, if only with moss and frost, and tearful. Icicles that are doleful drizzle from their boughs. As leaf, bud, blossom, and branch, Colin might also be considered isomorphic with the landscape, which is "made"—fashioned as or refashioned into—the mirror of his mind. Although the formal indication of comparison is present, "All so," landscape and singer are effectually fused in image and imagination, the one realizing—objectifying and spatializing—the other.

Andrewes's naked tree, "weather-beaten . . . desolate and forlorne," exists within an exegetical discourse and Colin's trees within a pastoral one. The first privileges symbol and word, the second landscape. It is therefore possible to distinguish their uses of metaphor in terms of their rationales. Spenser's trees have more context, both as features of a landscape and as the psychologically projected melancholy of the mournful swain. They are even depicted within the rudiments of a temporal context: once there were birds in their boughs and blossoms on their now frozen branches. Now, however, their barrenness, dreary icicles, and dry, sere leaves mirror a single emotional state. In themselves the trees are now subordinate rather than focal, and the more so if seen in the larger context of the eclogue. In contrast, Andrewes's desolate tree, as tree, is decontextualized, its origin a word, its settings abstract, and its meanings multiple. Its leaves are comforts, crowds, and disciples, and its fruit divine consolation. As the recurring image on which an expansive interpretation centers, it is set apart from its less iconic surroundings, both its desolation and its iconicity thus dramatized. It is altogether a more emblematic or formally symbolic object than Spenser's trees. In itself, it is significant and therefore more memorable.

Briefly, I would take these comparisons a step further by referring to the first quatrain of Shakespeare's Sonnet 73:

That time of year thou mayst in me behold
When yellow leaves, or none, or few, do hang
Upon those boughs which shake against the cold,
Bare [ruin'd] choirs, where late the sweet birds sang.

Here a tree or trees, symbolic illustrations of a time of year and time of life, are only synechdochized in lines 2 and 3, not even named outright. They are not merely subordinate to the speaker's condition; they have been absorbed into it: striking but unstable features of them — "yellow leaves, or none, or few" — move selectively and associatively across a screen of the speaker's projecting. As an image, the tree or trees are visually unstable; they have virtually no autonomy or objectivity. They have been taken into an interiorized context — recontextualized, in this sense. It does not matter to the coherence of the sonnet that its second quatrain should turn from the time of year to the time of day — a sunset — and its third to a glowing fire. "In me," repeated in each quatrain, is the axis on which the sonnet turns.

The contrast with Andrewes's focal image of a tree, originating in a biblical word, could hardly be greater, and yet it is exceeded by Shakespeare's striking but conventional use of metaphor in these famous lines from *Macbeth*:

I have liv'd long enough: my way of life
Is fall'n into the sear, the yellow leaf,
And that which should accompany old age,
As honor, love, obedience, troops of friends,
I must not look to have.[26]

Quoted in isolation, as here, the metaphor in these lines is essentially illustrative, its potential symbolism undeveloped. Although nature plays a significant part in the drama as a whole, and the sere and yellow leaf obviously relates to it, the larger meaning is not evident in a single, separable passage to the extent that it is with Andrewes's tree and to a progressively lessening extent with those in Spenser's eclogue and Shakespeare's sonnet. By contrast, the lines in *Macbeth* make the reified, raised image of Andrewes's tree stand out still more in the liminal space between conventional figure and animate object that the image occupies.

A powerful essay by Harry Berger on *"the order of the body"* and *"the order of texts,"* on interpretation in performances of Shakespeare and interpretation in the study, offers an additionally useful frame for Andrewes's methods.[27] Berger writes italically and self-reflexively — and in these respects like Andrewes — about *"iconic recoding,"* which he defines as "the transfer of meanings from verbal to extraverbal signifiers" (pp. 156, 160). To illustrate this recoding, he turns to Victor Turner's rendering of the ritual practices of the Zambian Ndembu, who effect a cure by transferring the meaning of a certain word (*isoma*) both to a patient's pathological condition and "to particular trees [i.e., the Zambian *mulendi* tree] whose capacity to manifest the meaning is what elevates them (on grounds of sympathic magic) to medicinal status." In this way, "semantic networks generated within language are . . . reified in — and as — 'nature,' " that is, in and as actual trees. Berger concludes that iconic recoding operates through "the principles of polarity and analogy" to bind meaning to the signifying object "in a nonarbitrary or motivated way because it commits them to the associational networks in which the object is perceived" (p. 160).[28]

Berger's conclusion bears provocatively on Andrewes's practice if we assume that the signifying object is a figure (*figura*) and hence verbal, rather than a physical tree. In the Ndembu culture, the *mulendi* tree is " 'prominent in rites and [therapeutic] treatments' " — shades of Agrippa. In contrast, Andrewes's tree is bodily embedded not in nature but in the word — *vindemiavit*. If it has a curative effect, this is imagined to be psychic and volitional, not transitive and physical. Whereas in Andrewes a medium of comprehension, the word itself, is the real text, the real tree to which it refers is not: meaning remains suspended in language, the tree significantly abstracted — textualized — in comparison with the magical *mulendi* tree. Through the accidents of history and culture, Andrewes's reality has thus been reoriented from nature to word. Here the word is the thing—at once the point and a thing in itself—and it is presumed to do more than merely gesture at its referent, whether the physical tree or the suffering Christ. This is all the more the case if our reading empties the word of its numen and finds in it only a fossilized structure of language.

———————

Fundamentally fictive yet proximate to magic, Andrewes's exposition of the iconic word relates to allegorical techniques and more generally to verbal objects—the kinds of "word-things" Terence Cave finds in Erasmus's writings. Andrewes often employs allegory in his sermons, sometimes extensively, and his high church example casts a historically revealing light on the practices of Renaissance allegorists and nonallegorists alike.[29] Choice specimens from the Renaissance arboretum—Spenser's allegory of Fradubio, the knight magically changed to a tree by Duessa in *The Faerie Queene*, and Prospero's story of Sycorax's magical imprisonment of Ariel in a tree in *The Tempest*—offer further cases in point. Both these arborealizing narratives displace the focus on the substantive word and its figuration that Andrewes's sermon has instanced, but with variant degrees of distantiation both also reflect it.[30]

In Spenser's story, Redcrosse and the nominally disguised Duessa travel together until they come "at last"

> Where grew two goodly trees, that faire did spred
> Their armes abroad, with gray mosse ouercast,
> And their greene leaues trembling with euery blast,
> Made a calme shadow far in compasse round.   (I.ii.28)

At first little distinguishes this landscape from a purely natural one, although several of its features invite a moment's pause: for example, the oddly specific number (the duplicity?) of the "two goodly trees"; the sense of significance inherent in their apparent isolation; the humanizing effect, however conventional, of their fair-spread "armes"; and the incongruity of the trembling of their leaves in the windy blasts with the calm, breadth, and depth of the shadow they cast "far in compasse round." Although muted, memories of the Wandering Wood also reverberate in this numerically more focused one, including the "shadie groue . . . Whose loftie trees . . . Did spred so broad, that heauens light did hide," and they resonate more generally from the incongruity between the pleasure "shrouded" within the Wandering Wood and the cruelty of "the tempest dred" outside it (I.i.7–8).

Such resonance and reverberation, a form of self-citation, help considerably to impart a substantive impression of this place, the site of the two trees: we recognize something about it. Even before more specific questions arise, the wood signals its significance, the fact that in some way it matters. Subsequently, of course, the text asks us fully to recognize Fradubio's grove as a common*place*, a topos instinct with the history of arboreal metamorphoses and their meanings: this place shadows the warning of danger given by Vergil's Polydorus to Aeneas and the grove of Dante's suicides, whose fates proleptically mirror the suicidal path Redcrosse pursues; more immediately shadowing his career, it also recalls the seduction of Ariosto's Astolfo by the false Alcina and Astolfo's futile warning to Rogero to avoid her power; and it glances as well at Ovid's account of the metamorphic fixation, figured arboreally, of Clymene's daughters and the arboreal desecration by Erysichthon in *The Metamorphoses*.[31] In psychological and theological terms, fixation and desecration have an obvious bearing on Redcrosse's situation at this juncture; and in terms of representation they bear on the iconic techniques that culturally and creatively inform it.

Again, the citationality of layered allusion imparts a seeming substance to the passage, which my own language in the preced-

ing paragraph — "some*thing*," "it *matters*," "common*place*" — has
reflected. Perhaps not surprisingly, it creates a fundamental condition of allegory. In such persistent encoding of former texts, the
rhetorical substance of the place achieves some measure of historical and cultural reality and simultaneously and ontologically
some measure of its lack. After all, we encounter the two trees in
the company of both Everyman and Duplicity, the Knight of the
Cross and the witch of double being (Duo-esse). The basic conditions of the poem thus invite divided responses.

But long before Redcrosse plucks a bleeding bough from Fradubio's trunk and thereby evokes the arborealized man's allusive
story, indeed, even before the stanza introducing the grove of Fradubio has finished, more specific doubts are raised about the
nature of this place: Why is the fearful shepherd "there aghast,"
for example, and why is its ground "vnlucky"? And why are
we back again in the pastoral landscape — one even affording
"pleasaunce" — that was renounced in the proem but then re-
introduced in the battle with Error within the Wandering Wood?
Such doubts further enforce attentive analysis of this place, and
they are intensified by imagery that intimates surplus meaning by
stressing the unmotivated ferocity of Phoebus, who "Hurled his
beame so scorching cruell hot, / That liuing creature mote it not
abide" (29). Phoebus's scorching hostility both complements
Jove's hideous rainstorm in canto i and gestures toward the fates
of Clymene's offspring, the overreaching Phaëton scorched and
the mournful Heliades metamorphosed into trees.[32] The plot —
or at least its setting — thickens.

It does so metaphorically, of course, but the metaphor is
grounded in perception, especially in memory; in the popular
conventions of critical language ("something about it," "it matters");[33] and in an allusively charged text. Here not the word as
such but the figuration of a landscape, a cultural place, is encoded
iconically. The difference between Andrewes's sacred word and
Spenser's textual place thus involves the evolving claims of fiction

and narrative. These claims are more substantial in Fradubio's grove, and memory is more crucial to them.

Fradubio's voice, finally emerging from within the arboreal setting, expresses the latent meaning of the place, which bypasses the Redcrosse Knight's comprehension. The knight fails to hear that this voice speaks within him:

> O spare with guilty hands to teare
> My tender sides in this rough rynd embard,
> But fly, ah fly far hence away, for feare
> Least to you hap, that happened to me heare,
> And to this wretched Lady, my deare loue,
> O too deare loue, loue bought with death too deare.
>
> (I.ii.31)

Characteristically, a paralleling of subject and object ("spare" / "teare", "to you hap" / "happened to me") and referential ambiguity in Fradubio's outcry underline the peril to Redcrosse: "guilty" in what sense, "heare" as adverb or imperative (*here* or *hear*), and "deare" meaning "cherished" or "costly." A memory of the Dwarf's warning to Redcrosse in canto i.13, "Fly, fly (quoth then / The fearefull Dwarfe)" also reverberates in Fradubio's, "fly, ah fly . . . for feare" in the present passage, and within another two stanzas, the declaration of Fradubio's name (Brother Doubt — "*mon semblable, mon frère*") and the account of his fate make explicit his allegorical figuration — his embodiment — of Redcrosse's progressive entrapment in the fallen nature from which only the redemptive waters of "a liuing well" can free him.[34]

An oddly resonant line in Fradubio's story occurs in Redcrosse's address to him: "Say on *Fradubio* then, or man, or tree" (34). A number of words in the line sound initially like fillers, and perhaps this is why it stands out. An uncertainty within Fradubio's story, "or man, or tree," at once reflects and transfigures a larger uncertainty within the poem involving the relationship between interior condition and exteriorized place, text and body, word and thing. Albeit submerged — sedimented — the cultural memories of magic inhere in this uncertainty. Within Fradubio's story, the doubter exists on the operative level of magic; he is a "liuing tree" who will eventually be healed by "a liuing well." Comparable to Andrewes's tree, he is thus an icon of reality. But Fradubio is also embedded — layered — within levels of textuality and therefore of fiction not found in Andrewes's sermon. His own voice exists within another's within a fairyland. Operative magic is still a memory somewhere in there, but its claims have been still further distanced from its bodily enactment in actual life.

Within Fradubio's own account of his arborealization there resides an instance of reflexivity that further enforces the uncertainty of relation between word and thing. This reflexivity seems to affirm and deny truth, at once revealing and obscuring it. According to Fradubio, Duessa deceives him in precisely the way Archimago has deceived Redcrosse: she replaces his love's true beauty with an illusion of ugliness, which the knight takes to be truth. The "foggy mist" and malignant power that she conjures up dim the "shining ray" of Fraelissa's beauty and "with foule vgly forme . . . disgrace" it (38). Through her false art she thus leads him to suppose that he uncovers the ugly reality when he actually embraces deception. His disillusionment, like Redcrosse's, leads only further into illusion.

Such parallels defy containment, whether within the poem or in the relation of the poem to its own production and to its reproduction in reading. When next Fradubio discovers Duessa's own disillusioning shape, "Her neather partes misshapen, monstruous" — the very shape that Redcrosse will see when Duessa is stripped — what is our warrant that this shape too is not just another deception and, more exactly, another product of the projecting or fictionalizing mind (41)? If illusion fails, is disillusionment reality?[35] And when the magic that lies at the roots of the iconic tree man is ironized into illusion, can the irony be kept from contaminating the "liuing well" and the warrant of truth that lies within it? Essentially absent from Andrewes's sermon, such questions everywhere inhabit the thickening substance and consequent uncertainty of the Spenserian text.

Both in subject matter — holiness — and in terms of allegorical method, Spenser's Book I nonetheless remains a natural analogue to Andrewes's verbally substantive sermons. Once easy arboreal associations are put aside, however, Shakespeare's *Tempest* is, or at least seems to be, quite a different matter. Prospero's story of Ariel's arborealization is already at a further remove from Andrewes than Spenser's is, since the recounting of it belongs wholly to one of the dramatis personae, to a figure within the fiction proper, rather than partly to a narrator whose voice is situated ambiguously with respect to it. Moreover, the arboreal-ization is merely recounted; the invitation to visualize rather than simply to remember it is minimal or nonexistent. Its status as an emblem or an emblematic part of a landscape has become the performance of a mnemonic act that is both purely self-reflexive and potently ironized, albeit not on the part of Prospero, its speaker.

As most editors of *The Tempest* insistently protest, this play is not allegorical in any easy sense. Yet protestation so notably con-spicuous begets doubt, and it is hard to believe that an allegorical heritage is not present in the play when we see Prospero, a secu-larized but not wholly demystified Everyman, silhouetted be-tween Ariel and Caliban, air and earth. An interpreter would have to be deaf not to hear the invitation to allegory in the contrapun-tal balance of Prospero's address to Ariel, "my spirit," with his acknowledgment that Caliban, "this thing of darkness," is "mine" (V.i.6, 275–76). Ariel, like his many arborealized precursors, has been affixed in bodily nature by Caliban's mother and stuck, as it were, in one "place" — a *topos* in both the physical and rhetorical senses.[36] I suspect it might be taken as an axiom that whenever editors of Shakespeare go out of their way to deny the presence of allegory, its threat breathes hotly upon them. Ariel and Caliban may not be the same as Faustus's Good and Bad Angels, but in a play in which the protagonist is a magician surrounded by good and bad characters, they descend from such Marlovian embodiments of motivation and awareness and thence, more distantly, from the morality play.

Aside from the names of Prospero, Miranda, Ariel, and Caliban — notably, all those who inhabit the enchanted island — and the conspicuous inclusion of a masque, the most allegorical aspect of *The Tempest* is structural and involves the counterpointing of the instincts, intuitions, aspirations, and skepticisms of human nature. Despite the undercurrent of Vergilian allusion that runs through the play, little in its surface resembles the layers of citation we find in *The Faerie Queene*.[37] There is not the same thickening, the same kind of substantializing found, with significant variations, in Spenser and Andrewes. But there is a memory of it, most blatantly in the claims of Prospero's magic, his faerie power, whose basis is here in question.[38]

Prospero's story of Ariel's arborealization is a significant part of his annoying and hence conspicuous insistence on memory and storytelling in the second scene of the play, first to Miranda and then to Ariel. Prospero insists on his power to interpret the past and thence to control the present. For example, when Ariel asks for freedom, Prospero counters with a question, "Dost thou forget / From what a torment I did free thee?" (I.ii.250–51). Even though Ariel replies that he remembers, an overly exercised Prospero responds, "Thou liest, malignant thing! Hast thou forgot / The foul witch Sycorax, who with age and envy / Was grown into a hoop? Hast thou forgot her?"[39] The word "thing," often overdetermined in a Shakespearean text, sounds threatening here in conjunction with lies and malignancy and, as the climactic term of negative characterization, suggests something formless and nondescript. Prospero's thrice-repeated question, accusing and demanding, dramatizes his investment in Ariel's remembering how he was bound and why he cannot (as yet) have freedom, but it also fails to account for the nature of this investment. Why is Prospero so exercised and at this point so worried about the rendition of the story that has to be told?

When Ariel, at Prospero's request, replies that Sycorax was born in Argier but expatiates no further, Prospero indicates that this is not the right response: "O, was she so? I must / Once in a month recount what thou hast been, / Which thou forget'st" (261–63). The word "which" reverberates oddly and ambiguously as the line continues, "This damn'd witch Sycorax . . ." Along with Prospero's denunciation of Ariel as a "malignant thing," this fleeting echo suggests a potential for virulence in the spirit, or at least Prospero's suspicion that such potential exists (conceivably identical possibilities).

Whatever the validity of Prospero's suspicion, the magician recites at length, not once but twice, how Sycorax in rage confined the spirit "Into a cloven pine, within which rift / Imprison'd, thou didst painfully remain / A dozen years . . . where thou didst vent thy groans / As fast as mill-wheels strike" (277–81).[40] When Prospero's tale gets to Caliban, the witch's son — "A freckled whelp, hag-born . . . not honor'd with / A human shape" — Ariel interrupts him, "Yes — Caliban her son" (283–84). Presumably, Ariel chorically assents to Prospero's description of Caliban as not fully human, although the intention of Ariel's remark is unclear and could also be construed either as disagreement with Prospero's judgment or, more likely, given Ariel's discomfort with Prospero's story of his confinement, as an attempt to shift the subject to Caliban as the unshaped, malignant thing worthy of Prospero's ire. Whichever reading prevails, Prospero's imme-

diate response, "Dull thing, I say so," is a puzzler. While it dramatizes the importance of "saying so" for this magician, the need to
state — in fact, "Once in a month recount" — the same story, and
while it further emphasizes the authority of his speech (*"I say
so"*), it remains at best doubtfully motivated, and it increases the
impression that there is something at once elliptical or overheard,
rehearsed and ritualistic, about the whole exchange. Once more
Ariel seems not to have gotten his assigned lines in the performance by heart.

So far, however, the story is actually Ariel's, a part of his past
before Prospero's presence on the island, and Ariel might well
have spoken the whole thing were the reciting of its words not in
effect to reconfine him. The process of reconfinement is why he
so obviously resists it and is so clearly relieved by its end: "I thank
thee, master" (I.ii. 293). The reiteration of this story of confinement and eventual benefaction exposes the method by which
Prospero keeps the spirit in control.[41] Memory, representation,
and reenactment are thus as basic to Prospero's power as they are
to Spenser's text — his rendering of a cultural *topos* — in the tale of
Fradubio.

The word "master" — *magister* — introduces further possibilities. While it suggests master-servant-slave relationships, it also
suggests the relationship of the master to his disciple or pupil.[42]
Numerous accounts of practices in Renaissance schools at all
levels — practices dependent on memorization, recitation, and
bullying — suggest their striking likeness to the exchange between Prospero and Ariel. The non sequiturs of this exchange,
the impression that motives are assumed and submerged within
it, result from the fact that we are overhearing elements of a
familiar ritual of shaping and fashioning the spirit.

Only Caliban in the play, though said to be confined to a cave
by Prospero's art, talks back to him. Prospero's offspring Miranda (or conceivably Prospero himself) has taught him language, and with it to know his own meaning, although ironically

not in the sense that the Prospero family might have intended.[43] Caliban forgets what Prospero would have him remember and remembers what he would have him forget: "This island's mine by Sycorax my mother, / Which thou tak'st from me" (I.ii.331–32). Unlike the potentially rebellious Ariel, moreover, Caliban speaks defiantly and at length:

> All the charms
> Of Sycorax, toads, beetles, bats, light on you!
> For I am all the subjects that you have,
> Which first was mine own king. (I.ii.339–42)

Caliban offers a more harshly critical perspective than Ariel on Prospero's storytelling, his construction of the past and consequent shaping of the present, and Caliban's assertion of his own version of the past highlights still more clearly the fabrication in the magician's design. From Caliban's point of view, the lines Prospero has earlier used to explain his brother's usurpation could be applied to Prospero himself, who is "like one":

> Who having into truth, by telling of it,
> Made such a sinner of his memory
> To credit his own lie — he did believe
> He was indeed the Duke, . . . (I.ii.99–103)

or, in this case, the rightful lord of the island.

Earlier, I suggested that Prospero's story of Ariel's arborealization had little in common with the rhetorical substance of the allegory of Fradubio in Spenser's first book. Except in an overly literal sense, this is perhaps an oversimplification. Aside from the nonspecific resemblance of Ariel's arborealization to earlier texts, its fiction, the twinned product of memory and storytelling, brings to the surface what in Spenser is enfolded in the more illusory substance of the text. It is as if this Shakespearean drama, like *Hamlet*, would deliberately explore memory and storytelling, the twinned powers and engines of allegory, and would critically expose the illusory but powerful magic that is in them.[44] To travel from Agrippa through Andrewes to Spenser and Shakespeare is thus to watch the shifting relations of animate verbal object to icon and allegory, to commonplace or cultural site, and to the processes of cultural and conceptual reflection of these and on these. It is to track something of the evolution and devolution, however uneven, of the substantive word.

Chapter 6

Weighing Words

I n preceding chapters, I have often invoked the practices of Spenser and Donne as points of reference on a linguistic map of Renaissance English. Spenser's writing has generally provided a model that circumvents or defers the identification of fictive word and referential thing, Donne's a model that identifies them, however problematical any such attempt proves to be. Taken together, the texts of these writers represent a broad spectrum of linguistic possibilities and a radical engagement with the substantiality of language, which informed everything their culture understood. In this way their texts motivate the sustained examination proposed in the sections that follow.

The Giant's Scales

Characteristically, *The Faerie Queene* contains perceived threats to its own assumptions and conditions of meaning; that is, it includes and ambivalently attempts to control them. This is especially true of questions concerning the fictionality or illusionism of art, such as those associated with the evil magicians of the poem, with the idealization of Elizabeth I, and with the substantiality of Faerie Land itself.[1] It pertains as well to Spenser's most outspoken treatment of words, which occurs in the episode of the leveling Giant that caps and comments on Artegall's initial exploits in Book V.

This episode opposes the materialism embodied in the Giant to the immaterial conceptions, ultimately founded on idealism or faith, that Artegall voices. It is hardly surprising that Artegall is allowed to win his debate with the Giant; it is perhaps surprising that his literally conclusive triumph should be figured in the material elimination of his opponent, who is summarily pushed from a cliff to destruction in the sea below. If this is justice, it operates in the Giant's own terms. The materialism of these terms recalls yet graphically exceeds and politicizes Harvey's "sinews in tropes" and "muscles and tendons in figures" and even the physical criteria of Hart's allegory of Esop, cited earlier. Artegall's rhetorical triumph, as its figuration suggests, is so enmeshed in ironic or otherwise disturbing nuances as to render it more problematic than first meets the eye. It is typical of Book V in this respect.

Artegall's debate with the Giant does not introduce the first signs of strain in this book between metaphorical and material dimensions of meaning, between concept and history, or between words and things, but it focuses them more sharply. This debate initiates conceptualization of the problem of embodying justice: the difficulty of fleshing it out in a real world. That such strains and problems exist self-reflexively in Book V has long been an established critical position, which Annabel Patterson has recently brought to bear on the relation of the fifth book to Spenser's *View of the Present State of Ireland*.[2] My present concern is with their more specific relation to language and to a question the Giant's challenge to Artegall poses: "How and how much do words weigh?" Verbal weight carries both a metaphorical and a material value here. The embodiment of justice implicates graphic and rhetorical characteristics in ideological, psychological, and historical ones. Moreover, they all revolve — at times dizzily — around the multivalence of *res*: the things of this world, higher things, and the things of rhetoric.

Artegall encounters the Giant just after having overseen the severing of Lady Munera's hands and feet and their display — "on high, that all might them behold" — as conspicuously material tokens for moral and political edification. From the outset, the Giant Artegall beholds is an emblematized and highly visible figure, standing "Vpon a rocke, and holding forth on hie / An huge great paire of ballance in his hand" (ii.26, 30). Despite the intervention of two stanzas to account for other matters — the drowning of the remainder of Lady Munera and the razing of her castle — the narrator's line of vision, along with Artegall's and our own, moves essentially from the dismembered tokens of Munera, hung on high, to the elevated Giant. It thus moves suggestively but ambivalently from the visual display of severed members to a gigantic embodiment of materialism. But what is being questioned in this ironic movement? The efficiency of Artegall's "great iustice"? The materialism of its means? Or the persistence of materialism itself? Like the Cave of Mammon, at whose core lies an inclusive and corrosive materialism, the Giant is a sight whose significance threatens containment, and the debate in which Artegall engages him is a profoundly disturbing locus of meaning in the poem. The appearance of the Giant questions the very province of symbolism and specifically that of the symbolism of justice, in which the resistance of matter (e.g., a woman's severed hands and feet) to higher meanings is peculiarly marked.

Consistently, the episodes preceding the sight of the Giant underline such resistance. In the first of these Artegall adjudicates between the conflicting stories of Sanglier and the Squire on the basis of the judgment of Solomon, but his decision, while correct, has two conspicuous loose ends that the biblical model noticeably lacks: a decapitated woman and her murderer. Sanglier's largely symbolic punishment — to bear the dead woman's head for a year as a mark of "shame" — ill fits the actual crime or the subsequent "ador[ation]" of Artegall's justice by the effusive squire (i.28, 30). Here the seam between literal and symbolic meanings or between material and generically romantic ones appears designed to exhibit severe signs of strain.

In the second episode, the defeat of Pollente and the execution of Munera, Artegall again establishes justice but at a cost to his own ideality. His victory over Pollente is punctuated by a reductive emphasis on the mundane and material that approaches mock epic. It includes attention to Artegall's prowess as a swimmer that is parodically digressive in length and focus ("But *Artegall* was better breath'd beside") and descriptions of combat whose imagery and rhythm similarly disappoint heroic and generic expectation: "They snuf, they snort, they bounce, they rage, they rore," thus enacting the sounds of mortal conflict between a dolphin and a seal.[3] Details of description are likewise designed to embarrass the justice of Lady Munera's execution. It is unclear, for example, whether Lady Munera's hands and feet are literally or symbolically gold and silver: her "hands of gold" could be gold-dispensing or her fingers richly adorned — "fretted with gold wyr" — like those of her prototype Lady Meed, and her feet could similarly be furnished with jewelry or net-work slippers of "choice" — Spenser's "trye" — silver.[4] The notion of "choice" silver itself points to either an aesthetic or a symbolic meaning. The distressing fact that Lady Munera is "holding vp her suppliant hands on hye" and "kneeling . . . submissiuely" when her extremities are summarily "Chopt off, and nayld on high" makes still harder the task of the apologist who — unlike even Artegall —

would ignore "her seemelesse plight." At once unseemly and seamless — perhaps "unseeming," or real, as well — her plight is a whole not separable into abstract and human segments or into concept and body, and to it Artegall proves conspicuously unable adequately to respond (V.ii.26–27).[5]

When, on the heels of Munera's dismemberment, the "mighty Gyant" enters the second canto, he is a looming physical presence whose figure focuses and mocks the cumulative incongruities between higher and lower meanings in the early episodes (30). Besides being an imposing sight, the Giant is a notably vocal figure — a talker, a boaster, and, with unwitting irony, in large part his own exegesis. Since he is physically a Giant, it is ironic that in principle he is also an egalitarian, one who would balance heaven with hell and "reduce vnto equality" all earthly things (32). To reinstate a presumed original justice he would reorder the components of the natural world, and from his reordering that of the social world would naturally follow:

> Therefore I will throw downe these mountaines hie,
> And make them leuell with the lowly plaine:
> These towring rocks, which reach vnto the skie,
> I will thrust downe into the deepest maine,
> And as they were, them equalize againe.
> Tyrants that make men subiect to their law,
> I will suppresse, that they no more may raine;
> And Lordings curbe, that commons ouer-aw;
> And all the wealth of rich men to the poore will draw.
>
> (V.ii.38)

Throughout, the Giant's argument is materialistic in the literal sense, since it is based on an injustice determined by quantity, appearance, and sight: "Seest not, how badly all things present bee," he demands, before continuing, "The sea it selfe doest thou not plainely see / Encroch vppon the land there vnder thee?" (37). Obviously, seeing is believing in these lines. But in them, insistent punning (see/sea), which is only nominally and inadvertently the Giant's, is also unusually obvious, and like the Giant's desire to reduce the high and mighty to the "lowly plaine," such punning anticipates — indeed, participates in — the leveling of the Giant himself, who is literally to be "thrust downe into the deepest maine" and "in the sea . . . dround" with narrative irony so blatant as to be vindictive (49).[6] The biblical scales on the Giant's eyes are thus to be eliminated — along with the Giant (Acts 9.18). Earlier, the Giant has been described as "mighty," in this context a word carrying the memory of its medieval force, which is not simply "powerful" in a brute sense but "capable of enacting"; for the medieval writers whom Spenser manifestly read, it is God who is (al)mighty.[7] Within the context of the present canto, the narrator's designation of the Giant's might is at once skeptical and frightened, ironic and anxious, a point to which I shall return.[8]

   In striking contrast to the pessimistic speaker of the proem to Book V, Artegall counters the Giant's perception of a fundamental injustice in the arrangement of the world and his desire to rectify it by asserting an underlying principle of Ptolemaic order — "The earth was in the middle centre pight" — and by affirming his own belief that this principle has been immutably established in accordance with "heauenly iustice" (35–36). In this connection, he both denies the possibility that significant change has ever occurred, for "mongst them al no change hath yet beene found," and categorically rejects its desirability: "All change is perillous, and all chaunce vnsound." His negative efforts anticipate Jove's absolute denial of presence and power to Mutability in the Cantos bearing her name, and they also recall such earlier moments as when Guyon and his Palmer fettered Occasion, implicitly and vainly trying to stop time and its inevitable concomitant, the forward movement of narrative and hence of the quest.[9]

More urgently and immediately, Artegall's premises oppose the historically grounded anxieties voiced conspicuously (paradox intended) by the speaker of the fifth proem:

> Me seemes the world is runne quite out of square,
> From the first point of his appointed sourse,
> And being once amisse growes daily wourse and wourse.
>
> . . . .
>
> Right now is wrong, and wrong that was is right,
> As all things else in time are chaunged quight.
> Ne wonder; for the heauens reuolution
> Is wandred farre, from where it first was pight.
>
> (V.Pro.1, 4)

The reemergence of this pessimistic view in the Giant's words and the extension of it to the social order further enforce its claim on our attention and impart a measure of authority to it within the narrative. Its reemergence also attests to the pressure of its historically material existence, which is well documented for the late sixteenth century and includes relevant causes ranging from new stars, prophecies, and seemingly irregular planetary movements to crop failures, inflation, enclosures, poverty, and vagrants in England, to worries about the importation of Anabaptist communism from the Continent and recurrent Irish uprisings somewhat closer to home.[10] In light of this persistently troubled view in both the historical *and* the Faerie contexts, that is, in the world and the poem, Artegall's unqualified absolutism is made to look suspect. In this it resembles the hyperbolic praise lavished on him in his early exploits, whose actual conduct and outcomes we have seen to be conceptually strained and recurrently touched by whiffs of parody.[11]

When the Giant is confronted with Artegall's categorical assertions, he, too, is stubborn, and he insists all the more on the evidence of his senses. Interestingly, his insistence causes Artegall to shift — to change — from an argument dependent on an immutable cosmos to a nearer and considerably more dynamic one based on a natural cycle of loss and recovery, flourishing and fading, birth and death:

> How euer gay their blossome or their blade
> Doe flourish now, they into dust shall vade.
> What wrong then is it, if that when they die,
> They turne to that, whereof they first were made?

(V.ii.40)

While this shift in the argument better accommodates the Giant's position regarding "things in sight" and could be construed as a generous or politic effort to reach him, it also represents a more complex and immediate engagement with matter. Insofar as it is merely a development of Artegall's original position, however, it exposes the underlying allegiance of his cyclical view to stasis: change might exist, but it makes no real difference; nothing *really* changes.

And even as the increased engagement with matter comes, as if to offset it Artegall more emphatically employs an argument based on faith. He slips easily from flowers and the biblical reso- nance of their fading into "dust" to the more human context of death and to a rhetoric exceeding the fate of flowers: now he depends on "the voice of the most hie," the "great Maker," to have ordained "What euer thing is done" (40–42). The authority of this voice is higher than the towering Giant, and the stanzas describing its action are, in Thomas Roche's apt words, "a tissue of biblical paraphrase."[12] They are so much so that they yield the poem's meaning to another context:

> They liue, they die, like as he doth ordaine,
> Ne euer any asketh reason why.
> The hils doe not the lowly dales disdaine;
> The dales doe not the lofty hils enuy.
> He maketh Kings to sit in souerainty;
> He maketh subiects to their powre obay;

He pulleth downe, he setteth vp on hy;
He giues to this, from that he takes away.

. . . .

Ne any may his mighty will withstand;
Ne any may his soueraine power shonne,
Ne loose that he hath bound with stedfast band.

(V.ii.41–42)

These lines, if not wholly unprecedented, do not represent the ordinary syntax and rhythm of Spenser's writing. They particularly contrast with the conversational quality of Artegall's words to Sanglier and the squire in the preceding canto (e.g., i.25) and with his exchanges with the Giant earlier in the present debate:

Thou that presum'st to weigh the world anew,
    And all things to an equall to restore,
    In stead of right me seemes great wrong doth shew,
    And far aboue thy forces pitch to sore.

. . . .

Thou foolishe Elfe (said then the Gyant wroth)
Seest not, how badly all things present bee,
And each estate quite out of order goth?   (V.ii.34, 37)

Unlike Artegall's biblical paraphrase, lines such as these are touched by the rhythm and diction of everyday living, and they actually participate in propositional debate.

In contrast, the ritualized rhythms of Artegall's paraphrase do not develop dialogue so much as they testify to the importation of meaning — literally, to its portability and imposition. What is "heard" in the passage is less truly a "voice" than a text, a rhythmically and allusively defined block of biblical writing, visibly and audibly a set piece that occupies the narrative and differs markedly from the immediate and larger contexts surrounding it in the poem. Such a text is broadly comparable to the "prefabricated unit of meaning" of which Nigel Barley has written in characterizing proverbial utterances and to the "sing-song effect" Maurice

Bloch calls intoning — a ritualized "repeating [of] what had been said before." Bloch's analysis is further relevant: he characterizes words in ritual as having little explanatory (or propositional) power and sees them performing "less as parts of a language and more as *things*, in the same way as material symbols." They are "frozen" statements, whose "repetition reminds us that we are not dealing with an argument, since an argument is a basis for another argument." Most tellingly in regard to Artegall's style of debating, Bloch interprets the frozen statement as "the use of form for power" — a politically potent substance.[13]

Effective as Artegall's biblical set piece is in its own right, its admissions sound also at times like an argument based merely on necessity or on fortune: "He pulleth downe, he setteth vp on hy; / He giues to this, from that he takes away." While other echoes of the rhetoric of Despair in Artegall's assertions — "When houre of death is come, let none aske whence, nor why" — might summarily be dismissed on the ground that the Knight of Justice argues for faith and not for suicide, dismissal begs the question. If there is one thing that the Book of Justice makes abundantly and explicitly clear, it is that in a real world faith is not identical with justice, the impersonal cardinal virtue which, by virtually any traditional definition — Aristotle's, Cicero's, Aquinas's, or Hooker's — concerns not an inner world of private virtues and beliefs but the material world of history.[14] Certainly from the point of view of the Giant and "the people" whom he represents, the self-abnegation of Artegall's faith must itself be a form of self-destruction: "What wrong then is it, if that when they die, / They turne to that, whereof they first were made" — dust into dust without any real sense of loss, let alone indignation. Faith is not an answer to the Giant's arguments to the same extent or in the same sense that a Ptolemaic position and a total denial of change would have been, had these proved credibly demonstrable. Artegall's shift from such "scientific" or relatively verifiable positions to an argument based wholly on faith is revealing, for in making it he discards the visual or perceptual criteria commonly used to theorize appearances into a "real" system that organizes matter from dense to rare.[15] Again his shift suggests the threatening historical reality of what the Giant so visibly and audibly — so materially — embodies.

Artegall's set piece in this debate has a natural association with other frozen pieces in the poem to which it is formally and thematically analogous, and these cast a proleptic or retrospective light upon it. The temptation of Despair in Book I, in which Redcrosse is counseled, "in true ballance . . . weigh thy state," affords a pertinent example (I.ix.45). As this episode shows, Despair can use and misuse Scripture, together with all the other sententious resources available in the period for moral guidance. Despair's temptation, like Artegall's invocation of faith, is itself a pastiche of traditional echoes — classical and proverbial, as well as scriptural — and even today, their familiarity conveys something of their cultural power:

> . . . . all ends that was begonne.
> Their times in his eternall booke of fate
> Are written sure, and haue their certaine date.
> Who then can striue with strong necessitie,
> That holds the world in his still chaunging state,
> Or shunne the death ordaynd by destinie? (I.ix.42)

Similarly drawing on the formulaic content and rhythm of traditional sources, the next stanza begins, "The lenger life, I wote the greater sin, / The greater sin, the greater punishment," and it subsequently explains that "life must life, and bloud must bloud repay. . . . For he, that once hath missed the right way, / The further he doth goe, the further he doth stray." The lines cited from these two stanzas recall eight proverbial sources and two scriptural ones, all of which strike me as being still available to cultural memory: for example, "Whatever has a beginning has an end"; "Blood will have blood"; "Death keeps no calendar"; "The time of death is certain"; "All men must die"; "The farther you go, the farther behind"; "The longer the life, the greater the misery"; "The force of necessity is irresistible."[16] Essentially, Despair's lines thus consist not merely of "vaine words," as Una characterizes them in her last-ditch effort to cancel their force, but of sentiments that carry considerable ideological "weight" — cultural and therefore unavoidably psychological weight, frozen matter (I.ix.53). In view of this fact, it makes sense that some critical doubt should have arisen as to whether Despair or Redcrosse speaks in a number of these lines.[17] Of course such ambiguity is symbolically appropriate in them, since Despair, the ghastly figure whose description mirrors that of the Knight rescued from Orgoglio's dungeon, now bids to become one with him. While the doubt that Despair's lines generate has meaning within the quest of Redcrosse, however, it also suggests the extent to which lines that recall the content and cadences of traditional sources can take on a life of their own, the poet's awareness of this fact, and his skill in utilizing it.[18] This poet knows how to use frozen words; his use, moreover, is not an innocent one.

Within the fifth book itself, a near example of such use occurs in an exchange between Artegall and Burbon, the knight who seeks to defend his possession of the lady Flourdelis and whose name alludes conspicuously to Bourbon, Henri de Navarre and subsequently Henri IV of France. When Burbon is challenged by a "rude rout" and throws away his battered shield in order to defend his lady more effectively, Artegall considers this act Burbon's dishonorable betrayal of his "honours stile," or knightly identity, and advises him to "Dye rather, then doe ought, that mote dishonour yield" (V.xi.44, 55). But Burbon answers Artegall's proverbial wisdom with some of his own, since he thinks that he can in time "resume" his former shield: he argues that "To temporize is not from truth to swerue, / Ne for aduantage terme to entertaine, / When as necessitie doth it constraine." Artegall, hardly to be outdone in this vein, replies by doubling the proverbial context: "Fie on such forgerie (said *Artegall*) / Vnder one hood to shadow faces twaine. / Knights ought be true, and truth is one in all" (56).[19] Again the weighted lines in which traditional wisdom is concentrated are problematical, and as Artegall's subsequent decision to assist Burbon suggests, neither view is without force and reason. Burbon's view favors temporal and material considerations, Artegall's ideal and absolute ones. It seems no accident that Artegall's words closely echo those he speaks earlier to the leveling Giant: "For truth is one, and right is euer one" (ii.48); nor accidental that his words to Burbon are followed almost immediately by his seemingly contradictory decision to assist the apostate knight, even though his doing so delays his already belated quest. The claim of unity, a single truth, is more and more entangled in irony, in doubleness and duplicity in the fifth book, a situation that extends into the sixth book and finally to the Mutability Cantos. Within this entanglement the claims of material existence — bodies in history — are increasingly real and persistently relevant to language, particularly when language is frozen into a thing, a material symbol or *res*.

While the biblical origin of the most formulaic portion of Artegall's words to the Giant may argue for immunizing them from the problems surrounding the other invocations of traditional wisdom I have cited, the fact that the sentiments introducing the Giant's proposal to curb aristocratic power and to redistribute wealth — "Therefore I will throw downe these mountaines hie, / And make them leuell with the lowly plaine" — also come from the Bible further complicates this argument.[20] The earlier gap between Artegall's own invocation of the judgment of Solomon and the actual situation in canto i adds yet another wrinkle (or Derridean fold) to it. The larger context of Book V and specifically the strains between material and ideal values everywhere evident in it argue still more strongly against such reductive immunization.

Accentuated and isolated by its form as well as its content, Artegall's frozen speech exists within a worldly frame that oddly both heightens and questions its difference from the material concerns and events of this world. In a book of Justice this is a crucial fact, for such a book, unlike those treating personal virtues, must deal with a world that is external and historical. When, in debating the Giant, Artegall shifts his focus from an utterly unchanging cosmos to the cyclical changes of the natural world, including the cycle of mortality, his belated admission of evident change, though ever so carefully balanced by a profession of personal faith, acknowledges the weight of material concerns and the persistent reality of matter. Once again, this episode anticipates the Mutability Cantos, yet in the penultimate stanza of Mutability, unlike the Artegallian debate, a sense of loss will outweigh the consolation of a recurring cycle:

> Which makes me loath this state of life so tickle
> And loue of things so vaine to cast away;
> Whose flowring pride, so fading and so fickle,
> Short *Time* shall soon cut down with his consuming sickle.[21]

In comparison to these lines, Artegall's guarded acknowledgment of materiality sounds detached ("How euer gay their blossome or their blade / Doe flourish now, they into dust shall vade") and defensive ("What wrong then is it, if that when they die, / They turne to that, whereof they first were made?"). In this context, his biblical paraphrase looks even more like a power play, a material assertion of form meant to compensate for the material vacuum his otherworldly beliefs have created.

As if uncomfortably aware of the likelihood of further debate once the ritual of biblical paraphrase recedes, Artegall takes the offensive and challenges the Giant of materialism directly. Brooking no response, he abruptly shifts the argument — in fact, the balance — once again from ponderable things to those imponderable:

For take thy ballaunce, if thou be so wise,
 And weigh the winde, that vnder heauen doth blow;
 Or weigh the light, that in the East doth rise;
 Or weigh the thought, that from mans mind doth flow.
 But if the weight of these thou canst not show,
 Weigh but one word which from thy lips doth fall.
 For how canst thou those greater secrets know,
 That doest not know the least thing of them all?
 Ill can he rule the great, that cannot reach the small.[22]

Presumably a word is "the least thing of them all." It is the ul-
timatum that is clearly on a continuum with greater things, and
the Giant's response indicates that he is specifically disconcerted
("abashed") at the prospect of weighing one, conceivably because this prospect hovers uncertainly between metaphorical and
material meanings—between "weigh" in the sense of evaluate or
consider, and "weigh" in the literal sense of relative poundage.
The Giant's abashment implicitly acknowledges something—
verbal *res*, a meaning—not strictly material. To this extent, like
Artegall, he shows some movement toward a healthier balance
between material and immaterial concerns.

But this is only momentary. He overcomes his abashment to
extend his materialism uncompromisingly to language, insisting
that "the least word that euer could be layd / Within his ballaunce, he could way aright" (44). Challenged by Artegall to
determine whether "right or wrong, the false or else the trew" is
heavier, he flings these into the balance, "But streight the winged
words out of his ballaunce flew." As in the initial idealism of
Rabelais's fable of the frozen words, these words are winged, like
Homer's; they participate in a reality that does not abide material measurement. The Giant, anticipating Bacon's desire to put
weights on the flights of the mind, dismisses their evidence
against him on grounds of the inherent—and, despite himself,
the figurative—lightness of words and tries instead, without suc-
cess, to weigh truth, essential truth, against falsehood. But all his

balance discovers is that "the false will [not] with the truth be wayd" (45). Falsehood, apparently incommensurable with truth, just slides off the scale, enacting itself as mere absence and denial, whether of truth, goodness, or positive being.

In a surprising turn Artegall tells the enraged Giant that the scales prove nothing, at best serving only to "betoken" right or wrong. His immediate point is that the scales are mechanically faultless, despite their finding against the Giant's view, yet his statement implies that the Giant's earlier weighing of the material world, which found for the Giant, is meaningless as well. The word *betoken* is slippery, however, and all the more so because Artegall's employment of it is unique in *The Faerie Queene*. Presumably, by it he means "signify," "denote," "indicate," "be a token of," but there is a basic ambiguity in the meaning of the substantive *token* that carries over into its verbal cognate: *token* means both "something that serves to indicate a fact" and "something serving as proof of a fact or statement; an evidence" — on the one hand, something that merely points to a thing and, on the other, something that has demonstrative validity in itself.[23] The latter meaning would grant a degree of autonomous authority to the evidence of the scales, as to other quantitative measurements, such as those by which phenomena that were irrational in a Ptolemaic order could be more clearly tracked and questioned. It would therefore grant some measure of definitive reality to the material realm. With an elusive, layered irony, the ambivalence of Artegall's word *betoken* thus weighs to an extent against him and the validity of his position. If the Giant's scales betoken that he cannot weigh words, they have earlier betokened that inequality exists.[24]

In invoking the word *betoken*, Artegall evidently means to argue that, while the Giant's scales can indicate relative weight — more exactly, weight relative to a fundamental principle — they are unable to determine the validity of the principles themselves according to which judgment must be rendered and material considerations weighed.[25] For

in the mind the doome of right must bee;
And so likewise of words, the which be spoken,
The eare must be the ballance, to decree
And iudge, whether with truth or falshood they agree.

(V.ii.47)

Like *vox*, "voice," the ear is here another material supplement of the mind; it listens, like the ear of a Renaissance jurist, to subjective intention, in which "both *mens* [*legislatoris*] and *ratio* [*legis*]" are conflated and found to be "not only beneath and behind the words of the law" but "also prior to the words" that express it.[26] Artegall's explanation is less about ears versus eyes, speech versus writing, than it is about mind versus mere matter — about "the doome" within the mind to which "words, the which be spoken," must be referred if they are to bear any true meaning — verbal *res*.

In terms of the broader basics being debated, Artegall's words — materially tripping him up, perhaps — further indicate not just the truism that human beings have minds as well as senses but a far stronger privileging of the "inward mind," repeatedly in this poem a phrase that implies the recesses of memory in Neoplatonic and Augustinian senses.[27] Artegall opts both for a subjective conception of truth as against an external and quantifiable one and for an interiorly valorized conception of language as against one that is material. His choice distinctly favors the Platonic end of the philosophic spectrum. Considered from this vantage point, his inward ear actually listens, like Augustine's, essentially to intuition.[28]

Within a context of idealism such as that attributed to Plato or Augustine, even to speak the inner word of truth, let alone to write it, is to subject it to a compromising degree of materialization. In *Letter VII*, a Platonic document sometimes identified with Plato himself, the epistler expresses his distrust of language most emphatically: "no intelligent man will ever be so bold as to put into language those things which his reason has contemplated." When he adds that this is particularly the case with written language, he does not erase the impression that *any* form of externalized expression obscures or distorts truth: for a Platonist, the "knowledge and understanding of real objects is not found in sounds nor in shapes but *in minds*; names, descriptions, bodily forms, and concepts do as much to illustrate the particular quality of any object as they do to illustrate its essential reality" (my emphasis). The Platonic epistler, anticipating his Neoplatonic successors, describes true knowledge as a "flash of understanding" in which the mind is "flooded with light."[29] Augustine similarly describes an understanding that floods the spirit in a rapid flash ("intellectus quasi rapida coruscatione perfundit animum"), and he repeatedly remarks how much actual speech, "the sound of our mouth," differs from it ("quantum distet sonus oris nostri ab illo ictu intelligentiae").[30] In his epistemology, true understanding is preverbal (with reference to ordinary human language), and the relation of the truth that shines within to the words we speak remains at best obscure.[31] Committed to time and space through syntax and figurality, any human language is for Augustine inherently flawed.[32]

In the context of debate with the Giant, Artegall's views, which are neither those of the proem to Book V nor necessarily co-extensive with Spenser's, are touched by the antilinguistic extremism of Platonism and by what I would imagine to be the projected anxieties of the poet. In an extreme form they also anticipate Ian Hacking's view, described in my Prologue, that language philosophy of the early modern period is radically ideational. As we have seen, however, Artegall's voice is neither unqualified by material considerations at this point nor unchallenged by other passages in the poem. While the Giant's fatal errors have first been to let Artegall radically shift the ground of argument from things seen to things unseen and then to suppose that words, concepts, and principles can be weighed in purely material terms, the Giant's failure has not affected visible, palpable inequalities in any way except to shift them from sight. Moreover, in doing so it has raised the classic specter of the failure of words to refer in some intrinsic way to things, or at least to material things.

Although Artegall invokes the mind and the ear and the Giant's arguments have been blatantly associated with matter and sight ("Seest not, how badly all things present bee, / . . . The sea it selfe doest thou not plainely see / Encroch vppon the land there vnder thee?"), these alignments are offset by other material considerations: by Artegall's earlier recourse to display — Pollente's head or Lady Munera's hands and feet, for example; by the assertions of his own weighted words, meant to suggest "the voice of the most hie," perhaps, but more evidently composing a portable piece of frozen rhetoric; and most dramatically by Talus's shouldering the Giant "from off the higher ground" of argument to the sea below:

> Like as a ship, whom cruell tempest driues
>   Vpon a rocke with horrible dismay,
>   Her shattered ribs in thousand peeces riues,
>   And spoyling all her geares and goodly ray,
>   Does make her selfe misfortunes piteous pray.
> So downe the cliffe the wretched Gyant tumbled;
>   His battred ballances in peeces lay,
>   His timbered bones all broken rudely rumbled,
> So was the high aspyring with huge ruine humbled.
>   (V.ii.50)

This stanza comes after Artegall wins his argument with the hapless Giant and serves as the materially conceived, conclusive expression of his victory. The terms of its conception contrast sharply with the knight's high-minded sentiment that "in the mind the doome of right must bee." Although at two nominal removes from Artegall — one through the intervention of a simile and another through that of Talus — the narrator's use of the adjective "cruell" in describing the Giant's fate participates in the recurrent association of Artegall with cruelty prior to his fall at

Radigund's hands and his subsequent rescue by Britomart.[33] According to traditional ethical theory, cruelty is the vice that specifically opposes justice, the wrong that negatively balances or — in view of the incommensurability of right and wrong Artegall urges to the Giant — perhaps fails to balance its right. Crucially and repeatedly in Book V, the narrative returns to this troubling question of balance, and as we have seen, it already implicates the matter of words, hence the poem itself, in its outcome.

How and how much do words weigh? From the first episode of Book V, when Artegall adjudicates the conflicting testimonies of Sanglier and the squire, through the last, the onslaught of Envy, Detraction, and the Blatant Beast, the relation of words to truth is at issue. In the early episodes words in themselves do not fare especially well; they are ineffectual, their testimony invariably superseded by more material considerations or by actions, as when the Giant is shouldered off the cliff. Artegall decides between Sanglier and the squire on the basis of "signes," not words as such; his words to the Giant are abruptly replaced by explosive force; when his own word conflicts with Braggadocchio's he invokes "signes"; and he requires "tokens" — material evidence — from Guyon to establish the latter's right to the stolen horse (i.24, ii.49, iii.21–22, 32). Correspondingly, the pleas of Lady Munera and the arguments of the Giant are brushed aside; the railings of Braggadocchio, that quintessential windbag, are rightly punished; and the mutual pledges of Amidas and Bracidas to their original loves are readily accommodated to fortune's redistribution of wealth through the action of the sea. In all these episodes, words prove themselves to be "the least thing of them all."

The later cantos of Book V are complexly and historically materialistic rather than crudely so like the early cantos, yet in them, although words may acquire more weight, they gain little more positive value. For example, Radigund advises her handmaid Clarinda to add "art" to her temptation of Artegall, "euen womens witty trade, / The art of mightie words, that men may charme," and Artegall remains Radigund's prisoner largely because he has imprudently pledged his word to her (V.v.49). What ultimately redeems him is his keeping his loyalty to Britomart; we might regard this as his keeping his word, but the poem never refers specifically in this way to his loyalty. It mentions only his inner troth, his loyalty or integrity (V.vi.2, cf. v.56). Even tokens become deceptive when Dolon mistakes Britomart for Artegall, but words still fare no better, for those that Dolon's vengeful sons speak to Britomart are simply "strange" — alien — to her ear (V.vi.34, 38). The words of rationalized interpretation that the priest of Isis imposes on Britomart's dream are similarly dubious, ill sorting with the powerful imagery of its passion. Malengin is "smooth of tongue," and Malfont "a welhed / Of euill words, and wicked sclaunders" (V.ix.5, 26). Strikingly, Malfont's tongue is nailed to a post as were Munera's hands and feet: the punishment for his transgression is thus the fixing, immobilizing, and thorough materialization of his speech. In a disturbing parody of an orthoepy like Hart's, his speech is reduced to an organ of utterance: Homer's "winged words" seem mocked and cynically monumentalized in his. Malfont's fate threatens both its opposites, whether unrestrained or immaterialized expression. Like the Giant of materialism, Malfont, whose name prophetically invokes the printing house, embodies an amorphous but very real danger, the meaning of which is hard to contain, though clearly this danger touches free expression — even language itself — to the quick.[34]

In a Lacanian essay that bears suggestively on Book V, Joan Copjec has described Vergil's Fama (rumor or report) as a paranoid image of the dismembered body that "appears at a point where the narration has reason to doubt its own omniscience, its own position as source of knowledge." It is at this point that "a cry [in the form of Fama] is torn from the throat of the narrative which [forcefully] reattaches it to the events of the world." Like Fama or like Malfont, the dismembered Giant who tumbles down the cliff can also be seen as "a hypostasized image of speech, an intrusion which is simultaneously the very *substance* of the narrative," its own self-reflexive commentary on its own mode of existence (p. 44; my emphasis). For Copjec, the paranoia of such nightmarish images inheres in the ordering and alienating impulses of speech itself (pp. 55–56). That paranoia should particularly inform moments in the heightened order of allegorical fiction would seem to follow: witness Fama.

The rest of Spenser's fifth book only strengthens the indictment of language, perhaps inevitably after such specters as Malfont and the Giant. In the trial of Duessa, Zeal, a figure bent essentially on winning, is characterized as one "that well could charme his tongue, and time his speach / To all assayes" (ix.39). Recalling Clarinda's art (not to mention Despair's), Zeal's charmed tongue is not entirely reassuring, and it is less so in view of the ambivalent behavior of Mercilla that succeeds its triumph (ix.50–x.4).[35] As earlier remarked, Artegall's second debate concerning justice, this time with Burbon, issues an affirmation of a univocal truth that his action promptly belies. Yet all these preceding reservations in Book V regarding the role of language pale in the face of its final episode, the assault on Artegall by Envy, Detraction, and the Blatant Beast, whose hundred braying tongues are sharpened by the "cursed tongs" and "bitter wordes" of these two hags (xii.41–42). Unlike the falsehood that merely slides off the Giant's scale, these words have a very real impact, stinging and piercing, biting and wounding. As Artegall passes "afore" Envy, her "halfe-gnawen snake . . . Bit him behind, that long the marke was to be read," and her poison is just the prelude to the "bitter wordes" of Detraction and the Beast (xii.39–42).

Like Artegall's shift from an outright denial of change to a recognition of material realities, however carefully hedged, this ugly episode acknowledges the biting reality of words, figurally, affectively, and also historically, since it blatantly alludes to the fate of Arthur, Lord Grey de Wilton; that is, it acknowledges the reality of words in terms that are fully material. Thus this episode, too, bitterly reattaches the narrative "to the events of the world." At the same time, however, the disfiguring end of Book V might also be seen to enable Book VI, in which words have real effects, whether physically, as when the Beast bites Timias and Serena, or ideally, as when the Graces materialize to dance on Mount Acidale. Less exuberantly, more nervously, even more backhandedly, Spenser's fables display a range of possibilities that recalls those of Rabelais in the episode of the frozen words. They seem to me finally weighted toward idealism but barely and painfully so.

The combination of capacious skepticism and provisional idealism in the closing books of *The Faerie Queene* will prove a sharp contrast to the insistence and extravagance of Donne's verbalism in the sections to follow. Yet the writings of Spenser and Donne alike inhabit the Rabelaisian universe in which words literally may become frozen forms. Always, for Donne, words are a substantial medium, and in the sermons of his later years they become realizations in about as radical a sense as can be entertained. In them verbal and material *res* might appropriately be termed consubstantial. Like Spenser's Giant, Donne, too, would weigh words, palpable words, but Donne's words, instead of flying out of his balance, will operate within its metaphor to translate *res* to another register.

Donne's Pre-deliberations, or Scaling the Heights

The way into Donne's sermons is through their ideas, but these quickly turn out to be verbal, not simply in the obvious sense that they are written but also in the sense that they are unreal without the substantiation of words. Words—audible, visible, material words — are "weighted" for Donne in a way that Spenser's Artegall would deny them. An example from Donne's fifth Prebend sermon puts this matter succinctly: "God had conceived in himselfe, from all eternity, certaine Idea's, certaine patterns of all things" but "these conceptions produced not a creature, not a worme, not a weed" until *"Dixit, & facta sunt*, God spoke, and all things were made" (VIII, 120). Donne continues, putting a notably un-Augustinian (and un-Artegallian) emphasis on the necessity for human beings of externalized utterance to fulfill the inner idea: "Inward speculations, nay, inward zeale, nay, *inward prayers*, are not full performances of our Duty" (my emphasis). The honoring of God demands the reality of language and further of actualized speech. Language so conceived is both material and efficacious.[36]

That God works according to a pattern, an idea, or a preconception and that we, made in God's image, should do likewise is a recurrent topic in Donne's sermons and one that he characteristically relates to utterance — to prayer and to preaching. The second Prebend sermon, like the fifth, aligns the presence of eternal preconceptions in God with verbal practice, whether human or divine. This sermon, too, begins by stressing the model itself: "First then, from the meanest artificer" — the meanest maker — "through the wisest Philosopher, to God himselfe, all that is well done, or wisely undertaken, is undertaken and done according to pre-conceptions, fore-imaginations, designes, and patterns proposed to our selves before-hand" (VII, 60). Even the rhythm of the chiasmus — "well done . . . wisely undertaken . . . undertaken and done" — here underscores deliberation: *deliberatio* or "well weighing." Donne next proceeds to apply the divine model — "And therefore let . . . [God] be our patterne for that, to worke after patternes" — and brings the application home to what he himself has deliberated and done: "If he aske me an Idea of my Sermons, shall I not be able to say, It is that which the Analogy of Faith, the edification of the Congregation, the zeale of thy worke,

the meditations of my heart have imprinted in me?" (VII, 61).[37]
Then he begins to broaden his reference, making the first-person
pronoun more representative: "But if I come to pray or to preach
without this kind of Idea, if I come to extemporall prayer, and extemporall preaching, I shall come to an extemporall faith, and
extemporall religion; and then I must looke for an extemporall
Heaven." An "extemporall Heaven" is a contradiction in terms,
an eternity ironically *ex tempore*, "rising out of the moment" and
therefore without basis in history and tradition.[38] The choice
and arrangement of words are again deliberate, well-weighed and
telling.

In the remainder of this section of the sermon Donne locates
the idea of a model more directly in the human past. He connects
it with ancient forms and beliefs, with what Janel Mueller has
described as "the corporate 'memory' of the continuing body of
Christ," and also connects it with his own formative meditations,
at once his specific preparations for this sermon and the more
generally formative influences that he brought to these.[39] In this
vein he continues, "for to that Heaven which belongs to the
Catholique Church, I shall never come, except I go by way of the
Catholique Church, by former Idea's, former examples, former
patterns, To beleeve according to ancient beliefes, to pray according to ancient formes, to preach according to former meditations" (VII, 61). The association between *form* and *former*, between shaping idea and ancient tradition, informs the language of
this passage, linking its words and ideas together. The passage
concludes aptly and self-reflectively: "God does nothing, man
does nothing well, without these Idea's, these retrospects, this
recourse to pre-conceptions, pre-deliberations." What has pre-
figured the present utterance is properly formative.

In this sermon Donne addresses the relation of preconception
to practice and simultaneously effects it. Developing it as subject
and word, *res* and *verbum*, he paradoxically renders language
something quite other than an incidental or a transparent system

of notations. Many of his words are imbued with their own history, weight, significance, and mnemonic resonance. Etymology and association are operative in his choice and deployment of them, and, it appears, in the way he thought not merely about but with them. His focus on and enforcement of individual words and phrases conspicuously make of them conceptual and tangible phenomena—in short, substantial *res*, things opaque and self-sustaining. Like Andrewes, Donne may be fascinated by the etymology of biblical names, finding in them an indication of the natures to which they refer (as in *Adam*, "redness," or "red earth"), and he may consider biblical Greek and Syriac, like Hebrew, privileged languages in which the Holy Ghost has chosen to speak, at times iconically, but his own practice in English and Latin, the two languages in which he had special expertise and the dominant languages of his sermons, exhibits a working view of language more complexly fictive than simple Cratylism or Adamicism would suggest.[40] Insofar as words participate in ideas, he *makes* them do so.

Donne's emphasis in the second Prebend sermon on the relation of preconception to verbal practice is central to his working view and underlies his language throughout the sermon. He draws the verse for this sermon from Psalm 63.7, "Because thou hast been my helpe, therefore in the shadow of thy wings will I rejoyce," and finds in it "the whole compasse of Time, Past, Present, and Future" (VII, 52). With glances at the recent exile of Londoners from the city on account of plague, his exposition of the biblical text moves from present affliction, David's exile in the wilderness, to God's past help, which becomes the underlying pattern of His relation to the faithful, to the present assurance of future joy. Present, past, and future thus constitute the three main divisions of the sermon, whose overall movement he conceives with reference to God's circularity—His regularity, sameness, and presence at any moment of time.

The initial section, time present, centers on the Latin phrase

"*Pondus Gloriae*," or "weight of glory," which comes from 2 Corinthians 4.17 and introduces a sometimes dizzying consideration of lightness and heaviness. As Donne indicates, the image of a scale is implicit in the Latin phrase: "It is a blessed Metaphore, that the Holy Ghost hath put into the mouth of the Apostle, *Pondus Gloriae*, That our *afflictions* are but *light*, because there is an *exceeding*, and an *eternall waight of glory* attending them" (VII, 53). He continues, "If it were not for that exceeding waight of glory, no other waight in this world could turne the scale, or waigh downe those infinite waights of afflictions that oppresse us here." Thus our afflictions are light but their weight is infinite, and yet this is outweighed by the weight of glory: two substantially different kinds of weight, one oppressing, the other alleviating—literally "lightening." The latent pun resolves the apparent contradiction between an "infinite" weight and one greater.

But not for long, for "*David* and *Solomon* have cryed out, That all this world is *vanity*, and *levity*," lightness, and Mary Magdalen's "lightnesse" was a worldly weight, a burden, as are beauty and riches and all other worldly goods. Indeed, "All our life is a continuall burden" and worse, adding "waight to waight . . . is this, That still the best men have had most laid upon them," as witness Job and Christ, the latter first "made partaker of the glory of heaven, . . . made now the Sewer of all the corruption, of all the sinnes of this world, as no Sonne of God, but a meere man, as no man, but a contemptible worme" (VII, 54–55). For two pages the enumeration of life's burdens continues. Their multiplication and increasing length—the sheer weight of disheartening examples on the page—offer material evidence of human misery.

"But then there is *Pondus Gloriae, An exceeding waight of eternall glory*," the next paragraph begins, "and that turnes the scale; for as it makes all worldly prosperity as dung, so it makes all worldly adversity as feathers" (VII, 55). As the first reference to the *Pondus Gloriae* introduced the consideration of temporal afflictions, so renewed reference now frames this consideration on its further side. Where before the Latin phrase was labelled a metaphor, now it comes unannounced and in the nick of time to balance the burden of affliction. Again, as when first invoked, *Pondus Gloriae* lightens affliction, but this time its effect has an even more remarkable power, for "it makes all worldly adversity as feathers." Now its effect touches directly the wings under whose shadow the faithful will rejoice, the base text of this sermon. Simply by repeating *"Pondus Gloriae"* without any further introduction or even the definite article, by which an English syntax might appropriate the phrase, Donne treats the phrase itself and not just its signification as a token with weight of its own as well as transformative imaginative power.

The fact that *Pondus Gloriae* is Latin contributes notably to its impact. The familiarity of Latin in varying degrees to many in Donne's audience in St. Paul's would not have lessened the distinction of this non-English phrase in the context of English, and the recurrent glossing of the phrase, whether for comprehension or emphasis, serves to point it more. Nor would familiarity with Latin have lessened the economy and force of the phonically interlocking Latin words in comparison to their English equivalents. Latin tags and focuses the phrase more effectively than would English alone and makes it a more detachable, portable, memorable unit.

But the significance of Latin here goes beyond rhetorical utility. Its very presence suggests the ancient forms and beliefs, the corporate memory of the faithful, that Donne recommends as a model. Donne's readiness to employ and to diverge from the Latin Bible, moreover, indicates that Latin is not for him, any more than it was for Erasmus, the language of Scripture so much as of the experience of Scripture, of the interpretive and translational tradition and of enlightened human response to the inexhaustible source.[41] In an earlier chapter, I noted relevant associations of Latin with tradition and stability by Donne's contemporaries, insofar as it is a language "shrined vp in books . . . [and] made immortall by the register of memorie."[42] Donne's recurrent and emphatic use of Latin phrases might be said to translate life, as he conceives, shapes, and delivers it to the congregation, into another language, one that is not "extemporall," to recall his own word in this sermon, and therefore one that transcends present time.[43]

This point is important enough to clarify by reference to Donne's similar but more striking use of Latinity to translate meaning to a different register in another sermon. This instance, the most radical of several related ones in the following citation, involves the adversative conjunction *veruntamen*. Because *veruntamen* lacks the metaphoric, imagistic content of *pondus gloriae* and has no equivalent nominal potential, its failure to fit the grammar and syntax of its English sentence is even more graphic:

> Christ goes as far in the passion, in his agony, and he comes to a passionate deprecation, in his *Tristis anima*, and in the *Si possibile*, and in the *Transeat calix*. But as all these passions were sanctified in the roote, from which no bitter leafe, no crooked twig could spring, so they were instantly washed with his *Veruntamen*, a present and a full submitting of all to Gods pleasure, *Yet not my will O Father, but thine be done*. (IV, 328)

Preaching this time at Whitehall, Donne can assume his dominant audience's familiarity both with Latin and with the Latin Bible, and yet his treatment of *"Veruntamen"* without direct, immediate translation into English exaggerates its independence, virtually hypostatizing it into the kind of allegorical figure a Langland might animate.[44] Try substituting a noun like *blood* for *Veruntamen* in the clause "washed with his *Veruntamen*," and the impression disappears that the word *Veruntamen* itself is symbolic, rather than simply its gist. Substitute the literal translation "But yet" or even "Nevertheless" for *Veruntamen*, and the efficacious substance of the word itself evaporates into nonsense or incongruity. Through the use of Latin Donne textualizes and, more exactly, verbalizes our comprehension.

Although it is a less radical case of such verbal transformation, *Pondus Gloriae* is a more complex and an imaginatively weighter one, precisely because it does have metaphoric, imagistic content. In the next and best-known part of the second Prebend sermon, Donne's dramatization of an affliction that borders on despair, its weight is crucial. Here Donne plays a precarious game, offsetting the most burdensome account of spiritual misery he can muster only by the *Pondus Gloriae*. His account, a paragraph of 38 lines, has the nature of an inset. It starts with a sudden switch into dramatic soliloquy, which, when performed, would have to have been preceded by a significant pause and an adjustment of face and voice. The paragraph that directly follows this soliloquy opens by commenting upon it: "This is the fearefull depth, this is spirituall misery, to be thus fallen from God" (VII, 57). Stepping out of the inset and distancing it, the preacher makes sure we see it as a dramatized exemplum.[45]

The opening of the inset signals that Donne is striking a pose, literally "placing" an attitude and embodying a rhetorical topos, in this case, affliction. It consists of a single long sentence on temporal affliction that is unhurried in its expansivenesss and secure in its pronounced, rhythmic symmetries of syntax and alliteration:

> Let me wither and weare out mine age in a discomfortable, in an unwholesome, in a penurious prison, and so pay my debts with my bones, and recompence the wastfulnesse of my youth, with the beggery of mine age; Let me wither in a spittle under sharpe, and foule, and infamous diseases, and so recompence the wantonnesse of my youth, with that loathsomnesse in mine age; yet, if God with-draw not his spirituall blessings, his Grace, his Patience, If I can call my suffering his Doing, my passion his Action, All this that is temporall, is but a caterpiller got into one corner of my garden, but a mill-dew fallen upon one acre of my Corne; The

body of all, the substance of all is safe, as long as the soule is safe. (VII, 56)

Strategically placed near the end of the sentence, the mildew and the caterpillar do not merely minimize temporal affliction; they transform it. These images are self-consciously artful, even playful, so much so that they suggest pastoralism. Seen through them temporal affliction is contained, reinterpreted, and a little unreal.

But the second sentence of the inset, constituting more than two-thirds of it, shifts from temporal to spiritual affliction and witnesses a marked change from easy assurance to urgency and fear:

> But when I shall trust to that, which wee call a good spirit, and God shall deject, and empoverish, and evacuate that spirit, when I shall rely upon a morall constancy, and God shall shake, and enfeeble, and enervate, destroy and demolish that constancy; when I shall think to refresh my selfe in the serenity and sweet ayre of a good conscience, and God shall call up the damps and vapours of hell it selfe, and spread a cloud of diffidence, and an impenetrable crust of desperation upon my conscience; when health shall flie from me, and I shall lay hold upon riches to succour me, and comfort me in my sicknesse, and riches shall flie from me, and I shall snatch after favour, and good opinion, to comfort me in my poverty; when even this good opinion shall leave me, and calumnies and misinformations shall prevaile against me; *when I shall need peace, because there is none but thou, O Lord, that should stand for me, and then shall finde, that all the wounds that I have, come from thy hand, all the arrowes that stick in me, from thy quiver*; when I shall see, that because I have given my selfe to my corrupt nature, thou hast changed thine; and because I am all evill towards thee, therefore thou hast given over being good towards me . . . (VII, 56–57; my emphasis)

The pace of successive clauses quickens until the cry "O Lord, that should stand for me" comes like a realization forced out of the speaker. This outcry defies rational syntax in order to redirect the clause in which it arises from the need of peace in the face of mounting worldly losses to the pain whose underlying cause is God. The immediacy of the cry itself "O Lord" is further enforced by the presence of the verb *should* or "ought to," which simultaneously asserts obligation and registers doubt.

We are never allowed to forget that the inset is art, however. The speaker's cry is self-consciously *like* a cry, a simulation of one that is framed by the regular recurrence of the future tense: "when I shall trust," "when I shall think," "when I shall need," "when I shall see." It is also followed directly by imagery that reasserts the presence of art: "all the wounds that I have, come from thy hand, all the arrowes that stick in me from thy quiver." This art derives from that of the Psalmist and specifically dramatizes the second verse of Psalm 38, one of Donne's favorites: "For thine arrows stick fast in me, and thy hand presseth me sore."[46] The seven temporal clauses in the present quotation remain oratorical as well. Marked rhythmic balance continues throughout them, although it becomes less pronounced after roughly their first half when the alliteration similarly diminishes.

The final portion of the inset, which adds a last temporal clause and concludes in two main clauses, most concerns us. Both main clauses weigh in on the side of affliction. In the first, God is the knowledgeable agent; in the second, we are the desperately helpless subjects and only "that *pondus gloriae*" in God's hand stands between us and total destruction:

> When it comes to this height, that the fever is not in the humors, but in the spirits, that mine enemy is not an imaginary enemy, fortune, nor a transitory enemy, malice in great persons, but a reall, and an irresistible, and an inexorable, and an everlasting enemy, The Lord of Hosts himselfe, The Almighty God himselfe, the Almighty God himselfe onely knowes the waight of this affliction, and except hee put in that *pondus gloriae*, that exceeding waight of an eternall glory, with his owne hand, into the other

scale, we are waighed downe, we are swallowed up, irreparably, irrevocably, irrecoverably, irremediably. (VII, 57)

As we have seen, the ensuing paragraph, which closes and effectively restricts the drama of this performance, also makes clear that its point is fear and spiritual misery. The weight of these is to be recognized and felt in the inset's conclusion and is not to be denied, diminished, or simply outweighed. Yet this carefully contrived sermon hardly slams the door on the spiritually afflicted, now broadened by the plural pronoun "we" to include us all. The word's promise, although conditional, subordinate, and seeming unlikely to be fulfilled, perceptibly lingers: "and except hee put in that *pondus gloriae*, that exceeding waight of an eternall glory, with his owne hand, into the other scale." Except.

The Latin phrase *"pondus gloriae"* and its reemphasizing gloss occur here for the third time in the sermon and for the second time as the redeeming alternative to an extensively exhibited burden of affliction. For the first time, however, its metaphorical content is fully exploited. Generating the metaphor of the scale, *pondus gloriae* controls the image in which the inset concludes, the balance in which the issue hangs, and the scriptural terms in which the experience is interpreted and understood. The Latinity of this phrase, its reemphasizing gloss, and its efficacy in earlier passages, moreover, all carry some weight of a significantly different, more conceptual or more purely verbal sort from the sheer mass — the bulky weight — of affliction preceding it. The demonstrative adjective "that," which introduces *"pondus gloriae"* and, in a second occurrence, its gloss, asserts the familiarity and substance of earlier uses of the Latin phrase, although appropriately at this juncture also their distance from the afflicted speaker (*"that pondus gloriae,"* not *this* one).

Of course the power of God in the inset's conclusion ensures the power of *pondus gloriae* to offset affliction. The infinitely powerful God who afflicts has equal power to relieve, reaching "that *pondus gloriae* . . . with his owne hand" and putting it into the scale of salvation.[47] The four heavily alliterating adverbs at the end of the inset, so overwhelmingly engulfing in the urgent voice of affliction, similarly cut two ways. Each of the four communicates hopelessness, but like the word *hopeless* itself, each is posited on the viability of the positive quality whose absence it observes; that is, hopelessness is posited on the possibility of hope, and a person uncalled must be in some sense callable, as even Calvin recognized.

Each adverb — "irreparably, irrevocably, irrecoverably, irremediably" — is painstakingly chosen, on the basis of its etymological roots, to resonate with the positive qualities of Christian redemption that the speaker's feeling of desperation nearly denies. *Irreparable*, Latin *irreparabilis*, derives from *re* + *paro*, negatived, and literally means "un*renew*able," "un*reviv*able"; *irrevocable*, Latin *irrevocabilis*, from *re* + *vocare*, negatived, means "un*recall*able"; *irrecoverable*, which derives from Latin *recuperare*, or *re* + *capere*, negatived, means "un*recup*erable," "un*obtain*able," "un*reviv*able"; and *irremediable*, Latin *irremediabilis*, from *remediare*, or *re* + *mederi*, negatived, means "in*cur*able," "*remedi*less." Renewal or new life, a call or summons, recovery, healing, or salvation — one could hardly assemble a list carrying stronger positive associations with Scripture and its interpretive tradition. These positive nuances contrast with the burden of meaning that otherwise equivalent words like *eternally* or *damnably* or even *irresistibly* would carry in the same context. They might instead be compared to the multiple verbal ironies in Herbert's poem "The Collar," which "At every [wilde] worde," including the title, calls the wayward speaker back to himself and his relation to God.[48] In conjunction with "that *pondus gloriae*" still within reach of God's "owne hand," the redemptive ironies of Donne's desperate adverbs recall the possibility of a saving plan. Like almost everything else written in the sermon, they belong to the "pre-conceptions, fore-imaginations, designes, and patterns proposed to . . . [the maker] beforehand." They suggest both the extent to which

Donne's sermons were premeditated, especially in their final, written form, and the extent to which Latin is a substratum of their thought, a tie to the former, formative patterns that make up the corporate memory of the Church.

The second division of the sermon, time past, makes more explicit its concern with language and particularly with composition. The preconceived model Donne now recommends is "a copy to write by, a patterne to worke by, a rule, or an example to proceed by" (VII, 60). While the word *copy* means "pattern" or "example," it also invokes its traditional association with rhetoric and words themselves (*copia*). Our copious pattern or model is to be "Gods former wayes" with us and, more exactly, what we "*have seene* and *heard*, and *read*" (VII, 60, 62). Again this "copy" is dominantly verbal, consisting chiefly of the reception and comprehension of Scripture through reading and preaching. Its further exposition develops from the observation that Hebrew, "That language in which God spake to man . . . hath no present tense," relying instead on the past or, more exactly, the past perfect (VII, 62). The grammar of a language that is itself retrospective, backward-looking and memory-like, thus provides the copy for our writing and the rule and reason of all our actions.

This grammar corresponds, however, to the creative working of God and thereby ensures the ultimate coincidence of *verba* with *res*. God works according to "an eternall pre-conception, an eternall Idea, in himselfe" beforehand: "Of which Ideaes, that is, pre-conceptions, pre-determinations in God, S. *Augustine* pronounces, *Tanta vis in Ideis constituitur*, There is so much truth, and so much power in these Ideaes as that without acknowledging them, no man can acknowledge God, for he does not allow God Counsaile, and Wisdome, and deliberation in his Actions, but sets God on worke, before he have thought what he will doe" (VII, 60). This divine model is basic to Donne's conception of meaning, and in order to validate it he sides with Augustinian readings of two biblical passages against those of his own church. Thus Augustine and other Fathers

> read that place, (which we read otherwise) *Quod factum est, in ipso vita erat*; that is, in all their Expositions, whatsoever is made, in time, was alive in God, before it was made, that is, in that eternall Idea, and patterne which was in him. So also doe divers of those Fathers read those words to the Hebrews, (which we read, *The things that are seene, are not made of things that doe appeare*) *Ex invisibilibus visibilia facta sunt, Things formerly invisible, were made visible*; that is, we see them not till now, till they are made, but they had an invisible being, in that Idea, in that pre-notion, in that purpose of God before, for ever before. (VII, 60–61)

The Latin quotations in this passage subsequently feed, like "fore-conceits," into Donne's own diction; for example, into the key sentence cited earlier that concludes this stage of the discussion: "God does nothing, man does nothing well, without these Idea's, these retrospects, this recourse to pre-conceptions, pre-deliberations" (VII, 61). *Pre-conceptions*, literally "before-engenderings," or, more loosely, "before births," recalls the *invisibilia* "alive in God" before they were created, as Donne renders Augustine's "in ipso vita erat."

In the same passage, *pre-deliberations*, both unique in the discussion of models to this point and emphatic as its weighted conclusion, glances still more retrospectively toward the crucial image of the scale in the sermon's first section. *Deliberation* (Latin *deliberatio*) derives from *de* + *librare*, "to weigh well," and thence from *libra*, or "balance," "pair of scales." The weighting of diction in Donne's lengthy sermons and its orientation to a preconceived idea is often uncanny. Here, the backward glance of *pre-deliberations* enacts the retrospection to the biblical model the sermon recommends for our writing.

Taking *pre-deliberations* as my example, I would linger over the extent to which Donne's emphasizing the word is a radically verbal event, as distinct from the imagistic phenomena our culture favors. Typographically, *pre-deliberations* is the last word in a paragraph, as well as rhetorically the last in the presentation of a topic. In addition, phonic repetition and rhythm heighten its stress. The three paragraphs preceding its appearance, like the sentence it culminates, are full of rhythmically and phonically reiterative sequences of synonyms, appositives, and other amplifiers: for example, "the copy, the patterne, the precedent"; "pre-conceptions, fore-imaginations, designes, and patterns proposed to our selves beforehand"; "Of which Ideaes, that is, preconceptions, pre-determinations in God, S. *Augustine* pronounces . . ." The reiteration of the letter *p* and specifically of the prefix *pre* is reinforced by that of other sounds, like the suffix *ion* and the letter *d* within the same sequences and by the persistent recurrence of the same sounds outside these. Other words resembling *pre-deliberations*, such as *pre-determinations*, *predetermined*, and *deliberation* itself, similarly prepare for the culminating appearance of this word and render its emphasis perceptible.

"Pre-deliberations," particularly God's, echoing "pre-determinations" and recalling a balance or scale, look forward as well as back. In the context of judgment that the sermon's scales have established, prior deliberations and determinations readily imply the idea of election, to which the sermon soon turns. When this pre-dictable subject emerges explicitly, however, it is, unlike the earlier, near-desperate image of the scale, found to be reassuring: "God had thee, before he made thee; He loved thee first, and then created thee" (VII, 63). Backing away from the hint of a Calvinistic theory of predetermined damnation, it rights the balance.

Concluding the consideration of time past, the second division of the sermon, Donne attends more directly to his base text, specifically glossing the word *help* in its opening clause: *"Because thou hast beene my helpe."* Handling a theologically hot topic gingerly, he argues the relation of human willingness to God's pre-conceptions: while "All inchoations and consummations, beginnings and perfectings are of God, of God alone[,] . . . there is a concurrence on our part" (VII, 64). Aided by God's "Auxiliant graces, Helping graces," even as we help ourselves, we nonetheless "cannot looke for his helpe, except" we help ourselves also (VII, 63). As before in this section, Donne swings his topic around to utterance and conveniently discovers in David's praise, which provides this sermon's base text, the model of human interaction with the divine: "*Lord open thou my lips,* sayes *David*; that is Gods worke intirely; And then, *My mouth, My mouth shall shew forth thy praise*; there enters *David* into the worke with God. And then, sayes God to him, *Dilata os tuum, Open thy mouth,* (It is now made *Thy mouth,* and therefore doe thou open it) *and I will fill it*" (VII, 64).

An awareness of language as a medium is never far distant in Donne's sermons. In the passages just cited, for example, it is evident in the ostentatiously Latinate diction that operates again and again as a running gloss and concurrent translation—a kind of instant transformation—of words more simply native or native-sounding. Graces are both "Auxiliant," from Latin *auxiliant-em,* and "helping," from Old English *helpan*; then "inchoations," from Latin *inchoation-em,* and "consummations," from Latin *consummation-em,* are counterpoised by "beginnings," from Old English *beginnan,* and "perfectings." Although "perfectings" is Latin in origin (*perfectus*), its suffix *-ing* is pure English, and arguably in this context, where "perfectings" is paired with "beginnings" and played off "consummations," it does not sound Latinate, an impression that the substitution of the Latinate form *perfections* for it tends to confirm. Other instances of bilingual doublets abound in Donne's sermons and may have resulted either from habit or deliberate technique. They could be explained as the accident of a sensitivity to sound or rhythm or as the product of a mind deeply influenced by the Renaissance practice of double translation (Latin to English to Latin) in language training. Yet this habit of doubling also correlates with larger movements and more clearly deliberated effects in the sermons, for example, the use of Latin words and phrases as graphic tokens. Like *pondus gloriae*, bilingual doubling, too, does its small part in the present sermon to textualize life by translating it into another language.

In the final division of the sermon, Donne turns to the future and to the main clause of his base text, "*therefore in the shadow of thy wings will I rejoyce.*" Here he first describes the kind of "refreshing," of "respiration" (another pair of English-Latin derivatives), to be found "*In velamento alarum,* under the shadow of Gods wings" (VII, 64). This is not to be a total invulnerability but, according to the "Metaphore in this Text, (*Sub umbra alarum, In the shadow of thy wings*) . . . a refreshing and consolation" (VII, 65–66). Within a page of one another, he thus cites two Latin variants of the prepositional phrase in his base text — the first, the Vulgate's *in velamento alarum* and the second, Sebastian Munster's "unique reading," *sub umbra alarum.*[49]

Oddly, Donne, who had Hebrew, cites these variants without either examining or remarking their difference or citing the Hebrew original, as he frequently does elsewhere in the sermons. It is therefore unlikely that accuracy of translation or of the manuscript tradition accounts for their presence. In view of his divergence from nonessential readings of the authorized version elsewhere, including this sermon, an unexpressed desire on his part to buttress the authorized English of his base text by the Vulgate's *in* and Munster's *umbra* is similarly implausible, since the Vulgate's *in* would have proved less a help than its *velamento,* or "covering," a hindrance. Although the unremarked presence of these variants reflects a sophisticated assumption of instability in the translational layers of the biblical text and again highlights the preacher's mediation, further motivation of it seems likely in a sermon as deliberately plotted and as attuned to Latin as this one.[50]

The alternative prepositions, *in* and *sub*, appear to make little difference, however. In citing them initially Donne exchanges their meanings, glossing *in* as "under" and *sub* as "in," as if to indicate their interchangeability, which is not without warrant in Latin. When *sub umbra alarum* is subsequently cited alone, he translates it "under," and in the last two iterations of the Psalmist's phrase, which come exclusively in English, he simply alternates between *in* and *under* (VII, 67–69). The gratuitousness of the word *velamento* is of more interest. Donne's argument neither requires nor openly exploits this word, and yet his inclusion of it suggests its formative role in what he is saying. In contrast to the *Pondus Gloriae*, *velamento* is a small if also noticeable matter in the sermon and perhaps the more significant precisely for this reason. I will return to it in treating Donne's conclusion, where it affords a remarkable instance of the thoroughness with which the graphically emphatic words of these sermons were preconceived and their subject matter textualized.

In the sermon's final stage, Donne urges his listeners actively to cultivate the joy that arises from "a religious Constancy," in God, a refreshing in "the shadow of his Wings" (VII, 68). Comparing the two hemispheres of this world to joy and glory, in turn conceived as the two hemispheres of heaven, he endeavors to make heaven seem close, spatially real, and even habitable in the present: "And as of those two Hemisphears of the world, the first hath beene knowne long before, but the other, (that of America, which is the richer in treasure) God reserved for later Discoveries; so though he reserve that Hemisphear of heaven, which is the Glory thereof, to the Resurrection, yet the other Hemisphear, the Joy of heaven, God opens to our Discovery, and delivers for our habitation even whilst we dwell in this world" (VII, 69).

Further developing the possibility of active movement from an earthly to a heavenly condition, the speaker (whose passage into a more dramatic role my shift in terminology acknowledges) returns through allusion to his base text, twice asking, in the Psalmist's words, *"Why art thou cast downe O my soule?"* and then remembering, "No man is so little, as that he can be lost under these wings, no man is so great, as that they cannot reach to him" (VII, 70). In the final moments of the sermon, "these wings" and two lines later "his Wings" and "those wings" become the vehicle of imaginative movement from an earthly to a heavenly joy.

Associatively, the speaker turns next to "The Holy Ghost, who is a Dove, [and] shadowed the whole world under his wings; *Incubabat aquis*, He hovered over the waters, he sate upon the waters, and he hatched all that was produced, and all that was produced so, was good" (VII, 70). Here Donne uses either the unique Tremellius-Junius translation of Genesis 1.2, as Mueller suggests, or an interpretive reading by St. Jerome, which differs from the Vulgate and which Donne discusses in greater detail in a later sermon.[51] In either case, his selection of the Latin verb *incubabat* shows a care that its English gloss accentuates: "He hovered over . . . he sate upon . . . he hatched" what was brought forth. Aside from the sheer fact of emphasis, operating here as a kind of *verbal* presence, the fertile act is what engages the speaker. This is further realized in the next sentence, where Donne, like Milton after him, would have the Holy Ghost brood over each member of his audience, as once over the primal waters: "Be thou a Mother," the speaker urges, "where the Holy Ghost would be a Father; Conceive by him; and be content that he produce joy in thy heart" (VII, 70). *Conceive*, like its earlier cognate *(pre)conceptions*, carries both the meaning "produce," as the reference to motherhood indicates, and the meaning "imagine, experience, or apprehend," as the reference to joy suggests and the immediately following sentence makes explicit. "First thinke," this sentence begins, and its successor continues, "And then thinke also." The remainder of the sermon now becomes the conception inspired in speaker and audience by the Holy Ghost — the thoughts, that is, they thus conceive.

As so often in Donne's writing, wordplay operates as a springboard for imaginative flight. The first exhortation to think ends in a pun: "God would not give . . . [a man] his physick, God would not study his cure, if he cared not for him." Latin *cura*, "care," underlies the word *cure* and affirms the relation of correction and love, affliction and affection. The second exhortation, to "thinke also," leads through antitheses to continuities, through the pairing of "howling" and "singing," "noyse" and "voyce," "hell" and "heaven" to the contrasting rhythm of a sentence showing that "true joy in this world shall flow into the joy of Heaven, as a River flowes into the Sea" (VII, 70). This exhortation passes unobtrusively into the sermon's second inset, which, unlike the first, is not framed and set off from its surroundings. Instead it follows immediately on the last phrase quoted: thus "as a River flowes into the Sea; This joy shall not be put out in death, and a new joy kindled in me in Heaven." This time the shift to a first person pronoun, "me," is almost unnoticed and would not demand a framing pause for effective delivery. This time, moreover, the inset ends not with a distancing technique, a reference to itself as a performance, but with the word "Amen," in the immediate presence of the congregation.

Remarkably, the word *conceive*, which produces movement into the inset, now recurs within it when the speaker describes his soul's ascent to heaven:

> This joy shall not be put out in death, and a new joy kindled in me in Heaven; But as my soule, as soone as it is out of my body, is in Heaven, and does not stay for the possession of Heaven, nor for the fruition of the sight of God, till it be ascended through ayre, and fire, and Moone, and Sun, and Planets, and Firmament, to that place which we *conceive* to be Heaven, but without the thousandth part of a minutes stop, as soone as it issues, is in a glorious

light, which is Heaven, (for all the way to Heaven is Heaven; And as those Angels, which came from Heaven hither, bring Heaven with them, and are in Heaven here, So that soule that goes to Heaven, meets Heaven here; and as those Angels doe not devest Heaven by comming, so these soules invest Heaven, in their going.) As my soule shall not goe towards Heaven, but goe by Heaven to Heaven, to the Heaven of Heavens, So the true joy of a good soule in this world is the very joy of Heaven . . . (VII, 70–71; my emphasis)

Just when the conception in these lines occurs, here and now or during the soul's actual ascent, and just what the relation of inner conception to outer place might be in them is unclear or "undistinguish'd," to borrow a word from Donne's "Second Anniversarie" that belongs to a strikingly similar enactment of elation.[52] Donne's own former conceptions obviously count as well as the Bible's.

Like the handling of spiritual affliction in the sermon's earlier inset, the soul's ascent in this one consists of a single astonishingly long sentence (thirteen lines beyond what I have quoted). But instead of the relentless reiteration of eight temporal clauses, each beginning with the word *when* ("when I shall trust," "when I shall think," etc.), in the soul's expansive ascent there are speed and variety: "But . . . as soone . . . nor . . . till . . . through . . . to that place . . . but without . . . as soone . . ." Many of these varied connectives are adverbs and prepositions that indicate time and place but that are employed in the service of instantaneity—a speed immeasurable by space and time and therefore inexpressible in the syntax of human speech. Whereas in the first inset numerous temporal clauses take on an oppressive and cumulative weight in their sameness (when . . . when . . . when), the phrases and clauses of the present inset intimate forward movement even while asserting immediate presence. A paraphrase of them, stripped of negative amplification, amounts to a single statement, twice reinforced: "immediately my soul is in heaven; it waits not to get there but is there right away." The speaker's negative amplification, an account of what the soul does not experience or do, is particularly effective when the soul does not stay "till it be ascended through ayre, and fire, and Moone, and Sun, and Planets, and Firmament"; his rhetoric sustains a sense of movement while denying it and defers arrival even while conveying its speed. Here Donne graphically takes time and space to affirm their inadequacy to his conception. Although otherwise invested, Jonson's negative way comes again to mind, as does Calvin's dictum that "humanly devised symbols . . . are images of things absent rather than marks of things present."[53]

Primarily, of course, Donne's speaker postpones arrival in order to enable the imaginative conception of its immediate joy. Consider, for example, how the following steps defer the fulfilling of his initial assertion that "my soule, as soone as it is out of my body, is in Heaven": "but," he first explains, "without the thousandth part of a minutes stop" and then adds re-emphatically, "as soone as it issues"; next he elaborates, "is in a glorious light," and finally and subordinately concludes, as if to understate the possibility of conclusion, "which is Heaven." The speaker's final relative clause, his arrival, becomes almost an unnoticed appendage, as syntactical rearrangement ("is in Heaven, which is a glorious light") would illustrate.

The parenthesis that directly follows this second, amplified arrival in heaven reveals the speaker's desire to sustain the sense of arrival still longer while simultaneously showing his necessary withdrawal from it: "(for all the way to Heaven is Heaven; And as those Angels, which came from Heaven hither, bring Heaven with them, and are in Heaven here, So that soule that goes to Heaven, meets Heaven here; and as those Angels doe not devest Heaven by comming, so these soules invest Heaven, in their going.)" Initially the parenthesis prolongs elation but in the course of its extended explanations and comparisons, the visionary impulse begins to subside, as it similarly does in the "Second Anniversarie."

Perhaps the single most striking fact about the present inset is the recurrence of the one word *heaven* — twenty times in the fourteen lines I have cited. The sheer insistent verbalism of this performance is extraordinary, and it is reinforced by the negative amplification that conveys reality by words that cannot convey it. Although these words have material referents — moon and sun, a minute's stop, a light — these are not their point or finally their meaning. They are made instead to be the medium of an immaterial idea: speed undistinguished, time immeasurable, luminous glory inexpressible.

Repeating the word *heaven* and surrounding it with amplifications, Donne attempts with English alone what he more often achieves with the help of Latin: namely, to give heaven substantial existence, at least as a word. Renaissance rhetorics accommodate the rudiments of a similar conception, of which Thomas Wilson's affords a trenchant example. Wilson describes a kind of amplification that "resteth in wordes." Ordinarily these are words "of great weight, wherein either is some Metaphore, or els some large vnderstanding . . . conteined"; ideally, they "fill the mouth and haue a sound" to them. "And sometimes," Wilson adds, his verbal imagination clearly falling short of Donne's twenty repetitions of *heaven*, "wordes twise spoken, make the matter appeare greater."[54] Agrippa's understanding of "iteration" as a factor in the perdurance and perfection of speech and especially of writing affords additional context, as do even Homer's "winged words," whether recalled from a fable by Rabelais or a Baconian allusion serving intellectual reform. In Donne's final inset words as realizations of understanding but also simply as words become a distinct kind of meaning, a self-sustaining level of symbolism, that seeks to translate "heaven here," as Donne twice puts it.

In its close, the second inset carries a reminder of the word *velamento*, "covering," and by extension "garment" or "veil," which appears so gratuitously at the outset of this final division of the sermon. A memory of *velamento* is incipient earlier in the inset in the noticeably paired words *devest* and *invest*, "put off" and "don," both of which derive from Latin *vestire*, "to cover with a garment, to clothe." It takes more explicit shape in the sermon's final lines, which describe positively the joy "that shall passe up, and put on a more *glorious garment* above, and be joy *super-invested* in glory" (VII, 71; my emphasis).

The word *super-invest* appears to be Donne's coinage from Latin *super*, "above, over and above, beyond," plus Latin *in* and, again, *vestire*, "to cover with a garment, to clothe." *Super-invest* is a coinage that attracts Donne. In *Devotions Vpon Emergent Occasions*, published two years before he preached the second Prebend sermon, he had written similarly of the general Resurrection: "Then wee shall all bee invested, reapparelled in our owne *bodies*; but they who have made just use of their former *dayes*, [shall] be super-invested with *glorie*; whereas the others, condemned to their *olde clothes*, their *sinfull bodies*, shall have *Nothing* added, but *immortalitie* to *torment*."[55] Again the tie to clothing, literally present in the root-form of *invest*, is not only evident but openly much on Donne's mind, as we have seen it to be in the sermon at hand when he combines *garment* (a word of Germanic origin, via Old French) with the reinforcing Latinate form *super-invested*.[56]

In Thomas's Latin-English lexicon, a standard reference work in Donne's time, *velamentum*, "covering," is equated with its cognate *velamen*, "covering, clothing, garment," both Latin words deriving from *velare*, "to cover." The two nouns, in fact, receive from Thomas a single entry and definition, which reads in part, "a covering, a garment, a veile." Like Thomas, Donne evidently considered the two nouns interchangeable. In a sermon written seven years before the second Prebend sermon, for example, he glosses Jerome's "*sub velamento*," as "clothed": "*sed novi Deum sub velamento carnis latentem* . . . but I know where there is a God clothed in mans flesh, and that person cannot die" (II, 207). In the second Prebend sermon, the cognates *velamentum* and *velamen*, "covering, clothing, garment," seem to merge with the word *vestire*, "to cover with a garment, to clothe," and its cognate *vestis*, "clothing" or "vesture." Although *velamentum* and *vestio* are not now thought to be etymologically related, they are obviously linked by sound and meaning, sufficient evidence of relationship by Minsheu's lights. The linkage by meaning in the sermon, moreover, appears to be the product of a predeliberated attention to verbal root-forms and literal meanings, in this case those of *devest*, *invest*, and *super-invest*, all of which occur in roughly the last sixteen lines of the sermon. In small, the words *velamento* and *super-invest*, which appear unobtrusively at the beginning and end of the sermon's last division, contain between them the relation of the covering wings to investiture in heaven and the relation of rejoicing *in velamento alarum* to heavenly joy.

Never, perhaps, did Coleridge's characterization of Donne's writing as "meaning's press and screw" apply more aptly than to this sermon, and I would not imagine that the intricate details of its verbal subtlety would be accessible to an auditor or a casual reader.[57] We have reason to suppose, however, that Donne was a reasonably successful preacher in various pulpits and that the written version of his sermons resembles them spoken. Although drama can be inferred in his delivery of the sermons, we have to assume a considerable level of verbal comprehension and appreciation by his audiences (as, indeed, by Shakespeare's). The distracting image of John Donne the canonical coterie poet notwithstanding, the sermons are historical, relatively popular documents, whose relevance to the popular drama is as readily demonstrated as that of Andrewes's work, and even more than his they testify to a remarkable awareness of words.[58]

Izaak Walton's *Life of Donne* reports that Donne ordinarily spent the better part of the preceding week readying each sermon: "for as he usually preached once a week, if not oftner, so after his Sermon he never gave his eyes rest, till he had chosen out a new Text, and that night cast his Sermon into a form, and his Text into divisions; and the next day he betook himself to consult the Fathers, and so commit his meditations to his memory, which was excellent. But upon Saturday he usually gave himself and his mind a rest from the weary burthen of his weeks meditations" (p. 67). Donne had additional opportunities for reflection on the base texts of his Prebend sermons, since, as a Prebendary of St. Paul's Cathedral, he was required to recite daily a portion of the five Psalms assigned to him, and from these Psalms he selected each of his Prebend texts.

Analysis of Donne's textual practice exhibits verbal procedures and associations underlying the sermons and therefore traces of the structure of thought that produced them. These suggest what the meditation, mnemonic keying, reconsideration, and final re-casting that Donne himself and his biographers ascribe to his preparation actually meant, and they especially bring home the far-reaching linguistic and perceptual implications of the simultaneous awareness of English and Latin words that characterizes educated writing in the period. But again, perhaps most strikingly, these "pressings and screwings" make *the awareness of words themselves* as a meaningful and substantial medium almost seem real.

Donne's Final Word or Last Character: Life Lived and Life Written

When Donne undertook "Deaths Duell," his last sermon, he had even more particular and unusual opportunities for reflection than in his Prebend sermons, and "Deaths Duell" surpasses even their verbal claims. According to Walton, Donne, weakened by his fatal illness, returned to London specifically to preach this, *"his own Funeral Sermon,"* or as Walton explains, "to discharge his memory of his preconceived meditations, which were of dying" (p. 75). Not surprisingly for a seventeenth-century divine, Donne seems to have spent the closing months of his illness meditating on holy dying, yet the extent to which he planned and virtually orchestrated his death exceeds normal expectations. Most famous is his posing for a funeral portrait in his own winding-sheet, his body rising from the funeral urn as if to enact the resurrection of the body, his head turned symbolically " 'toward the East, from whence he expected the second coming of his and our Saviour Jesus.' "[59] His preparation for the end becomes his "nightly meditation," and the funeral portrait his "hourly object" (pp. 76, 78). When he dies, Walton reports, "he closed his own eyes; and then disposed his hands and body into such a posture, as required not the least alteration by those that came to shroud him" (pp. 81–82).[60]

Donne's sermons and *Devotions* indicate that he had been thinking about such exemplary and symbolic gestures for a long time.[61] Crucial among these, "Deaths Duell" is at once the culmination of his role as a preacher and a radically verbal gesture of self-characterization in every sense of the word *character*: representation, inscribed symbol, and definitive biographical form. In this sermon, he enters words and texts as if actually to become one with them and thence with the Word. To an amazingly literal extent, words — as such and in themselves — become the final, defining expression and extension of his life and being. They are his bid to abolish the borders of *verba* and *res* and to assert ultimate control over his own meaning. The introduction and conclusion of the sermon, which I propose to examine in detail, offer a conceptual frame for his effort to make of life and text, of character and characterizing form, a single entity.

Like the second Prebend sermon, "Deaths Duell" treats a verse drawn from the the Book of Psalms, which Donne held in special regard because he saw in it the essence of Scripture. This time his text is the end of the twentieth verse of Psalm 68: "*And Unto God The Lord Belong The Issues Of Death. i.e. From Death.*"[62] From the beginning Donne cites the final prepositional phrase of his text conspicuously in two English versions, first the Geneva translation "of death" and second the authorized translation "from death." Within the first twenty lines of the sermon, moreover, he twice again emphasizes the openness of his text to interpretation. He refers to "three divers acceptations of the words" of his text among its expositors and then describes the authorized version as "the most obvious and most ordinary acceptation of these words" (X, 230).

For most modern readers, the interpretive openness of Donne's text is unexpected. Intuitively, most see in the word *issues* the meaning "outcomes" or even "questions," rather than the more literal "outgoings," "egresses," or "exits."[63] Although the basic meaning "outgoings" is as available to us as to the seventeenth century, our culture tends to deliteralize and abstract the word where context allows it, as here to distance *issues* from its Latin roots, *ex*, "out," and *ire*, "to go." Donne's method is just the opposite in this sermon: the entire base text, not just parts of it, recurs with slight variations seventeen times, in five of which the Latin "*Domini Domini sunt exitus mortis*" reduplicates and reemphasizes the English. Additionally, of course, the single phrase "*exitus mortis*" with its English equivalent "issue(s) of death" recurs better than another half dozen times and is further reinforced by variations on it, also repeated, such as "*exitus à morte.*" More exclusively and insistently than is usual even for Donne, the base text becomes in whole and in part a tag and refrain, throughout the sermon a recurrent platform of meaning.

More exactly, Donne fixes on the word *issues* itself—issues variously from, in, and by or through death—as the sermon's center and effectual idea. It is not on the static nothingness of death or even on death itself that his attention rivets but on the goings, passings, and flowings out, the passages from one state to another. He understands these passages in terms of both living and writing, of existence and words, as is evident in one of the best-known examples from the sermon: "As the first part of a sentence peeces wel with the last, and never respects . . . the parenthesis that comes betweene, so doth a good life here flowe into an eternall life, without any consideration, what manner of death wee dye" (X, 241).[64]

The sermon begins with an architectural image that gives a visual shape and causal function to the base text and asks for our rational assent to the paradox that God is the God of salvation and hence of life precisely *because* He is the God of death, or the issues of death. Carefully establishing the image upon which the sermon will build, Donne first explains that "Buildings stand by the benefit of their foundations that susteine and support them, and of their butteresses that comprehend and embrace them, and of their contignations [or joinings of beams and boards] that knit and unite them." A building sustained, comprehended, embraced, and united implies human relevance and anticipates Donne's identification, a sentence later, of the main body of the building that concerns him. He identifies this building as the "former part" of the verse from which he has drawn his base text, namely "*hee that is our God is the God of all salvations,*"[65] and he finds in his base text itself, "*And unto God the Lord belong the issues of death,*" the foundations, buttresses, and contignations of this building of salvation (X, 230–31).

Donne then elaborates each of the three supports by which salvation stands and with each explanation again cites both his base text on the issues of death and the salvific text it accompanies and upholds. Each time, moreover, he cites the two texts in a way that reinforces the functional nature of their relationship. The citations are formulaic: each time the salvific text is introduced as "this building" and the base text is introduced as and equated with either a noun or the demonstrative pronoun *this*. Each time the solidity of the base text as a structure is thus insisted upon:

"the foundation of this building, (That *our God is the God of all salvations*) is laid in this; that *unto this God the Lord belong the issues of death*"; "the butteresses that comprehend and settle this building, That *hee that is our God, is the God of all salvation*, are thus raised; *unto God the Lord belong the issues of death*"; "the contignation and knitting of this building, that *hee that is our God is the God of all salvations*, consists in this, *Unto this God the Lord belong the issues of death*" (X, 230–31). The base text takes on the substantiality of a building block, and in the second instance, the buttresses, that of an actively causal power: the buttresses not only consist in the base text but are also "raised" or erected by it.

Every time the base text is reaffirmed as structurally basic in the opening paragraph, it is immediately followed by a gloss beginning "that is" and proceeding to an exposition of the sense in which the base text functions as foundation, buttress, or contignation. Donne glosses the foundations as God's "power to give us an issue and deliverance" from all forms of death and hence as *liberatio à morte*, a deliverance *from* death; the buttresses he glosses as God's care for "the disposition and manner of our death" and thus for our deliverance *in* death, *"liberatio in morte"*; and the contignations he glosses as God's delivery of us *by* and *through* His own death on the Cross, *"liberatio per mortem."* These three understandings of the base text, which are identified with the supporting structures of a building, at once correspond to the tripartite structure of salvation and provide the three divisions of Donne's sermon. In this way salvation and sermon coalesce.

Predictably, Donne's long introductory paragraph also aligns each understanding of the base text and thus each of the three enabling structures with the Trinity, belief in which he considers essential to salvation. The father, "God of power," is identified with the foundation; the Holy Ghost, "God of comfort," with the buttresses; and the Son, "God of mercy," with the contignations or joinings. In developing the structure that introduces *and* underlies the sermon and therefore in every sense frames it, Donne assigns particular significance to the contignation, or Incarnation of the Son, as we should reasonably expect him to do in the context of salvation. In the sermon's first sentence, he describes the contignations as the components of a building that "knit and unite" it, thereby holding it together. Later in the same paragraph, he locates "the contignation and knitting of this building" in the fact that "God the Lord having united and knit both natures in one, and being God, having also come into this world, in our flesh . . . could have no other meanes to save us . . . [and] could have no other issue out of this world, nor returne to his former glory, but by death" (X, 231). The words *united* and *knit* that describe the hypostatic union thus mirror those twice used earlier in the paragraph to describe the function of the contignations within the body of the building. In this reflexive wordplay the body of the building itself — salvation — becomes coextensive with the incarnate Word, Jesus Christ. Verbally, Christ is thus both inside the architectural image and outside it in history. Analogously, having "knit both natures in one," He unites Word with flesh, promise and image with actuality, and salvation with the issue of death. Risking a pun, I should characterize both contignation and Incarnation as crucial in every respect.

Donne's introductory paragraph concludes with a reinforcing summary of the ground covered to this point:

> And these three considerations, our deliverance *à morte, in morte, per mortem, from death, in death*, and *by death*, will abundantly doe all the offices of the foundations, of the butteresses, of the contignation of this our building; That *he that is our God, is the God of all salvation*, because *unto this God the Lord belong the issues of death*. (X, 231)

The difference between Donne's presentation of his paired texts now and earlier in the paragraph is marked and significant. Since the texts are now linked logically and syntactically to one another by the word "because," both are, in effect, in appositional relation to the phrase "this our building," the one directly and the other indirectly. Presenting the two texts, Donne omits a rationalizing expression like "that is to say" or "namely" (e.g., "namely, 'That *he that is*'"), and he also omits a demonstrative pronoun that would acknowledge his reifying the text by pointing to it, as, for example, the pronoun did when he first identified the architectural image with salvation ("The body of our building is in the former part of . . . [the] verse: It is *this, hee that is our God is the God of salvation*" [X, 230]). Now he makes an immediate equation between the building and both texts and, in comparison to the earlier examples, treats the salvific text less as an appositive than as something itself visibly real to which something else, the base text, can be affixed. His omitting an expression like *namely* and at the same time introducing the texts with the conjunction "That" ("That *he that is*") radically emphasizes the nominal status—hence again the substantiality—of the paired texts that follow.[66]

As noted already, the way Donne presents the relationship between his paired texts also differs from his practice earlier in the paragraph. Emphatically linking the texts of salvation and death with the conjunction *because*, he encapsulates and focuses sharply in this one word all that has gone before: the building of salvation stands *because* of its founding, supporting, and uniting structures, as Donne has so carefully defined them. And because the base text, the issues of death, has repeatedly been shown to support salvation, not just in an abstract sense but in one made visual and tangible, at this point of summation the word *because* itself carries a literal force—"by the cause that"—which ordinarily drops from sight. The literal meaning of this common word is recharged in a way it would not have been had the same sentence occurred near the beginning of the paragraph. The word, as word, comes to life and becomes in itself significant, an assurance of the necessary relation of salvation to the issues of death. This word, moreover, is interpretive and neither the Bible's in Latin nor in English, whose *Et* or *And* Donne replaces with his translation of *Quia*, based on an interpretation of Psalm 68 in Augustine's *De Civitate Dei.*[67]

In a landmark analysis of "Deaths Duell," Stanley Fish looks in Donne's opening paragraph for "a statement that will ask for our rational assent," but instead, confessing frustration, he discovers only "bald repetition[s]" of the base text that assert "the self-sufficiency of the revealed Word."[68] Reading its last paragraph, he, too, observes how all its weight "falls squarely on 'because'" in its final sentence, but he takes this as an invitation "to transfer its burden [of meaning] to the reason that will presumably follow" (p. 52). What he doesn't notice is that *because* is itself the reason. Fish denies to this word, as word, the substantiality that Donne attributes to it.

The presence of the conjunction *because* between Donne's paired texts fulfills another dimension of meaning, earlier latent but not explicit. While the phrase "this our building" in the concluding sentence refers primarily to the divinely appointed structure of salvation, the fact that the usual equivalent of "our building," the text *"God is the God of salvation,"* is here literally extended by the word *because* to encompass the issues of death indicates that "this our building" also refers to Donne's explanatory process—the "building" of his sermon itself. He can extend the meaning of "this our building" to the constructions of understanding as well as to those of reality precisely because of the explanations and identifications that have systematically led up to this point. The role of Donne as builder of the sermon now mirrors that of the God of salvation; his role as knitter or uniter of the paired texts more closely resembles that of the incarnate Christ.[69] Whereas this sermon begins in ritual subservience to the biblical word, in its course the interpreter's claims increase greatly. Insofar as *verba* and *res* are one within it, as creator and knitter, preacher and writer, he embodies their unity.[70]

In any sense of the word *rational* Donne would have recognized—whether "rightly reasoned" or "planned, ordered, relational" (from Latin *ratio*)—Fish's influential analysis is thus awry.[71] The charge of "bald repetition" simply ignores Donne's whole explanatory procedure, which, by employing conspicuous ordering devices like "first," "secondly," and "lastly," asks to be taken whole. But Fish's phrase "the self-sufficiency of the revealed Word," despite its connotations of mindlessness, is also on the right track. Language *is* sufficient in the sermons, but human language, fictive and constructive, cooperates in them with the revealed Word. If Fish's phrase can be seen not as a means of blocking or bypassing but of enabling comprehension, it does suggest the way in which Donne ascribes to words—and not only to revealed words—substantiality and self-sustaining import. As far as he is able, in a remarkably literal and tangible way, he would make words his reality in this sermon.

When Donne turns from the introduction to the body of the sermon, he begins to consider in detail what I earlier called the sermon's effectual idea, the issues of death or passings from one state to another. The whole sermon becomes a sustained meditation on the meaning of these issues belonging to God. It becomes an effort to comprehend and thereby in some sense to contain them and, as such, an integral part of the death Donne so carefully planned, directed, and tried to control. Ezra Pound once wrote that in cogitation, or discursive thought, "the mind flits aimlessly about the object"; in meditation "it circles about . . . [the object] in a methodical manner"; in contemplation "it is unified with the object."[72] One thinks again of Donne's funerary portrait, his figure shrouded, half crouching, enacting the body's resurrection, which became his "hourly object" until his death. His attention similarly fixed on the issues of death in his last sermon, he circles methodically around the text—the issues—as is customary in meditation. He proves remarkably intent on examining from every conceivable angle not only the idea of "issues" but also the object-like word itself.

The climactic instance of this examination comes in the final paragraph of the sermon, which comprises nearly a hundred lines. In this paragraph, Donne reaches through words — particularly through those on which he has focused — for the final experiences that words can convey, the experiences of death and delivery, the basic *issues*. Introducing the paragraph, he asks his audience "to *dwell here*, in this consideration" of Christ's "*issue of death* that day"; by *dwell here* he really means "reside and live here," rather than simply "linger over in thought" (X, 245). His invitation to live *here* in *this* consideration, in these words and this text, makes life and verbal text one. In the final paragraph itself he considers the events of the Passion from "the passeover upon Thursday" through the hour of Christ's death, with which the sermon ends. With each event he exhorts his listeners to consider whether they have spent their last day "in a conformity" with Christ and for this purpose employs the word *conformity* and its cognates *conform* and *conformable* some seven times: in reference to Christ's praying in the Garden of Gethsemane, for example, he observes, "If that time [last night] were spent in . . . a submission of thy will to . . . [God's], it was spent in a *conformity* to him"; and, in reference to the scourging of Christ and His crowning with thorns, "But this redeem'd him not, they pressed a crucifying. . . . [And] wee presse an utter Crucifying of that sinne that governs thee; and *that conformes* thee to Christ" (X, 246–47). The entire paragraph recalls the end of a much earlier sermon Donne preached to the Lords on Easter Day when King James was dangerously ill: "if I come to a true meditation upon Christ, I come to a *conformity with Christ*," he had observed upon that occasion, one to which I shall return (II, 212).[73]

As Donne approaches his conclusion in "Deaths Duell," he depicts the Crucifixion itself as if present — "There now hangs that sacred Body upon the Crosse" — and then turns to the actual issue of death, the delivery of Christ's soul into the hands of the Father (X, 247–48). He stresses that the new Adam, the son of God who had "come a new way unto us in assuming our nature, delivers" his soul

> by a new way, a *voluntary emission* of it into his Fathers hands; For though *to this God our Lord, belong'd these issues of death*, so that considered in his owne contract, he must necessarily dye, yet at no breach or battery, which they made upon his sacred Body, *issued* his soule, but *emisit*, hee gave up the Ghost, and as God breathed a soule into the first Adam, so this second Adam breathed his soule into God, into the hands of God. (X, 248)

The issue of death *belongs* to this new man in a new way, for He now wills and thereby possesses it; now He controls His *exitus*. At the same time that the word *belong* is thus redefined as control, the word *issued* is redefined as the Vulgate's more active *emisit*.[74] Literally *emisit* means "to send out or forth, to emit," which in the usage of Donne's time is also a meaning of the verb *issue* when it carries a transitive force: in *The Merchant of Venice*, for example, "Every word in it [is] a gaping wound / Issuing life-blood."[75]

This kind of control in death and indeed a "voluntary" death have engaged Donne's pen before. In *Biathanatos*, Donne's treatise on "self-homicide," which he never wished published but no less wished preserved, he had examined with particular interest the death of Samson, whom he considered unambiguously both a suicide and a type of Christ. In this early work, Donne cites approvingly the opinion that Samson had "the same reason to kill himselfe, which hee had to kill . . . [the Philistines], and the same authoritie, and the same priviledge, and safeguard from sinne. And he dyed . . . with the same zeale as Christ, unconstrained; for *In this manner of dying, as much as in any thing els, he was a Type of Christ*."[76] He had as much reason, we might add, recalling the end of "Deaths Duell," to "Crucify the sinne" that governed him and thereby to conform himself to Christ.

Hardly by coincidence, explicit reference to Samson occurs earlier in "Deaths Duell," when Donne cautions his audience not to assume God's disfavor in the face of an unquiet death: for God "received Sampson, who went out of this world in such a manner . . . as was subject to interpretation hard enough.[77] Yet the holy Ghost hath moved S. Paul to celebrate Sampson in his great Catalogue, and so doth all the Church" (X, 241). The conformity Donne envisions between Samson and Christ or between ourselves and Christ does not depend on a literal or physical crucifixion. It is enough to be "dispositively in a readiness to shed blood for his glory in necessary cases" and internally to crucify sin (X, 246–47). The essential imitation is inward and dispositive — voluntary and attitudinal.

The conformity between Samson and Christ in willing or controlling their deaths reminds one again of Donne's own "controlled" death — the funerary portrait, the nightly meditations, "Deaths Duell" itself, and the final moments — his closing his own eyes and disposing "his hands and body into such a posture, as required not the least alteration by those that came to shroud him." The word *disposing* is Walton's, in this context its pun on English *pose* irresistible and its derivation from Latin *ponere*, "to place," suggestive of a topos. Decades earlier in a poem called "The Triple Foole," Donne had written, "Griefe brought to numbers cannot be so fierce, / For, he tames it, that fetters it in verse." In view of Donne's handling of his own death, I would extend the second of these verses to any outward expression that has artistic and hence controlled form, not least, of course, the Dean's "*own Funeral Sermon*."[78] As earlier remarked, comprehension is in some sense containment, in this case of the issues belonging to God.

The end of that earlier sermon by Donne in which he observes how "a true meditation upon Christ" is "a *conformity with Christ*" has further relevance in this light to "Deaths Duell." Donne explains in it that the death is precious by which we apply Christ's "blood to our selves, and grow strong enough by it, to meet Davids question, *Quis homo?* what man? with Christs answer, *Ego homo*, I am the man, in whom whosoever abideth, shall not see death" (II, 212). In this extraordinary answer, which concludes the sermon, the speaker's conformity with Christ is complete, and, representative as the preacher may be, he is also dramatically present and physically real.[79] This identification of the speaker with Christ is definite enough and literal enough to startle a modern sensibility. In terms of "Deaths Duell," it is a contignation — a joining or knitting — of the speaker with the word of Christ that again mirrors Christ's own joining of Word to flesh, promise to actuality, salvation to the issues of death.

The final sentence of "Deaths Duell," which directly follows the second Adam's breathing his soul into the hands of God, is initially less startling for the conformity to Christ in it is less complete, as yet, perhaps, unfinished. The sentence admits of two readings: one that is rhetorically natural and distinctly accessible; the other submerged, even dubious, yet fascinating. In the first of these, Donne's leave-taking, his final public departure or issue, affords priestly counsel to the congregation. He leaves them in trusting reliance on the redemptive sacrifice of Christ:

> There wee leave you in that blessed dependancy, to hang upon him that hangs upon the Crosse, there bath in his teares, there suck at his woundes, and lye down in peace in his grave, till hee vouchsafe you a resurrection, and an ascension into that Kingdome, which hee hath purchas'd for you, with the inestimable price of his incorruptible blood.

With the words "There wee leave *you*," rather than "Let *us* hang upon him who hangs upon the cross," Donne distances himself from his listeners, and tactfully indicates that his own mind has now passed beyond the cross to the resurrection and ascension, the ultimate issues of death.

In this reading the initial word "There," which is a distancing expression (as the word "here" would not have been), both situates Donne's audience at the scene of the crucifixion and anticipates the phrase "that blessed dependancy," which is defined appositionally by the phrase beginning "to hang upon him." Since the phrase "that *blessed dependancy*" is stressed by italicization in the seventeenth-century text that presumably follows Donne's own practice and by the demonstrative adjective "that," it requires a clear and definite point of reference, which the phrase "to hang upon him that hangs upon the Crosse" provides.[80] In effect this phrase defines the word "dependancy," which comes from Latin *dependere*, "to hang from or on" or, in the instance of a word (or Word), "to be etymologically derived from." Like the word "There," which is repeated in the sentence, the demonstrative adjective "that" (i.e., not "this dependency") also serves to distance the immediate speaker from the location and condition to which his words point. The expressions "vouchsafe *you*" and "purchas'd for *you*" (my emphasis) that follow the phrase beginning "to hang" emphatically enforce the reference of the crucifixion to those now being left behind by the speaker.

That the ultimate issues of death should be the resurrection and ascension rather than the crucifixion not only accords with the movement of Donne's sermon but also recalls the stress on Christ's "other [or heavenly] Crowne" and on God's redemptive purpose in the final stanza of Donne's "Hymne to God my God, in my sicknesse," a poem presumably occasioned by an earlier illness.[81] In neither work is death, even Christ's, the final *issue* of death; resurrection and ascension are. It is in these that the presence of the word as Word is finally realized.

The alternative reading of Donne's concluding sentence suggests an undermining of such rational control. It depends on the possibility of syntactical ambiguity in the relationship of the phrase "to hang upon him that hangs upon the Crosse" to the initial clause "There wee leave you in that blessed dependancy."[82] If the infinitive "to hang" is taken to refer to the pronoun "wee," rather than either to "you" or to "that blessed dependancy," then for an ambiguous moment Donne aligns himself directly with the crucifying of Christ. Although this reading accords with his counsel earlier in the sermon to crucify sin and recalls both his desire to embrace (and be embraced by) "the last Adams blood" and his appropriation of Christ's "thornes" in "Hymne to God my God," rationally there are a number of difficulties with it. Even as we recognize the ambiguity, the rest of the sentence resists it. Perhaps more important, the initial clause ("There . . . dependancy") works rhetorically against our noticing that the ambiguity is present: both "There" and "dependancy" lack an immediately clear point of reference if it is Donne who is "to hang" upon the crucified Christ. Similarly, the more proximate and therefore more logical antecedents of the phrase beginning "to hang" are first "dependancy" and second "you," rather than "wee." Albeit after the ambiguous fact, the portion of the sentence that follows the phrase beginning "to hang" creates additional problems: if Donne were aligning himself with Christ's sacrifice, his hanging "upon him . . . till hee vouchsafe you a resurrection, and an ascension into that Kingdome, which hee hath purchas'd for you" would invite us for lack of other meaning to see Donne's inclusion of his own suffering, or, worse, his own intercession, in the redemptive work of Christ's suffering. For a Protestant minister, this blasphemous meaning is hardly conceivable. Hardly.[83]

When all is said, the syntactical ambiguity of Donne's final sentence is submerged to begin with and erased in the end. And yet for a flickering and irrational moment as we read or listen to the first half of the sentence, it *is* possible and present.[84] Once noticed, it is a possibility whose exclusion requires deliberate effort and one that could account for Donne's strongly emotional investment in the rendering of human relation to the suffering of Christ: "there bath in his teares, there suck at his woundes." As a possibility it may testify subtly, almost subliminally, to the weakness of human control even in the context of a controlled *exitus*, to the final treachery of human syntax and order, and to the older, Roman Catholic habits of thought inscribed in Donne's own linguistic choices.[85] At the same time, however, this poignant weakening of control in the sentence conforms to and becomes one with the crucified Christ's own weakness or suffering, with His "woundes" and "teares," with His pain and then the release from it.[86] Thus, by either of the readings examined, the one controlled and rational, the other not so, the end of "Deaths Duell" is a rehearsal for the events in Donne's life that are to follow it, and its words are an approach to the presence of the Word. Humanly it would be hard to bring life lived and life written and then spoken and posthumously printed into closer conjunction or to imagine a substantiation of the word that is more thoroughly radical: at once fictive, conceptual, and material.[87]

In a number of ways, Donne's practice in "Deaths Duell" recalls conceptions of meaning examined earlier in these chapters, and occasions review of them. The living ("animées") words Rabelais attributes to Homer, Panurge's recollection of the biblical voices seen sensibly ("sensiblement"), and Pantagruel's Manor of Truth come to mind first, followed by Agrippa's mystical sense of the material perdurance of writing as the final realization of meaning, and by Hart's more pedestrian sense of the same thing. Given Donne's conspicuous building of salvation in "Deaths Duell," these general recollections are followed in more pointed succession by Harvey's "domiciles of argument," his rhetorical topoi or places, and by the historicized notion of a "prefabricated unit" for the construction of meaning — "exaedificationem constructionemque," as the preface to Estienne's *Thesaurus* has it. Not far behind are Jonson's discursive and poetic comparisons of a verbal construct to a dwelling and his well-squared stones, which have "the fastning, and force of knitting, and connexion . . . [and] will rise strong a great way without mortar." Jonson's dictum returns the matter specifically to words, where the issue has focused.

Although the sufficiency of words in Donne's sermons contrasts markedly with the skepticism regarding them in Spenser's fifth book, the recollections in the previous paragraph sketch linguistic ground shared by their writings, and an additional corner of it is worth emphasis. While both writers' texts variously employ ritual methods — Spenser's in Artegall's litany of biblical echoes, Donne's in the continual iteration of biblical verses — they are fundamentally committed to argument and exposition, not just to intoning. The mix of belief and doubt, inquiry and exploration, differs radically between them, but both are committed to imaginative process and not, finally, to "freezing," to what Vives regarded as a *rigor frigidior*, a rigidity stiffer than ice. Their perdurable words are essentially instruments, "in-builders," of understanding, which is in itself an expansive and hence temporal conception. From as unlikely a position as Donne's funeral sermon, the fact of imaginative process brings within distant sight the probing mind of Rabelais, the irreverent monk, whose "intermediate word-world" has much in common with that of the Dean of St. Paul's, albeit even more with that of the ironized speaker of Donne's "Canonization": "As well a well wrought urne becomes / The greatest ashes, as half-acre tombes."[88] For this speaker, "Becomes," meaning either "adorns" or "turns into," openly acknowledges material reality, the monuments that crumble and the words that melt.

———————

Modifying Ian Hacking's vision of early modern language philosophy as the heyday of ideas, I have argued throughout this book for a heyday of sub-sentential units of various sorts, such as individual words, proverbs, Latin phrases, lexical entries, and rhetorical tropes and schemes. Increasingly apparent in this emphasis on the sub-sentential has been a tendency to objectify words, a sense of their substantiality and weight as things, as *res* in meaningful ways material, and this reification has also extended to larger units of semantic senténce that instantiate topoi, formulae, and other forms of frozen language. Whereas Hacking argues abstractly that language only comes to matter when sentences replace ideas as the medium of knowledge and when the public discourse of the linguistically constituted subject replaces the mental discourse of the Cartesian ego, I have attempted to show historically that words, notably lexicalized and printed words, matter significantly and problematically long before then.

They matter as currency and commodity; as vow, memento, inspiration, and sacrament; they matter as graphic character, as icon, as template, as *topos* or "place." They matter increasingly as the basis of meaning shifts from essence to word and logic to lexicon. They are the matter of fiction — the well-defined substance of Jonson's lyric forms and the substantial medium of Andrewes's "liberty," Spenser's Faerie, or Prospero's magic; they are the matter of equality and justice and the matter of salvation, belief, and perdurance. Arguments about them in this period are often figuratively matters of life and death and they are equally often literally so — all through the letter.

Reference Matter

Notes

For full forms of citations, see the Works Cited.

Prologue

1. *Why Does Language Matter?*, p. 187; also pp. 19, 29, 161–62, 166. G. A. Padley finds the roots of later seventeenth-century thinking about language planted firmly in the preceding centuries, although, coming to them with a grammatical rather than a philosophical focus, he sees a shift from a word-basis to a sentence-basis in the mid-seventeenth century grammar of Port Royal: *Grammatical Theory in Western Europe, 1500–1700: Trends in Vernacular Grammar*, I, 298–300, and chaps. 4–5. But the word-basis of Renaissance grammar is what matters to my argument, and, as Padley everywhere insists, it is endemic to the Renaissance.

2. Mueller's *Native Tongue and the Word* affords a distinguished example of the linguistic and stylistic assumption that the sentence is the fundamental unit in early modern English: e.g., chap. 1, esp. p. 5.

3. In taking Middle English "sentence" (ca. 1395) to mean a grammatically formal "séntence" as well as sententious expression, Mueller seems to me to stretch her case, particularly since "séntence" now turns out to mean something in her argument more like "phrasal form" than

"grammatically complete, isolable unit": pp. III–12, cf. "sentence form," p. 126. The *MED*, s.v. *Sentence n.*, does not recognize the modern grammatical meaning. The *OED*, s.v. *Sentence sb.*, situates the first instance of it in 1447 and cites a second instance in 1526. Arguably, the 1447 example is ambiguous. Latin *sententia*, of course, has a range of meanings, including "opinion," "judgment," "meaning," "aphorism," "a thought," and "a period," the last normally conceived in semantic or rhetorical terms. Translated to English, its sense in early modern times tends to be verbal, tropological, or schematic rather than formal. Padley distinguishes sharply between the "sentence," or *oratio* (after Priscian), which is normally understood in the Renaissance as a semantically "complete thought," and the sentence understood formally or structurally: *Grammatical Theory in Western Europe, 1500-1700: The Latin Tradition*, p. 32. His distinction applies to the royally authorized grammar bearing the name of William Lily, which rarely uses the word *sentence* and when it does uses it semantically. This grammar even introduces instruction about grammatical agreement in a "sentence" under the heading "The Concordes of Latine Speache" — "speech" here suggesting *oratio*, a complete thought: *A Shorte Introduction of Grammar* (1567; rpt. New York: Scholars' Facsimiles & Reprints, 1945), Ciiiiʳ. Unless otherwise specified, subsequent reference will be to this edition of the *Grammar*.

4. Wimsatt, *Verbal Icon*, p. 217.

5. Marcus's essay, pp. 41–63, is entitled "Renaissance/Early Modern Studies."

6. For a relevant but less extraordinary instance, see *Renaissance News & Notes* VII, no. 2 (1994), 9: "Early Modern Culture 1450-1850. 2nd Annual Meeting of the Group for Early Modern Cultural Studies."

Chapter 1

1. *Plutarch's Moralia*, I, 418–21.

2. I use the term *sententia* (*sententiae*) loosely and inclusively to mean sententious saying, a designation it could carry in the Renaissance. For comprehensive discussion, see McCutcheon, *Sir Nicholas Bacon's Great House Sententiae*, esp. pp. 22–25.

3. Castiglione, *Book of the Courtier*, pp. 166–67; Calcagnini, *Opera Aliquot*, p. 638; Rabelais, *Gargantua and Pantagruel*, Bk. 4, chaps. 55–56, pp. 566–70. References to the original French of Rabelais are to *Le Quart Livre*.

4. Calcagnini's version reads, "Quom pater forte audisset duo cele-
berrima esse in orbe terrarum gymnasia, in quibus adolescentes erudiri
solerent: ad Indos alterum, in quo ob caloris magnitudinem auditorum
aures semper paterent, sed uoces ita liquescerent, ut uel statim uel certe
mox effluerent: ad Hyperboreos alterum, ubi frigoris ui uoces adeo tor-
pescerent et congelascerent, ut uix demum superueniente aestate resolu-
tae auditorum aures transmearent: consulebat Solonem ad eorum utrum
filium disciplinae gratia mitteret.at Solon, optio tua sit, sed ego Hyperboreos malim" (p. 638).

5. I thank Anne Prescott for calling my attention to the possibility of
Donne's knowing the episode of the frozen words in Rabelais. This
possibility is based on the reference to "'words spoken in those frosty
places where they are not heard till the next thaw'" in a letter that
Evelyn M. Simpson attributes to Donne: *Prose Works of John Donne*, p.
310. Simpson notes a more definite reference to the Rabelais episode "in
the verses headed '*Incipit Ioannes Dones*' prefixed to Coryat's *Crudities*,
1611, sig. f.5 verso (ll. 11–13): 'It's not that *French* which made his *Gyant*
see / Those vncouth Ilands where wordes frozen bee, / Till by the thaw
next yeare they'r voic't againe'" (p. 310, n. 1). Donne clearly had some
knowledge of the work of Rabelais, since he refers in "Satire 4," vs. 59,
specifically to Panurge's linguistic powers: *Satires, Epigrams and Verse
Letters*.

6. Scaliger, *Poetices libri septem*, p. 55. The discussion of this passage
by Heninger in *Sidney and Spenser*, pp. 211–14, is extremely helpful, but
Heninger may multiply Scaliger's inconsistencies by identifying *substan-
tia/substantialis* only with matter (*materiam*).

7. Marichal, ed., glosses *la pate* as "base" and calls Rabelais's usage
unique. He refers the reader to Du Cange, *Glossarium mediae* : s.v. 2.
Pata, Du Cange gives the definition "Turris seu aedificii pars ima."
Screech, *Rabelais*, p. 420, translates *la pate* as "the hearth."

8. *Sic: siecle*. Screech, *Rabelais*, p. 423, cites as a gloss the recurring
phrase *consummatio saeculi* in the Gospel of Matthew.

9. Virtually nothing is known about the Greek philosopher Petron.
The content of Pantagruel's myth is Platonic or Pythagorean. The translation here, as elsewhere, is mine; at points it coincides with Cohen's or
with the translations of Screech. My account of language in Rabelais is
indebted to Screech's discussion, pp. 411–439, but I have considerable
difficulty with his assertion (p. 432, cf. pp. 422, 426) that only inspired

words are termed *parolles* by Rabelais; while this is true of Pantagruel's Platonized myth, repeatedly it is not the case in chap. 56 of the *Quart Livre*, a fact that Screech does not adequately address.

10. Rabelais's *Works*, II, p. 355, renders *catarrhes* "rheums and mildews." Screech, pp. 424–26, remarks Rabelais's allusion to *katarrhoos* at the end of Plato's *Cratylus*; but see also Walker's review of Screech's *Rabelais* in *Music, Spirit and Language*, section XVI, pp. 1–7. Although in the *Cratylus* Socrates initially and hopefully pursues the possibility that there is real knowledge in language and appears to favor Cratylus's linguistic view, he eventually becomes deeply skeptical about this position: *Dialogues of Plato*, ed. Hamilton and Cairns, p. 474 (440a–e): unless otherwise specified, Plato's works are cited from this edition.

11. This paragraph is largely drawn from Screech, *Rabelais*, pp. 378–96; the reference to Niso comes from pp. 384–85.

12. See Augustine, *On Christian Doctrine*, Book II.xxv: "everyone seeks a certain verisimilitude in making signs so that these signs, in so far as is possible, may resemble the things that they signify. But since one thing may resemble another in a great variety of ways, signs are not valid among men except by common consent." Also Isidore of Seville, *Etymologiarum sive Originum*, I, Book I.xxix: "All names, however, have not been imposed by the ancients according to the nature of things, but certain ones according to whim, just as we sometimes give names that strike our fancy to our servants and possessions. Hence it is that all the secrets of etymology are not to be discovered—because certain things receive names not according to their natural cause [*non secundum qualitatem, qua genita sunt*] but in consequence of the decision of the human will." Isidore's views are thus mixed, although the entire weight of his *Etymologiae* is on the side of Cratylism. Screech does not note the relevance of Augustine's and Isidore's work to Rabelais's fable.

13. The irony of the *Cratylus* was not generally appreciated in Renaissance Europe; in accordance with numerous Renaissance citations of Cratylus's position, I have simplified it here. In Plato's dialogue, the linguistic realism of Cratylus ultimately leads to his reassertion of the doctrine of Heraclitan flux, whereas Socrates' belief in unchanging ideal Forms finally leads him to distrust the correspondence of language to reality. Screech, *Rabelais*, p. 396, notes that Renaissance translations of the *Cratylus* were not as tentative about a real relation of words to things as is the version known to us.

14. The Vulgate text reads, "Cunctus autem populus videbat voces et lampades, et sonitum buccinae, montemque fumantem."

15. Cohen translates the French *dragée perlée* (here "crystallized sweetmeats") as "crystallized sweets" (p. 569). Essentially *perlée* means "crystallized" in this context and suggests human making—more exactly, confecting. I have translated *dragée* "sweetmeats" in order more strongly to suggest the nut (almond, hazlenut, etc.) that typically is sugared to produce the confection—the kernel within, as it were. A tempting alternative translation would be "crystallized confections"; but although the word "confection" (cf. Latin *conficere*) would convey the confecting power—combinatory and creative—of language, it would not convey the notion of substance within.

16. The text puns on *gueule*, meaning "mouth," and *gueles*, meaning "heraldic red." Screech's rendering of the pun as "gullet words" (p. 435) comes close, since it plays on the comparison of the frozen words to sweetmeats, but it does not capture the fact that *gueule* particularly applies to the function of the mouth in speaking or crying out. Cohen translates *des motz de gueule* as "some words gules, or gay quips," thus missing the substance of the words but catching their nature as utterances (p. 569). As Anne Prescott has reminded me, Randle Cotgrave similarly translates *mot de gueule* as "A wanton or waggish ieast, an obscene or lasciuious conceit" in his *Dictionarie*.

17. Lily, *A Shorte Introduction of Grammar*, 1567, A.v^r: I have capitalized "Manus," etc., beyond its initial letter to indicate a change in font, in this case from black letter to a larger roman. *Vnderstande* is an archaic form of the past participle current until the final quarter of the sixteenth century; by 1600 modern *understood* had generally replaced it (*OED*, s.v. *Understand*). Priscian's definition of the noun is fairly close to Lily's (actually Colet's): "Nomen est pars orationis, quae unicuique subiectorum corporum seu rerum communem vel propriam qualitatem distribuit" (from Padley, *Latin Tradition*, p. 264, but cf. pp. 32–43, esp. p. 33). Although "Lily's" *Grammar* was compiled by a committee using many sources besides Lily, I have retained the work's traditional attribution to him. On the methods of the compilers, see Allen, "Sources"; Flynn, "Grammatical Writings"; and Baldwin, *"Small Latine & Lesse Greek,"* I, 97–98.

18. Cf. Padley, *Latin Tradition*, pp. 39, 44; also, his *Vernacular Grammar*, I, 75. Anne Ferry observes that the grammarian John Brinsley's

lesson about the noun reveals an earlier interpretation of Lily in carefully distancing itself from the assumption that a hand itself is a noun: "Q. Is a hand a Noune? A. A hand it selfe is not a Noune: but the word signifying a hand, is a Noune": *Art of Naming*, pp. 38–39; and *Posing of the Parts*, pp. 1–2. Brinsley's lesson essentially reasserts an Aristotelian distinction, however: "A *name* [noun] is a spoken sound significant by convention . . . because no name is a name naturally but only when it has become a symbol" (*De interpretatione*, 16a 19, 27–28, in Aristotle, *Works*, I, 25). See also Plato's *Cratylus*, 432b: "the image [i.e., word], if expressing in every point the entire reality, would no longer be an image" (p. 466).

19. I would reemphasize that the comma merely accentuates rather than creates an uncertainty inhering in the syntax; by modern criteria Renaissance punctuation is notoriously arbitrary. In other printings and editions of Lily's *Grammar* that I have seen the comma between "thing" and "that" is sometimes present and sometimes absent, but it continues to suggest hesitation about the grammatical structure of the sentence and the appropriate voicing of it. Cf. Lily and Colet,: *A Short Introduction of Grammar*, 1549: the definition in English of a noun, given in Appendix I, is taken from a 1557 edition of the grammar; in it, the relevant comma disappears. In the editions printed by Reginald Wolfe in 1567 and 1568 it reappears, along with a comma after "Noune" in the latter. The comma after "thing" also appears in Francis Flowar's edition of 1574 but disappears in his edition of 1590. It emerges again in John Battersbie's edition of 1597. In John Norton's edition of 1606, it is gone, however, as it is in the other early seventeeth-century editions I have sampled — Cantrell Legge's in 1621, Bonham Norton's in 1630 and 1633, and Roger Norton's in 1636.

20. There is considerable evidence in the Renaissance, notably in Shakespeare's dramas, of comic or playful readings of Lily's *Grammar*. For exemplary discussions, see Parker, *Literary Fat Ladies*, pp. 26–31; and Pittenger, "Dispatch Quickly," esp. pp. 397–400.

21. In a classic discussion, Summers describes the disintegration of metrical, syntactical, and even verbal form in "Church-monuments," in *George Herbert*, pp. 129–35.

22. From the second part or *Breuissima Institutio*, Av^r, of Lily. R. R.'s edition of Lily translates the Latin as follows: "A Noun is a part of speech, which signifieth a thing, without any difference of time or person": *Grammar, 1641*, p. 6. The Folger Library copy of the 1606 edition of

Lily's *Grammar*, published by John Norton, is interleaved with heavily annotated pages, among which the translation of the Latin definition of the noun, presumably dictated by a schoolmaster, suggests the conceptual dominance of the English one: "A Noune is a part of speech w[hi]ch nameth a thing without any Difference in time, place, or person, as Manus, a hand, Domus, an house." Like the translation of *significat* as "nameth," the examples cited come from the English version.

23. Relevantly, Aristotle defines a noun or name as "a spoken sound significant by convention, without time, none of whose parts is significant in separation": *De interpretatione*, 16a 19–20, in *Works*, I, 25. Cf. Donatus's definition of a noun: "Pars orationis cum casu corpus aut rem proprie communiterve significans" (A part of speech which signifies with the case a person or a thing specifically or generally), pp. 28–29, in *Ars Minor of Donatus*, trans. Wayland Johnson Chase.

24. Padley, *Latin Tradition*, pp. 38–39.

25. On the *pars orationis*, which was implicitly a grammatical element rather than simply a lexical entry, see Padley, *Latin Tradition*, pp. 264, 266; and Bursill-Hall, *Speculative Grammars*, pp. 73–77.

26. Padley, *Latin Tradition*, p. 26, identifies Donatus, with an admixture of Priscian, as major influences on Lily's *Grammar*. C. G. Allen, "Sources," names Lily and Colet as the chief sources for the English section and Lily, Linacre, Melancthon, Despauterius, Aldus, Erasmus, and Listrius as the more immediate Renaissance sources for the Latin one.

27. Padley notes hints of this awareness in the English section of Lily as well but dismisses their import: *Latin Tradition*, p. 43.

28. R. R.'s edition of 1641 translates the Latin definition of a noun and prints it sequentially with the English one without acknowledging any discrepancy, unless R. R.'s including both definitions suggests hesitation on his part about their equivalence. The effect of two different definitions, one after the other, is peculiar, as are other features of R. R.'s hybrid edition of Lily. The possibility that R. R. did hesitate, sensing a discrepancy, gains some credence from the fact that the meaning of *significat* and the difference between it and *is* (Latin *est*) are involved in the numerous controversies of the period regarding the Eucharist, as, for example, in Lancelot Andrewes's criticism of Zwingli's position: "To avoid *Est* . . . he fell to be all for *Significat*, and nothing for *Est* at all" (*Two Answers to Cardinall Perron*, in *Works*, XI, 14). Unless otherwise specified, subsequent reference to Andrewes's writings is to this edition.

29. The preceding quotation is from Padley, *Latin Tradition*, p. 45; the present one from Cohen, *Sensible Words*, p. xxiv. See also Salmon, *Study of Language*, e.g., pp. 144–45.

30. *Linguistics and Literary History*, p. 21. Spitzer's statement need not imply that linguistic nominalism had no place in the Middle Ages but rather that its implications had an increasing effect as the early modern period developed.

31. *De doctrina christiana*, I.ii, p. 19: having identified words as signs, Augustine continues, "Quamobrem omne signum etiam res aliqua est; quod enim nulla res est, omnino nihil est" ("Wherefore every sign is also a thing, because what is not a thing is nothing at all").

32. Sidney, "A Defence of Poetry," pp. 78–79; Spenser, *Works of Edmund Spenser: A Variorum Edition*, II: II.Pro.1; cited hereafter as *Var.*, with *The Faerie Queene* cited as *FQ*.

33. Bacon, *Advancement of Learning*, in *Works*, VI, 119–20.

34. Cave, *Cornucopian Text*, p. 21.

35. In different terms, Elsky finds both kinds of reification coexisting in Herbert's pattern poetry: *Authorizing Words*, pp. 146–68. Herbert's poetry, like Augustine's linguistics, seems to me to work against such coexistence. Increasingly it seeks to affirm the purity of its conceptual foundation in a denial of the substantiality of language. For Herbert to have doubled Puttenham's triangle (Puttenham, *Arte of English Poesie*, p. 107), calling the result "Easter Wings," was to have insisted on a materially imitative form. Elsky's view is similarly modified by Andrew M. Cooper in "Collapse of the Religious Hieroglyph."

36. See Summers, *George Herbert*, pp. 129–35.

37. The numerology, or Pythagorean isomorphism, of Spenser's *Epithalamion* comes closer to some of Herbert's and Donne's practices. In asserting the shared concerns of Spenser and Herbert, I join the overwhelming chorus of voices rejecting, for England, Michel Foucault's sharp division between the sixteenth and seventeenth centuries in his early work *The Order of Things*.

38. The kabbalistic belief, which derives from much older traditions in Judaism, is based on subsequent chapters of Exodus in which Moses spends forty days and nights on the Mount, but these are not separable from the delivery of the Commandments from the Mount in Exodus 20.18. See Scholem, *On the Kabbalah*, pp. 29–31, 38, 47–48, 62–63; also Blau, *Christian Interpretation of the Cabala*, pp. 5–6. Although Screech

rejects the possibility that the allusion to Exodus has a "serious theological point," he suggests some points anyway: for St. Ambrose "*voces* ['voices'] refers to the inner sense of the words 'seen' spiritually; in the New Testament St. John did see the word incarnate (I John 1, 1–2), and so on" (p. 435).

39. The terms *dialectic* and *logic* were often used interchangeably, as they are by Vives: *In Pseudodialecticos*, ed. and trans. Charles Fantazzi, p. 17. On their relation, see Jardine, "Lorenzo Valla."

40. Jardine's *Erasmus*, pp. 16–20, comments relevantly on the polemics shared by Erasmus and Vives against the contemporary practice of logic, and, I would add, against the freezing of language more generally. But her "point" (p. 20) that their polemics concern Louvain, not Paris, is perhaps unhappily phrased, since the local project appears to overwhelm the larger one, and the nuance the general meaning. Surely Louvain is important, but Paris is clearly implicated as well.

41. Plutarch, *Moralia*, p. 421; Vives, *In Pseudodialecticos*, p. 88.

42. Cooper and Ross, "Word Order," in *Parasession on Functionalism*, pp. 63–111; cited in Ferry, *Art of Naming*, pp. 79, 189. The conclusions of Cooper and Ross suggest that freezing has psychological (cognitive-emotive) as well as linguistic importance. On the recognizable rhythm of "sayings," cf. Havelock, *Prologue to Greek Literacy*, pp. 27–31.

43. Barley, "Structural Approach to the Proverb," pp. 740–41, citing E. Ardener (1970) and M. McLeod (1972). Barley's expertise combines linguistics with folklore.

44. Barthes, *Elements of Semiology*, pp. 19, 62. The preceding quotations from Barthes come from *S-Z*, p. 100; cf. Pierre Bourdieu's inclusion of proverbs and other kinds of sayings in the doxic structure of cultural practice: *Theory of Practice*, p. 167. Nigel Barley also finds the syntagmatic nature of the proverbial expression evident in "the way it lends itself to limited restructuring and variation" and finds "its paradigmatic nature . . . [in] the comic effect of these changes" ("Structural Approach to the Proverb," p. 741).

45. Empson, *Structure of Complex Words*, p. 39.

46. Lakoff and Johnson, *Metaphors*; for examples, see pp. 10–11, 46, 98–99, 126.

47. This is not to claim that the codes based on such grounding are the same: e.g., for some cultures the future is in back of us, rather than in front (Lakoff and Johnson, *Metaphors*, p. 14). Bourdieu, *Theory of Prac-*

tice, pp. 89–92, 119, corroborates and extends these observations about "body geography." Roy Wagner, *Symbols*, argues an even more sweeping extension of metaphor to the study of cultures.

48. Lakoff and Johnson, *Metaphors*, p. 190; Aristotle, *Poetics*, 1459a, in *Works*, *II*. Lakoff's and Johnson's insight regarding metaphor is hardly unique in recent years, but its terms are particularly useful to my argument. Obvious touchstones for a similar insight are Black, *Models and Metaphors*, pp. 25–47; Ricoeur, *Rule of Metaphor*; and Derrida, "White Mythology" and "The Retrait of Metaphor."

49. Cf. Ong, *Ramus*, p. 69: "The economy of the human mind thus bears inexorably toward substances or substance-like conceptualizations (substantives)." For a moment Ong sounds like a precursor of Derrida but adds, "Such hypostatization can be controlled not by being avoided, but only by being recognized for what it is." Derrida's more radical and avowedly impossible project is avoidance.

50. Emile Benveniste, *Problems in General Linguistics*, pp. 131–44, here 138, 143. Arguing that a nominal assertion is complete in itself and should not be described as lacking the copula, Benveniste makes the point that *omnis homo mortalis* is symmetrical with *omnis homo moritur* rather than with *omnis homo est mortalis* (pp. 137–38). I have translated the nominal assertion with the [not-missing] copula in this instance, because it affords the nearest nominal equivalent in modern English.

51. Sparrow, *Visible Words*, passim, here pp. 92, 102.

52. For the political implications of such monumentality, see Hedrick's suggestive essay "Literacy and Democracy," pp. 24–27, on the force for democracy or tyranny of inscriptions in Athenian society.

53. Respectively, Ong, *Ramus*; Cohen, *Sensible Words*; Eisenstein, *Printing Press*; Norton, *Ideology and Language of Translation*; Elsky, *Authorizing Words*; Goldberg, *Writing Matter*. I am grateful for and indebted to all these works, but particularly to Eisenstein and Elsky.

54. On medieval practices of emphasis and notation, see Carruthers's rich study, *Book of Memory*, passim (e.g., pp. 93–96, 107–14, 146, 217). On the basis of the medieval neuropsychology of memory and mnemonic techniques current in the period, Carruthers denies that medieval educators had any less "visual and spatial" an "idea of *locus*" than a "Ramist had" (p. 32). In *"Statim invenire"* Rouse and Rouse document changes in the ordering and indexing of information from the twelfth to thirteeth centuries onward. They trace the introduction of "artificial order as a finding device" (i.e., alphabetical order), as opposed to "ra-

tional" (i.e., natural, thematic) ordering devices, which, they argue, were keyed to mnemonic systems. While their conclusions qualify Carruthers's interpretation of the essentially mnemonic purpose of manuscript markings, they support the case for a greater *degree* of perceptual continuity between the later Middle Ages and the Renaissance. See also Daly and Daly, "Some Techniques"; Alford, "The Role of Quotations"; and C. J. Mitchell, "Quotation Marks," pp. 359–84, here 362.

55. Regularly in the Middle Ages a charter was not even dated, possibly because it was considered a mnemonic aid, secondary and posterior to the actual transaction, rather than its warrant and legal realization: for other possible explanations, see Clanchy, *From Memory*, pp. 299–304. As Clanchy indicates, the function of costly illuminated manuscripts with exquisite calligraphy was likely to be ceremonial and symbolic (pp. 278–83). While Clanchy's book is invaluable, it should be noted that literacy in the twelfth to the thirteenth centuries looks more advanced relative to the eleventh century, his primary point of measurement, than to the early modern period.

56. Ibid., p. 269. Clanchy's observation is not significantly affected by the fact that silent reading, sometimes complementing or alternating with communal reading, became a common literate practice in the later Middle Ages: see *Culture of Print*, ed. Chartier, p. 2.

57. Elsky, pp. 110–46, has an impressive chapter on "Space and Textuality" in the Renaissance, in which he writes of the "spatially rationalized page" and the "visualization of language" (p. 128). He also treats the page as an object in space, although I find his visual illustrations of this topic (pp. 117–21) more ambiguous than his interpretation of them: e.g., the illustration of a manuscript page with rents in it revealing country scenes may portray the page as an object, but it also depicts the page as a flat ground through which one looks to something outside or beyond it. In a second illustration, perspective directs the viewer's gaze to a point beyond the page, again suggesting that the page serves something beyond it.

58. On controversy surrounding the translation of *Logos*, see Boyle, *Erasmus on Language*; and on the reality of bread, Lancelot Andrewes's *Responsio ad apologiam Cardinalis Bellarmini*, in *Works*, VIII, p. 265: "Ea nempe conjunctio inter Sacramentum visibile, et rem Sacramenti invisibilem, quae inter humanitatem et divinitatem Christi, ubi, nisi Eutychen sapere vultis, humanitas in divinitatem non transubstantiatur"; somewhat freely, "Truly there is the same union between the visible

bread and wine of the sacrament and its invisible reality that exists between the humanity and divinity of Christ, where, unless you wish to smell of Eutyches, the humanity is not changed into the divinity." The primacy of Scripture was anticipated in the later Middle Ages, for example, by Jean Gerson (1363–1429), a conciliarist based in Paris (Guy, *Tudor England*, p. 123); an emphasis on preaching is also associated with the earlier establishment of the friars. The doctrine of substantiation had certainly encountered its skeptics over the centuries as well, and, with striking relevance, in the fourteenth-century heresiarch John Wycliffe, who believed that the bread remained on the altar after the words of consecration had been spoken: see Hudson, *Premature Reformation*, pp. 281–90, esp. pp. 281–82; also Rubin, *Corpus Christi*, chap. 1 and pp. 320–34; Stock, *Implications of Literacy*, chap. 3 and p. 524. Put simply, most of the Reformation was anticipated by the later Middle Ages. Nonetheless, there was a radical development of attitudes, ideas, and institutions in the early modern period that realized these earlier, less normative signs of change.

59. See, for example, Elsky, *Authorizing Words*, pp. 16–19, 33–37; and Waswo, *Language and Meaning*, pp. 110, 204. A great strength of Elsky's book is his ability lucidly to organize an impressive range of materials to support the thesis that Humanist language theory was essentially Aristotelian; lesser weaknesses, to my mind, are his minimizing Augustinian and Platonic influences on language theory in the period and his overlooking the linguistic relevance of fiction to it.

60. Hoskyns, *Direccions for Speech and Style*, in *The Life, Letters, and Writings of John Hoskyns, 1566–1638*, ed. Osborn, pp. 153–54; unless otherwise specified, reference is to this edition. Hoskyns, objecting to the excessive use of sententiae, acknowledges that a sentence (i.e., *sententia*) "is a pearle in a discourse" but asks whether it is "a good discourse that is all pearle" and then continues, "and if a sentence were as like to be an hand in the text, as it is commonlie noted with a hand in the margent, yet I should rather like the text that had noe more hands than *Hercules*, than that which had as many as *Briarcus* [i.e., Briareus]." Despite the reference to speech in the title of Hoskyns's work, he has writing primarily in mind here, as more often than not elsewhere; he makes this fact explicit: "why would the writers of these daies, imprison themselues in the straightnes of these maximes?" (Osborn, ed., dates *Direccions* between 1598–1603, with 1599 the "likely date of composition.") For more general discussion of marginalia in the period, see Slights, "Edifying Mar-

gins"; and his " 'Marginall Notes that spoile the Text' "; and Tribble, *Margins and Marginality.*

61. Cited from Udall's "To the Reader," introducing his edition of Erasmus's *Apophthegmes* (1564), *iii^r; subsequent reference is to this edition, but the 1542 edition is essentially the same. Similar examples are abundant: for a striking and much later instance of textual mapping, see the markings in John Minsheu's Spanish dictionary, bound with *Ductor in Linguas, (Guide into the Tongues)* (1617; rpt. Scholars' Facsimiles and Reprints, 1978). Minsheu's key to abbreviations and other indexical markers in the Spanish dictionary affords a summary of the markings: in part, it reads, when you see "in this Dictionarie *in the Spanish word* Abríl, *figured* p. 313. n.8354 — e *looke into the* Etymologicall Dictionarie of ele-uen Languages, *the* 313. page, and *the number of wordes* 8354. *and* you *shall* finde *the word* Moneth, *and in the* margine *or* middle *of that page* you shall likewise *find following that number* 8354. *the letters* b,c,d,e, etc. set before *the deriuatiue wordes,* then looke in — e, *and you shall finde* Abríl *with his* and *other* Etymologies." Ong, *Interfaces of the Word,* pp. 88, 204, discusses the impact of indices on noetic processes and the suitability of indices to books produced in large quantities, as opposed to differently paginated manuscripts, each of which would require its own index.

62. Martin Irvine's *Making of Textual Culture* serves to underline both the similarity of Udall's methods and aims to medieval ones and their difference from them. While the medieval page is visually struc-tured to convey a coded message — at once the role of interpretation and its containment — the limiting code is antecedent to the page and exter-nal to it as well, being "acknowledged" by the layout on the page itself (pp. 392–93). Thus the page is less road map than mirror. Regrettably, Irvine's study came too late for me to make fuller use of it.

63. The revisions of John Withals's popular *Dictionarie for Yonge Be-gynners* (1553) afford another instance of concern for authorship. Abra-ham Fleming, the second reviser, advertises that "What is added in this edition which none of the former at any time had, these markes ¶.★. may sufficiently shew": *A Shorte Dictionarie in Latine and English, verie profit-able for yong beginners,* title page. William Clerk, the third reviser, notes that his additions will be indicated with reverse quotation marks: *A Dic-tionarie in English and Latine for Children, and yong beginners,* A4^{r-v}.

64. Hunter, "The Markings of *Sententiae*," pp. 171–88; Ong, *Rhet-oric, Romance, and Technology,* p. 72. As noted earlier, different scripts were at times employed in medieval manuscripts — to distinguish text

from glosses, for example — but spatially they were less rational and discrete than the arrangement and appearance of type faces on the Renaissance page. Perhaps more important, their use was not as common and
standardized.

65. From Goldberg, *Writing Matter*, p. 228. I have found Goldberg's
discussion of handwriting in the Renaissance remarkably illuminating,
although finally, to my mind, metaphorically based, as suggested below.

66. Generalizations about manual or typographic writing in the two
periods are perilous, since there are always exceptions to them. A crudely
printed Renaissance book, for example, hardly wins a competition for
visibility with a prize manuscript in medieval bookhand, like the Ead-
wine Psalter.

67. Goldberg argues that the materiality of (hand)writing has priority with respect to other materialisms and that even the historical
materialism of Marx and Engels can be resituated *within* a deconstructive
reading of origins (*Writing Matter*, pp. 311–16). But the materiality he
grounds in the human hand (always already the hand written and writing as well) is more complexly conceptual than what might be considered a basic definition of matter — something that occupies space and is
available to sense perception. Such a definition is all I intend here by
"purely material fact" and by "material" in the next sentence.

68. Done, *Polydoron: or A Miscellania of Morall, Philosophicall, and
Theologicall Sentences*, p. 38. Simpson, *Prose Works*, p. 357, rejects the poet
Donne's authorship of this work.

69. Lowry's translation, in *World of Aldus Manutius*, p. 234. Aldus
refers to exemplars, "quae dilaceranda impressoribus traderentur per-
irentque ut pariens vipera": Orlandi, *Aldo Manuzio editore*, I, 16. Lowry
(pp. 234, 240) characterizes Aldus's unsentimental attitude toward the
manuscript as his normal one; since Aldus is not much beyond an exclusively manuscript culture, his attitude is particularly telling, and evidence
suggests that his contemporary Froben, working with Erasmus, shared it
(Lowry, p. 246). Rouse, "Copy-specific Features of the Printed Book:
What to Record and Why," notes that "As printed books replaced manuscripts, the latter became redundant, were cut up as useful material, and
put to use as binder's scrap" (p. 205). On the marking and scarcity of
surviving copytexts and the use of printed books as copytexts both for
revisions and manuscripts (!), see also Blake, *Caxton*, pp. 86, 88, 91–92;
and his "Manuscript to Print," pp. 403–32, esp. 416; Hellinga, "Notes on
the Order of Setting," pp. 64–69, esp. 64; and her "Manuscripts in the

Hands of Printers," pp. 3–11, esp. 3–4; also Jardine, *Erasmus*, pp. 24–25. Cf. also Greg's speculations about manuscript "value," evidently personal rather than commercial: "An Elizabethan Printer and His Copy," pp. 102–18, here 108.

70. From Bullokar's Prologue to his *Booke at Large* in *Booke at Large and Bref Grammar*, C.i^r. The lines by Shakespeare cited just above are from Sonnet 18 (my emphasis added): *The Riverside Shakespeare*; subsequent reference to Shakespeare's writing is to this edition.

71. The conclusion of Ovid's *Metamorphoses* provides a familiar instance of the motif: "Iamque opus exegi, quid nec Iovis ira nec ignis / nec potuerit ferrum nec edax abolere vetustas" ("And now my work is done, which neither the wrath of Jove, nor fire, nor sword, nor the gnawing tooth of time shall ever be able to undo"); ed. and trans. Frank Justus Miller, II, Bk. XV, 871–72.

72. *Sermons of John Donne*, III, 188; X, 196. Except where otherwise specified, subsequent reference to Donne's sermons is to this edition.

73. Taken from Mynors, *Durham Cathedral Manuscripts*, p. 9. A radically abbreviated paraphrase of this passage is cited in Clanchy, *From Memory*, pp. 116–17.

74. For another medieval example, consider this simile from Bersuire's *Repertorium Morale*: "For Christ is a sort of book written into the skin of the virgin. . . . That book was spoken in the disposition of the Father, written in the conception of the mother, exposited in the clarification of the nativity, corrected in the passion, erased in the flagellation, punctuated in the imprint of the wounds, adorned in the crucifixion above the pulpit, illuminated in the outpouring of blood, bound in the resurrection, and examined in the ascension": cited in Gellrich, *Idea of the Book*, p. 17, epigraph. To a modern sensibility, the extension of Bersuire's simile ("a sort of") seems forced or "artificial." Increasingly it displays its figurality as opposed to literalness.

75. The preceding quotation is from Carruthers, *Book of Memory*, p. 31. Cf. Goody, *Domestication*, p. 9: "the material concomitants of the process of mental 'domestication' . . . also shape its future forms" (cf. pp. 51, 76–77). Havelock also believes that "Alphabetic literacy . . . had to await the invention of the printing press": *Origins of Western Literacy*, p. 73. While I think the claims of Goody and Havelock have some bearing on a Renaissance culture that valorized the printed word, I agree with Street's trenchant objection to Goody's use of "technological determinism" to discriminate between the cognitive abilities of "literate" and

"non-literate" cultures: *Literacy in Theory and Practice*, e.g., pp. 1, 29, and chap. 2. As Street argues, technology is not ideologically neutral, yet he overstates his case in suggesting that technology is virtually irrelevant to cultural difference. In frequent citation of Clanchy he overlooks a number of relevant factors, for example, the fact that the term "literacy," as Clanchy uses it, can simply mean participation in literate conventions (possession of a charter or letter) rather than the ability to read and write, or Clanchy's awareness of the interaction of culture and material means: "The gentry were not going to read until documents were available and necessary"; or "A particular technology of writing shapes and defines the uses of literacy in a region or culture" (Clanchy, *From Memory*, pp. 78, 114–15; cf. pp. 154, 185). More recently, Stock has also minimized the impact of technology, in this case printing; utilizing the broadest (Derridean) sense of *writing*, he asserts that there was "no orality without an implied textuality" in the Middle Ages, a situation that "was mechanized, but not substantively altered, by printing": *Listening for the Text*, pp. 4, 20; but cf. p. 36. Whether or not printing made a real difference is becoming, perhaps ironically, a matter of slippery semantics.

76. *Hall's Chronicle*, by Edward Hall, pp. 762–63: Packington urges Tunstall to buy "the stampes," or printing types, but not the punches and matrices — let alone the technology — to make more of them or, for that matter, the remaining varieties of types already in the printer's shop.

77. *FQ*, I.i.20. In a paper read at "Spenser at Kalamazoo" (May 1992), Lawrence F. Rhu also aligns Hall's story with Spenser's Error ("a sort of apocalyptic bookmobile"), although he does so for the more specific purpose of illustrating the dangers of limitless interpretation of Scripture. See also Gregerson, "Protestant Erotics."

78. Erasmus, *Adages*, p. 165. For the preceding statistics, see Daniel Kinney, "Erasmus' *Adagia*," pp. 169–92, here 169; and Erasmus, *Parabolae*, trans. R. A. B. Mynors, pp. lxiv–lxv; XXXI, trans. Margaret Mann Phillips, with notes by R. A. B. Mynors, p. xiii.

79. McCutcheon, *Sir Nicholas Bacon's Great House Sententiae*, pp. 12, 21; Lancelot Andrewes, *Sermons*, ed. G. M. Story, p. xxxiv; *Oxford Dictionary of English Proverbs*, p. xxii, also pp. xx–xxi; *Advice to a Son*, ed. Wright; Hoskyns, p. 152; and Hoyt H. Hudson, ed., *Directions for Speech and Style*, by John Hoskyns, p. xi. For additional examples see Zeitlin, "Commonplaces," and William G. Crane, *Wit and Rhetoric*, pp. 33–48. The latter observes that biblical books like Proverbs and Ecclesiastes were printed separately in the period, as in 1550 was an epitome of

"pointed texts" in the Bible, and in 1578 *A Treatise of Heauenly Philoso-phie*, another collection of biblical *sententiae*, by Thomas Palfreyman (p. 37).

80. On the orality of sayings, see Ong, *Rhetoric, Romance, and Tech-nology*, pp. 46, 155; but for a considerable refinement of Ong's view, see Goody, *Domestication*, p. 116. On the essentially humane nature of Eras-mus's engagement with sayings, see Greene's persuasive essay "Eras-mus's 'Festina lente,'" pp. 132–48; also Hoskyns, *Direccions*, pp. 152–53. Carruthers's study *Book of Memory* amply supports the identity of *senten-tiae* with traditional wisdom.

81. Peacham, *Garden of Eloquence*, pp. 29–31; cf. pp. 86–87.

82. Whigham, *Ambition and Privilege*, pp. 25–31; and Mary Thomas Crane, *Framing Authority*, chap. 1. The latter relates the selection and accumulation of "sayings" to specific societal developments like Human-ist education, economic capitalization, and the growth of the Tudor bureaucracy and preferment within it. While I admire Crane's interpreta-tion of the commonplace tradition, I have reservations about some as-pects of its historicity: virtually all the topoi she considers definitive of Renaissance practices belong to the commonplace tradition in the Mid-dle Ages, a period with different social and economic determinants (e.g., pp. 32, 56–58, 62–63); cf. Carruthers, *Book of Memory*, pp. 16–45. Al-though Carruthers's arguments do not disqualify Crane's, they suggest that the historical causes Crane identifies may be too direct and specific. The international character of the commonplace tradition in the six-teenth century and its ultimately classical roots also exert pressure on any narrowly cultural view of causation. Halpern, who emphasizes Eras-mus's influence on the commonplace tradition, sees the ideological work of *copia* (which includes commonplaces) as "merely negative": *Poetics of Primitive Accumulation*, pp. 47–48.

83. McCutcheon, *Sir Nicholas Bacon's Great House Sententiae*, pp. 68–69; I have eliminated the copula and reversed the positions of the initial noun and adjective in McCutcheon's translation. The capital letters in the Latin *sententia* reproduce McCutcheon's text and the style of the inscription itself.

84. Puttenham, *The Arte of English Poesie*, p. 243. Quotations in the preceding sentence are from Kirshenblatt-Gimblett, "Proverb Meaning," p. 821; and Tilley, *A Dictionary of the Proverbs*, p. vi. The emphasis in both quotations is mine. Cf. Havelock, *Prologue to Greek Literacy*, who ob-serves that the rhythms of preservable speech, for example, sayings, para-

bles, and fables, "come . . . to a stop"; they do not "admit of extended statement; none of them are open-ended" (p. 30).

85. Cf. Kirshenblatt-Gimblett, "Proverb Meaning," p. 826. Greene, in "Erasmus's 'Festina lente'" eloquently argues that Erasmus situates the proverbs historically and socially in the *Adagia*, and to the extent that Erasmus does so, his work resists the temporal and spatial fixity of other compilations. Simultaneously, however, it advances the perception that there are linguistic nuggets to be quarried. Cf. also Daniel Kinney, "Erasmus' *Adagia*," and Seitel, "Proverbs." In addition to specific compilations of proverbs or *sententiae* more generally, dictionaries of the period also included separate citations of proverbs, sometimes marked with an asterisk or other distinguishing sign.

86. Medieval *florilegia* are an obvious example of such roots: see Rouse and Rouse, "Florilegia"; and "The *Florilegium Angelicum*," in *Medieval Learning and Literature*, ed. J. J. G. Alexander and M. T. Gibson.

87. Ascham, *The Scholemaster*, p. 214; my emphasis. Although I have hesitated to use the term "practical consciousness" here, Anthony Giddens's definition has relevance: "Practical consciousness consists of all the things which actors know tacitly about how to 'go on' in the contexts of social life," *Constitution of Society*, pp. xxii–xxiii. More relevant is his insistence that "The line between discursive and practical consciousness is fluctuating and permeable" (p. 4, cf. p. 26). There appears to be no name for the intermediate state that exists, as here, between Ascham's (discursive) language and his explicit awareness.

88. Harvey, *Gabriel Harvey's Ciceronianus*, trans. Clarence A. Forbes, p. 89; my emphasis.

89. Quoted from p. 41 of Harvey's *Ciceronianus*. The physicality of John Hart's conception of letters is similarly striking. Hart compares his project of reforming letters (orthography) to "thorder of Phisicke, which is, first to vnderstand the complexion, disposition and parts of the body, and then to know the nature of the causes which doe offende, whereby the Doctor may proceede without daunger to minister purgations of the vicious humors, with certaine remedies, and then to prescribe the pacient a wholesome diet and order to be preserued from falling into the like againe": *An Orthographie*, 10^{r-v}. Cf. also Ben Jonson's treatment of the flesh, blood, bones, and sinews of style in *Timber, or Discoveries*, in *Works*, VIII, 626.

90. Harvey, *Ciceronianus*, p. 83; Bacon, *Novum Organum*, in *Works*, VIII, 138. In *The Advancement of Learning*, Bacon distinguishes between

copious words and "weight," more exactly, "the weight of matter, worth of subject, soundness of argument, life of invention, or depth of judgment." His association of weight with matter, as distinct from worthy subject, accentuates his association of *res* with materiality (*Works*, VI, 119).

91. Howell, *"Res et Verba,"* pp. 131–42, here p. 131. Howell locates this slippage in the seventeenth century; as we have repeatedly seen, however, it is discernible in the sixteenth century as well, although it is by no means as generally pronounced there.

92. Describing efforts to correlate "the taxonomy of linguistic elements and the natural order of things in the world," Cohen, *Sensible Words*, pp. 20–21, draws a useful distinction between two ideas of nature current in the seventeeth century: the first, associated with Adamic naming, endeavors to find a correspondence between "the shapes and sounds of linguistic elements" and natural essences; the second, associated with Baconian empiricism, sees language reproducing "through mostly arbitrary symbols, the composition and coherence of things in nature." In practice, however, this distinction is hard to maintain, since both ideas correlate with nature. Bacon's writings (invoked just above) often indicate his regret that current words are not tied firmly to the nature of things and his desire either to secure them as nearly as possible to it or to replace them altogether with less ambiguous visual symbols, which, while they might not have "any *secure* foundation" in the material world, are nonetheless to be keyed to it: quotation from Elsky, *Authorizing Words*, p. 179; my emphasis. On pp. 172–74, Elsky seems to acknowledge a similar position. The broader context of my discussion in *Biographical Truth*, pp. 124–25 and chap. 9, is relevant. Cf. also Padley, *Vernacular Grammar*, I, 326–31.

93. Cited from a 1536 edition of *De tradendis*, p. 250: "Eodem referuntur prouerbia, et sententiae: omnia denique quae ex quorundam animaduersione annotata, in populo remanserunt tanquam publicae opes in aerario communi." I have consulted but generally not followed Foster Watson's translation in *Vives: On Education*, pp. 38–39.

94. Relevant is Cave's discussion of the derivation of *copia*, the copiousness so valued in the Renaissance, from Latin *ops*, "material riches," associated with affluence, military power, and rhetorical fluency (pp. 3–9). *Oxford Latin Dictionary*, s.v. *Aerarium*, and s.v. *Aerarius*. In connection with memory, Carruthers (*Book of Memory*) locates meanings in the Middle Ages analogous to those of Vives, although *aerarium* (from *aes*,

aeris, "copper, brass") is not one of the terms she connects with memory. *Aerarium* carries a strongly material and specifically monetary meaning. *Thesaurus*, "treasury," the word that most commonly occurs in connection with memory, often carries a more general reference to a chamber, storehouse, or repository, not necessarily for money and including immaterial things. Other words for memory Carruthers treats — *arca, sacculus, scrinium* (whence English *shrine*) — include monetary associations. Cf. Halpern, *Poetics*, p. 91.

95. Tilley, *Dictionary of the Proverbs*, p. vii; Bacon, *De Augmentis*, vi.1, *Works*, IX, 110: "For we are handling here the currency (so to speak) of things intellectual, and it is not amiss to know that as moneys may be made of other material besides gold and silver, so other Notes of Things may be coined besides words and letters." Cf. Jonson, *Timber*, pp. 620, 622.

96. A fairly close medieval analogy occurs in William Langland's *Piers Plowman*: "Thow myꝫtest bettre meete myst on Maluerne hilles / Than gete a mom of hire [the barristers'] mouþ til moneie be shewed": *Will's Visions of Piers Plowman*, Pro.211–16. The linguistic emphasis of this passage and of Langland's late medieval poem as a whole is another instance of the extent to which this "morning star of the Reformation" (to quote a Renaissance editor of *Piers Plowman*) anticipates sixteenth-century concerns. Yet the focus of Langland's passage, unlike Rabelais's, remains primarily moral rather than linguistic.

97. According to Starnes, the *Thesauri* of Cooper and Estienne were "part of the standard equipment of school libraries and individual libraries" in the period: *Estienne's Influence*, pp. 99–100, cf. pp. 10–11, 104; Watson describes Estienne's (i.e., Stephanus's) *Thesaurus* as "the great general dictionary" of the period: *English Grammar Schools*, p. 387; cf. also Baldwin, *"Small Latine & Lesse Greek,"* I, 422, 528–31. Although dictionaries existed in the Middle Ages, in the absence of the printing press they were subordinate to a mnemonic tradition: see Daly and Daly, "Some Techniques," pp. 229–39; and Gabriele Stein, *The English Dictionary*, pp. 114–15. Other sixteenth-century dictionaries with names that allude to the earlier mnemonic tradition while belonging to a pervasive printed one are Simon Pelegromius's *Synonymorvm Sylva* and John Baret's *Alvearie or Triple Dictionarie* (*Quadruple Dictionarie* in its second edition, 1580); cf. Carruthers, *Book of Memory*, pp. 33, 35–36, 62. Addressing the reader in a preface, Baret explains *Alvearie* ("beehive") in a way that shifts its meaning from the trained memory to the written and eventually

printed externalization of it. Withals's *Shorte Dictionarie for Yonge Begynners*, described by Stein (pp. 194–95) as being "in the lexicographical tradition of the medieval vocabularies," is the exception that proves the rule. Withals's prologue emphasizes memory and the laying up of treasure in it. Not surprisingly, this work is brief (appropriate for the memories of young students), and its arrangement of entries is topical rather than alphabetical like that of most other dictionaries of the period.

98. *Traicté de la conformité dv langage françois auec le Grec* (Paris: Robert Estienne, 1569), **.vᵛ. For the date of Estienne's treatise, see Clément, *Henri Estienne*, p. 506. The first quotation from the *Traicté* is cited by Norton, *Ideology and Language of Translation*, p. 259. See also the discussion of *propriety/proprietas* in Bloch, *Etymologies and Genealogies*, chaps. 1–2, e.g., pp. 40–41, 85.

99. Webbe, *An Appeale to Truth*, pp. 14 (my emphasis) and 34.

100. See Margaret Mann Phillips, trans., *Erasmus on His Times*, p. 3: "Proverbs," Erasmus explains, "should be as clear–cut as gems"; their "force and significance which are contained in the concision" of their words "should recur on every monument everywhere."

101. Aristotle, *De interpretatione*, in *Works*, I, 25. Augustine, *The Trinity*, XLV, 475, 477–78: Bk. XV.x.18–20, xi.20; and Augustine, *Sermons*, XXXVIII, 15: Sermon 187, 3. Waswo, *Language and Meaning*, pp. 88–113, maintains that Lorenzo Valla's notion of language was relational rather than referential, but his book also suggests that Valla's *theorized* position was exceptional rather than normative in the period. Gravelle, "The Latin-Vernacular Question," argues that other Humanists besides Valla "sought . . . to prove that language determines culture and thought" (p. 386). For an indication of how fiercely contested this issue is, see the highly charged exchange between Monfasani, "Was Lorenzo Valla an Ordinary Language Philosopher?" and, in the opposing camp, Waswo, "Motives of Misreading," and Gravelle, "A New Theory of Truth."

102. Spenser, *Var.*, X, 119.

103. Bacon, *Novum Organum*, in *Works*, VIII, 86.

104. *Life and Letters of John Donne*, II, 16.

105. See Stein, *English Dictionary*, pp. 128, 184–86: for an example of such an entry, consider the headword "Crampe, whych is a defecte of the synnowes and muscles, whereby somtyme the whole bodye, and sometyme parte therof is stretched, if it be in parte of the bodye, then it is thus Englished, crampe: if it be in the entier body (whych is rare) the name therof in oure mother tonge is not knowen." The translation equivalent

now follows, "*Conuultio. onis, Spasmus*, (?) graece σπασμός [*sic*]. Some learned man maye Englyshe it" (cited from Richard Huloet, *Abecedarium Anglico-Latinum*).

Chapter 2

1. A curiously relevant example of the weighted use of *locus* in a modern English environment can be found in Weimann, *Shakespeare and the Popular Tradition*, pp. 74ff. *Locus* occurs, of course, in the dramatic documents Weimann examines.

2. Based on Gravelle, "The Latin-Vernacular Question," p. 377; the Bruni-Poggio debate occurred in 1435. Mary Thomas Crane's remarks on the ambivalent position of Latin in Humanist education, *Framing Authority*, pp. 12–15, are illuminating. Cf. also Slights, "Scriptural Annotation," pp. 264–65; and Ong, "Latin Language Study."

3. Cited from the Scolar Press edition, p. 154 (diagram), pp. 158–61 ("artificiall" as a synonym for "Ciceronian"); see also pp. 147–48, 152 (the "vexation," "paine," and "feare" of mastering "true Latine and pure *Tully*").

4. See Orme, *English Schools*, pp. 88–98, here 96–99; also White, ed., *The Vulgaria*; Stanbridge, *Accidence* (ca. 1496); Horman, *Vulgaria* (1519). Watson, *Grammar Schools*, pp. 233, 253, notes that John Anwykyll (1483) and John Holt (ca. 1497) also wrote printed Latin grammars in English. The first surviving grammatical treatise to include limited explanations in English is John Cornwall's *Speculum grammaticale* in 1346 (Orme, p. 95).

5. White, ed., *The Vulgaria*, pp. lx–lxi. See also Jones, *Triumph of the English Language*, pp. 277–84. Cf. the instance of R. R.'s translation of Lily, chap. 1, n. 22. Padley, *Vernacular Grammar*, I, 147–53, lists ten elucidations of Lily in English between 1590 and 1660; such translations were a means of circumventing Lily's monopoly on the instruction of Latin, with its presentation in English of the rudiments only. Helgerson explores the politics of Elizabethan views of language in *Forms of Nationhood*, chap. 1.

6. See Stein, *English Dictionary*, pp. 2–3, 121–22. Also Starnes, *Renaissance Dictionaries*; and Starnes and Noyes, *English Dictionary*.

7. Tambiah, "The Magical Power of Words," pp. 180, 181: examples of disjunctive religious languages are "Latin in the occidental Catholic Church, Hebrew for Jews, Vedic Sanskrit for Hindus[, Pali for Bud-

dhists,] and Arabic for Muslims." On ritualized language, see also Bloch, "Symbols, Song, Dance."

8. Essentially this is Watson's translation of Vives in *On Education*, p. 91, but I have altered it at several points to bring it closer to the Latin: "Sacrarium est eruditionis lingua, et siue quid recondendum est, siue promendum uelut proma quaedam conda. Et quando aerarium est eruditionis, ac instrumentum societatis hominum, e re esset generis humani unam esse linguam, qua omnes nationes communiter uterentur" (*De tradendis*, p. 285).

9. Dante, *Il convivio*, ed. Bruna Cordati (Torino: Loescher, 1968), 1.5: "lo latino è perpetuo e non corruttibile" (p. 20); also Gravelle, "The Latin-Vernacular Question," p. 375. The Modistae extended and further rationalized Aristotle's view that words are symbols of mental experiences (affections in the soul) which are in turn images of things in the external world. Aristotle also held that since the external world is the same for all, then the inner world affected by it is the same as well, and only the sounds of the various languages are different. The Modistae went on to argue more specifically that grammar, which mirrors the structure of reality as grasped by the understanding, is not only universal but also universally that found in the Latin language. In the words of Bursill-Hall, *Speculative Grammars*, Latin was "thus raised to the status of a metalanguage," a universal language expressing "the universality of things as conceived and understood by the universality of human reason" (p. 38).

10. *Mulcaster's Elementarie*, pp. 177, 269. Mulcaster (1530?–1611) was headmaster of Merchant Taylors' School from 1561 to 1586 and of St. Paul's from 1596 to 1608.

11. I refer here to Dante's idealization of Latin in *Il convivio*, as cited above, rather than to his (inconsistent) views elsewhere. In *De vulgari eloquentia*, I.i (p. 7), Dante contradicts his characterization of Latin (and Greek) in *Il convivio* as the noblest of languages by declaring the vulgar tongue nobler ("nobilior est vulgaris"); his reasons for doing so are based predominantly on origin ("prima") and naturalness ("naturalis," not "artificialis"), although, sandwiched between these two reasons, he both notes and qualifies the vernacular's currency ("totus orbis ipsa perfruitur, licet in diversas prolationes et vocabula sit divisa"). Linguistic change is gradual and uneven.

12. "Alexander Gil's *Logonomia Anglica*," trans. Dorothy Dixon, p. 333. I have derived the cognate "consecration" from Gil's "sacratae sunt"

("are consecrated"). The rest of Gil's Latin statement reads, "sacratae sunt hae linguae [i.e., Hebrew, Greek, Latin]. . . . Atque ideo Sacrosanctus ille Christi spiritus, qui doctorum Christianorum coetum vniuersum regit, per unam linguam Latinam, nulli genti vulgarem, ideoque mutationibus non obnoxiam . . . linguarum peritiam induxit": *Logonomia Anglica*, p. 151.

13. "To the Reader," *A Worlde of Wordes, or Most Copious, and exact* Dictionarie *in Italian and* English, 1598; printed as the appendix to the facsimile of Florio's second edition, *Queen Anna's New World of Words, or Dictionarie of the* Italian *and* English *tongues* (1611). In the *Scholae grammaticae*, Peter Ramus also refers to Latin as a "book language": cited in Padley, *Vernacular Grammar*, I, 26–27. In the 1660s, John Wilkins similarly explains that "*learned* Languages [like Latin] which have now ceased to be *vulgar*, and remain onely in Books, by which the purity of them is regulated, may, whilst these Books are extant and studied, continue the same without change": *An Essay Towards a Real Character*, p. 6.

14. See, for example, Abraham Wright, *Five Sermons*; and the discussion by Davies, *Worship and Theology in England from Andrewes to Baxter and Fox, 1603–1690*, pp. 135–36. Wright gives examples of Anglican, Presbyterian, and Independent preaching.

15. Perkins, *Workes*, II, 670–71; cf. Thomas Cranmer's remonstrances in a letter to Queen Mary: Foxe, *Acts and Monuments*, VIII, 93; likewise, Lawrence Chaderton's sermon at Paul's Cross in 1578: "many ['stuffe their sermons'] with curious affected figures, with Latine, Greeke, and Hebrue sentences, without any iust occasion offered by their texte" (cited by Harold Fisch, "Puritans," p. 232). On the connection between religious iconoclasm and verbal images, see W. J. T. Mitchell, *Iconology*, p. 113 and chap. 1; and Watt, *Cheap Print*, chap. 4. Commenting on the methods of the Rheims editors of the Bible, Tribble in *Margins and Marginality* notes its heavy reliance on Latin forms (e.g., "exaniniated") and concludes that the editors seek to introduce "unfamiliarity and difficulty" into the biblical text, pp. 47–48. Her evaluative terms suggest a Reformation point of view. Peter Blayney has pointed out to me the extent to which Reformation polemics in Elizabethan England pointedly employed a *roman* font to represent Catholic positions and black letter, a good native font, to represent more enlightened Protestant ones.

16. "The Idolatrous Eye," p. 287. Stubbes is cited from Arthur Freeman's facsimile of the May 1, 1583, edition, Lv.

17. Andrewes, *Ninety-Six Sermons*, in *Works*, V, 61.

18. From Rider, "Directions for the Reader," *Bibliotheca Scholastica*. Rider's dictionary was subsequently revised and enlarged by Francis Holyoke, and it saw 23 reissues and editions in the first 60 years of the seventeenth century. Significantly, in revising Rider, Holyoke added a Latin-English dictionary, taking considerable material from Thomas's dictionary, with which the Rider-Holyoke dictionary then competed. Eventually, in the 1620s, the Rider-Holyoke version appears to have become dominant in the market. The fact that it offered an English-Latin as well as a Latin-English lexicon may bear on its increasing popularity. On the extensive debt of both Rider and Holyoke to Thomas's dictionary, see Starnes, *Renaissance Dictionaries*, pp. 218–71, esp. 224, 243–47; and for editions of Rider-Holyoke, see Stein, *English Dictionary*, pp. 419–31.

19. Miles Smith has been identified as the writer of this preface; see Opfell, *King James Bible Translators*, pp. 61–62 and chap. 10. On Andrewes's role in translating the authorized version, see chaps. 1, 3.

20. *The Holy Bible Conteyning the Old Testament, and the New*, 1611, Bii[r-v]. Tribble, *Margins and Marginality*, pp. 54–55, citing a portion of the translators' preface, interprets their concern with variants as containment. I admire Tribble's book, but coming to the translators' preface from the perspective of language, I cannot agree.

21. In a provocative discussion of Andrewes's writing, Shuger, *Habits of Thought*, pp. 65–67, puzzles over two of his polemical works, *A Discourse of Ceremonies* and *Two Answers to Cardinall Perron*, that indicate considerable historical and anthropological sophistication regarding the origin of religious ritual. She characterizes them as shockers and "experiments in humanist demystification" but essentially dismisses their challenge to a totally mystified attitude toward language on Andrewes's part. She finds them instances of the intellectual fragmentation endemic to the period. Much as I like Shuger's work, I suspect that such compartmentalization of Andrewes's interests oversimplifies his position.

22. Kinney, *Humanist Poetics*, p. 36; cf. p. 31.

23. On medieval dictionaries, see Daly and Daly, "Some Techniques," pp. 229–39; Orme, *English Schools*, pp. 92–94, Stein, *English Dictionary*, pp. 53–121.

24. Quotation from Starnes, *Renaissance Dictionaries*, p. 107. Unless otherwise indicated, reference is to Cooper's 1565 edition, rpt. 1969.

25. Cf. the comprehensive bilingual *Catholicon Anglicum* of the late Middle Ages, which includes verses describing differences in meaning

that were clearly meant as mnemonic aids: see Stein, *English Dictionary*, pp. 114–15.

26. As Cooper explains the paragraph sign, "Vbicunque repereris hanc notam ascriptam.¶.ibi scito vel significationem, vel usum dictionis nonnihil discrepare ab eo, quod proxime superius praecesserat": from "Annotationes Quibus studiosi lectores . . ." [(*)3ᵛ]. Commentary suggests some uncertainty about this explanation. I borrow the translation "thing" for *dictio* from Starnes's "paraphrase" (in pseudo-Elizabethan English), *Renaissance Dictionaries*, p. 102, since the Latin word signifies "meaning," rather than simply acoustic image (Padley, *Latin Tradition*, p. 264). My rendering of *nonnihil* comes directly from Cooper's exclusive translation equivalent of this word in his *Thesaurus*: "somewhat, a little."

27. Stein, *English Dictionary*, p. 210; I have drawn on pp. 209–16 for the present discussion. Starnes, *Renaissance Dictionaries*, p. 52, similarly refers to an "etymological arrangement" of derivatives.

28. Between 1565 and 1587, Cooper's *Thesaurus* went through five editions, according to Stein; the prefatory note to the Scolar facsimile notes as well a printing of Cooper in 1584 that Stein does not record. Between 1587 and 1644, Thomas's dictionary went through sixteen re-issues or editions. These figures speak not only to the popularity of both works but also to the increasing popularity of dictionaries themselves. Stein lists editions on pp. 410–31; see also p. 313. Citations to Thomas will be to the 1587 edition.

29. In comparison to Cooper's *Thesaurus*, Thomas's dictionary is considerably more compact and easier to handle, a fact pertinent to repeated referential use. Like the Thomas dictionary, Rider-Holyoke is alphabetically arranged and, particularly in Holyoke's section, which first appeared in 1606, looks relatively modern. Likewise alphabetical in arrangement is Calepine's (i.e., Ambrogio Calepino's) popular *Dictionarium*, which was first published as a Latin dictionary in 1502 but was combined with various vernacular languages as the century progressed. English was added to "the Calepine" in 1585. The most popular dictionary of the sixteenth century was John Withals's *Shorte Dictionarie for Yonge Begynners*, an English-Latin topical vocabulary first published in 1553. Withals's is a beginning school text and in no sense a comprehensive dictionary—indeed, in Starnes's view in *Renaissance Dictionaries*, pp. 182–83, according to standards in place by the 1580s, it is not even a dictionary, properly speaking.

30. *An Alvearie or Triple Dictionarie*, 1574, Cʳ: my emphasis on "how-

soeuer . . . reast" and "(they say)." I have also italicized proper names and references where the original has either italic or roman type, as distinct from the black letter of the main body of text.

31. In 1604 Robert Cawdrey published the first monolingual English dictionary, a work in the "hard word" tradition rather than the comprehensive one. Cawdrey's work was aimed at the marginally literate, namely, "Ladies, Gentlewomen, or any other vnskilfull persons." Although Cawdrey advised his readers to "learne the Alphabet . . . perfectly without booke, and where euery Letter standeth" in order to make use of his own book, he nonetheless found it appropriate to entitle his work *A Table Alphabeticall of Hard Usual English Words*, thus implying that alphabetical order was a familiar idea. Edmund Coote's *English Schoole-Maister*, a pre–grammar school book similarly intended for the "vnskilfull," explains both basic numbering (i.e., 1, 2, 3, 4, etc.) and how to use the alphabetical list of hard words included (pp. 65, 72–73). On pp. 1–2, Coote provides material found in a hornbook, namely, printings of the alphabet in six different typefaces and simple rudiments of spelling. In view of the purpose, intended audience, and explanations by Cawdrey and Coote (e.g., A4^{r-v}), I am puzzled by the weight Ferry, in *Art of Naming*, pp. 19–21, gives their works in asserting the unfamiliarity of alphabetical order to the Renaissance reading public, as well as by her similar use, p. 21, of Withals's *Shorte Dictionarie for Yonge Begynners*, rev. William Clerk. Withals's book, first revised in the sixteenth century by Lewis Evans and then by Abraham Fleming, and early in the seventeenth century by Clerk, is topically organized, although it introduces alphabetical headings (A, B, C, etc.) near its end, employing mnemonic, etymological, associative, and contrastive, as well as alphabetical, groupings beneath these: *A Shorte Dictionarie most profitable for Yong Beginners*, rev. Lewis Evans, 1568, pp. 71^{v}ff. Further augmenting Withals and in the process obscuring (but retaining) the structure of its groupings, Clerk thought appropriate an apology for the overall topical organization: "And though . . . [this dictionary] leadeth not, as do the rest, by the way of the *Alphabet*, yet hath it . . . the fittest *order*, and the fittest method for yong beginners" (preface to the 1608 edition of *A Dictionarie in English and Latine for Children, and yong beginners*). Classification of the various revisions of Withals can be confusing: e.g., Ferry, p. 21, refers to Clerk as the author of Withals 1602.

32. Quotation from Hart's *Orthographie*, 9^r; the complete title of Hart's book speaks for itself: *An Orthographie, conteyning the due order*

and reason, howe to write or paint thimage of mannes voice, most like to the life or nature; subsequent reference is to this edition except where specified otherwise. Cf. Smith, *De recta et emendata linguae Anglicae scriptione*, 5ᵛ: "Est autem scriptura, imitatio sermonis, vt pictura corporis . . . vt vere possit dici scriptionem esse vocum picturam." Jones aptly encapsulates Smith's view in the phrase *"ut pictura, orthographia"* (*Triumph of the English Language*, p. 145). Baret refers to Smith in *An Alvearie* when discussing the letters *H* and *S*, for example, and to "Maister H. Chesters booke" (i.e., to Hart) when treating the letter *I*.

33. Stein, *English Dictionary*, pp. 8, 14–15, describes the alphabetization of Glossaries in the eight and ninth centuries. According to Rouse and Rouse, an early medieval example of alphabetical ordering dates from the middle of the eleventh century, and by the thirteenth century, "all significant" collections of *distinctiones* were alphabetized (*"Statim invenire,"* pp. 201–25, here pp. 203, 210). The early lexicons Daly and Daly describe in "Some Techniques" are all alphabetized to an extent and one, the *Catholicon* of 1286, is even alphabetized throughout words, rather than just through their first three letters. Widely known examples of alphabetization are abundant in both the vernacular and Latin traditions of the Renaissance period (e.g., the index of proverbs in Erasmus's *Adagia*).

34. Harris's work has been formative to my thinking about these matters, and I am indebted to it here: *The Language-Makers*, pp. 133–34.

35. Peacham's explanation of tropology clearly invites application of Derrida's notion of the supplement. Cf. Derek Attridge's illuminating discussion of the supplement in Puttenham's analysis of Renaissance rhetoric: *Peculiar Language*, pp. 17–45.

36. See Rouse and Rouse, *"Statim invenire,"* pp. 201–25; and Stein, *English Dictionary*, pp. 8–50.

37. Singer, "Hieroglyphs," comments incisively on this development: "The language problem of the early seventeenth century occurred when it was thought that words had slipped out of their rightful place and slipped in between ideas and nature" (p. 67).

38. I.e., Joseph and Julius Caesar. Fungerus (Johannes Fungeri) (d. 1612), a Dutch educator, published *Etymologicum Latinum ex probatissimis philologis, philosophis* in 1605 and *Etymologicon trilingue, Latinum, Graecum et Hebraicum* in 1607: van der Aa, ed., *Biographisch Woordenboek der Nederlanden*, V, 84.

39. Estienne died in Geneva in 1559; this preface, dated 1561, is attributed to Albert Burer, alias Johannes Albertus Burerus or Burerius (Basel: Froben, 1578), I, A2ʳ: "Haud secus habet cum eo, qui orationis exaedificationem constructionemque meditatur: eum enim necesse est primum formae, deinde materiae habere rationem [regardless of the style he wants to effect — copious or brief]. . . . Verum haec omnia frustra excogitasset, nisi materiam, ex qua ipsa construatur, et in qua forma eluceat, aptam compararet. Materia autem orationis, partim est in verbis, partim in rebus ipsis." Burer evidently worked with Beatus Rhenanus, editing Latin texts for Froben: see D'Amico, *Theory and Practice*, pp. 59–60; also Woodmin, ed., *Velleius Paterculus* (2.41–93), p. 1 et passim. Analogously, in his preface "To the Reader," William Lily thinks of grammar as the foundation of a building: "no buyldynge [can] bee perfecte, when as the foundacion and grounde worke is readye to fall, and vnable to vphold the burthen of the frame" (1567 edition: A.iiʳ). Elsky mentions Lily's comparison and also points out that the spelling reformer Thomas Smith employs the word *exaedificare* to refer to the composition of words from letters (*Authorizing Words*, pp. 10–11). Examples could be multiplied indefinitely.

40. Scaliger's *Poetices libri septem*, p. 55, provides a striking analogue to the 1578 preface of Estienne's *Thesaurus*. Quintilian is a notable common source behind both works: "*Omnis autem oratio constat aut ex iis, quae significantur, aut et iis, quae significant, id est rebus et verbis*": *Institutio oratoria*, trans. H. E. Butler, I, 396–97: "Every speech, moreover, consists at once of that which is signified and that which signifies, that is, of things [subject matter] and words" (Bk. III.v.1). In the interest of clarity, I have altered Butler's translation. See Heninger, *Sidney and Spenser*, pp. 211, 545, n. 130.

41. Cited from Harris, *The Language-Makers*, p. 133, which again influences my argument. Harris sees in these developments "the psychological foundation . . . for all modern forms of structuralism." The phrase "psychological foundation" is a careful hedge, one that spans centuries of development, including those that follow the Renaissance. Harris is not primarily concerned with immediate historical context and the slow, uneven development of the changes he describes. He ties these changes more closely to the specific development of the monolingual dictionary than I think the evidence warrants, perhaps because his attention focuses on the eventual formulation of Saussurean structuralism (p. 156).

42. Cf. Arthur F. Kinney, *Humanist Poetics*, p. 24; in pp. 8–22, Kinney demonstrates the motivation of fiction by Humanist practices of education.

43. Puttenham, *Arte of English Poesie*, p. 157. By "English Dictionaries" Puttenham presumably refers to bilingual and polyglot dictionaries that included English, since no monolingual dictionaries as yet existed. Starnes, *Renaissance Dictionaries*, p. 110, goes further: "There being no English dictionaries, it is fairly certain that the Latin-English of Elyot and Cooper in a measure filled that lack, and were intended to do so." (Thomas Elyot published a Latin-English *Dictionary* in 1538.) Whether referring to English or to Latin, the 1568 preface of Lewis Evans's revision of the brief English-Latin Withals *Dictionarie* for children is also suggestive: "I haue weeded oute a number of barbarous wordes, and in their places I haue planted, wordes which be in vse, and well allowed" (ii^v).

44. Levins, "The Preface to the Reader," *Manipulus Vocabulorum*, p. 3 (my emphasis on *set*). See Stein, *English Dictionary*, pp. 166–68, 230: in 1552, the *Dictionariolum puerorum tribus linguis Latina, Anglica and Gallica conscriptum*, John Veron's redaction of Robert Estienne's earlier Latin-French dictionary, follows Estienne's practice of indicating accent for Latin words, but Levins's dictionary is the first to indicate accentual stress for the vernacular. Levins also indicates that certain words cited are archaic and not for general use, and he formulates some rules for spelling (Stein, pp. 229–30, 240). All the sixteenth-century orthographers of note advocated the marking of accent (or stress) in English words: namely, Sir Thomas Smith, John Hart, William Bullokar, and Richard Mulcaster (only in the case of ambiguity), in 1568, 1569, 1580, and 1582, respectively.

45. Cf. Ricoeur, *Rule of Metaphor*, pp. 290–91 (*tête, testa*); this issue figures in Ricoeur's debate with Derrida concerning metaphor. For an account of it sympathetic to Derridean (de)constructions, see LaCapra's review essay, "Who Rules Metaphor?"

46. The influx of new words into English during this period is relevant to the instability of the language and to the desire to arrest it. Bateson has reported that "An analysis of forty pages of the *Shorter Oxford Dictionary* has shown that of every 100 words in use in 1600, 39 were introduced between 1500 and 1600": *English Poetry*, p. 31, n. 1. Scragg, *History of English Spelling*, pp. 53–81, discusses both the printers' accep-

tance between 1550 and 1650 of a stable system of spelling and the unevenness of such acceptance during much of this period.

47. Bullokar, *Short Introduction*, p. 1 (1580) and p. 1 (1581). See *OED*, s.v. *Stay, sb.²*, 1: "Something that supports or steadies something else; also 1b, 1c; and *Stay, sb.³*, 1, 3, 6, 7, 7b: "A permanent state or condition." On p. 20 of the 1581 edition, Bullokar clearly uses *staied* to mean "stopped, stabilized," or the like: "whereas men be of opinion, that our language is at this present time in perfect and sensible use: my opinion is, that it is the great goodnes of God, if the same be now staied in that perfectnes, *which may continue as long as letters shall endure*" (my emphasis).

48. For another example, see Thomas Wilson, *The Rule of Reason*, 1553, p. 37: "A difinicion of the substaunce, is a speache, whiche sheweth the very nature of the thing." By "speache," Wilson means a logical definition or predicated statement.

49. Quotation from Scragg, *History of English Spelling*, p. 63.

50. See Slaughter, *Universal Languages*, p. 86. Also Wilkins, *An Essay*, p. 385, who explains that speech came first and writing was afterwards its "figure," or representation, and "in order of time subsequent to it; yet in order of *Nature* there is no priority between these: But *voice* and *sounds* may be as well assigned to Figure, as *Figures* may be *Sounds*."

51. "Epistle Dedicatorie" to *A Worlde of Wordes*, from the Appendix to *Queen Anna's New World of Words*. The works by Citolini, Garzoni, and Alunno that Florio mentions in connection with his title are all sources he used in compiling his dictionary. In Florio's words, *La tipocosmia* ("The Type or Figure of the World") and *La piazza vniversale di tvtte le professioni del mondo, e nobili et ignobile* ("The Universal Piazza of all the professions of the world, both noble and ignoble") have between them more "words concerning euerie seuerall trade, arte, or occupation for euerie particular toole, or implement belonging vnto them, then euer any man heeretofore . . . collected in any booke" ("Epistle Dedicatorie"). *La fabrica del mondo* ("The Frame or Fabric of the World") consists of topically organized quotations and features material from Dante, Petrarch, and Boccaccio; it also offers an alphabetical table of words cited from these and other authors.

52. Michaell de Montaigne, *The Essayes*, trans. John Florio, A5ᵛ; the succeeding citation occurs in the same passage.

53. Florio's metaphor recalls the bins, pigeonholes, treasure chests,

and the like associated anciently and in the Middle Ages with memory (Carruthers, *Book of Memory*, pp. 33, 36–37). They testify again to the gradual, progressive supplementing and displacing of the mnemonic thesaurus by the printed one — in this case, by the comprehensive dictionary.

Chapter 3

1. Quotation from Padley, *Vernacular Grammar*, I, 156. As Padley observes, even Ben Jonson's English *Grammar*, which is based mainly on the Latin grammar of Peter Ramus, maintains that "single words must by their very nature be treated prior to any syntactic discussion" (p. 59). See Jonson, *Works*, VIII, 466: "*Dictionis natura prior est, posterior orationis.*" Cf. Salmon, *Study of Language*, p. 31.

2. Donaldson repeatedly remarked this change: for background to it see his second edition of *Chaucer's Poetry*, pp. 1043, 1138, 1140. Greene has an excellent and more extensive discussion of its pertinence to Wyatt's lyrics, and I am close to his reading here: *The Light in Troy*, pp. 254–56. The meaning of *trouth* is a recurrent theme in Chaucer's poetry and an urgent issue in Langland's, yet even in *Piers Plowman* questions about the nature and location of truth have a firmer moral and religious frame of reference than in the work of Wyatt and other writers in the sixteenth century.

3. Goody, *Domestication of the Savage Mind*, pp. 74–111, has a chapter on the implications of listing that is useful despite his tendency to make the objectifying function of a list abstractly causal, rather than subject to cultural perception, of which in this case the dictionary itself might be labeled "exhibit A." The circularity I invoke by this statement is analogous to that everywhere present in Bourdieu's argument that practices *are* perceptions: e.g., *Theory of Practice*, chap. 4. See also Wagner, *Symbols*, chap. 6.

4. My use of the word *narrative* reflects that of Lyotard, who puts the connection of narrative with customary knowledge in opposition to the implications of *technology*: *Postmodern Condition*, p. 19 et passim. On the growing interest in etymology that characterizes the late sixteenth and seventeenth centuries, see Starnes, *Renaissance Dictionaries*, pp. 235, 258–60; and Weekley, "Our Early English Etymologists." Cf. also Grafton, *Joseph Scaliger*, I, 116–17.

5. Pages 386, 21. I am stepping outside the Renaissance parameters

of my project to discuss Wilkins's *Essay* dated 1668, just four years before his death; the *Essay* extends ideas Wilkins purports to find in the work of Bacon—hardly surprising in view of Wilkins's birth near the beginning of the seventeenth century.

6. In a wide-ranging and thoroughly illuminating essay, Coudert demonstrates the mystical and magical ideas of language that underlie the conception of a real or natural language in the seventeenth century: "Some Theories of a Natural Language."

7. Agrippa, *Three Books*, p. 153. To the first of the citations from Agrippa, cf. Mulcaster, *Elementarie*, p. 188: "For euen God himself, who brought the creatures, which he had made, vnto that first man, whom he had also made, that he might name them, according to their properties, doth planelie declare by his so doing, what a cunning thing it is to giue right names, and how necessarie it is, to know their forces, which be allredie giuen, bycause the word being knowen, which implyeth the propertie the thing is half known, whose propertie is emplyed."

8. Wilkins, *An Essay*, p. 5, explains that the Hebrew known to fallen human beings is "not . . . the same which was con-created with our first Parents, and spoken by *Adam* in *Paradise*."

9. For a culturally central example, besides Mulcaster, *Elementarie*, p. 188, see Camden, *Remaines, concerning Britaine*, pp. 34–35: Camden explains that "the *Etymology* or reason whence many . . . [English words] are deriued" is as readily found "as in the learned tongues" and gives such examples as the derivation of *God* from *good*, *summer* from *sun*, and *sayle* from *sea-haile*. Subsequently, however, he refers ironically to "the Mint-masters of our *Etymologies*" who have "merily forged" such whimsies as "*Flatter* from flie-at-her," "*Mayd* as my ayd," and "*Symony* [as] *See-mony*." He mentions relevant views of Isidore, Varro, Plato, the Pythagoreans, the Jews, the magicians (the power ascribed to the word "abradacarba," as the 1614 edition spells it) and later concludes, "For this is to be taken as a granted verity, that names [in the limited sense] among all nations and tongues . . . are significatiue, and not vaine senslesse sounds" (pp. 52–53, cf. p. 47). Cf. Camden, *Britain*, "The Author to the Reader," 4ᵛ: "*Plato in his* Cratilus *commandeth that we recall the originals of names to the barbarous tongues (for so he called all but Greek) as being most ancient*." Another historian, George Buchanan, scorns "this Enquiry after the Original of Words," but even he maintains that the names of nations and cities, are significant, since "they were not *rashly* imposed at the begin-

ning, but . . . by general and deep advice and consent by their *Founders*, . . . [and they] receive no alteration without a mighty Perturbation of the whole": *History of Scotland*, pp. 3, 62.

10. From the 1543 edition (Paris: Robertus Stephanus [i.e., Estienne]): "Suapte natura, inquit Valla, ponderosum significat: vt Graue saxum, grauis sarcina, grauia arma, graue scutum, quod scilicet grauat nos in ferendo, et quod aegre, et cum molestia fertur. Inde per abusionem transferimus ad senectutem, ad morbum, ad laborem, ad dolorem: quia hi qui molestiam ex senectute, morbo, caeterisque sentiunt, quasi onere intolerabili premuntur, quod cupide velut graue pondus a se vellent deponere. Neque solum ad molestias corporis translatio haec fit, verum etiam ad molestias animi, vt grauis contumelia, grauis iniuria, grauis moeror, grauis iactura, quae animum genere quodam ponderis premunt. Itaque vnus modus est, quae corpori aut animo molesta sunt, ea grauia appellare. Eoque molestia a mole, id est a re magna, magnique ponderis vocitata est. Alter modus est, quod quemadmodum grauia saxa et grandes trunci non facile loco mouentur, sed ad omnem temporis mutabilitatem haerent: ita homines constantes, ac praediti sapientia, merito per figuram graues nominantur, quod nec precibus, nec minis, nec vanitate, nec promissis ab aequo et iusto summouentur: ut hi faciunt quos leues vocamus, qui in similitudinem pulueris et palearum ad omnem auram ventilantur."

11. Rand's essay on Coleridge's "Geraldine" affords useful parallels to Estienne's practice: *Untying the Text*, pp. 280–316.

12. By "Elyot," I refer both to the three editions of *The Dictionary of Syr Thomas Eliot knight* (1538, 1542, 1545, the latter two with the title *Bibliotheca Eliotae: Eliotis Librarie*) and the three subsequent revisions, including substantial augmentations, by Thomas Cooper (1548, 1552, 1559). Cooper utilized "much of the matter of the 1559 *Bibliotheca*" in his 1565 *Thesaurus* but vastly expanded it with material drawn from various other sources (Starnes, *Renaissance Dictionaries*, p. 233). Further reference to Elyot's dictionary will be to the 1538 edition.

Compare Estienne's definition of *gravis* given above with that of Cooper: "Heauy: greuous: peinfull: sore: substantiall: weightie: of good importance: graue or hauing grauitie: sage: discrete: sure, constant, plentious or full: stinkyng or hauyng a strong and ill sauour: difficile: hard: olde: aged." Aside from Elyot's *Bibliotheca*, Cooper's major source is Robert Estienne's Latin-French dictionary, based in turn on

Estienne's earlier Latin *Thesaurus* (Starnes, *Renaissance Dictionaries*, pp. 91, 93, 233).

13. From the title page of *Ductor in Linguas* (1617). Derek Attridge's essay on etymology is relevant and provocative: "Language as history/history as language."

14. I.e., "as Earth comes from lifting up, mountain from shaking" (A^{v}). Minsheu's Latin to this point reads, "*Nunc vero ad reprehensionem* vallae *vel* aliorum *qui ineptias aestimant* Etymologias; *opinor neminem esse qui affirmarit* vallam *dixisse* de sana et vera Etymologia, sed de facetis allusionibus et ridiculis illiterationibus *quales saepe apud* Varronem, *dum omnia* a Latinis *infeliciter trahit et* Petrum Lvmbardum."

15. Isidore, *Etymologiarum sive Originum*, I, Bk. I.xxix.

16. On purchasers of Minsheu's dictionary, see, in addition to catalogue(s) in the dictionaries themselves, Franklin B. Williams, Jr., "Scholarly Publication." Rosier characterizes Minsheu's dictionary as "one of the most common Jacobean books extant today"; 125 copies of the 1617 edition exist, and there could be more of the second edition: "Sources and Methods," p. 75.

17. I have benefited from Slaughter's study of the relationship of botanical taxonomy to the universal language movement in the seventeenth century; cf. *Universal Languages*, p. 9.

18. A partial exception, perhaps, is Isidore's tenth book, which explains the etymologies of words organized alphabetically according to their initial letter alone, yet even in this book, all the words have been topically selected; all pertain to human beings (*Etymologiae*, X.1). For a contemporary analogue to Minsheu's practice that is not lexical, see Camden's *Britain*, 4^{v}: interested more in discriminating than including, Camden apologizes for having once or twice offered two conjectures for the same name, since he believes that the name should be consonant to the thing and if "A sound, a forme, and colour [he declares himself perplexed as to how to capture the meaning of Plato's Greek] . . . *discover not themselves in the name I reiect the coniecture*."

19. I.e., "to raise or lift up, to elevate, because it [heaven] is raised and elevated above all things." In citing Minsheu's etymological entries (only), I have employed bold type for his emphatic black letter and italic emphasis for his roman type, and I have left his tiny italic undistinguished. To my eye, this scheme best suggests the relative emphases and effect of his text, and it avoids a confusing reversal of the modern con-

ventions of linguistic emphasis generally employed in this book. I have also indicated my expansions of Minsheu's abbreviations with brackets, as is not my practice elsewhere, because many of his abbreviations are part of his method or apparatus rather than simply conventional. My citations from Minsheu's preface and other explanations observe the usual conventions of modern typography, e.g., italic receives emphasis, and roman (or black letter, if present) does not. I have not attempted to represent the typography of the other early lexicons I treat.

20. Rosier, "Sources and Methods," p. 68, notes Minsheu's frequent (derivative) use of Old English to explain an etymology and, pp. 74–75, describes his characteristic methods. In the examples adduced for each method, the meaning is clearly the bottom line from which Minsheu's associative methods start. In a useful article, "John Minsheu: Scholar or Charlatan?" Schäfer observes that Minsheu employs all four major theories of linguistic origin in his etymologies — Latin, Greek, Hebrew, and Dutch — and then reproaches him for inconsistency. Yet Schäfer overlooks Minsheu's criticism of Varro for restricting his etymons to Latin and dismisses as "window dressing" his citation in the *Prima epistola lectori* of Joseph Scaliger's work on etymology (pp. 29–30). Scaliger's discovery of several "matrices" or families of linguistic origin, even if imperfectly understood by Minsheu, illuminates his effort to find rational etymons for English words in several languages presumed to be original.

21. Harris, *Language-Makers*, pp. 147–48. Quine's statement is in *From a Logical Point of View*, p. 22. See also William and Martha Kneale, *The Development of Logic*, pp. 6, 21, 94.

22. Modern logicians are likely to hold that Aristotelian logic is really about words, not reality. Emile Benveniste has demonstrated that Aristotle's categories actually depend on Greek grammar (pp. 56–62). Generally this is not a Renaissance perception, although there are suggestions of it in Bacon's distrust of language and in his contempt for Scholastic logic. For a more complex assessment of Aristotle's view, see Larkin, *Language in the Philosophy of Aristotle*, pp. 43–44; and McKeon, "Aristotle's Conception of Language," *Classical Philology* 41 (1946), and 42 (1947). Also Kneale and Kneale, *The Development of Logic*, pp. 26–27, and Maclean, "The Interpretation of Natural Signs," pp. 231–52, here p. 245.

23. Harris's need, *Language-Makers*, p. 128, to overlook medieval lexicons, despite his evident suspicion that they are relevant to modern ones, is a giveaway; he also does not seem aware of the Papias dictionary (1053), which is "close to modern theory and practice," or aware of its

relatives and successors in the Middle Ages: see Daly and Daly, "Some Techniques," esp. pp. 229–35.

24. I have borrowed the *sheep/mouton* example from Jonathan Culler's somewhat different use of it in *Ferdinand de Saussure*, , p. 43; and the *arbor/arbre* example from Norton, *Ideology and Language of Translation*, pp. 128–29.

25. In Cicero, *De inventione, De optimo genere oratorum, Topica*, trans. H. M. Hubbell, IV.26, VIII.35–37: "Definitio est oratio quae id quod definitur explicat quid sit." Cf. *Topica*, II.11–13, IV–VIII passim.

26. *Institutio oratoria*, I.vi.29–30: "in definitionibus assignatur etymologiae locus."

27. *De duplici copia verborum ac rerum commentarii duo*, by Desiderius Erasmus of Rotterdam: *On Copia of Words and Ideas*, p. 67. The Latin reads, "etymologia . . . finitionis ceu species quaedam est": *De duplici copia verborum ac rerum*, ed. Betty I. Knott, *Opera Omnia*, I–6, p. 230 (Bk II.824). Knott, in her translation, renders the Latin more loosely, "[the] exposition of the meaning of a word [*etymologia*] . . . is a form of definition": *"Copia": Foundations of the Abundant Style*, XXIV, 606. *De copia* was a basic school text in the Renaissance.

28. Cited from p. 37: "generall" in Sprague's edition reads "gererall"; I have emended this obvious misprint. Compare with Wilson's view the distinction between logical and merely verbal definition of the Ramist Dudley Fenner: *"Notation* . . . is the interpretation of a name, which appertaineth not to Logike but to Dictionaries": *Artes of Logike and Rhetorike*, Aiii[r]. Fenner also rigorously distinguishes a "perfect Definition" (genus and species) from a "description" (any other distinguishing "Reason," i.e., characteristic or cause): Biii[r-v].

29. Bacon, *De Augmentis*, in *Works*, IX, 101 (Bk. V.iv).

30. Ibid., IX, 69 (Bk. V.ii).

31. Calvin, *Institutes of the Christian Religion*, I, 108 (Bk. I.xi). Aston, *England's Iconoclasts*, I, 437, 453, notes this and another relevant statement by William Perkins in *A Warning against the Idolatrie of the last times*: "the right way to conceive God, is not to conceive any form, but to conceive in mind his properties and proper effects. So soon as the mind frames unto itself any form of God . . . an idol is set up in the mind."

32. See Aristotle, *De interpretatione*, 16b 19–22, in *Works*, I, 26; and Larkin, *Language in the Philosophy of Aristotle*, pp. 31–32, which I follow here. Larkin notes that the term *name* or *noun* ("ὄνομα") includes not only verbs, but also "all the declinable parts of speech except perhaps the

relatives" and speculates that "the reason for this is that 'case' as used by Aristotle is broader than the present grammatical usage," comprising "tense, number, and voice of verbs," "genders and cases of nouns," "adjectives derived from the noun and the adverb derived from the adjective," and "the singular and plural forms of nouns." In addition, of course, "adjectives and adverbs are reduced to the noun and the verb," a practice with ramifications for grammatical categories themselves throughout antiquity, the Middle Ages, and the Renaissance.

33. Another passage Ferry invokes in *Art of Naming*, p. 65, is conceptually similar to the one concerning accidents and similarly challenges her interpretation when restored to its context. In it, Wilson discusses "woordes annexed, or knit to the substaunce," and Ferry excerpts the following example of the blurring of noun with verb: "As nobilitie, powre, fame, aucthoritie. To bee an Oficer, a Maior, A Sherief." Restored to its context, this example reads, "As touchyng wordes knit, ye maie vnderstande, that thei are ioigned outwardly to the subiect, and geue a name vnto him, accordyng as thei are. As richesse are ioigned to a riche man. For where as Crassus, is called a man by his awne substaunce, yet notwithstandyng by his richesse, he is called a riche man." Further examples follow, including wearables, moods, conditions, and "al soche as are casuall to man." But some things are annexed to man, Wilson continues, that are "farther of" than "thinges worne vpon his backe . . . and rather perceiued by vnderstandyng then knowen by yie sight. As nobilitie, powre, fame, aucthoritie. To bee an Officer, a Maior, a Sherief, Lorde Chauncelour, Comptroller, or any other officer in the common weale, al these are annexed to their inferiour, ouer whom thei haue aucthoritie" (pp. 116–17). "To bee an Officer" is obviously an accidental or qualitative distinction as Wilson uses it and one that the pointing of the sixteenth-century text separates, just enough to avoid grammatical confusion (in the modern sense), from the nouns, "nobilitie" and the like, that precede it.

Another example of grammatical insensitivity Ferry cites, p. 65, comes from the Withals *Shorte Dictionarie*, rev. William Clerk, but as she seems to recognize on p. 21, this dictionary for beginners employs other principles besides grammar and the alphabet for its organization — principles variously topical, etymological, synonymous, antonymous, analogous. Instead of indicating an indifference to grammatical categories, its organization shows consideration for the knowledge and abilities of children. (In the successive revisions of Withals's work between 1553 and

1634, there is a significant evolution of content and organization, which invites more attention than space allows here, but see n. 31, Chap. 2.)

34. Stein, *English Dictionary*, pp. 323–24. Thomas's headwords are in a roman font, and his definitions in an italic one.

35. Bruner et al., *Studies in Cognitive Growth*, pp. 2, 8. In this connection, Bruner cites the work of A. R. Luria, *The Role of Speech in the Regulation of Normal and Abnormal Behavior*. In a postmodern context, Bruner's phrase "under the control of language" is more loaded (e.g., with Lacanian nuances) than when he wrote it.

36. I regard the unparalleled achievement of the *OED* and the extraordinary comprehensiveness of the *MED* as exceptions to the standard modern form, and my generalizations do not include them. Their equivalents, even loosely considered, did not exist in the Renaissance.

37. Calepino, *Dictionarium octolingue*: "Ouid. 1 *Metamorph*. Pronaque quum spectent animalia caetera terram, Os homini sublime dedit, caelumque videre Iussit et erectos ad sydera tollere vultus." The translation, by Frank Justus Miller, is from the Loeb edition, I, 9.

38. *Webster's New World Dictionary*, 2nd ed. My purpose is not to trace the meaning of *man* in the present century. I have used a 1974 definition rather than a more recent one, because this older usage of *man* offers a more illuminating comparison with Renaissance *homo* than does either the rectified usage or an alternative word. For much the same reason, modern definitions in the remainder of this section also come from this dictionary unless specified otherwise. My emphasis is on the general or covering definitions of words in relatively popular lexicons.

39. *Riders Dictionarie* corrected and augmented by Francis Holyoke.

40. Minsheu's Latin reads, "Est quae *per se substat, et fundamentum praebet accidentibus*, quae fine illa subsistere non possunt."

41. The Latin in Estienne's quotation reads, "Materia, et quasi essentia et soliditas, ac nerui cuiusque rei." The full quotation in Minsheu reads, "Quandoque etiam *substantia* ponitur pro *materia et argumento*, circa quae versatur cardo, totius rei." This reference and subsequent ones in the present chapter are to Estienne's 1543 edition.

42. Calepine's Latin reads, "Nobilissima animae facultas, qua vna a caeteris animantibus homo secernitur, et a qua rationalis appellatur." Estienne's reads, "Est illa vis animi, qua a caeteris animalibus homo disiungitur, iisque praepollet atque imperat."

43. The translation is by Walter Miller, I.xxviii.101.

44. This statement resembles Ferry's view that language in the Renais-

sance referred to objective reality, but emphatically does not resemble her view that language is somehow external to the mind: see Ferry, *Art of Naming*, p. 79, also p. 31. As a further qualification of her position (e.g., p. xvii), I would note that the views described in this paragraph are formulated in the first half of the sixteenth century; in the latter half they coexist with alternative lexical views, such as the one described in the paragraph that follows; in the first half of the seventeenth century, they continue to coexist with other views, if we are to judge from the continuing popularity of Calepine, in particular. I have addressed both positive and negative aspects of Ferry's book more extensively in a review of it in *JEGP* 1990.

45. Thomas's definition in this facsimile edition (1587) differs slightly from that in the 1596 edition (Fig. 5).

46. If Thomas's repetition of *counsell* is not a printer's error, it presumably supposes a different shade of meaning, e.g., "guidance," as distinct from "opinion." The use of the colon to distinguish the different senses of a word is more evident in Rider-Holyoke's abbreviated Latin-English version: "reason, purpose, counsell, care, consideration: the cause, the matter, the state, the meanes, or way: the fashion, or proportion, a rule, a trade: the manner and sort: an account, or reckening, business." Further distinctions among the senses listed would be made in a modern dictionary.

47. Starnes, *Renaissance Dictionaries*, p. 259, credits Rider-Holyoke with giving "prominence . . . [to etymology] through the first half of the seventeeth century." Minsheu's dictionary is not part of Starnes's project. Rosier, p. 69, notes the influence of Minsheu on Blount's *Glossographia* (1656), on Skinner's *Etymologicon* (1671), and on Junius's *Etymologicon* (1743). He also notes Minsheu's citation as an authority in Bailey's *Universal English Dictionary* (1721) and even in Skeat's *Etymological Dictionary* (1st ed., 1879–82).

Chapter 4

1. As Elsky argues, Jonson's understanding of language is thoroughly Aristotelian, but it is also nuanced in ways that are both more complex or complicated and less neat than an inflexible adherence to Aristotelianism would suggest: "Words, Things, and Names"; and *Authorizing Words*, pp. 81–109, esp. 82–83.

2. Bacon, *Novum Organum*, in *Works*, VIII, 86. Elsky, *Authorizing Words*, also discusses the alignment of Jonson with Bacon.

3. Don E. Wayne's suggestion that Jonson's simile implies "a refusal of the connotative dimensions of language" is fascinating, although perhaps overstated; Jonson's control or shaping of language is pronounced but not so limited or extreme as "refusal" indicates: *Penshurst*, p. 35; but see also pp. 36–37 for provocative commentary.

4. My emphasis. *The Grammar* is cited from *Works*, VIII, 466.

5. "*Ben Jonson's* Conversations with William Drummond of Hawthornden," in *Works*, I, 143.

6. Jonson, *Works*, VIII, 126.

7. Peterson, "Imitation and Praise," p. 289; also Kamholtz, "Ben Jonson's Green World," p. 176; and Crane, "'His Owne Style,'" p. 37.

8. Fowler, "The Silva Tradition," pp. 165, 173–74. Wayne translates *silva* as "pieces of raw material": "Jonson's Sidney," p. 231.

9. The views Jonson expresses in his prose works often parallel Scaliger's and occasionally refer specifically to them; for explicit evidence of Jonson's knowledge of the *Poetice*, see *Works*, VII, 225n; X, 347.

10. Jonson, *Works*, VIII, 309 (vs. 85–90), 308 (vs. 60–63); cf. inflected and cognate forms of *silva* on pp. 321, 327 (vs. 355ff., 479ff.), 320, 326 (vs. 250ff., 335ff.). Van den Berg conceives of the entire *Forrest* as an "imitation of the forms and temper of Horatian poetry": *Action of Ben Jonson's Poetry*, p. 113 and chap. 5 passim.

11. "Ben Jonson's Poetry," a strong essay by Friedberg, is a partial exception. Other discussions of Jonson's poetry that are especially helpful regarding his concern with language are Peterson's ("Imitation and Praise"), Wayne's (*Penshurst* and "Jonson's Sidney"), Greene's (*Light in Troy*, chap. 13), and Elsky's (*Authorizing Words*, pp. 81–109); also McCanles, *Jonsonian Discriminations*, chap. 1.

12. Greene's provocative observations about the differing values Jonson characteristically attributes to nouns and to verbs are relevant: *Light in Troy*, pp. 276–77.

13. After more than two decades, Raymond Williams's remarks on the negative definitions of "Penshurst" are still compelling: *The Country and the City*, pp. 26–34. See also Wayne, *Penshurst*, pp. 38–44; and Friedberg, "Ben Jonson's Poetry," p. 128. For an engaging recent treatment of Jonson's technique of negation as an expression of courtly *sprezzatura*, see Catherine Bates, "Much Ado about Nothing," pp. 29–33.

14. Cf. Goldberg, *James I and the Politics of Literature*, pp. 223–26.

15. The influence of Juvenal's Satire IV, lines 68–69, is usually invoked to soften or explain the unsettling rhetoric of the passage. But

Juvenal's rhetoric has little relevance to Jonson's, and if the Latin lines are read in their immediate context they actually intensify questions about Jonson's. In the satire, a huge fish is presented to the Emperor with a flattering speech that ends, "ipse capi voluit" ("The fish himself wanted to be caught"). But the satire continues, "quid apertius? et tamen illi / surgebant cristae; nihil est quod credere de se / non possit cum laudatur dis aequa potestas" ("Could flattery be more gross? Yet the Monarch's comb began to rise: there is nothing that divine Majesty will not believe concerning itself when lauded to the skies!"): *Juvenal and Persius*, trans. G. G. Ramsay. Cf. *Martial: Epigrams*, II, 176–77 (X.xxx.19–24). Cf. Marshall, "Addressing the House," pp. 68–69, for a recent alternative assessment of Jonson's lines about the fish, of his poem more generally, and of the leading ideological critiques of it.

16. See Schoenfeldt's acute observations in "'The Mysteries of Manners, Armes, and Arts,'" pp. 71, 75. Schoenfeldt, too, seems to want the "clandestine criticism" in "Penshurst" to be there without Jonson's permission, but his statements on the subject vary (p. 75).

17. On the recycling of building materials, particularly monastic ones, in early modern England, see Clifton-Faber, *Pattern of English Building*, p. 300; Howard, *Early Tudor Country House*, pp. 17–18, 136–62, esp. 136, 138–39; Airs, *The Making of the English Country House*, pp. 16–19; *Three Chapters of Letters*, ed. Thomas Wright, pp. 107, 111; Aston, "English Ruins," pp. 238–39, 241. On the currency of the subject of monastic despoliation in Jonson's time, see Keith Thomas, *Religion and the Decline of Magic*, pp. 96–104, esp. 96–98, 100–101. On the despoliation of villages and the recycling of their materials from the Middle Ages through the time of the ravages of Cromwell's army, especially see Beresford, *Lost Villages of England*, esp. pp. 57–58, 65, 97–99, 120–21, 138–39, 153, 172–73; peripherally, *Deserted Medieval Villages*, ed. Beresford and Hurst, is also of interest: e.g., pp. 94, 128, 176.

18. Stone for the orchard wall was quarried locally in 1612: see *Historical Manuscripts Commission*, 77; *Report on the Manuscripts of Lord De L'Isle*, IV, 240; V, 45–47; cf. II, 164. Referring to the L'Isle letters, J. C. A. Rathmell has suggested that completion of the wall in May 1612 might bear on the dating of "Penshurst": "Johnson, Lord Lisle, and Penshurst," pp. 252–53. See also Wayne's chapter in *Penshurst* on "The House," pp. 81–115; the other Sidney additions to Penshurst "were built of the same [country] stone from local quarries as the medieval house" (p. 99). Wayne's observation is evidently based on Marcus Binney's four-part

article in *Country Life*, 1972, of which the installments of March 9 (pp. 554–58, esp. 556), March 16 (pp. 618–21), and April 27 (pp. 994–98) are relevant.

19. For identification and discussion of additional instances of negation in "Penshurst," see Wayne, *Penshurst*, pp. 45–80. While these instances add further dimensions to the poem, they are unnecessary to my argument in this chapter.

20. *Works*, I, 133. If Jonson had any acquaintance with Minsheu's *Ductor in Linguas*, it would have to have been in manuscript form, since publication of *The Forrest* (1616) preceded that of the *Ductor* (1617).

21. *OED*, s.v. *Dwell v.*

22. See Marckwardt's edition of Nowell.

23. On Jonson's relations with antiquarians like Robert Cotton, owner of the celebrated library, and John Selden, see, for example, David Riggs, *Ben Jonson*, pp. 16, 56, 93, 193.

24. *OED* and *MED*, s.v. *Dwellen v.* The quotation is taken from *Workes*, ed. Thomas Speght (London: Adam Islip, 1602), fol.82^v; this is the Folger copy of Chaucer's works with markings in Jonson's hand. See Robert C. Evans, "Ben Jonson's Chaucer." Osselton, "Ben Jonson's Status," p. 207, notes that 20 percent of Jonson's acknowledged citations in his *Grammar* to illustrate English syntax come from Chaucer's work.

25. Quotations are from Wilson's second edition (London: William Jaggard, 1616). Cf. Harp, "Jonson's 'To Penshurst,'" pp. 73–89, esp. p. 78, where Harp, too, invokes Wilson.

26. Martial's fiftieth epigram in Book XII, ending "quam bene non habitas" is usually cited (after Herford and Simpson) as a gloss on the final couplet of "Penshurst" (*Epigrams*, II, 352–55); actually, the whole of this epigram would be a more appropriate gloss on the opening of the poem. In no way does it account for Jonson's choice and subsequent deployment of the particular English word *dwell* at the end of his poem.

27. Helgerson, *Forms of Nationhood*, p. 40, ascribes political weight to Penshurst as a Gothic place, contrasted to its neoclassic rivals. His observation could be extended to conspicuously nonclassical features of Jonson's language in *The Forrest*: e.g., *dwell, live, still*.

28. By an "anaphoric field," I mean a cluster of words repeated significantly. I have appropriated this term from a theory of oral narrative (e.g., in Old English) and bent it to my own purpose: Foley, *Immanent Art*, pp. 9–10, 57–58. In Foley's discussion, the term refers to a field of meaning that the individual work/performance invokes but which

greatly exceeds it. In Jonson's writing, the significance of the anaphoric field is self-contained and largely self-generating. In part this is possible because of the literacy (vs. dominant orality) of his culture. As comparison with Spenser will subsequently suggest, in part it is also more specifically Jonsonian.

29. On the value Jonson attaches to the word *home*, see Wayne, *Penshurst*, pp. 24–27 et passim.

30. For excellent discussion of the contrast between stasis and movement and centricity and dispersion, see Greene, "Ben Jonson," pp. 325–48; and Peterson, "Imitation and Praise," pp. 284–88.

31. Cf. Patterson, *Censorship and Interpretation*, p. 146: "In certain positions, 'still' has the ability to suggest temporal and ethical marginality."

32. On Jonson's metrics, see Trimpi, *Ben Jonson's Poems*, pp. 122–33; but also McCanles, *Jonsonian Discriminations*, pp. 5–6. The entirety of McCanles's excellent discussion of Jonson's punctuation, pp. 4–21, is relevant: "Jonson's punctuation introduces . . . emphases that would not normally occur without" it (p. 9); McCanles similarly describes the function of Jonson's enjambments (p. 18). See also his discussion of punctuation by Herford and Simpson, eds., pp. 220–22, n. 6, and Donovan, "Jonson's Texts," pp. 23–37, esp. p. 25.

33. Cf. William E. Cain, "Mirrors, Intentions, and Texts," pp. 11–23, esp. 19–21.

34. *OED*, s.v. *Decline v.*: II, 11a, c; 20a, b. Elsky's incisive discussion of the epistle to Lady Aubigny, *Authorizing Words*, pp. 104–5, parallels my own, although our overarching aims differ, as do a number of the passages we discuss. Peterson, "Imitation and Praise," pp. 285–86, aligns Jonson's use of the verb *decline* with a Senecan epistle that describes the "swerving" (*declinare*) of the wicked from the right way of nature. His argument is a difficult one, not only because Jonson employs the verb to describe a turning away from vice to virtue but also because *decline*, meaning "withdraw," "avert," or "turn aside from," appears not to have been an unusual English usage in Jonson's lifetime; the same is true of the meaning "inflect."

35. The appeal of silence for Jonson is howlingly sexist from my vantage point, but it is only fair to note that there were times when he thought silence golden for men: "*How* much better is it, to bee silent; or at least, to speake sparingly," he exclaims in *Timber* when he considers the

behavior of clients who frequent the tables and houses of the great (VIII, 612–13).

36. The fact that young William Sidney was dead when Jonson published this ode to him makes the phrase "in graues but dwell" and the idea of waiting "To liue vntill to morrow" peculiarly ironic.

37. The bracketed insertions are mine. See William Kerrigan's exhaustive reading of "To Heaven," which seems to me both sensitive and basically right: "Ben Jonson Full of Shame and Scorn," pp. 199–217, here p. 207.

38. *OED*, s.v. *Heaven*, 6a, b.

39. See my essay "The Knight and the Palmer in *The Faerie Queene*"; and Carscallen, "The Goodly Frame of Temperance."

40. Discussion of the word *permanent* and subsequently of the word *scrine* is taken from my essay " 'Myn auctour.' "

41. The word *permanent* occurs one other time in Spenser's poetic corpus, in *Amoretti* 79, the sonnet immediately preceding the one in which Spenser mentions having composed six books of *The Faerie Queene*.

42. *Webster's New World Dictionary*, s.v. *Manor*; Charlton T. Lewis and Charles Short, *A Latin Dictionary*, s.v. *Maneo*.

43. Trans. Roland Kent, VI.49: "Meminisse a memoria, cum [in] id quod remansit in mente rursus movetur; quae a manendo." Cf. Thomas, *Dictionarium*, s.v. *Maneo*: "To tarie, staie, abide, stand still, remaine, continue, or persist . . . *also* to stick to, or to stick at: to remember, not to forget." Thomas has obviously been reading Varro, whether directly or through an intermediary. For further discussion of Spenser's secret sources and their connection with memory and thought, see Anderson, " 'Myn auctour,' " passim.

44. Greene, *Light in Troy*, pp. 143–44, 264–93.

45. Thomas H. Cain, *Praise in "The Faerie Queene*," pp. 49–50. Richard Rambuss also discovers in these lines a reference to the Queen as the secret of the muse's (i.e., poet's) scrine and the "cynosure of *The Faerie Queene*'s every story": *Spenser's Secret Career*, pp. 64–69.

46. Estienne's Latin reads, "A secernendo, Dicitur locus in quo seruantur pretiosa ac secreta" (1543, 1573). Later editions of Cooper's *Thesaurus* differ from that cited, 1565, only in accidentals.

47. *OED*, s.v. *Scrine*; Du Cange, *Glossarium mediae et infimae Latinitatis*, s.v. *Scrinium*; *MED*, s.v. *Shrin(e)*.

48. *Catullus*, ed. Merrill, XIV.17–18 and notes, p. 33: for my purpose

the notes in this edition are most pertinent; for corroboration see *Catullus: A Commentary*, by Fordyce, pp. 137–38, nn. 17–18.

49. Lewis and Short, *Latin Dictionary*, s.v. *Scrinium*.

50. Du Cange, *Glossarium*, s.v. *Scrinium*; also Latham, *Revised Medieval Latin Wordlist*. I am indebted on this point to a conversation with Mary Carruthers.

51. Du Cange, *Glossarium*, s.v. *Scrinium*.

52. Sidney, *Defence*, pp. 100–101: since the Duncan-Jones–van Dorsten reading "treasure" makes inferior sense, I have emended it to "treasurer," the reading of the editions both of Gregory Smith and Geoffrey Shepherd. Cf. Thomas Wilson, *Arte of Rhetorique*, p. 415: "The memorie [is] called the Threasure *of the mynde*" (my emphasis). Cornford, *Plato's Theory of Knowledge*, pp. 2, 27–28; Gilson, *Christian Philosophy*, pp. 71–76, 99–105. In *Aristotle on Memory* Richard Sorabji asks "why Aristotle should have devoted half his treatise" on memory to recollection or reminiscence (*anamnesis*) and then explains that "recollection played a major role in Plato's metaphysics and epistemology. And though Aristotle did not accept the metaphysics and epistemology, he did inherit [from Plato] the interest in recollection" (p. 35).

53. Berger, *Allegorical Temper*, p. 79, makes a similar observation about the written documents in Eumnestes' chamber. Likewise, Murrin, *Veil of Allegory*, p. 82.

54. Bacon, *Works*, VI, 182; VIII, 408, 426, 433; II, 187–88, 206, 214–15. Aristotle, *Works: Metaphysics* I.i.980b26–981a21, 981b30–982a2; *Nicomachean Ethics* II.i.1103a14–16; *Poetics* IX.1451b5–9. Aquinas, *Summa Theologica*, trans. Fathers of the English Dominican Province, X, II–II.47.16, 49.1; also *Summa Theologiae*, XXXVI: "Sed ad generationem prudentiae necessarium est experimentum, quod fit ex multis memoriis, ut dicitur in princ. *Meta.*" (II–II.47.16); "Quid autem in pluribus sit verum oportet per experimentum considerare. Unde et Philosophus dicit quod *virtus intellectualis habet generationem et augmentum ex experimento et tempore*. Experimentum autem est ex pluribus memoriis, ut patet in I *Meta.*, unde consequens est quod ad prudentiam requiritur plurium memoriam habere" (II–II.49.1). On Spenser's allegory of prudence, see *Books I and II of "The Faerie Queene,"* ed. Kellogg and Steele, p. 343, n. 47.8–9; Mills, "Spenser, Lodowick Bryskett, and the Mortalist Controversy"; Reid, "Alma's Castle."

55. Cf. Thomas Wilson, *Rhetorique*, ed. Thomas Derrick, p. 414: "The same is memorie to the mynde, that life is to the body."

56. Whether the muse of *The Faerie Queene* is Clio or Calliope is a perennially vexed question. I suspect that Spenser saw his muses as he saw his Venuses, as so many expressions of a single power, in this case the power of mnemonic song. When the Spenserian poet does not specifically name his muse, she is likely to be a composite figure, as in the first proem and in the present quotation (VI.Pro.2–3), where the "muse" is the focal referent for the power of the "sacred ymps, that on *Parnasso* dwell." A generally useful discussion of the muses is Wesley Trimpi's *Muses of One Mind*, pp. i, xvii. Referring to Hesiod's *Theogony*, Trimpi observes that the poet's office embodies "the collective activities of the Muses," who themselves exist as "various aspects" of each other, "one implying all the others."

57. Jonson, *Timber*, VIII, 618; *Letter-Book of Gabriel Harvey, 1573–80*, pp. 82–83.

58. Bruns, *Inventions*, p. 43.

59. Padley, *Latin Tradition*, p. 84; also Osselton, "Ben Jonson's Status," p. 209.

Chapter 5

1. For a recent discussion of expansive and restrictive, essential and historical definitions of magic, see Kieckhefer, "Specific Rationality of Medieval Magic," pp. 813–14, 827 (current debate) and pp. 824, 832–33 (historical usage). Thomas M. Greene's discussion of "coercive magic, shamanistic magic, . . . literalized performance," as distinguished from metaphor, "the characteristic trope of modern poetry" that is "by definition the trope of fleeting correspondence," is also suggestively relevant to the more immediately historized distinctions I am attempting in this chapter: "Poetry as Invocation," pp. 502, 507–8; see also his *Poésie et magie*.

2. Cf. Coudert, "Some Theories," p. 67; Vickers, "Analogy Versus Identity," p. 117; Kristeller, *Philosophy of Marsilio Ficino*, p. 94. My view has been influenced by each of these works.

3. Walker, *Spiritual and Demonic Magic*, pp. 12–13, 14, 80–81.

4. Ficino, *Three Books on Life*, ed. and trans. Carol V. Kaske and J. R. Clark, p. 359. The following passage clarifies the fact that Ficino essentially has the words as well as the notes of a song in mind: "you will win over . . . [the gods] by using their songs, especially if you supply musical notes that fit their songs." He also advises the practitioner to "declaim aloud by singing and playing in the manners we have specified" (p. 361).

5. This translation is mine, since the seventeenth-century translation is not accurate enough; Agrippa, *De occulta philosophia lib. III*, pp. 147–48 (Bk. I, chap. LXXIV), reads, "veluti sacramenta quaedam et vehicula rerum explicatarum, illarum essentiam et vires vbique; secum ferentes." Perhaps avoiding a literal translation of *sacramenta*, J.F.'s translation renders the passage "as certain Signs, and vehicula's [*sic*] of things explained carrying with them every where their essence, and vertues" (p. 161). The rendering of Wayne Shumaker, *Occult Sciences*, cited by Vickers, p. 106, is close to the eighteenth-century French rendering, namely, "comme de certains secrets ou sacremens qui expliquent les choses, et portent leur essence et leur force par tous les profonds secrets, les pensées mysterieuses, et les significations admirables de ces choses se trouvent dans ces caracteres": *La Philosophie occulte*, p. 206. Each of these translations involves significantly different nuances of meaning.

6. Shumaker, *Occult Sciences*, p. 135. Cf. Scholem, *On the Kabbalah*, pp. 36, 77; also Blau, *Christian Interpretation*, pp. 5–6, 36. On the influence of Kabbala in seventeenth-century England, see David S. Katz, *Philo-Semitism*, chap. 2.

7. E.g., Donne, *Essays in Divinity*, pp. 13–14. Cf. also Gundersheimer, "Erasmus, Humanism, and the Christian Cabala."

8. The Latin reads "unius," that is, "alone" (pp. 145–46).

9. Woodbridge, "Patchwork," pp. 39–40.

10. In a cruder manuscript version of the printed text, Hart calls the allegory an "Analogie," and the main character "Tulli" rather than "Esop": *John Hart's Works*, I, 123.

11. Goldberg, *Writing Matter*, pp. 199–200, makes similar observations about Hart's allegory; cf. also pp. 225–29; Elsky, *Authorizing Words*, pp. 44–45; Ferry, *Art of Naming*, pp. 32, 38, 78–79, 93.

12. Cf. Vickers, "Analogy Versus Identity," p. 136: "The occultist will say, 'this is not just a trope, but reality.'"

13. Agrippa was also a physician, though he became one midway between writing *De occulta philosophia* (1510) and publishing it (1533). For that matter, Dr. Rabelais was one as well.

14. Wind, *Pagan Mysteries*, passim (e.g., chaps 3–4); and Strong, "From Picture Boxes to the Cabinet"; cf. Patricia Fumerton, "'Secret' Arts."

15. *Works*, II, 373 (Sermon XI of the Resurrection): in the interest of clarity, I have inserted commas after Andrewes's words *so* and *this*. The

text for the sermon is 1 Peter 1:3–4: *"Blessed be God and the Father of our Lord Jesus Christ, Which according to His abundant mercy hath begotten us again unto a lively hope, by the resurrection of Jesus Christ from the dead, To an inheritance incorruptible and undefiled, and that fadeth not away, reserved in Heaven for you"* (*"Benedictus Deus et Pater Domini nostri Jesu Christi, Qui secundum misericordiam Suam magnam regeneravit nos in spem vivam, per resurrectionem Jesu Christi ex mortuis, In haereditatem incorruptibilem, et incontaminatam, et immarcescibilem, conservatam in caelis in vobis"*).

16. *Works*, XI, 14. While I have found Shuger's discussion of Andrewes, *Habits of Thought*, pp. 47–58, immensely helpful, I also think it misleading in some respects. Her comparison of Andrewes's thinking to that of Levy-Bruhl's "primitive" raises all sorts of distracting issues, the meaning of "primitive" not least among them: e.g., see Terence Turner, "'We Are Parrots,'" pp. 131–33, 151, 156, 158. These issues are also clarified in an essay Shuger herself cites: Robin Horton's "African Traditional Thought and Western Science," pp. 155–56, 159–60; cf. Kieckhefer, "Specific Rationality of Medieval Magic," pp. 832–33. Perhaps a touchstone of our difference can also be situated in Shuger's statement that Andrewes "unequivocally, accepts the doctrine of the real presence of Christ in the Eucharist" (p. 54). While I am unsure what the highly ambiguous phrase "the real presence" (conceptually real? mystically? materially? and why "the," not "a"?) means in this instance, Shuger's discussion of Andrewes's language suggests that she intends the radically physical interpretation identified with the Roman *est* or else with the modified doctrine of Luther (similarly real but not transubstantiated or lasting) rather than the *significat* (absent presence) of Zwingli or Calvin, who also asserted a "communication of Christ's body" in the sacrament but meant something different by it: e.g., Calvin, *Institutes*, II, Bk. IV.19–21, here pp. 1384, 1385. Historically, the various shades of meaning given the idea of godly "presence" in communion bear fundamentally on ideas of language in the period. See, for example, Waswo, *Language and Meaning*, pp. 235–84; Boyle, *Erasmus on Language*, chap. 1 and passim; and for further historical perspective, Rubin, *Corpus Christi*, chap. 1 and pp. 322, 333, 352–53.

17. Andrewes, *Works*, XI, 17. Cf. John Calvin: "The Papists . . . 'pretend there is a magical force in the sacraments, independent of efficacious faith'"; cited by Keith Thomas, *Religion and the Decline of Magic*, p. 53.

18. Walker, *Spiritual and Demonic Magic*, p. 13. See also Ficino, *Three Books on Life*, pp. 246–47: "This quintessence can be ingested by us more and more if a person knows . . . how to use those things often which are filled with it, especially in its purer form. Such things are: choice wine, sugar, balsam, gold, precious stones, myrobalans, and things which smell most sweet and which shine, and especially things which have in a subtle substance a quality hot, moist, and clear; such, besides wine, is the whitest sugar, especially if you add to it gold and the odor of cinnamon and roses."

19. Andrewes, *Works*, II, 139 (Sermon II of the Passion). The text for the sermon is Lamentations 1:12: "*Have ye no regard, O all ye that pass by the way? Consider, and behold, if ever there were sorrow like My sorrow, which was done unto Me, wherewith the Lord did afflict Me in the day of the fierceness of His wrath*" ("*O vos omnes, qui transitis per viam, attendite et videte si est dolor sicut dolor Meus: quoniam vindemiavit Me ut locutus est Dominus in die irae furoris Sui*").

20. Andrewes, *Works*, II, 143: I have substituted "it" for "is" in this quotation from *Works*. The latter is an obvious error, as is evidenced by the 1604 version of this sermon, which reads, "*and it left naked and bare*": *The Copie of the Sermon preached on Good Friday last before the Kings Maiestie*, A6ᵛ; the 1604 reading is confirmed by that of *XCVI Sermons*, p. 353. It should also be noted that *tree* can be interchanged with *vine*; see *OED*, s.v. *Tree*, I.1.b: "A single plant or tree of this species or genus."

21. The figural meaning of *tree* is sufficiently common to be cited by the *OED* as an established meaning in the Renaissance, as well as before and after it: s.v. *Tree*, 4.a.

22. My view that the phrase "si fuerit sicut" could be Andrewes's is based on a check of sixteen Latin Bibles in the Folger Library, including those of Sebastian Munster (1546), Immanuel Tremellius and Franciscus Junius (1580, 1581, 1585, 1593, 1628), Franciscus Vatablus (1540, 1564), and Santis Pagnini (1528, 1542, 1564). The phrase is not, of course, in the earlier cited Vulgate version, "si est dolor sicut dolor Meus," which most of the other Bibles in my sample follow; the variations are Munster's ("si est dolor similis dolori meo") and Tremellius-Junius ("an sit dolor par dolori meo"). I am grateful to Tamara Goeglein for checking this data.

23. Seven times on an earlier page in this same sermon, Andrewes uses *stay* to mean "delay" or "wait": *Works*, II, 141. Twice on a single page in Sermon XI of the Nativity, he also uses *stay* this way: first as a verb,

"Where stayed it?" and then as a noun, "to satisfy Justice upon whom all the stay is" (I, 182). See *OED*, s.v. *Stay, sb.*²: 1; *sb.*³: 4, 6.

24. See *OED*, s.v. *Leave, sb.*: 2.a; cf. 3, 4. Also Shakespeare's *Richard II*: "Then let us take a ceremonious leave / And loving farewell of our several friends" (I.iii.50–51).

25. Andrewes, *Works*, II, 147. Shuger, *Habits of Thought*, pp. 50–51, discusses the arboreal passages of the sermon at greater length, but with a somewhat different emphasis. She does not situate them in relation to readings of similar passages in the period. While I have greatly benefited from her analysis, I think it overly mystifies Andrewes's treatment of the biblical text. I sympathize with her apology, p. 48, for the fact that quotations from the work of Andrewes inevitably "suffer from being both annoyingly long and annoyingly fragmentary," but I find her omissions particularly significant in treating this sermon: they minimize the rationality of Andrewes's method and exaggerate its affective features. This is even more the case with the most compelling evidence of Andrewes's "primitivism" that Shuger cites from another sermon: every biblical word "is *verbum vigilans*, as St. Augustine speaks, 'awake all;' never an one asleep among them" (p. 47). Even though Andrewes is quoting Augustine, this passage as cited sounds like Ficino or Agrippa. But it does not sound this way if restored to its context: see *Works*, I, 420 (Sermon VII of Repentance and Fasting); cf. II, 142. On the iconicity of Andrewes's language, see also Carrithers, *Donne at Sermons*, pp. 72–73; also Opie, "The Devil, Science, and Subjectivity"; Berry, *Process of Speech*, pp. 45–46; and McCullough, "Lancelot Andrewes and Language," pp. 304–16.

26. Shakespeare, V.iii.22–26. For a different comparative purpose, Watkins, *Shakespeare and Spenser*, pp. 279–82, cites the passages from Spenser and Shakespeare to which I have referred.

27. Berger, "Bodies and Texts," p. 147.

28. See also Victor W. Turner, *Ritual Process*, chap. 1, esp. pp. 25–26, 42: "in the semantics" of Ndembu symbolism there is "a union of ecology and intellect that results in the materialization of an idea" (p. 26). In a sense this is true of Andrewes's tree as well, and yet there is also a material difference between the physical tree that is part of an actual landscape and the figural tree whose site is language.

29. Andrewes's sermon on Psalm 85:10–11: "Mercy and Truth shall meet; Righteousness and Peace shall kiss one another" is the best known of his allegorical sermons: *Works*, I, 175–95. Much of this sermon could have come right out of Langland's *Piers Plowman*.

30. Since Spenser's work precedes Andrewes's prominence as a Jacobean preacher, I do not imply a chronological evolution (or devolution) in moving from one writer to another. Taken together, their texts suggest an uneven process of change in attitudes toward language. That of Andrewes, the most conservative attitude of them, exemplifies a high church model.

31. Spenser, *Variorum*, I, 202–204, affords a convenient listing of sources; see also Ovid, *Metamorphoses*, I, 83–85.

32. On Phaëton, see Ovid, *Metamorphoses*, I, 61–83: Bk. II.1–328.

33. On these conventions, Lakoff and Johnson are persuasive, passim, esp. chap. 17.

34. French quotation based on T. S. Eliot's *Wasteland*, in *The Complete Poems and Plays*: the complete line reads, "You! hypocrite lecteur! — mon semblable, — mon frère!" (vs. 76). Kennedy, "Rhetoric, Allegory, and Dramatic Modality," has further demonstrated the paralleling between Fradubio and Redcrosse. Particularly relevant are pp. 361–62, including the echo of I.i.13 in I.ii.31.

35. I am grateful to Kenneth Gross for suggesting this reading of the episode to me.

36. On the allegorical relation of Ariel and Caliban to Prospero, see Berger, "Miraculous Harp," pp. 255–61; also Watkins, *Shakespeare and Spenser*, p. 98; and Colie, *Shakespeare's Living Art*, p. 287. Berger, clearly reading *The Tempest* through Spenserian lenses, interprets Ariel's arborealization as entrapment "in the tree of fallen human nature" (p. 257); Sundelson finds in it "imprisonment in a constricting womb," with "overtones of castration": "So Rare a Wonder'd Father," p. 39. Such diverse but homologous interpretations suggest the basic, pervasive presence of allegorical structure in the play. My own view of the arborealization as entrapment in bodily nature or more simply in matter (*silva*, the Vergilian forest, traditionally the material stuff of this world) avoids importing a religious dimension more specific than the text warrants. (Logically, such a dimension would imply that Ariel is the redeemed Christian spirit, rather than more neutrally spirit, and would return us to untenable Christian readings of the play.) Note 39, below, buttresses a reading of the imprisoning tree as bodily matter.

37. See, for example, Wiltenburg, "The 'Aeneid' in 'The Tempest.'"

38. In IV.i.196–97, 212, Ariel is actually termed a fairy by Stephano and Trinculo.

39. I.ii.257–58; cf. Prospero's subsequent threat to Ferdinand, "I'll

manacle thy neck and feet together" (I.ii.462), thus turning him into a hoop, in effect, and fettering his head to his feet and therefore his spirit to matter.

40. Frank Kermode, ed., draws an analogy between Ariel's fate and that of Spenser's Fradubio at this point: *The Tempest*, 6th ed., p. 27*n*. The analogy is general, rather than verbally specific.

41. On Prospero's catechizing Ariel, see Berger, "Miraculous Harp," p. 268; Breight, " 'Treason doth never prosper,' " p. 10; Skura, "Discourse and the Individual," p. 65; Francis Barker and Peter Hulme, " 'Nymphs and reapers heavily vanish,' " p. 199; and especially Brown, " 'This thing of darkness I acknowledge mine,' " pp. 59–60, 63–64. My concern with the evolving manifestations of magic is more general and more encompassing than Brown's emphasis on colonialism, an obvious element in the play.

42. See, for example, Erasmus, *Praise of Folly*, p. 90 (magistral bullies) and p. 101: "It is a sacrilege, they [the masters of theology in the schools] say, to write MAGISTER NOSTER in small letters." In another extensive passage relevant to *The Tempest*, Erasmus's Folly suggests that the philosopher-king, like Prospero, is a plague to the state and that he should "imitate Timon and retire to some wilderness where he may enjoy his wisdom alone" (pp. 62–63). Erasmus's work is clearly in the background of *The Tempest*. For a humane example of Renaissance schooling, see Brinsley, *Ludus Literarius*, chaps. 5, 22, et passim.

43. At I.ii.351–62, where Miranda angrily denounces Caliban for repaying her efforts to teach him language with an attempted rape, some editors have attributed the speech to Prospero, whose character it better fits; unfortunately, they have done so without textual warrant.

44. Greenblatt's examination of the theatrical appropriation of the exorcist's power is relevant to the shift from Agrippa's operative magic to Andrewes's iconicity and to mnemonic reflection in Spenser and Shakespeare: *Shakespearean Negotiations*, pp. 120, 126–28. But cf. Woodbridge, "Patchwork," p. 32.

Chapter 6

1. See Wofford, *Choice of Achilles*, pp. 230–31, 236; also Nohrnberg, *Analogy of "The Faerie Queene,"* pp. 758–59; and DeNeef, *Spenser and the Motives of Metaphor*, pp. 95–97.

2. "The Egalitarian Giant: Representations of Justice in History/ Literature," in *Reading between the Lines*. Patterson builds on the percep-

tion that Spenser examines "the contradiction between [the] principle and practice" of justice (p. 89); for an earlier argument advocating this view, see Anderson, "'Nor Man It Is'"; *Growth of a Personal Voice*, pp. 154–55, 164–73, 184–86; and s.v. "Artegall," in *Spenser Encyclopedia*, ed. Hamilton, et al., pp. 62–64. Another relevant essay is Greenblatt's "Muring Peasants," pp. 19–23; Greenblatt identifies Artegall's responses with "Spenser's" too unproblematically, however.

3. The quotations come from *FQ* V.ii.15, 17. For a description of Artegall's swimsmanship that is digressive in length, see stanza 16, especially lines 6–9:

> For *Artegall* in swimming skilfull was,
> And durst the depth of any water sownd.
> So ought each Knight, that vse of perill has,
> In swimming be expert through waters force to pas.

4. Langland's description of Lady Meed's fingers is taken from *Piers Plowman*, II.11. Like Munera, Meed is an ambivalent figure. The medieval adjective *try* ("trye") appears to have been rare at best by Spenser's time and its archaic coloring further suggests the intertextual influence of Langland's poem at this point.

5. Foucault, *Discipline and Punish*, is pertinent: "the great spectacle of punishment ran the risk of being rejected by the very people to whom it was addressed" (p. 63, also pp. 59–69).

6. My use of the words *narrator, narrative*, and *poet* in this chapter is deliberate. Their relation in *The Faerie Queene* is complex, but it is not an issue that I can examine here, as I hope to do elsewhere. For the most impressive recent treatments of it, see Berger, "Narrative as Rhetoric"; and "'Kidnapped Romance.'" Berger privileges narrative, equating the narrator with it. *Poet* becomes either an irrelevant term, similarly replaced by *narrative* (or *discourse*) or else the historical Spenser, upstaged and subverted by his poem.

7. *OED*, s.v. *Mighty adj.*, 1. "Possessing 'might' or power"; s.v. *Might, sb.*: 1.a. "The quality of being able (to do what is desired); operative power"; 3. "Great or transcendent power or strength; mightiness."

8. Goldstein's description of the pathological anxiety triggered by perceived threats to the human sense of order and by actual disorder aligns itself suggestively with Artegall's response to the leveling Giant and at times, as here, with that of the narrative or narrator as well: *Organism*, pp. 35–55, 291–306; *Human Nature*, pp. 85–119. Goldstein's

data remain relevant, although their cultural implications would likely be interpreted as being more repressive today. For a Lacanian interpretation of the paranoid confusion of Real and Symbolic inherent in an anxious or overbearing sense of order, see Copjec, "The Anxiety of the Influencing Machine," esp. pp. 52–56.

9. Strikingly, when Occasion is bound in II.iv, the characters just stand around talking to one another: action stops, and the incursion of Atin is needed to get it going again. I have treated this episode further in "The Knight and the Palmer."

10. On stars and planets, see Johnson, *Astronomical Thought*, passim, e.g., p. 214: Johnson observes that the physical foundations of the Aristotelian system were "disastrously shattered" by "the new star of 1572, the comet of 1577, and the other comets that appeared in the last two decades of the sixteenth century." Cf. Toulmin and Goodfield, *Fabric of the Heavens*, pp. 184–98. Mattingly, *Defeat of the Spanish Armada*, pp. 159–68, offers a telling example of the readiness of Europeans to respond to prophecy as the *fin de siècle* approached. On the agricultural and more generally economic difficulties experienced by the English in the 1590s, see Guy, *Tudor England*, p. 456; Sharp, *In Contempt of All Authority*, pp. 10–11, 13, 36–40; and Rappaport, *Worlds within Worlds*, pp. 13–15, 136–37, 148–50. Although Rappaport is anxious to emphasize the stability of Tudor society and to deemphasize the impoverishment of its members, he acknowledges that the 1590s were "a decade of exceptional hardship," indeed, the only one in which London's problems conceivably threatened public order (p. 378). With respect to Ireland, even a glance at Spenser's *View* is enough to indicate the imminent turmoil that surrounded the poet there. Aside from pressures in England and Ireland, the episode of the Giant has also been associated with the perceived threat of the Anabaptist movement: *Var.*, V, 175–76. The growing number of impoverished vagrants in England, the dispossessed and famished inhabitants of the Irish countryside, and the Anabaptists all seemed to embody the cosmic disturbances near at hand.

11. See *Personal Voice*, pp. 184–86, for my assumptions regarding the historical grounding of the speaker's view in the fifth proem and "'Nor Man It Is,'" pp. 450–54, for those regarding the parodic elements of Artegall's early exploits.

12. See Roche's edition of *The Faerie Queene*, p. 1193; also the biblical citations in Hamilton's edition, p. 541. In addition to the biblical references they cite, I would invoke the cadence of Ecclesiastes, e.g., 3.1–8.

13. "Symbols, Song, Dance," pp. 69, 75–76, 79.

14. Anderson, "'Nor Man It Is,'" pp. 447–70, esp. 461–66.

15. Alexandre Koyré describes the implications of the "scientific and philosophical revolution" of the early modern period in terms that illuminate what underlies Artegall's argument with the Giant: "the disappearance, from philosophically and scientifically valid concepts, of the conception of the world as a finite, closed, and hierarchically ordered whole [a cosmos] . . . and its replacement by an indefinite and even infinite universe" whose components inhabit a single level of being. Such a universe "implies the discarding by scientific thought of all considerations based upon value-concepts" and "the utter devalorization of being, the divorce of the world of value and the world of facts": *Closed World*, p. 2.

16. See Smith, *Spenser's Proverb Lore*, nos. 53, 68, 155, 160, 179, 240, 472, 570. For the scriptural references, see the annotations of Roche, ed., Hamilton, ed., *The Faerie Queene*; and Naseeb Shaheen, *Biblical References*, p. 82.

17. Hamilton, ed., *The Faerie Queene*, and Alpers, *Poetry of "The Faerie Queene*," pp. 354–55.

18. Cf. George T. Wright on the "sacralizing character of verse": "An Almost Oral Art," pp. 159–69, e.g., pp. 166–67.

19. See Smith, *Spenser's Proverb Lore*, nos. 157, 231, 791, 891.

20. See Luke 3.5, "Every valley shall be filled, and every mountain and hill shall be brought low," cited by Hamilton, ed., *The Faerie Queene*, p. 541. As Hamilton observes, the Giant's context is apocalyptic.

21. In the interest of the evident ambiguities of these lines, I have dropped the comma at the end of the first of them. For discussion, see Berger, "The *Mutabilitie Cantos*," p. 172; and Anderson, *Personal Voice*, p. 201.

22. *FQ* V.ii.43; my emphasis. This stanza recalls 2 Esdras 4.5, 10–11; unlike the impersonally intoned ritual dominant in the preceding stanzas, it is addressed directly and primarily to the Knight's opponent and exhibits other rhetorical characteristics of dialogic exchange. (In the Geneva Bible, the books of Esdras are considered apocryphal.)

23. *OED*, s.v. *Betoken*, 1.*trans*., 2, 3, 4; s.v. *Token*, 1.a, 3.a. While *Betoken* occurs uniquely in Spenser's fifth book, the form *betokening* appears in *Amoretti* LXII, vs. 4, where it means "being a sign, or omen of," "giving promise of," "auguring" (*OED* 3): "with shew of morning mylde he [the new year] hath begun, / betokening peace and plenty to

ensew." Interestingly, *token(s)* is a word that occurs with unusual frequency in Book V. Versions of this word, including *betoken*, occur ten times in V, out of a total of twenty times in the other books, including VII. The 1596 addition, plus the Mutability Cantos, accounts for sixteen of the twenty occurrences. The various ways of "betokening" clearly engaged Spenser's interests to a greater extent as the relation of Faerie to the everyday world became more problematical.

24. Annabel Patterson, *Reading*, p. 95, recognizes "clear narrative and iconic indications that the confrontation between Knight and Giant is not simply a case of right versus wrong."

25. I am unaware of an adequate gloss on the first five lines of stanza 47 and therefore offer my own. In recent years, Roche's edition affords the fullest gloss on the Giant's efforts to weigh truth and falsehood and specifically concerns stanzas 48–49, but his gloss merely cites *Var.*, V, 180. Hamilton's edition invokes the Aristotelian doctrine of the mean as early as stanza 45. Cf. as well the narrator's disapproval of Avarice in Book I, who "right and wrong ylike in equall ballaunce waide" (iv.27). As Roche remarks, the weighing episode in Book V is strained—I think significantly so.

26. See Maclean, *Interpretation and Meaning*, pp. 142–58, here 155, 157, on the mentalism of Renaissance jurisprudence and its corollary, the supplemental role of words; similarly, pp. 181, 183, 202, and Thorne, ed., *A Discourse*, pp. 57–62, 77.

27. *FQ* IV.viii.26. For further discussion of this point, see Anderson, "'Myn auctour,'" pp. 16–31, esp. pp. 27–28. Cf. also Augustine, *On Christian Doctrine*, pp. 70–71 (Bk. II.xxxv). Wofford, *Choice of Achilles*, p. 346, characterizes the "inward turn" of the allegory at this point as an evasive effort "to transform the giant from political to moral allegory."

28. See Ferguson, "Saint Augustine's Region of Unlikeness," pp. 842–64, here pp. 861–62, on the inward ear; pp. 847 and 853 are also particularly relevant.

29. See Larkin, *Language*, p. 17 (preceding quotation), and Letter VII, 342e–343a, 344b, in Plato, *Collected Dialogues*, pp. 1590–91. Plato's letters are often characterized as "doubtfully genuine." Among them, Letter VII has been given the most credence: see Bury, trans., in *Plato*, VII, 391–92, 472; and Morrow, trans., in *Plato's Epistles*, pp. 5, 9, 14, esp. 16. Morrow suggests that the letters "were written, if not by Plato himself, at least by some well-informed member of the Platonic circle, at a date very shortly after the death of Plato" (p. 13). Ludwig Edelstein

rejects Plato's authorship of Letter VII but describes this letter as an "important interpretation of Plato's life and doctrine which must go back to the first decades after his death": *Plato's Seventh Letter*, pp. 4, 76–85. The letters have long been a part of the Platonic tradition: e.g., early Hellenistic catalogues of Plato's writings include a collection of letters; Timaeus, an early historian, makes use of them; and Cicero quotes and refers to Letter VII as Plato's (Morrow, p. 13; Edelstein, p. 1). Berger's recent essays on Plato's dialogues have interpreted them as proto-Derridean inscriptions, deeply distrustful of logocentrism: e.g., "Levels of Discourse," pp. 75–100; and "*Phaedrus* and the Politics of Inscription." For all these reasons, I have emphasized a tradition of Platonic interpretation in the present paragraph—a tradition of which Augustine is a notably influential exemplar (and Calvin after him).

30. *De catechizandis rudibus*, in *Patrologia Latina*, XL, 311–12.

31. See Markus, "St. Augustine on Signs," pp. 60–83, esp. p. 77. While these views are debated in the secondary literature on Augustine, I do not see how any reading of his actual works can avoid them. For a classic statement of Augustine's position, see *The Trinity*, pp. 475, 477–78, 487; Bk. XV.x.19, xi.20, xiv.24: e.g., the "word cannot be uttered in sound nor thought in the likeness of sound, such as must be done with the word of any language; it precedes all the signs by which it is signified" (p. 478, xi.20). Linda Gregerson's stimulating essay "Protestant Erotics" assumes the relevance of Augustine to Spenser's first book but does not acknowledge the ambivalence at best of Augustine's attitude to any kind of human language and not merely to its written forms.

32. See Ferguson, "St. Augustine's Region of Unlikeness," pp. 847, 853: Augustine acknowledges "that his own language traps him" because "there is something in the nature of language which necessitates a spatial understanding of a difference—an unlikeness—that is not spatial . . . at all."

33. E.g., *FQ* V.ii.15, 18; iii.22; v.13; vii.22. After Radegone, the remarkably few instances in which cruelty touches Artegall are qualified by circumstances and explicable in the terms I have argued in *Personal Voice*, pp. 168–73.

34. *OED*, s.v. *Font sb.*², gives 1676 as the first meaning of *font* to refer to the casting of type; also s.v. *Fount*², 1683; I suspect that the usage occurs earlier. For recent commentary on Malfont, see Bieman, *Plato Baptized*, pp. 182–85; Suzuki, *Metamorphoses of Helen*, pp. 193–95; and Krier, *Gazing on Secret Sights*, pp. 214–15. Lately the number of com-

mentators who do *not* treat Malfont in a significant way is surprising: for a tantalizing three-liner, however, see McCabe, *Pillars of Eternity*, p. 78.

35. O'Connell's discussion of Mercilla's behavior remains useful: *Mirror and Veil*, pp. 150–54.

36. Merrill contrasts Donne's view that the Word must be preached with both Hooker's and Andrewes's, and maintains that as a preaching theorist, Donne was a Puritan, for whom "The sermon was, in effect, if not in name, a sacramental rite which was an *ipso facto* effective channel of divine grace": "John Donne and the Word of God," p. 598. But see also Donne, *Sermons*, IV, 102: "God spake then in the Creation, but he spake *Ineffabiliter*, says St. *Augustine*, without uttering any sound. He spake, but he spake *Intemporaliter*, says that Father too, without spending any time in distinction of syllables." And *Sermons*, VII, 80: "With one *word, One Fiat*, . . . nay with one *thought* of *God* cast toward it, (for *Gods* speaking in the *Creation*, was but a *thinking*,) *God* made all of *Nothing*." It is difficult to find theoretical consistency in Donne's statements, a fact that probably explains the pronounced disagreements concerning his theoretical position(s). Baumlin, *John Donne and the Rhetorics*, chap. 1, offers a useful review of recent criticism and the sensible opinion that Donne's theoretical position is complex, comprehensive, and unstable. For a convenient anthology of Donne's statements in his sermons about language, see *John Donne and the Theology of Language*, ed. Stanwood and Asals. Asals's excellent essay "John Donne and the Grammar of Redemption," pp. 125–39, is also relevant, although I would associate Donne's assertion that Christ is most often defined by "*The Word Sermo*, Speech" with Erasmus, rather than with Augustine, as she suggests (p. 125): see Chap. 1, above, and Boyle, *Erasmus on Language*, pp. 12–20.

37. On Donne's practices in preparing and revising sermons, see Sparrow, "John Donne and Contemporary Preachers," pp. 144–78, esp. pp. 166–67; Walton, "The Life of Dr. John Donne," in *Lives*, p. 67; and Donne, *Sermons*, I, 48.

38. *Oxford Latin Dictionary*, s.v. *Tempus*, 10: "The circumstances existing at a particular time, the occasion, moment"; 10b: "On the spur of the moment; in accordance with the needs of the moment." Cf. s.v. *Ex*, 18, 21. Also *OED*, s.v. *Extempore adv. a.* and *sb.* "[lit. 'out of time']," B: "Arising out of the moment"; although the *OED*'s first citation for this meaning is 1639, it was clearly available to a Latinist like Donne.

39. Quotation from Mueller's edition of *Donne's Prebend Sermons*, p. 34; cited subsequently as Mueller, ed.

40. Chamberlin, *Increase and Multiply*, pp. xiii–xiv, 7, asserts that Donne's view of language is iconic and realist (as opposed to conventionalist); p. xiii affords a helpful review of arguments that Donne's words have a "sacramental" or "emblematic" reality. Carrithers, *Donne at Sermons*, pp. 79–82, denies that Donne's view of language is iconic. Webber observes that life for Donne "has reality only when it becomes verbal": *The Eloquent "I"*, p. 47. She often remarks Donne's reification of words or his use of them in a sacramental way, but she generally avoids aligning his practice with the historical development of theories of linguistic origin: *Contrary Music*, pp. 40, 123–25. Again, Baumlin's view that Donne holds no single view of language is relevant: see n. 35, this chapter. On Adamicism, see Chap. 1, n. 92, and Chap. 3, pp. 74–75, above.

41. On Donne's view of the Latin Bible, see *Sermons*, III, 315–16; cf. H. J. de Jonge, ed., in Erasmus, *Opera Omnia*, IX–2, p. 3: "for Erasmus himself and for most sixteenth-century readers of . . . [his 1516 New Testament], its most important constituent was not the Greek text, but the new Latin version of the New Testament." Don Cameron Allen also discusses Donne's attitude toward the Latin Bible in "Dean Donne Sets His Text," pp. 222–25.

42. Mulcaster, *Elementarie*, p. 177; Gil, *Logonomia Anglia*, pp. 333–34.

43. On Donne's use of Latin phrases, cf. Webber, *Contrary Music*, pp. 52–53, and Michael L. Hall, "Searching the Scriptures," p. 220.

44. Cf. Quinn, "Donne's Christian Eloquence": "The Biblical phrase is only a vehicle, not the subject. . . . But he [Donne] does not wish us to forget the vehicle, the text; he wishes us to be conscious of the words as *things*. Where there is no image Donne will work with the word itself as an image, not merely as a conventional sign" (p. 292).

45. For a recent discussion of Donne's impersonations, see Harland, "Dramatic Technique and Personae," pp. 709–26; pp. 709–10 review relevant criticism, and pp. 714–16 concern the second Prebend sermon.

46. Donne preached six extant sermons on Psalm 38.

47. Bettie Anne Doebler observes the traditional "conceit of Christ as *weight* on the cross" or alternatively as the balance itself and Donne's frequent use of it in his sermons: *Quickening Seed*, pp. 117–18. Cf. *Sermons*, V, 383, for another instance of Donne's use of the image of the scale in a positive relation to the glory of God.

48. E.g., "suit," "thorn," "wine," and "wilde" itself, rhyming with the reaffirmative "Child": *Works of George Herbert*, pp. 153–54.

49. Mueller, ed., *Donne's Prebend Sermons*, p. 238, ll. 537–38, 579–80. The Geneva Bible translates the phrase "vnder" in accordance with Munster's preposition.

50. Cf. *Sermons*, IX, 71–72, where "Words, and less particles then words have busied the whole Church. In the Councell of *Ephesus*, . . . the strife was but for a word. . . . In the Councell of *Chalcedon*, . . . It was but for a syllable, whether *Ex*, or *In*." Donne continues with other examples — "but for one letter" in the Council of Nice — reflects on the significance of "transposing of words, or syllables, or letters," and asks rhetorically, "how much doth an accent vary a sense? An interrogation, or no interrogation will make it directly contrary." Donne's attention to the details of Scripture and its interpretation and translation is meticulous.

51. Mueller, ed., *Donne's Prebend Sermons*, p. 243, l. 704; *Sermons*, IX, 98.

52. Lines 175–218 of the "Second Anniversarie" are relevant; "undistinguish'd" occurs in line 208: Donne, *The Epithalamions, Anniversaries and Epicedes*. The relation between the "Anniversarie" and the Prebend sermon is often noted in Donne criticism. Several features of it are particularly germane. In the "Anniversarie," elation is readied by repeated exhortations to the speaker's own soul to "thinke" on "thy self" and on death. With similar timing, the speaker shifts from urging and directing thought to enacting it, and his enactment of the immediate nearness and presence (again the two are not distinguished) of heaven to the soul at the moment of death anticipates the sermon even verbally. Cf. Smith, "Moments of Being": Donne sees "time as a series of disjunctive segments" that can be bridged in "a significant moment," such as death (p. 3, also pp. 15–18).

53. Calvin, *Institutes*, II, Bk. IV.xvii.21. In *Sermons*, IV, 87, Donne expresses a similar view, not limited to verbal images but instead extended to constructs of the human intellect more generally: "How barren a thing is Arithmetique? (and yet Arithmetique will tell you, how many single graines of sand, will fill this hollow Vault to the Firmament). . . . How weak a thing is Poetry? (and yet Poetry is a counterfait Creation, and makes things that are not, as though they were) How infirme, how impotent are all assistances, if they be put to expresse this Eternity?"

54. *Wilson's Arte of Rhetorique, 1560*, ed. G. H. Mair, p. 114. The discussion of iteration and reduplication in the section "More of Form Is More of Content" from Lakoff and Johnson's *Metaphors* is relevant as well (pp. 127–28).

55. Donne, *Devotions*, p. 76.

56. Donne returns repeatedly to the idea of "vesting"—to putting on and taking off, to what is inside and what outside. Cf. *Sermons*, V, 158–60: "There is then a double *Induere*, a twofold clothing; we may *Induere*, 1. *Vestem*, put on a garment; 2. *Personam*, put on a person. We may put on Christ so, as we shall be *his*, and we may put him on so, as we shall be *He*" (p. 158).

57. Coleridge, *Miscellaneous Criticism*, p. 131.

58. On the relevance of Donne's linguistic methods to drama, see my essay "'But we shall teach the lad another language,'" esp. pp. 187–93. The essay is concerned with Donne's poetry, which is more ironic than the sermons, but its argument is relevant to them. The play by Ford the essay examines is *Perkin Warbeck*, a play centrally concerned with the relation of rhetoric to material reality.

59. See Bald, *John Donne*, pp. 535–36: "the shrouded figure [of Donne] is rising from the funeral urn, and what seems at first glance to be a crouching attitude suggests rather that he is still emerging" in resurrection.

60. Cf. *Sermons*, VIII, 190: "those Pictures which are deliver'd in a minute, from a print upon paper, had many dayes, weeks, Moneths time for the graving of those Pictures in the Copper; So this Picture of that dying Man, that dies in Christ, that dies the death of the Righteous, that embraces Death as a Sleepe, was graving all his life; All his publique actions were the lights, and all his private the shadowes of this Picture. And then this Picture comes to the Presse, this Man to the streights and agonies of Death, thus he lies, thus he looks, this he is." Notable is Donne's interest in the technology of reproduction as well as in the topos or "pose" of holy dying.

61. Some five years before, in the second Prebend sermon, Donne had remarked how David and Daniel in exile turned always in prayer "towards the Temple" and how "*Hezekias* turning to the wall to weepe, and to pray in his sick bed, [is] understood to be to that purpose, to conforme and compose himselfe towards the Temple": *Sermons*, VII, 58; cf. V, 290.

62. On Donne's regard for the Psalms, see *Sermons*, VI, 292, for example. In citing "Deaths Duell" (*Sermons*, X, 230–48) I have reluctantly omitted the seventeenth-century italicization. Except for biblical verse, whose variant forms I have re-italicized to approximate Donne's

own practice, any other italicization or typographical pointing has been added in order to clarify or to emphasize my argument.

63. Standard modern editions of the Bible in English translate *exitus mortis* either "escape from death" or "passageways of death," thereby avoiding the ambiguity (and the potentially resonating dimensions) of the translation "issues."

64. Cf. Webber, *Contrary Music*, pp. 125–26.

65. This version of the former or building-text I cite comes later in the paragraph (l. 39) but is more representative than Donne's initial version.

66. That Donne frequently employs such a construction ("That he that is") does not eliminate its effects here or elsewhere. For another example in this sermon, see p. 240, l. 366.

67. *Sermons*, X, 242: "But why did he [the Lord] dye? . . . *Quia Domini Domini sunt exitus mortis* (as Saint *Augustine* interpreting this *text* answeres that question) because *to this God our Lord belong'd the issues of death*." The reference to Augustine is identified marginally: "lib. 17. c. 18."

68. *Self-Consuming Artifacts*, pp. 50–51.

69. Discussing William Empson's claim, based on Donne's poem "The Relique," that the figure (i.e., person) of Christ is iterable for Donne, Docherty suggests instead that the figure (i.e., symbol), or more precisely the name, is iterable in this way: *John Donne, Undone*, pp. 175–76. I would modify the suggestion further by broadening it: Christ, perhaps, is more generally iterable *linguistically* for Donne.

70. Cf. *Sermons*, II, 250–51: "For first there is *verbum in carne*, the word came in the flesh, in the Incarnation; and then there is *caro in verbo*, he that is made flesh comes in the word, that is, Christ comes in the preaching thereof." This radically incarnational view of preaching appears somewhat modified, however, in a later sermon: "The Word of God is made a Sermon, that is, a Text is dilated, diffused into a Sermon; but that whole Sermon is not the word of God" (V, 56). Since Donne's pronouncements on preaching are various, any single excerpt can prove incomplete or misleading, particularly without adequate examination of his practice. Donne's statement, earlier cited, that a "perplexity in the words . . . cast[s] a perplexity upon the things," and therefore that language has a constitutive effect on meaning, is also relevant: *Life and Letters*, II, 16.

71. Cf. *Sermons*, V, 345: "a prayer . . . hath a *Quia*, a Reason, upon which it is grounded." And again, "It is but a Parenthesis, that might be left out . . . if it have not a *Quia*, a Reason, a ground for it." Grammatically a conjunction, not a noun, a *quia*, "because" has an emphatically nominalized or otherwise reified status more than once in Donne's writing.

72. Pound, *Guide to Kulchur*, p. 77.

73. The date of this sermon is March 28, 1619.

74. See Matthew 27:50 in the Vulgate.

75. *OED*, s.v. *Issue v.*, II. 7; *The Merchant of Venice*, III.ii.265–66.

76. Donne, *Biathanatos*, p. 201.

77. While the relevance of Donne's argument to his own death from a wasting illness is evident, we should note that the point he makes here is traditional: see Doebler, *Quickening Seed*, pp. 105–6 and chap. 3, passim. For a radically different, psychologically oriented view of Donne's treatment of death in his poetry and prose, see Carey, *John Donne*, chap. 7.

78. Donne, *Elegies and The Songs and Sonnets*, p. 52.

79. On the impact of Donne's bodily visibility in preaching, see Carrithers, *Donne at Sermons*, pp. 11–17.

80. On the authority of italics in "Deaths Duell," see *Sermons*, X, 272–75.

81. Donne, *Divine Poems*, p. 50.

82. I thank David Evett for raising the possibility of this syntactical ambiguity. He also questioned the referent of the pronoun "wee," which I take to be a "royal" or, more accurately, a tactful priestly usage: in any case, I don't see how "wee" can refer to both Donne and Christ *before* the syntactical ambiguity occurs, and when it does occur, "wee" cannot reasonably "hang upon him that hangs upon the Crosse," if this pronoun includes Christ.

83. Terry G. Sherwood, invoking the Pauline notion of Donne and, more exactly, of Donne's suffering body as an exemplary member of the Church as the Body of Christ, argues that Donne's suffering fulfills "the suffering of Christ in his own flesh for the Body's sake": *Fulfilling the Circle*, p. 196. This still seems to me a Roman Catholic reading. Cf. Baumlin, *John Donne and the Rhetorics*, p. 46: "the language of Roman Catholicism remains a continuous, if subversive, presence in his [Donne's] writing." Also see Carey, *John Donne*, pp. 29–31.

84. In *Donne, Milton*, pp. 188–89, Sloane assumes the ambiguous

reading as the obvious (and seemingly exclusive) one. His doing so confirms its possibility for readers or auditors. Sloane also aligns Donne's emotional investment in the ending of "Deaths Duell" with the notion of "conformity" as a technique of persuasion (p. 187).

85. In *Iconoclasm and Poetry*, chap. 5, Gilman's discussion of Donne's "ambivalent regard" for images is suggestively analogous to these linguistic choices.

86. Donne's weakness correlates as well with the image he presents in Walton's "Life" when, faint, hollow voiced, tearfull, and emaciated, he appeared in the Pulpit for the last time. Little more than a month from death, he looked like a man who came "not to preach mortification by a living voice: but, mortality by a decayed body and a dying face" (pp. 74–75).

87. I agree with Bald's conclusion in *John Donne* that Donne must have written "Deaths Duell" out in full before he delivered it, "since it is unlikely that it would have been subsequently prepared for publication" (p. 525).

88. Donne, *Elegies and The Songs and Sonnets*. On Donne's speaker, see Anderson, "History and Rhetoric"; also Herz, "'An Excellent Exercise of Wit,'" pp. 3–14; and, conversely, Rajan, "'Nothing Sooner Broke,'" pp. 805–28. Also Fish, "Masculine Persuasive Force," pp. 223–52, esp. pp. 250–51.

Works Cited

Journal abbreviations and acronyms follow the standard forms listed in the *MLA International Bibliography*, volume 1.

Advice to a Son: Precepts of Lord Burghley, Sir Walter Raleigh, and Francis Osborne. Ed. Louis B. Wright. Ithaca, N. Y.: Cornell University Press, 1962.

Agrippa von Nettesheim, Henry Cornelius. *De occulta philosophia lib. III*. Lyons: Deringos Fratres, 1600.

———. *La Philosophie occulte de Henr. Corn. Agrippa*. La Haye: R. Chr. Alberts, 1727.

———. *Three Books of Occult Philosophy*. Trans. J. F. London: R. W., for Gregory Moule, 1651.

Airs, Malcolm. *The Making of the English Country House, 1500–1640*. London: Architectural Press, 1975.

Alexander, J. J. G., and M. T. Gibson, eds. *Medieval Learning and Literature: Essays Presented to Richard William Hunt*. Oxford: Clarendon, 1976.

Alford, John A. "The Role of Quotations in *Piers Plowman*." *Speculum* 52 (1977): 80–99.

Allen, C. G. "The Sources of 'Lily's Latin Grammar': A Review of the Facts and Some Further Suggestions." *The Library*, 5th series, 9 (1954): 85–100.

Allen, Don Cameron. "Dean Donne Sets His Text." *ELH* 10 (1943): 208–29.

Alpers, Paul J. *The Poetry of "The Faerie Queene."* Princeton: Princeton University Press, 1967.

Alunno, Francesco. *La fabrica del mondo*. Venice: Paolo Gherardo, 1556.

The American Heritage Dictionary. 2nd ed. Boston: Houghton Mifflin, 1985.

Anderson, Judith H. *Biographical Truth: The Representation of Historical Persons in Tudor-Stuart Writing*. New Haven, Conn.: Yale University Press, 1984.

——. "'But we shall teach the lad another language': History and Rhetoric in Bacon, Ford, and Donne." *RenD* 20 (1989): 169–96.

——. *The Growth of a Personal Voice: "Piers Plowman" and "The Faerie Queene."* New Haven, Conn.: Yale University Press, 1976.

——. "The Knight and the Palmer in *The Faerie Queene*, Book II." *MLQ* 31 (1970): 160–78.

——. "'Myn auctour': Spenser's Enabling Fiction and Eumnestes' 'immortall scrine.'" In *Unfolded Tales: Essays on Renaissance Romance*, ed. George M. Logan and Gordon Teskey, pp. 16–31. Ithaca, N.Y.: Cornell University Press, 1989.

——. "'Nor Man It Is': The Knight of Justice in Book V of Spenser's *Faerie Queene*." In *Essential Articles for the Study of Edmund Spenser*, ed. A. C. Hamilton, pp. 447–70. Hamden, Conn.: Archon, 1972.

——. Review of *The Art of Naming*, by Anne Ferry. *JEGP* 89 (1990): 542–45.

Andrewes, Lancelot. *The Copie of the Sermon preached on good Friday last before the Kings Maiestie*. London: R. Barker, 1604.

——. *XCVI Sermons*. London: by George Miller, for Richard Badger, 1629.

——. *Sermons*. Ed. G. M. Story. Oxford: Clarendon, 1967.

——. *The Works of Lancelot Andrewes*. 11 vols. 1854. Rpt. New York: AMS, 1967.

Aquinas, Saint Thomas. *Summa Theologiae*. Blackfriars Edition (Latin and English). 60 vols. London: Eyre and Spottiswoode, 1964–76.

——. *The "Summa Theologica."* Trans. Fathers of the English Domini-

can Province. 2nd rev. ed. 22 vols. London: Burns, Oates & Wash-
bourne, 1916–29.

Aristotle. *The Complete Works of Aristotle*. Ed. Jonathan Barnes. 2 vols.
Princeton: Princeton University Press, 1984.

Asals, Heather Ross. "John Donne and the Grammar of Redemption."
ESC 5 (1979): 125–39.

Ascham, Roger. *The Scholemaster*. In *English Works*, ed. William Aldis
Wright, pp. 171–302. Cambridge: Cambridge University Press, 1904.

Aston, Margaret. *England's Iconoclasts*. 2 vols. Oxford: Clarendon, 1988.

——. "English Ruins and English Story: The Dissolution and the Sense
of the Past." *JWCI* 36 (1973): 231–55.

Attridge, Derek. "Language as history/history as language: Saussure
and the romance of etymology." In *Post-structuralism and the Question
of History*, ed. Derek Attridge, Geoff Bennington, and Robert Young,
pp. 183–211. Cambridge, Eng.: Cambridge University Press, 1987.

——. *Peculiar Language: Literature as Difference from the Renaissance to
James Joyce*. Ithaca, N.Y.: Cornell University Press, 1988.

Augustine, Saint. *De catechizandis rudibus*. In *Patrologia Latina*, ed. J. P.
Migne. Vol. XL. Paris: Garnier, 1887.

——. *De doctrina christiana*. In *Patrologia Latina*, ed. J. P. Migne. Vol.
XXXIV. Paris: Garnier Fratres, 1887.

——. *On Christian Doctrine*. Trans. D. W. Robertson, Jr. 1958. Rpt.
Indianapolis: Bobbs-Merrill, 1984.

——. *Sermons on the Liturgical Seasons*. Trans. Sister Mary Sarah Mul-
downey. In *The Fathers of the Church*. Vol. XXXVIII. Washington,
D.C.: Catholic University of America Press, 1963.

——. *The Trinity*. Trans. Stephen McKenna. In *The Fathers of the
Church*. Vol. XLV. Washington, D.C.: Catholic University of America
Press, 1963.

Bacon, Francis. *The Works of Francis Bacon*. Ed. James Spedding, Robert
Leslie Ellis, and Douglas Denon Heath. 15 vols. Boston: Brown and Taggard [imprint varies; vols. 6–10: Taggard and Thompson], 1860–64.

Bacon, Nicholas. *Sententiae*. See McCutcheon, Elizabeth, trans.

Bald, R. C. *John Donne: A Life*. Ed. Wesley Milgate. Oxford: Oxford
University Press, 1970.

Baldwin, T. W. *William Shakespere's "Small Latine & Lesse Greek."* 2 vols.
Urbana: University of Illinois Press, 1944.

Baret, John. *An Alvearie or Triple Dictionarie, in Englishe, Latin, and
French*. London: Henry Denham, 1574.

———. *An Alvearie or Quadruple Dictionarie*. London: Henry Denham, 1580.

Barker, Francis, and Peter Hulme. "Nymphs and reapers heavily vanish: the discursive con-texts of *The Tempest*." In *Alternative Shakespeares*, ed. John Drakakis, pp. 191–205. London: Methuen, 1985.

Barley, Nigel. "A Structural Approach to the Proverb and Maxim with Special Reference to the Anglo-Saxon Corpus." *Proverbium* 20 (1972): 737–50.

Barthes, Roland. *Elements of Semiology*. Trans. Annette Lawes and Colin Smith. New York: Hill & Wang, 1967.

———. *S-Z*. Trans. Richard Miller. New York: Hill & Wang, 1974.

Bates, Catherine. "Much Ado about Nothing: The Contents of Jonson's *Forest*." *EIC* 42 (1992): 29–35.

Bateson, F. W. *English Poetry and the English Language*. 1934. Rpt. New York: Russell and Russell, 1961.

Baumlin, James S. *John Donne and the Rhetorics of Renaissance Discourse*. Columbia: University of Missouri Press, 1991.

Benveniste, Emile. *Problems in General Linguistics*. Trans. Mary Elizabeth Meek. Coral Gables, Fla.: University of Miami Press, 1971.

Beresford, Maurice. *The Lost Villages of England*. New York: Philosophical Library, 1954.

———, and John G. Hurst, eds. *Deserted Medieval Villages*. London: Lutterworth, 1971.

Berger, Harry, Jr. *The Allegorical Temper: Vision and Reality in Book II of Spenser's "Faerie Queene."* New Haven, Conn.: Yale University Press, 1957.

———. "Bodies and Texts." *Representations*, nos. 17–20 (1987): 144–66.

———. "'Kidnapped Romance': Discourse in *The Faerie Queene*." In *Unfolded Tales: Essays on Renaissance Romance*, ed. George M. Logan and Gordon Teskey, pp. 208–56. Ithaca, N.Y.: Cornell University Press, 1989.

———. "Levels of Discourse in Plato's Dialogues." In *Literature and the Question of Theory*, ed. Anthony J. Cascardi, pp. 75– 100. Baltimore: The Johns Hopkins University Press, 1987.

———. "Miraculous Harp: a Reading of Shakespeare's Tempest." *ShakS* 5 (1969): 253–83.

———. "The *Mutabilitie Cantos*: Archaism and Evolution in Retrospect." In *Spenser: A Collection of Critical Essays*, ed. Harry Berger, Jr., pp. 146–76. Englewood Cliffs, N.J.: Prentice-Hall, 1968.

——. "Narrative as Rhetoric in *The Faerie Queene.*" *ELR* 21 (1991): 3–48.

——. "*Phaedrus* and the Politics of Inscription." In *Plato and Postmodernism*, ed. Steven Shankman. Glenside, Penn.: Aldine, 1994.

Berry, Boyd M. *Process of Speech: Puritan Religious Writing & Paradise Lost*. Baltimore: The Johns Hopkins University Press, 1976.

Bieman, Elizabeth. *Plato Baptized: Towards the Interpretation of Spenser's Mimetic Fictions*. Toronto: University of Toronto Press, 1988.

Black, Max. *Models and Metaphors: Studies in Language and Philosophy*. Ithaca, N.Y.: Cornell University Press, 1962.

Blake, N. F. *Caxton: England's First Publisher*. New York: Barnes & Noble, 1976.

——. "Manuscript to Print." In *Book Production and Publishing in Britain, 1375–1475*, ed. Jeremy Griffiths and Derek Pearsall, pp. 403–32. Cambridge, Eng.: Cambridge University Press, 1989.

Blau, Joseph Leon. *The Christian Interpretation of the Cabala in the Renaissance*. New York: Columbia University Press, 1944.

Bloch, Maurice. "Symbols, Song, Dance and Features of Articulation." *European Journal of Sociology* 15 (1974): 55–81.

Bloch, R. Howard. *Etymologies and Genealogies: A Literary Anthropology of the French Middle Ages*. Chicago: University of Chicago Press, 1983.

Bourdieu, Pierre. *Outline of a Theory of Practice*. Trans. Richard Nice. Cambridge, Eng.: Cambridge University Press, 1977.

Boyle, Marjorie O'Rourke. *Erasmus on Language and Method in Theology*. Toronto: University of Toronto Press, 1977.

Breight, Curtis. " 'Treason doth never prosper': *The Tempest* and the Discourse of Treason." *SQ* 41 (1990): 1–28.

Brinsley, John. *Ludus Literarius*. 1612. Rpt. Menston, Eng.: Scolar, 1968.
——. *The Posing of the Parts*. 1612. Rpt. Menston, Eng.: Scolar, 1967.

Brown, Paul. " 'This thing of darkness I acknowledge mine': *The Tempest* and the Discourse of Colonialism." In *Political Shakespeare: New Essays in Cultural Materialism*, ed. Jonathan Dollimore and Alan Sinfield, pp. 48–71. Ithaca, N.Y.: Cornell University Press, 1985.

Bruner, Jerome S., et al. *Studies in Cognitive Growth*. New York: John Wiley, 1966.

Bruns, Gerald. *Inventions: Writing, Textuality, and Understanding in Literary History*. New Haven, Conn.: Yale University Press, 1982.

Buchanan, George. *The History of Scotland*. Trans. J. Fraser. London: E. Jones, for A[wnsham] Churchill, 1690.

Bullokar, William. *Booke at Large (1580) and Bref Grammar for English (1586)*. Delmar, N.Y.: Scholars' Facsimiles & Reprints, 1977.

——. *A Short Introduction or Guiding 1580–1581*. In *The Works of William Bullokar*, ed. B. Danielsson and R. C. Alston. University of Leeds School of English. Oxford: Truex, 1966.

Burerus, Albertus Johannes. Preface to Robert Estienne's *Thesaurus linguae Latinae*. Basel: Froben, 1578.

Bursill-Hall, G. L. *Speculative Grammars of the Middle Ages: The Doctrine of "Partes Orationes" of the Modistae*. The Hague: Mouton, 1971.

Cain, Thomas H. *Praise in "The Faerie Queene."* Lincoln: University of Nebraska Press, 1978.

Cain, William E. "Mirrors, Intentions, and Texts in Ben Jonson." *Essays in Literature* 8 (1981): 11–23.

Calcagnini, Caelio. *Opera Aliquot*. Basle: Froben, 1544.

Calepino, Ambrogio. *Dictionarium octolingue*. Geneva: Matthaei Berjon, 1620.

——. *Dictionarium vndecim linguarum*. Basel: Sebastian Henrici Petri, 1598.

Calvin, John. *Institutes of the Christian Religion*. Trans. Ford Lewis Battles. Ed. John T. McNeill. 2 vols. London: S.C.M., 1961.

Camden, William. *Britain*. Trans. Philemon Holland. London: George Bishop and John Norton, 1610.

——. *Remaines, concerning Britaine: But especially England, and the Inhabitants thereof*. London: by John Legatt for Simon Waterson, 1614.

Carey, John. *John Donne: Life, Mind and Art*. New York: Oxford University Press, 1981.

Carrithers, Gale H., Jr. *Donne at Sermons: A Christian Existential World*. Albany: SUNY Press, 1972.

Carruthers, Mary J. *The Book of Memory: A Study of Memory in Medieval Culture*. Cambridge, Eng.: Cambridge University Press, 1990.

Carscallen, James. "The Goodly Frame of Temperance: The Metaphor of Cosmos in *The Faerie Queene*, Book II." *UTQ* 37 (1968): 136–55.

Castiglione, Baldassare. *The Book of the Courtier*. Trans. Sir Thomas Hoby. 1561. Rpt. London: David Nutt, 1900.

Catullus. *Catullus*. Ed. Elmer Truesdell Merrill. Cambridge, Mass.: Harvard University Press, 1893.

Cave, Terence. *The Cornucopian Text: Problems of Writing in the French Renaissance*. Oxford: Clarendon, 1979.

Cawdrey, Robert. *A Table Alphabeticall of Hard Usual English Words.* 1604. Rpt. Gainesville, Fla.: Scholars' Facsimiles & Reprints, 1966.

Chamberlin, John S. *Increase and Multiply: Arts-of-Discourse Procedure in the Preaching of Donne.* Chapel Hill: University of North Carolina Press, 1976.

Chaucer, Geoffrey. Works, in *The Riverside Chaucer,* ed. Larry D. Benson. 3rd ed. Boston: Houghton Mifflin, 1987.

Cicero. *De inventione, De optimo genere oratorum, Topica.* Trans. H. M. Hubbell. 1949. Rpt. London: Heinemann, 1976.

———. *De officiis.* Trans. Walter Miller. 1931. Rpt. London: Heinemann, 1961.

Citolini, Alessandro. *La tipocosmia.* Venice: Vincenzo Valgrisi, 1561.

Clanchy, M. T. *From Memory to Written Record: England, 1066–1307.* 2nd ed. Oxford: Blackwell, 1993.

Clément, Louis. *Henri Estienne et son oeuvre française.* 1898. Rpt. Geneva: Slatkine, 1967.

Clerk, William, reviser. See Withals, John.

Clifton-Faber, Alec. *The Pattern of English Building.* London: Faber and Faber, 1972.

Cohen, Murray. *Sensible Words: Linguistic Practice in England 1640–1785.* Baltimore: The Johns Hopkins University Press, 1977.

Coleridge, Samuel Taylor. *Miscellaneous Criticism.* Ed. Thomas Middleton Raysor. Cambridge, Mass.: Harvard University Press, 1936.

Colie, Rosalie. *Shakespeare's Living Art.* Princeton: Princeton University Press, 1974.

Cooper, Thomas. *Thesaurus linguae Romanae et Britannicae.* 1565. Rpt. Menston, Eng.: Scolar, 1969.

———. *Thesaurus linguae Romanae et Britannicae.* London: Henry Bynneman, 1578.

Cooper, Andrew M. "The Collapse of the Religious Hieroglyph: Typology and Natural Language in Herbert and Bacon." *RenQ* 45 (1992): 96–118.

Cooper, William E., and John Robert Ross. "Word Order." In *Papers from the Parasession on Functionalism,* ed. Robin E. Grossman, L. James San, and Timothy J. Vance, pp. 63–111. Chicago: Chicago Linguistic Society, 1975.

Coote, Edmund. *The English Schoole-Maister.* 1596. Rpt. Menston, Eng.: Scolar, 1968.

Copjec, Joan. "The Anxiety of the Influencing Machine." *October* 23 (1982): 43–59.

Cornford, Francis MacDonald. *Plato's Theory of Knowledge.* 1934. Rpt. New York: Liberal Arts Press, 1957.

Cotgrave, Randle. *A Dictionairie of the French and English Tongues.* 1611. Rpt. Menston, Eng.: Scolar, 1968.

Coudert, Allison. "Some Theories of a Natural Language from the Renaissance to the Seventeenth Century." In *Magia naturalis und die Entstehung der modernen Naturwissenschaften, Studia Leibnitiana,* sonderheft 7, pp. 56–114. Wiesbaden: Franz Steiner, 1978.

Crane, Mary Thomas. *Framing Authority: Sayings, Self, and Society in Sixteenth-Century England.* Princeton: Princeton University Press, 1993.

———. "'His Owne Style': Voice and Writing in Jonson's Poems." *Criticism* 32 (1990): 31–50.

Crane, William G. *Wit and Rhetoric in the Renaissance: The Formal Basis of Elizabethan Prose Style.* 1937. Rpt. Gloucester, Mass.: Peter Smith, 1964.

Culler, Jonathan. *Ferdinand de Saussure.* Rev. ed. Ithaca, N.Y.: Cornell University Press, 1986.

The Culture of Print: Power and the Uses of Print in Early Modern Europe. Ed. Roger Chartier. Trans. Lydia G. Cochrane. Princeton: Princeton University Press, 1987.

Daly, Lloyd W., and B. A. Daly. "Some Techniques in Medieval Latin Lexicography." *Speculum* 39 (1964): 229–39.

D'Amico, John F. *Theory and Practice in Renaissance Textual Criticism: Beatus Rhenanus between Conjecture and History.* Berkeley: University of California Press, 1988.

Dante, Alighieri. *Il convivio.* Ed. Bruna Cordati. Torino: Loesher, 1968.

———. *De vulgari eloquentia.* Ed. Sergio Cecchin. Torino: TEA, 1988.

Davies, Horton. *Worship and Theology in England from Andrewes to Baxter and Fox, 1603–1690.* Princeton: Princeton University Press, 1975.

de Jonge, H. J., ed. See Erasmus, Desiderius of Rotterdam.

DeNeef, A. Leigh. *Spenser and the Motives of Metaphor.* Durham, N.C.: Duke University Press, 1982.

Derrida, Jacques. "The Retrait of Metaphor." *Enclitic* 2 (1978): 5–33.

———. "White Mythology: Metaphor in the Text of Philosophy." *NLH* 6 (1974): 5–74.

Deserted Medieval Villages. Ed. Maurice Beresford and John G. Hurst. London: Lutterworth, 1971.

Docherty, Thomas. *John Donne, Undone*. London: Metheun, 1986.

Doebler, Bettie Anne. *The Quickening Seed: Death in the Sermons of John Donne*. Salzburg: Universität Salzburg, 1974.

Donaldson, E. Talbot, ed. *Chaucer's Poetry: An Anthology for the Modern Reader*. New York: Ronald Press, 1975.

Donatus the Grammarian. *The Ars Minor of Donatus*. Trans. Wayland Johnson Chase. University of Wisconsin Studies in the Social Sciences and History, no. 11. Madison, 1926.

Done, John. *Polydoron: or a Miscellania of Morall, Philosophicall, and Theologicall Sentences*. London: Thomas Cotes, for George Gibbes, 1631.

Donne, John. *Biathanatos*. [1646?]. Rpt. New York: National Process, 1930.

———. *Devotions Vpon Emergent Occasions*. Ed. Anthony Raspa. Montreal: McGill-Queen's University Press, 1975.

———. *The Divine Poems*. Ed. Helen Gardner. 2nd ed. Oxford: Clarendon, 1978.

———. *Donne's Prebend Sermons*. Ed. Janel M. Mueller. Cambridge, Mass.: Harvard University Press, 1971.

———. *The Elegies and The Songs and Sonnets*. Ed. Helen Gardner. 1965. Rpt. Oxford: Clarendon, 1970.

———. *The Epithalamions, Anniversaries and Epicedes*. Ed. W[esley]. Milgate. Oxford: Clarendon, 1978.

———. *Essays in Divinity*. Ed. Evelyn M. Simpson. 1952. Rpt. Oxford: Clarendon, 1967.

———. *John Donne and the Theology of Language*. Ed. P. G. Stanwood and Heather Ross Asals. Columbia: University of Missouri Press, 1986.

———. *The Life and Letters of John Donne*. Ed. Edmund Gosse. Vol. II. New York: Dodd, Mead, 1899.

———. *The Satires, Epigrams and Verse Letters of John Donne*. Ed. W[esley]. Milgate. Oxford: Clarendon, 1967.

———. *The Sermons of John Donne*. Ed. George R. Potter and Evelyn M. Simpson. 10 vols. 1953. Rpt. Berkeley: University of California Press, 1984.

Donovan, Kevin J. "Jonson's Texts in the First Folio." In *Ben Jonson's 1616 Folio*, ed. Jennifer Brady and W. H. Herendeen, pp. 23–37. Newark, N.J.: University of Delaware Press, 1991.

Du Cange, Charles du Fresne. *Glossarium mediae et infimae Latinitatis.* Rev. Léopold Favre. 10 vols. Paris: Librairie des Sciences et des Arts, 1937–38.

Edelstein, Ludwig. *Plato's Seventh Letter.* Leiden: E. J. Brill, 1966.

Eisenstein, Elizabeth. *The Printing Press as an Agent of Change: Communications and Cultural Transformations in Early-Modern Europe.* 2 vols. Cambridge, Eng.: Cambridge University Press, 1979.

Eliot, T. S. *The Complete Poems and Plays.* 1930. Rpt. New York: Harcourt, Brace, 1952.

Elsky, Martin. *Authorizing Words: Speech, Writing, and Print in the English Renaissance.* Ithaca, N.Y.: Cornell University Press, 1989.

———. "Words, Things, and Names: Jonson's Poetry and Philosophical Grammar." In *Classic and Cavalier: Essays on Jonson and the Sons of Ben,* ed. Claude J. Summers and Ted-Larry Pebworth, pp. 91–104. Pittsburgh: University of Pittsburgh Press, 1982.

Elyot, Thomas. *The Dictionary of Syr Thomas Eliot knight.* London: Thomas Berthelet, 1538.

Empson, William. *The Structure of Complex Words.* London: Chatto & Windus, 1951.

Erasmus, Desiderius of Rotterdam. *Adages IiI–Iv100.* Trans. Margaret Mann Phillips, with notes by R. A. B. Mynors. In *The Collected Works of Erasmus.* Vol. XXXI. Toronto: University of Toronto Press, 1982.

———. *Adagia.* Venice: P. Manuzio, 1585.

———. *Apologia ad annotationes Stunicae.* In *Opera Omnia,* IX–2. Ed. H. J. de Jonge. Amsterdam: North Holland, 1983.

———. *Apophthegmes.* Trans. Nicholas Udall. London: Richard Grafton, 1542.

———. *Apophthegmes.* Trans. Nicholas Udall. London: John Kingston, 1564.

———. *"Copia": Foundations of the Abundant Style.* Trans. Betty I. Knott. In *The Collected Works of Erasmus.* Vol. XXIV, ed. Craig R. Thompson. Toronto: University of Toronto Press, 1978.

———. *De duplici copia verborum ac rerum commentarii duo.* Ed. Betty I. Knott. In *Opera Omnia,* I–6. Amsterdam: North Holland, 1988.

———. *On Copia of Words and Ideas.* Trans. Donald B. King and H. David Rix. Milwaukee: Marquette University Press, 1963.

———. *Parabolae.* Trans. R. A. B. Mynors. In *The Collected Works of Erasmus.* Vol. XXIII, ed. Craig R. Thompson. Toronto: University of Toronto Press, 1978.

———. *The Praise of Folly*. Trans. Leonard F. Dean. 1946. Rpt. New York: Hendricks House, 1969.

Estienne, Henri. *Traicté de la conformité dv langage françois auec le Grec*. Paris: Robert Estienne, 1569.

Estienne, Robert. *Thesaurus linguae Latinae*. Paris: Robertus Stephanus, 1543.

———. *Thesaurus linguae Latinae*. Basel: Froben, 1576–78.

Evans, Robert C. "Ben Jonson's Chaucer." *ELR* 19 (1989): 324–45.

Fenner, Dudley. *The Artes of Logike and Rhetorike*. [Middleburgh: Richard Schilders?], 1584.

Ferguson, Margaret W. "Saint Augustine's Region of Unlikeness: The Crossing of Exile and Language." *Georgia Review* 29 (1975): 842–64.

Ferry, Anne. *The Art of Naming*. Chicago: University of Chicago Press, 1988.

Ficino, Marsilio. *Three Books on Life*. Ed. and trans. Carol V. Kaske and John R. Clark. Binghamton, N.Y.: Medieval and Renaissance Texts and Studies, 1989.

Fisch, Harold. "The Puritans and the Reform of Prose Style." *ELH*, 19 (1952): 229–48.

Fish, Stanley. "Masculine Persuasive Force: Donne and Verbal Power." In *Soliciting Interpretation: Literary Theory and Seventeenth-Century English Poetry*, ed. Elizabeth D. Harvey and Katharine Eisaman Maus, pp. 223–52. Chicago: University of Chicago Press, 1990.

———. *Self-Consuming Artifacts: The Experience of Seventeenth-Century Literature*. Berkeley: University of California Press, 1972.

Florio, John. *Queen Anna's New World of Words, or Dictionarie of the Italian and English tongues*. 1611. Rpt. Menston, Eng.: Scolar, 1968.

Flynn, Vincent Joseph. "The Grammatical Writings of William Lily." *Papers of the Bibliographical Society of America* 37 (1943): 85–113.

Foley, John Miles. *Immanent Art: From Structure to Meaning in Oral Epic*. Bloomington: Indiana University Press, 1991.

Fordyce, C. J. *Catullus: A Commentary*. Oxford: Clarendon, 1961.

Foucault, Michel. *Discipline and Punish: The Birth of the Prison*. Trans. Alan Sheridan. New York: Random House, 1977.

———. *The Order of Things: An Archeology of the Human Sciences*. 1970. Rpt. New York: Random House, 1973.

Fowler, Alastair. "The Silva Tradition in Jonson's *The Forrest*." In *Poetic Traditions of the English Renaissance*, ed. Maynard Mack and George deForest Lord, pp. 163–80. New Haven, Conn.: Yale University Press, 1982.

Foxe, John. *The Acts and Monuments*. Vol. VIII. Ed. George Townsend. New York: AMS, 1965.

Friedberg, Harris. "Ben Jonson's Poetry: Pastoral, Georgic, Epigram." *ELR* 4 (1974): 111–36.

Fumerton, Patricia. " 'Secret Arts': Elizabethan Miniatures and Sonnets." In *Representing the English Renaissance*, ed. Stephen Greenblatt, pp. 93–133. Berkeley: University of California Press, 1988.

Garzoni, Thomaso. *La piazza vniversale di tvtte le professioni del mondo, e nobili et ignobile*. Venice: Battista Somascho, 1586.

Gellrich, Jesse M. *The Idea of the Book in the Middle Ages: Language Theory, Mythology, and Fiction*. Ithaca, N.Y.: Cornell University Press, 1985.

The Geneva Bible: A Facsimile of the 1560 Edition. Madison: University of Wisconsin Press, 1969.

Giddens, Anthony. *The Constitution of Society: Outline of the Theory of Structuration*. Berkeley: University of California Press, 1984.

Gil, Alexander. "Alexander Gil's *Logonomia Anglia* Edition of 1621." Trans. Dorothy Dixon, Ph.D. diss., University of Southern California, 1951.

———. *Logonomia Anglia*. 2nd ed. London: John Beale, 1621.

Gilman, Ernest B. *Iconoclasm and Poetry in the English Reformation*. Chicago: University of Chicago Press, 1986.

Gilson, Etienne. *The Christian Philosophy of Saint Augustine*. Trans. L. E. M. Lynch. 1960. Rpt. New York: Random House, 1967.

Goldberg, Jonathan. *James I and the Politics of Literature: Jonson, Shakespeare, Donne, and Their Contemporaries*. Baltimore: The Johns Hopkins University Press, 1983.

———. *Writing Matter: From the Hands of the English Renaissance*. Stanford: Stanford University Press, 1990.

Goldstein, Kurt. *Human Nature in the Light of Psychopathology*. Cambridge, Mass.: Harvard University Press, 1940.

———. *The Organism: A Holistic Approach to Biology Derived from Pathological Data in Man*. New York: American Book, 1939.

Goody, Jack. *The Domestication of the Savage Mind*. Cambridge, Eng.: Cambridge University Press, 1977.

Grafton, Anthony. *Joseph Scaliger: A Study in the History of Classical Scholarship*. Vol. I. Oxford: Clarendon, 1983.

Gravelle, Sarah Stever. "The Latin-Vernacular Question and Humanist Theory of Language and Culture." *JHI* 49 (1988): 367–86.

———. "A New Theory of Truth." *JHI* 50 (1989): 333–36.

Greenblatt, Stephen. "Murdering Peasants: Status, Genre, and the Representation of Rebellion." In *Representing the English Renaissance*, ed. Stephen Greenblatt, pp. 1–29. Berkeley: University of California Press, 1988.

———. *Shakespearean Negotiations: The Circulation of Social Energy in Renaissance England*. Berkeley: University of California Press, 1988.

———, and Giles Gunn, eds. *Redrawing the Boundaries*. New York: The Modern Language Association, 1992.

Greene, Thomas M. "Ben Jonson and the Centered Self." *SEL* 10 (1970): 325–48.

———. "Erasmus's 'Festina lente': Vulnerabilities of the Humanist Text." In *Mimesis: From Mirror to Method, Augustine to Descartes*, ed. John D. Lyons, pp. 132–48. Hanover, N.H.: University Press of New England, 1982.

———. *The Light in Troy: Imitation and Discovery in Renaissance Poetry*. New Haven, Conn.: Yale University Press, 1982.

———. *Poésie et magie*. Paris: Juilliard, 1991.

———. "Poetry as Invocation." *NLH* 24 (1993): 495–517.

Greg, W. W. "An Elizabethan Printer and His Copy." *The Library*, 4th series, 4 (1923): 102–118.

Gregerson, Linda. "Protestant Erotics: Idolatry and Interpretation in Spenser's *Faerie Queene*." *ELH* 58 (1991): 1–34.

Gundersheimer, Werner. "Erasmus, Humanism, and the Christian Cabala." *JWCI* 26 (1963): 38–52.

Guy, John. *Tudor England*. Oxford: Oxford University Press, 1988.

Hacking, Ian. *Why Does Language Matter to Philosophy?* Cambridge, Eng.: Cambridge University Press, 1975.

Hall, Edward. *The Vnion of the Two Noble and Illustre Famelies of Lancastre and Yorke*. 1548. Rpt. in *Hall's Chronicle*. London: for J. Johnson et al., 1809.

Hall, Michael L. "Searching the Scriptures: Meditation and Discovery in Donne's Sermons." In *New Essays on Donne*, ed. Gary A. Stringer, pp. 211–38. Salzburg: Universität Salzburg, 1977.

Halpern, Richard. *The Poetics of Primitive Accumulation: English Renaissance Culture and the Genealogy of Capital*. Ithaca, N.Y.: Cornell University Press, 1991.

Hamilton, A. C., ed. See Spenser, Edmund; also *The Spenser Encyclopedia*.

Harland, Paul W. "Dramatic Technique and Personae in Donne's Sermons." *ELH* 53 (1986): 709–26.

Harp, Richard. "Jonson's 'To Penshurst': The Country House as Church." *JDJ* 7 (1988): 73–89.

Harris, Roy. *The Language-Makers*. Ithaca, N.Y.: Cornell University Press, 1980.

Hart, John. *John Hart's Works on English Orthography and Pronunciation* (1551, 1569, 1570). Vol. I. Ed. Bror Danielsson. Stockholm: Almqvist & Wiksell, 1955.

——. *An Orthographie*. 1569. Rpt. Menston, Eng.: Scolar Press, 1969.

Harvey, Gabriel. *Gabriel Harvey's Ciceronianus*. Trans. Clarence A. Forbes. Introduction and notes by Harold S. Wilson. Lincoln: University of Nebraska, 1945.

——. *The Letter-Book of Gabriel Harvey, 1573–80*. Ed. Edward John Long Scott. Camden Society, n.s. 33. Westminster: Nichols and Sons, 1884.

Havelock, Eric A. *Origins of Western Literacy*. Toronto: Ontario Institute for Studies in Education, 1976.

——. *Prologue to Greek Literacy*. Cincinnati: University of Cincinnati Press, 1971.

Hedrick, Charles W. "Literacy and Democracy." *Humanities* 14 (1993): 24–27.

Helgerson, Richard. *Forms of Nationhood: The Elizabethan Writing of England*. Chicago: University of Chicago Press, 1992.

Hellinga, Lotte. "Manuscripts in the Hands of Printers." In *Manuscripts in the Fifty Years after the Invention of Printing*, ed. J. B. Trapp, pp. 3–11. London: Warburg Institute, 1983.

——. "Notes on the Order of Setting a Fifteenth-Century Book." *Quaerendo* 4, no. 1 (1974): 64–69.

Heninger, S. K., Jr. *Sidney and Spenser: The Poet as Maker*. University Park, Penn.: Pennsylvania State University Press, 1989.

Herbert, George. *The Works of George Herbert*. Ed. F. E. Hutchinson. 1941. Rpt. Oxford: Clarendon, 1959.

Herford, C. H., and Percy and Evelyn Simpson, eds. See Jonson, Ben.

Herz, Judith Scherer. "'An Excellent Exercise of Wit that Speaks so Well of Ill': Donne and the Poetics of Concealment." In *The Eagle and the Dove: Reassessing John Donne*, ed. Claude J. Summers and Ted-Larry Pebworth, pp. 3–14. Columbia: University of Missouri Press, 1986.

Historical Manuscripts Commission, 77; Report on the Manuscripts of Lord De

L'Isle and Dudley Preserved at Penshurst Place. 6 vols. London: His Majesty's Stationery Office, 1925–66.

The Holy Bible Conteyning the Old Testament, and the New. London: Robert Barker, 1611.

Holyoke, Francis, reviser. *Riders Dictionarie*. London: Adam Islip, 1606.

Horman, William. *Vulgaria*. 1519. Rpt. Amsterdam: Theatrum Orbis Terrarum, 1975.

Horton, Robin. "African Traditional Thought and Western Science." In *Rationality*, ed. Bryan R. Wilson, pp. 131–71. Oxford: Blackwell, 1970.

Hoskyns, John. *Direccions for Speech and Style*. In *The Life, Letters, and Writings of John Hoskyns, 1566–1638*, ed. Louise Brown Osborn. New Haven, Conn.: Yale University Press, 1937.

———. *Directions for Speech and Style*. Ed. Hoyt H. Hudson. Princeton: Princeton University Press, 1935.

Howard, Maurice. *The Early Tudor Country House: Architecture and Politics 1490–1550*. London: George Philip, 1987.

Howell, A. C. "*Res et Verba*: Words and Things." *ELH* 13 (1946): 131–42.

Hudson, Anne. *The Premature Reformation: Wycliffe Texts and Lollard History*. Oxford: Clarendon, 1988.

Huloet, Richard. *Abecedarium Anglico-Latinum*. 1552. Rpt. Menston, Eng.: Scolar, 1970.

Hunter, G. K. "The Markings of *Sententiae* in Elizabethan Printed Plays, Poems, and Romances." *The Library*, 5th series, 6 (1951): 171–88.

Irvine, Martin. *The Making of Textual Culture: "Grammatica" and Literary Theory 350–1100*. Cambridge, Eng.: Cambridge University Press, 1994.

Isidore of Seville. *Isidori Hispalensis Episcopi Etymologiarum sive Originum*. Ed. W. M. Lindsay. 2 vols. 1911. Rpt. Oxford: Clarendon, 1971.

Jardine, Lisa. *Erasmus, Man of Letters: The Construction of Charisma in Print*. Princeton: Princeton University Press, 1993.

———. "Lorenzo Valla and the Intellectual Origins of Humanist Dialectic." *Journal of the History of Philosophy* 15 (1977): 143–64.

Johnson, Francis R. *Astronomical Thought in Renaissance England: A Study of the English Scientific Writings from 1500–1645*. 1937. Rpt. New York: Octagon, 1968.

Jones, Richard Foster. *The Triumph of the English Language*. 1953. Rpt. Stanford: Stanford University Press, 1966.

Jonson, Ben. *Workes*. Ed. Thomas Speght. London: Adam Islip, 1602.

———. *Works*. Ed. C. H. Herford and Percy and Evelyn Simpson. 11 vols. 1925–52. Rpt. Oxford: Clarendon, 1963–75: vols. I–VIII from corrected sheets.

Juvenal. *Juvenal and Persius*. Trans. G. G. Ramsay. Rev. ed. London: Heinemann, 1940.

Kamholtz, Jonathan Z. "Ben Jonson's Green World: Structure and Imaginative Unity in *The Forrest.*" *SP* 78 (1981): 170–93.

Katz, David S. *Philo-Semitism and the Readmission of the Jews to England, 1603–1655*. Oxford: Clarendon, 1982.

Kennedy, William J. "Rhetoric, Allegory, and Dramatic Modality in Spenser's Fradubio Episode." *ELR* 3 (1973): 351–68.

Kerrigan, William. "Ben Jonson Full of Shame and Scorn." *SLitI* 6 (1973): 199–217.

Kieckhefer, Richard. "The Specific Rationality of Medieval Magic." *American Historical Review* 99 (1994): 813–36.

Kinney, Arthur F. *Humanist Poetics: Thought, Rhetoric, and Fiction in Sixteenth-Century England*. Amherst: University of Massachusetts Press, 1986.

Kinney, Daniel. "Erasmus' *Adagia*: Midwife to the Rebirth of Learning." *JMRS* 11 (1981): 169–92.

Kirshenblatt-Gimblett, Barbara. "Toward a Theory of Proverb Meaning." *Proverbium* 22 (1973): 821–27.

Kneale, William and Martha. *The Development of Logic*. 1962. Rpt. Oxford: Clarendon, 1984.

Koyré, Alexandre. *From the Closed World to the Infinite Universe*. Baltimore: The Johns Hopkins University Press, 1957.

Krier, Theresa M. *Gazing on Secret Sights: Spenser, Classical Imitation, and the Decorums of Vision*. Ithaca: Cornell University Press, 1990.

Kristeller, Paul Oskar. *The Philosophy of Marsilia Ficino*. Trans. Virginia Conant. New York: Columbia University Press, 1943.

LaCapra, Dominick. "Who Rules Metaphor?" *Diacritics* 10 (Dec. 1980): 15–28.

Lakoff, George, and Mark Johnson. *Metaphors We Live By*. Chicago: University of Chicago Press, 1980.

Langland, William. *Will's Visions of Piers Plowman, Do-Well, Do-Better and Do-Best: The B Version*. Ed. George Kane and E. Talbot Donaldson. London: Athlone, 1975.

Larkin, M[iriam]. T[herese]. *Language in the Philosophy of Aristotle*. The Hague: Mouton, 1971.

Latham, Ronald E. *Revised Medieval Latin Wordlist*. London: Oxford University Press, 1965.

Levins, Peter. *Manipulus Vocabulorum: A Rhyming Dictionary of the English Language*. Ed. Henry B. Wheatley. EETS 27. London: Trübner, 1867.

Lévy-Bruhl, Lucien. *How Natives Think*. Trans. Lilian A. Clare. 1910. Rpt. Princeton: Princeton University Press, 1985.

Lewis, Charlton T., and Charles Short. *A Latin Dictionary*. 1879. Rpt. Oxford: Clarendon, 1966.

Lily, William. *An English Grammar, 1641*. By R. R. Menston, Eng.: Scolar, 1972.

——. *A Shorte Introduction of Grammar*. 1567. Rpt. New York: Scholars' Facsimiles & Reprints, 1945.

——. *A Shorte Introduction of Grammar*. London: Reginald Wolfe, 1567, 1568.

——. *A Short Introduction of Grammar*. London: Francis Flowar, 1574, 1590.

——. *A Short Introduction of Grammar*. London: John Battersbie, 1597.

——. *A Short Introduction of Grammar*. London: John Norton, 1606.

——. *A Short Introduction of Grammar*. Cambridge, Eng.: Cantrell Legge, 1621.

——. *A Short Introduction of Grammar*. London: Bonham Norton, 1630, 1633.

——. *A Short Introduction of Grammar*. London: Roger Norton, 1636.

Lily, William, and John Colet. *A Short Introduction of Grammar*. 1549. Rpt. Menston, Eng.: Scolar, 1970.

Lowry, Martin, trans. *The World of Aldus Manutius: Business and Scholarship in Renaissance Venice*. Ithaca, N.Y.: Cornell University Press, 1979.

Lyotard, Jean-François. *The Postmodern Condition: A Report on Knowledge*. Trans. Geoff Bennington and Brian Massumi. Minneapolis: University of Minnesota Press, 1984.

Maclean, Ian. *Interpretation and Meaning in the Renaissance: The Case of Law*. Cambridge, Eng.: Cambridge University Press, 1992.

——. "The Interpretation of Natural Signs: Cardano's *De subtilitate* versus Scaliger's *Exercitationes*." In *Occult and Scientific Mentalities in the Renaissance*, ed. Brian Vickers, pp. 231–52. Cambridge, Eng.: Cambridge University Press, 1984.

Manutius, Aldus. See Lowry, Martin, trans.

Marcus, Leah. "Renaissance/Early Modern Studies." In *Redrawing the Boundaries*, ed. Stephen Greenblatt and Giles Gunn, pp. 41–63. New York: The Modern Language Association, 1992.

Marichal, Robert, ed. See Rabelais, François.

Markus, R. A. "St. Augustine on Signs." *Phronesis* 2 (1957): 60–83.

Marshall, Thomas D. "Addressing the House: Jonson's Ideology at Penshurst." *TSLL* 35 (1993): 57–78.

Martial. *Martial: Epigrams*. Trans. Walter C. A. Ker. 2 vols. Rev. ed. London: Heinemann, 1968.

Mattingly, Garrett. *The Defeat of the Spanish Armada*. 1959. Rpt. London: Jonathan Cape, 1970.

McCabe, Richard A. *The Pillars of Eternity: Time and Providence in "The Faerie Queene."* Kill Lane, Blackrock, County Dublin, Ireland: Irish Academic Press, 1989.

McCanles, Michael. *Jonsonian Discriminations: The Humanist Poet and the Praise of True Nobility*. Toronto: University of Toronto Press, 1992.

McCullough, Peter E. "Lancelot Andrewes and Language." *Anglican Theological Review* 74 (1992): 304–16.

McCutcheon, Elizabeth, trans. *Sir Nicholas Bacon's Great House Sententiae. ELR Supplements* 3, 1977.

McKeon, Richard. "Aristotle's Conception of Language and the Arts of Language." *Classical Philology* 41 (1946): 193–206.

——. "Aristotle's Conception of Language and the Arts of Language." *Classical Philology* 42 (1947): 21–50.

Merrill, Thomas F. "John Donne and the Word of God." *NM* 69 (1968): 597–616.

Mills, Jerry Leath. "Spenser, Lodowick Bryskett, and the Mortalist Controvery: *The Faerie Queene*, II.ix.22." *PQ* 52 (1973): 173–86.

Minsheu, John. *Ductor in Linguas (Guide into the Tongues)*. 1617. Rpt. Delmar, N.Y.: Scholars' Facsimiles & Reprints, 1978.

——. *Ductor in Linguas, The Guide Into Tongues*. London: John Brown, 1617.

Mitchell, C. J. "Quotation Marks, National Compositorial Habits, and False Imprints." *The Library*, 6th series, 5 (1983): 359–84.

Mitchell, W. J. T. *Iconology: Image, Text, Ideology*. Chicago: University of Chicago Press, 1986.

Monfasani, John. "Was Lorenzo Valla an Ordinary Language Philosopher?" *JHI* 50 (1989): 309–23.

Montaigne, Michaell de. *The Essayes*. Trans. John Florio. London: Edward Blount, 1603.

Morrow, Glenn R., trans. See Plato.

Mueller, Janel M., ed. *Donne's Prebend Sermons*. See Donne, John.

———. *The Native Tongue and the Word: Developments in English Prose Style 1380–1580*. Chicago: University of Chicago Press, 1984.

Mulcaster, Richard. *Mulcaster's Elementarie*. Ed. E. T. Campagnac. Oxford: Clarendon, 1925.

Murrin, Michael. *The Veil of Allegory: Some Notes toward a Theory of Allegorical Rhetoric in the English Renaissance*. Chicago: University of Chicago Press, 1969.

Mynors, R. A. B. *Durham Cathedral Manuscripts to the End of the Twelfth Century*. Oxford: Oxford University Press, 1939.

Nohrnberg, James. *The Analogy of "The Faerie Queene."* Princeton: Princeton University Press, 1976.

Norton, Glyn P. *The Ideology and Language of Translation in Renaissance France and Their Humanist Antecedents*. Geneva: Droz, 1984.

Nowell, Laurence. *Vocabularium Saxonicum*. Ed. Albert H. Marckwardt. Ann Arbor: University of Michigan Press, 1952.

O'Connell, Michael. "The Idolatrous Eye: Iconoclasm, Anti-Theatricalism, and the Image of the Elizabethan Theater." *ELH* 52 (1985): 279–310.

———. *Mirror and Veil: The Historical Dimension of Spenser's "Faerie Queene."* Chapel Hill: University of North Carolina Press, 1977.

Ong, Walter J. *Interfaces of the Word: Studies in the Evolution of Consciousness and Culture*. Ithaca, N.Y.: Cornell University Press, 1977.

———. "Latin Language Study as a Renaissance Puberty Rite." *SP* 56 (1959): 103–24.

———. *Ramus: Method and the Decay of Dialogue*. 1958. Rpt. Cambridge, Mass.: Harvard University Press, 1983.

———. *Rhetoric, Romance, and Technology: Studies in the Interaction of Expression and Culture*. Ithaca, N.Y.: Cornell University Press, 1971.

Opfell, Olga S. *The King James Bible Translators*. Jefferson, N.C.: McFarland, 1982.

Opie, B. J. "The Devil, Science, and Subjectivity." *ELR* 6 (1976): 430–52.

Orlandi, Giovanni. *Aldo Manuzio editore*. Vol. I. Milan: Polifilo, 1975.

Orme, Nicholas. *English Schools in the Middle Ages*. London: Methuen, 1973.

Osselton, N. E. "Ben Jonson's Status as a Grammarian." *Dutch Quarterly Review of Anglo-American Letters* 12 (1982): 205–12.

Ovid. *Metamorphoses*. Ed. Frank Justus Miller. 2 vols. 1916. Rpt. London: Heinemann, 1964.

Oxford Dictionary of English Proverbs. Compiled by William George Smith, with an introduction by Janet E. Heseltine. 2nd rev. ed., by Paul Harvey. Oxford: Clarendon, 1948.

Oxford Latin Dictionary. 8 vols. Oxford: Clarendon, 1968–82.

Padley, G. A. *Grammatical Theory in Western Europe, 1500–1700: The Latin Tradition*. Cambridge, Eng.: Cambridge University Press, 1976.

——. *Grammatical Theory in Western Europe, 1500–1700: Trends in Vernacular Grammar*. 2 vols. Cambridge, Eng.: Cambridge University Press, 1985.

Parker, Patricia. *Literary Fat Ladies: Rhetoric, Gender, Property*. London: Methuen, 1987.

Patterson, Annabel. *Censorship and Interpretation: The Conditions of Writing and Reading in Early Modern England*. Madison: University of Wisconsin Press, 1984.

——. *Reading between the Lines*. Madison: University of Wisconsin Press, 1993.

Peacham, Henry. *The Garden of Eloquence*. 1577; 1593. Rpt. New York: Scholars' Facsimiles & Reprints, 1954.

Pelegromius, Simon. *Synonymorvm Sylva*. London: John Norton and John Bill, 1612.

Perkins, William. *Workes*. 3 vols. London: John Legatt, 1612–13.

Peterson, Richard S. "Imitation and Praise in Ben Jonson's Poems." *ELR* 10 (1980): 265–99.

Phillips, Margaret Mann, trans. *The "Adages" of Erasmus: A Study with Translations*. Cambridge, Eng.: Cambridge University Press, 1964.

——. *Erasmus on His Times: A Shortened Version of the Adages of Erasmus*. London: Cambridge University Press, 1967.

Pittenger, Elizabeth. "Dispatch Quickly: The Mechanical Reproduction of Pages." *SQ* 42 (1991): 389–408.

Plato. *The Collected Dialogues of Plato*. Ed. Edith Hamilton and Huntington Cairns. New York: Random House, 1961.

——. *Plato*. Vol. VII. Trans. R. G. Bury. London: Heinemann, 1929.

———. *Plato's Epistles*. Trans. Glenn R. Morrow. Rev. ed. Indianapolis: Bobbs-Merrill, 1962.

Plutarch. *Plutarch's Moralia*. Vol. I. Trans. Frank Cole Babbit. London: Heinemann, 1927.

Pound, Ezra. *Guide to Kulchur*. Norfolk, Conn.: New Directions, 1938.

Puttenham, George. *The Arte of English Poesie*. 1589. Rpt. Kent, Ohio: Kent State University Press, 1970.

Quine, W. V. O. *From a Logical Point of View*. Rev. ed. Cambridge, Mass.: Harvard University Press, 1961.

Quinn, Dennis. "Donne's Christian Eloquence." *ELH* 27 (1960): 276–97.

Quintilian. *Institutio oratoria*. Trans. H. E. Butler. 4 vols. London: Heinemann, 1920–22.

R. R. *An English Grammar*. See Lily, William.

Rabelais, François. *The Histories of Gargantua and Pantagruel*. Trans. J. M. Cohen. 1955. Rpt. New York: Penguin, 1985.

———. *Le Quart Livre* [des faicts et dicts héroiques du bon Pantagruel]. Ed. Robert Marichal. 1947. Rpt. Geneva, Droz, 1967.

———. *Works*. Trans. Sir Thomas Urquhart and [Peter] Motteux. Vol. II. London: G. H. Bohn, 1855.

Rajan, Tilottama. "'Nothing Sooner Broke': Donne's *Songs and Sonets* as Self-Consuming Artifact." *ELH* 49 (1982): 805–28.

Rambuss, Richard. *Spenser's Secret Career*. Cambridge, Eng.: Cambridge University Press, 1993.

Rand, Richard A. "Geraldine." In *Untying the Text: A Post-Structuralist Reader*, ed. Robert Young, pp. 280–316. Boston: Routledge & Kegan Paul, 1981.

Rappaport, Steve. *Worlds Within Worlds: Structures of Life in Sixteenth-Century London*. Cambridge, Eng.: Cambridge University Press, 1989.

Rathmell, J. C. A. "Jonson, Lord Lisle, and Penshusrt." *ELR* 1 (1971): 250–60.

Reid, Robert L. "Alma's Castle and the Symbolization of Reason in *The Faerie Queene*." *JEGP* 80 (1981): 512–27.

Ricoeur, Paul. *The Rule of Metaphor*. Trans. Robert Czerny. Toronto: University of Toronto Press, 1977.

Rider, John. *Bibliotheca Scholastica*. 1589. Rpt. Menston, Eng.: Scolar, 1970.

———. *Riders Dictionarie*. See Holyoke, Francis, reviser.

Riggs, David. *Ben Jonson: A Life*. Cambridge, Mass.: Harvard University Press, 1989.

Roche, Thomas P., Jr., ed. See Spenser, Edmund.

Rosier, James L. "The Sources and Methods of Minsheu's *Guide Into the Tongues*." *PQ* 40 (1961): 68–76.

Rouse, M. A., and R. H. Rouse. "Florilegia of Patristic Texts." In *Les Genres littéraires dans les sources théologiques et philosophiques médiévales*, pp. 165–80. Louvain-La-Neuve: University Catholique de Louvain, Publications de l'Institut d'Etudes Médiévales, second series 5 (1982).

———. "The *Florilegium Angelicum*: Its Origin, Content, and Influence." In *Medieval Learning and Literature: Essays Presented to Richard William Hunt*, ed. J. J. G. Alexander and M. T. Gibson, pp. 66–114. Oxford: Clarendon, 1976.

———. "*Statim invenire*: Schools, Preachers, and New Attitudes to the Page." In *Renaissance and Renewal in the Twelfth Century*, ed. Robert L. Benson and Giles Constable, pp. 201–25. Cambridge, Mass.: Harvard University Press, 1982.

Rouse, Richard. "Copy-specific Features of the Printed Book: What to Record and Why." In *Bibliography and the Study of 15th Century Civilization*, ed. Lotte Hellinga and John Goldfinch, pp. 202–15. London: British Library, 1987.

Rubin, Miri. *Corpus Christi: The Eucharist in Late Medieval Culture*. Cambridge, Eng.: Cambridge University Press, 1991.

Salmon, Vivian. *The Study of Language in 17th-Century England*. Amsterdam: John Benjamins, 1979.

Scaliger, Julius Caesar. *Poetices libri septem*. 1561. Rpt. Stuttgart: Friedlich Frommann, 1964.

Schäfer, Jürgen. "John Minsheu: Scholar or Charlatan?" *RenQ* 26 (1973): 23–35.

Schoenfeldt, Michael C. "'The Mysteries of Manners, Armes, and Arts': 'Inviting a Friend to Supper' and 'To Penshurst.'" In *"The Muses Common-Weale": Poetry and Politics in the Seventeenth Century*, ed. Claude J. Summers and Ted-Larry Pebworth, pp. 62–79. Columbia: University of Missouri Press, 1988.

Scholem, Gershom. *On the Kabbalah and Its Symbolism*. Trans. Ralph Manheim. New York: Schocken, 1965.

Scragg, D. G. *A History of English Spelling*. New York: Barnes & Noble, 1974.

Screech, M. A. *Rabelais*. Ithaca, N.Y.: Cornell University Press, 1979.

Seitel, Peter. "Proverbs: A Social Use of Metaphor." *Genre* 2 (1969): 143–61.

Shaheen, Naseeb. *Biblical References in The Faerie Queene*. Memphis: Memphis State University Press, 1976.

Shakespeare, William. *The Riverside Shakespeare*. Ed. G. Blakemore Evans et al. Boston: Houghton Mifflin, 1974.

———. *The Tempest*. Arden edition. Ed. Frank Kermode. 1954. Rpt. London: Methuen, 1984.

Sharp, Buchanan. *In Contempt of All Authority: Rural Artisans and Riot in the West of England, 1586–1660*. Berkeley: University of California Press, 1980.

Sherwood, Terry G. *Fulfilling the Circle: A Study of John Donne's Thought*. Toronto: University of Toronto Press, 1984.

Shuger, Debora Kuller. *Habits of Thought in the English Renaissance: Religion, Politics, and the Dominant Culture*. Berkeley: University of California Press, 1990.

Shumaker, Wayne. *The Occult Sciences in the Renaissance: A Study in Intellectual Patterns*. Berkeley: University of California Press, 1972.

Sidney, Philip. *A Defence of Poetry*. In *Miscellaneous Prose of Sir Philip Sidney*, ed. Katherine Duncan-Jones and Jan van Dorsten. Oxford: Clarendon, 1973.

Simpson, Evelyn M. *A Study of the Prose Works of John Donne*. 2nd ed. Oxford: Clarendon, 1948.

Singer, Thomas C. "Hieroglyphs, Real Characters, and the Idea of Natural Language in English Seventeenth-Century Thought." *JHI* 50 (1989): 49–70.

Skura, Meredith Anne. "Discourse and the Individual: The Case of Colonialism in *The Tempest*." *SQ* 40 (1989): 42–69.

Slaughter, M. M. *Universal Languages and Scientific Taxonomy in the Seventeenth Century*. Cambridge, Eng.: Cambridge University Press, 1982.

Slights, William W. E. "The Edifying Margins of Renaissance English Books." *RenQ* 42 (1989): 682–716.

———. " 'Marginall Notes that spoile the Text': Scriptural Annotation in the English Renaissance." *HLQ* 55 (1992): 255–78.

Sloane, Thomas O. *Donne, Milton, and the End of Humanist Rhetoric*. Berkeley: University of California Press, 1985.

Smith, Charles G. *Spenser's Proverb Lore*. Cambridge, Mass.: Harvard University Press, 1970.

Smith, Julia J. "Moments of Being and Not-Being in Donne's Sermons." *Prose Studies* 8, no. 3 (1985): 3–20.

Smith, Thomas. *De recta et emendata linguae Anglicae scriptione.* 1568. Rpt. Menston, Eng.: Scolar Press, 1968.

Sorabji, Richard. *Aristotle on Memory.* Providence: Brown University Press, 1972.

Sparrow, John. "John Donne and Contemporary Preachers." *E&S* 16 (1931): 144–78.

———. *Visible Words: A Study of Inscriptions in and as Books and Works of Art.* Cambridge, Eng.: Cambridge University Press, 1969.

Spenser, Edmund. *Books I and II of "The Faerie Queene."* Ed. Robert Kellogg and Oliver Steele. New York: Odyssey, 1965.

———. *The Faerie Queene.* Ed. A. C. Hamilton. London: Longman, 1977.

———. *The Faerie Queene.* Ed. Thomas P. Roche, Jr. 1978. Rpt. New Haven, Conn.: Yale University Press, 1981.

———. *The Works of Edmund Spenser: A Variorum Edition.* 11 vols. Ed. Edwin Greenlaw, Charles Grosvenor Osgood, and Frederick Morgan Padelford. Baltimore: The Johns Hopkins Press, 1932–57.

The Spenser Encyclopedia. Ed. A. C. Hamilton, et al. Toronto: University of Toronto Press, 1990.

Spitzer, Leo. *Linguistics and Literary History: Essays in Stylistics.* Princeton: Princeton University Press, 1948.

Stanbridge, John. *Accidence.* 1496. Rpt. Menston, Eng.: Scolar, 1969. See also White, Beatrice, ed.

Starnes, DeWitt T. *Renaissance Dictionaries: English-Latin and Latin-English.* Austin: University of Texas Press, 1954.

———. *Robert Estienne's Influence on Lexicography.* Austin, Tex.: University of Texas Press, 1963.

Starnes, DeWitt T., and Gertrude E. Noyes. *The English Dictionary from Cawdrey to Johnson, 1604–1755.* Chapel Hill: University of North Carolina Press, 1946.

Stein, Gabriele. *The English Dictionary before Cawdrey.* Tübingen: Max Niemeyer, 1985.

Stock, Brian. *The Implications of Literacy: Written Language and Models of Interpretation in the Eleventh and Twelfth Centuries.* Princeton: Princeton University Press, 1983.

———. *Listening for the Text: On the Uses of the Past.* Baltimore: The Johns Hopkins University Press, 1990.

Street, Brian V. *Literacy in Theory and Practice*. Cambridge, Eng.: Cambridge University Press, 1984.

Strong, Roy. "From Picture Boxes to the Cabinet." In *The English Miniature*, ed. John Murdock et al., pp. 73–84. New Haven, Conn.: Yale University Press, 1981.

Stubbes, Philip. *The Anatomie of Abuses* (1583). Ed. Arthur Freeman. New York: Garland, 1973.

——. *The Anatomie of Abuses*. London: Richard Jones, 1583.

Summers, Joseph H. *George Herbert: His Religion and Art*. 1954. Rpt. Binghamton, N.Y.: Center for Medieval and Early Renaissance Studies, 1981.

Sundelson, David. "So Rare a Wonder'd Father: Prospero's *Tempest*." In *Representing Shakespeare: New Psychoanalytic Essays*, ed. Murray M. Schwartz and Coppélia Kahn, pp. 33–53. Baltimore: The Johns Hopkins University Press, 1980.

Suzuki, Mihoko. *Metamorphoses of Helen: Authority, Difference, and the Epic*. Ithaca, N.Y.: Cornell University Press, 1989.

Tambiah, S. J. "The Magical Power of Words." *Man* 3 (1968): 175–208.

Thomas, Keith. *Religion and the Decline of Magic: Studies in Popular Beliefs in Sixteenth and Seventeenth Century England*. London: Weidenfeld and Nicolson, 1971.

Thomas, Thomas. *Dictionarium linguae Latinae et Anglicanae*. 1587. Rpt. Menston, Eng.: Scolar, 1972.

——. *Dictionarium linguae Latinae et Anglicanae*. Cambridge, Eng.: John Legat, 1594.

——. *Dictionarium linguae Latinae et Anglicanae*. Cambridge, Eng.: John Legat, 1596.

Thorne, Samuel E., ed., *A Discourse upon the Exposicion and Understanding of Statutes, with Sir Thomas Egerton's Additions*. San Marino: Huntington Library, 1942.

Three Chapters of Letters Relating to the Suppression of Monasteries. Ed. Thomas Wright, for the Camden Society. London: John Bowyer Nichols and Son, 1843.

Tilley, Morris Palmer. *A Dictionary of the Proverbs in England in the Sixteenth and Seventeenth Centuries*. 1950. Rpt. Ann Arbor: University of Michigan Press, 1966.

Toulmin, Stephen, and June Goodfield. *The Fabric of the Heavens: The Development of Astronomy and Dynamics*. New York: Harper & Row, 1961.

Tribble, Evelyn B. *Margins and Marginality: The Printed Page in Early Modern England*. Charlottesville: University Press of Virginia, 1993.

Trimpi, Wesley. *Ben Jonson's Poems: A Study of the Plain Style*. Stanford: Stanford University Press, 1962.

———. *Muses of One Mind: The Literary Analysis of Experience and Its Continuity*. Princeton: Princeton University Press, 1983.

Turner, Terence. "'We Are Parrots,' 'Twins Are Birds': Play of Tropes as Operational Structure." In *Beyond Metaphor: The Theory of Tropes in Anthropology*, ed. James E. Fernandez, pp. 121–58. Stanford: Stanford University Press, 1991.

Turner, Victor W. *The Ritual Process: Structure and Anti-Structure*. Chicago: Aldine, 1969.

Udall, Nicholas, trans. See Erasmus, Desiderius of Rotterdam.

van den Berg, Sara J. *The Action of Ben Jonson's Poetry*. Newark, N.J.: University of Delaware Press, 1987.

van der Aa, Abraham Jacob, ed. *Biographish Woordenboek der Nederlanden*. Vol. V. Haarlem: J. J. van Brederode, 1852–78.

Varro. *De lingua Latina*. Trans. Roland Kent. 2 vols. London: Heinemann, 1938.

Vickers, Brian. "Analogy Versus Identity: The Rejection of Occult Symbolism, 1580–1680." In *Occult and Scientific Mentalities in the Renaissance*, ed. Brian Vickers, pp. 95–106. Cambridge, Eng.: Cambridge University Press, 1984.

Vives, Juan Luis. *De tradendis disciplinis*. Cologne: Joannes Gymnicus, 1536.

———. *In Pseudodialecticos*. Ed. and trans. Charles Fantazzi. Leiden: E. J. Brill, 1979.

———. *Vives: On Education*. Trans. Foster Watson. 1913. Rpt. Totowa, N.J.: Rowman and Littlefield, 1971.

Wagner, Roy. *Symbols That Stand for Themselves*. Chicago: University of Chicago Press, 1986.

Walker, D. P. Review of M. A. Screech's *Rabelais*. In *Music, Spirit and Language in the Renaissance*, ed. Penelope Gouk, section XVI, pp. 1–7. London: Variorum Reprints, 1985.

———. *Spiritual and Demonic Magic from Ficino to Campanella*. London: Warburg Institute, University of London, 1958.

Walton, Izaak. "The Life of Dr. John Donne, Late Dean of St. Paul's Church, London" (1675). In *The Lives of John Donne, Sir Henry Wot-*

ton, *Richard Hooker, George Herbert, and Robert Sanderson*, pp. 1–89. 1927. Rpt. London: Oxford University Press, 1966.

Waswo, Richard. *Language and Meaning in the Renaissance*. Princeton: Princeton University Press, 1987.

——. "Motives of Misreading." *JHI* 50 (1989): 324–32.

Watkins, W. B. C. *Shakespeare and Spenser*. 1950. Rpt. Cambridge, Eng.: Walker-de-Berry, 1961.

Watson, Foster. *The English Grammar Schools to 1600: Their Curriculum and Practice*. Cambridge, Eng.: Cambridge University Press, 1908.

Watt, Tessa. *Cheap Print and Popular Piety: 1550–1640*. Cambridge, Eng.: Cambridge University Press, 1991.

Wayne, Don E. "Jonson's Sidney: Legacy and Legitimation in *The Forrest*." In *Sir Philip Sidney's Achievements*, ed. M. J. B. Allen, Dominic Baker-Smith, and Arthur F. Kinney, with Margaret M. Sullivan, pp. 227–50. New York: AMS, 1990.

——. *Penshurst: The Semiotics of Place and the Poetics of History*. Madison: University of Wisconsin Press, 1984.

Webbe, Joseph. *An Appeale to Truth, In the Controuersie between Art, & Vse; About the best and most expedient Course in Languages*. London: George Latham, 1622.

Webber, Joan. *Contrary Music: The Prose Style of John Donne*. Madison: University of Wisconsin Press, 1963.

——. *The Eloquent "I": Style and Self in Seventeenth-Century Prose*. Madison: University of Wisconsin Press, 1968.

Webster's New World Dictionary. 2nd ed. New York: William Collins and World, 1974.

Weekley, Ernest. "Our Early English Etymologists." *The Quarterly Review* 257 (1931): 63–72.

Weimann, Robert. *Shakespeare and the Popular Tradition in the Theater: Studies in the Social Dimension of Dramatic Form and Function*. Ed. Robert Schwartz. Baltimore: The Johns Hopkins University Press, 1978.

Whigham, Frank. *Ambition and Privilege: The Social Tropes of Elizabethan Courtesy Theory*. Berkeley: University of California Press, 1984.

White, Beatrice, ed. *The Vulgaria of John Stanbridge and the Vulgaria of Robert Whittinton*. EETS 187. London: Kegan Paul, Trench, Trubner, 1932.

Whittinton, Robert. See White, Beatrice, ed.

Wilkins, John. *An Essay Towards a Real Character and a Philosophical Language.* 1668. Rpt. Menston, Eng.: Scolar, 1968.

Williams, Franklin B., Jr. "Scholarly Publication in Shakespeare's Day: A Leading Case." In *Joseph Quincy Adams: Memorial Studies,* ed. James G. McManaway, Giles E. Dawson, and Edwin E. Willoughby, pp. 755–73. Washington, D.C.: Folger Shakespeare Library, 1948.

Williams, Raymond. *The Country and the City.* New York: Oxford University Press, 1973.

Wilson, Thomas (1525?–1581). *The Arte of Rhetorique.* Ed. Thomas J. Derrick. 1553. Rpt. New York: Garland, 1982.

——. *The Rule of Reason Conteinying the Arte of Logique.* 3rd ed. 1553. Ed. Richard S. Sprague. Northridge, Calif.: San Fernando Valley State College, 1972.

——. *Wilson's Arte of Rhetorique, 1560.* Ed. G. H. Mair. Oxford: Clarendon, 1909.

Wilson, Thomas (1563–1622). *A Christian Dictionary.* 2nd ed. London: William Jaggard, 1616.

Wiltenburg, Robert. "The 'Aeneid' in 'The Tempest.'" *ShS* 39 (1986): 159–68.

Wimsatt, W. K., Jr. *The Verbal Icon: Studies in the Meaning of Poetry.* 1954. Rpt. n.p.: Noonday, 1960.

Wind, Edgar. *Pagan Mysteries in the Renaissance.* Rev. ed. Harmondsworth, Middlesex, Eng.: Penguin, 1967.

Withals, John. *A Dictionarie in English and Latine for Children, and yong beginners.* Rev. William Clerk. London: Thomas Purfoot, 1608.

——. *A Shorte Dictionarie for Yonge Begynners.* London: Thomas Berthelet, 1553.

——. *A Shorte Dictionarie in Latine and English, verie profitable for yong beginners.* Rev. Abraham Fleming. London: Thomas Purfoote, 1584.

——. *A Shorte Dictionarie most profitable for Yong Beginners.* Rev. Lewis Evans. London: Thomas Purfoote, 1568.

Wofford, Susanne Lindgren. *The Choice of Achilles: The Ideology of Figure in the Epic.* Stanford: Stanford University Press, 1992.

Woodbridge, Linda. "Patchwork: Piecing the Early Modern Mind in England's First Century of Print Culture." *ELR* 23 (1993): 5–45.

Woodmin, A. J., ed. *Velleius Paterculus: The Caesarian and Augustan Narrative* (2.41–93). Cambridge, Eng.: Cambridge University Press, 1983.

Wright, Abraham. *Five Sermons in Five Several Styles; or Waies of Preaching*. London: Edward Archer, 1656.

Wright, George T. "An Almost Oral Art: Shakespeare's Language on Stage and Page." *SQ* 43 (1992): 159–69.

Zeitlin, Jacob. "Commonplaces in Elizabethan Life and Letters." *JEGP* 19 (1920): 47–65.

Index

In this index an "f" after a number indicates a separate reference on the next page, and an "ff" indicates separate references on the next two pages. A continuous discussion over two or more pages is indicated by a span of page numbers, e.g., "57–59." *Passim* is used for a cluster of references in close but not consecutive sequence. Notes are indexed only if the reference is substantive.

Library of Congress Cataloging-in-Publication Data
Anderson, Judith H.
Words that matter : linguistic perception in Renaissance English /
Judith H. Anderson.
    p.   cm.
Includes bibliographical references and index.
ISBN 0–8047–2631–0 (cloth : alk. paper)
    1. English literature — Early modern, 1500–1700 — History and
criticism.   2. English language — Early modern, 1500–1700 —
Lexicology.   3. English language — Early modern, 1500–1700 —
Semantics.   4. Language and culture — England — History — 16th
century.   5. Language and culture — England — History — 17th century.
6. English language — Early modern, 1500–1700 — Style.   7. Rhetoric —
History — 16th century.   8. Rhetoric — History — 17th century.
9. Renaissance — England.   I. Title.
PR421.A53   1996
820.9'003 — dc20
96-3159   CIP